Sailing

Sailing

3rd Edition

JJ Fetter and Peter Isler
with Marly Isler

Sailing For Dummies®, 3rd Edition

Published by: **John Wiley & Sons, Inc.**, 111 River Street, Hoboken, NJ 07030-5774, www.wiley.com

For general information on our other products and services, please contact our Customer Care Department within the U.S. at 877-762-2974, outside the U.S. at 317-572-3993, or fax 317-572-4002. For technical support, please visit https://hub.wiley.com/community/support/dummies.

Wiley publishes in a variety of print and electronic formats and by print-on-demand. Some material included with standard print versions of this book may not be included in e-books or in print-on-demand. If this book refers to media such as a CD or DVD that is not included in the version you purchased, you may download this material at http://booksupport.wiley.com. For more information about Wiley products, visit www.wiley.com.

Library of Congress Control Number: 2022940419

ISBN 978-1-119-86723-4 (pbk); ISBN 978-1-119-86724-1 (ebk); ISBN 978-1-119-86725-8 (ebk)

SKY10035008_062822

Contents at a Glance

Table of Contents

Introduction

There is nothing — absolutely nothing — half so much worth doing as simply messing about in boats.

—*WATER RAT TO MOLE*, THE WIND IN THE WILLOWS, *BY KENNETH GRAHAME*

What gives sailing such enchanting prospects? Water Rat certainly had a piece of the puzzle. Messing about in a boat — any kind of boat — is great fun. You escape the cares and stresses of everyday life, conveyed on a craft powered solely by the forces of nature. The spell that the wind casts on the sails of a boat is bewitching to behold.

Maybe the best part of sailing is the part that your imagination can latch onto, conveying your mind to places you've never been, promising experiences yet untold. And no matter how experienced you become or how much water passes beneath your keel, sailing still has more to offer. The sport is so vast that no one can experience all of sailing's facets in a single lifetime.

But enough generalizing. After all, you wouldn't have picked up this book if you weren't already at least intrigued by the allure of sailing.

About This Book

In this book, you can find all the information you need to go sailing. This book is a textbook, user manual, and reference book all in one. We start with basic sailing skills and move on to cover more advanced topics for when you widen your horizons to activities such as chartering a boat and going cruising. You get to practice tying knots, and you find out about sailing such diverse crafts as a kiteboard and a catamaran. You'll learn how to forecast the weather, as well as how to have a fun and safe day at anchor. You even discover the basics of sailboat racing. We cover all you need to know to be safe on the water, and we make the whole process easy and fun!

This third edition of *Sailing For Dummies* is full of new and revised information. In addition to new photos, we've

- **»** Revised the text on safety equipment and navigation with the most current information
- **»** Updated the sailboat-racing chapter and our advice on what to wear and bring
- **»** Added the best apps and websites for sailing, navigation, and safety
- **»** Invited our daughter, Marly, to revise and expand our chapter on windsurfing to include kiteboarding and foiling

Have you ever listened in on the conversation of two sailors? Sailing has so many specific words that sailors can sound like they're speaking a foreign language. But don't let the jargon turn you off. The language of sailing has an old and rich tradition, and as you become more comfortable in a sailboat, you gradually pick up more and more of the language and become part of the sailing tradition yourself.

In this book, we try to avoid using sailing jargon, but we can't get around it completely, because some of the terms are very important for safety. When the skipper plans a maneuver that requires a coordinated crew effort, for example, using and understanding the exact sailing term allows everyone on the boat to know what's happening and what to do.

We use the following conventions to help you understand everything that we're discussing and to stay consistent:

- **»** We *italicize* boat names and new terms, and follow them with easy-to-understand definitions. We also list most of the italicized terms in the glossary so that you can brush up on sailing terminology.
- **»** We **boldface** important keywords in bulleted lists as well as the action parts of numbered lists.

Finally, in this book we simply refer to *boats* or *sailboats.* Sometimes, we further differentiate between big sailboats with keels *(keelboats)* and small sailboats with centerboards *(dinghies)* as necessary for the subject we're covering. (In the United States, a *yacht* is the snobby cousin of the boat, but in New Zealand and much of the current and former British Empire, the word *yacht* has no elitist connotations.)

Foolish Assumptions

The most foolish assumption we made when we wrote the first edition of this book was that only our parents and a few close friends would ever read it. We've been overwhelmed by the positive responses to the first two editions, and we hope that you enjoy all the new information we've crammed into this book. We assume one or more of the following things about you, our reader:

- You've been given this book as a gift by a friend who wants to take you sailing.
- You get dragged out on the water by your sailing-loving family, and you don't really know what to do.
- You've always been intrigued by the sea.
- You may have had a bad experience on the water, but now you want to give sailing another try.
- Your child has been bitten by the sailboat-racing bug, and you want to figure out what you're watching.
- You love the water and enjoy powerboats, but a sailboat seems to be better for the environment (and cheaper).
- You discovered the basics of sailing at summer camp and haven't sailed since then, but now you want to charter a boat in the Caribbean.
- You already enjoy sailing and want a good, complete reference book and ideas for exploring some new directions in the sport.

We wrote this book to lure you into the sport that we love — no matter how you came to turn that first page.

Icons Used in This Book

You may notice icons, or cute little pictures, in the margins of this book. Those icons do more than just break up the white space; they also tell you something about that particular paragraph.

WARNING

This symbol helps you avoid common mistakes while you're starting and alerts you to potential dangers. As a sailor, you need to have a healthy respect for the power of the wind and the sea.

REMEMBER

This icon points out information that we don't want you to forget. Store it in your brain for quick recall at a later time.

TIP

In sailing, because you're letting the wind do the work, the easy way is the right way. These tips can help you find the easy way.

TECHNICAL STUFF

This icon highlights more detailed information that isn't critical but that can enhance your knowledge and make you a better sailor.

Beyond the Book

In addition to the hundreds of pages of information in this book, you can access more tips, advice, and reference material online. Just go to `www.dummies.com` and type "Sailing For Dummies Cheat Sheet" in the search box.

Where to Go from Here

Where you start is up to you. If you're brand-new to the world of sailing, just turn the page and start with Chapter 1. If you've been around boats before, browse the table of contents and pick a chapter that interests you.

But do start somewhere. The faster you start, the faster we can share our love of sailing with you. While cruising, we've explored some of the most remote and beautiful parts of the world. While racing, we've had the chance to challenge ourselves in international competitions and make friends around the globe. Who knows? Maybe on a future voyage, we'll even get a chance to meet you.

1

Before You Get Your Feet Wet

IN THIS PART . . .

Get a formal introduction to a sailboat.

Discover where you can take sailing lessons.

Find out what you should wear and what kind of equipment you need.

Study what you need to know before you leave the dock.

IN THIS CHAPTER

» Exploring the essentials of beginning sailing

» Dissecting the parts of a sailboat

» Answering basic sailing questions

» Describing where sailing can take you

Chapter 1

Ready, Set, Go: Time to Start Sailing

It is an interesting biological fact that all of us have, in our veins, the exact same percentage of salt in our blood that exists in the ocean, and therefore, we have salt in our blood, in our sweat, in our tears. We are tied to the ocean. And when we go back to the sea, whether it is to sail or to watch it — we are going back from whence we came.

—JOHN F. KENNEDY

Water covers nearly three-quarters of the planet. Over the course of human history, the oceans (as well as lakes and rivers) have served as pathways upon which trade and civilization have developed. Getting away from shore, you feel a link to those ancient mariners who set off over the horizon. When you're flying across the water, you're harnessing the same forces of nature that powered the early explorers.

Why are humans drawn to the sea? President John F. Kennedy had a poetic answer. Generations before you have felt the call of the wind and waves, beckoning to accept their offer of unknown possibilities — adventure and serenity.

Even in today's high-tech, fast-paced world, sailing regularly rates high on pollsters' lists of desirable activities. So if you ever find yourself dreaming of packing it all in and setting sail over the horizon or of simply having your own boat to sail near home on a warm, breezy afternoon, you're not alone. And this chapter shows you that getting out on the water is easier than you think.

What You Need to Start Sailing

Starting sailing is a little different from starting most sports. In basketball, you can start to learn the basic moves, such as dribbling and shooting, without worrying about the "playing field" — the court boundaries or the height of the basket. But the sailor's "playing field" — the wind and the water — is constantly changing. The wind changes strength and direction, while waves and/or current change the water conditions. Sailing is harnessing the power of Mother Nature, and sailors need a healthy respect for her power. So in this section, we cover some important weather and safety considerations you need to know before you start sailing.

Also in this section, we encourage you to begin your sailing career by taking lessons from a qualified instructor — we both did — so you can focus on learning the basic moves while the instructor makes sure that the conditions are suitable for learning.

Taking lessons

You can find sailboats near almost every body of water. And where you find sailboats, you can find sailing schools and/or a sailing club with experienced sailors looking for crew. Most boats longer than 15 feet (5 meters) are meant to be sailed with more than one person, and the average 30-foot (9-meter) sailboat is best sailed with at least four crew members. So go down to the local marina, check out the bulletin board, and ask around. The offers you get to go sailing may pleasantly surprise you.

WARNING

Although having friends to take you sailing can make practicing and progressing easy, we strongly recommend taking lessons from a sailing school with certified instructors before you head out on your own. For a variety of safety reasons, we don't recommend sailing alone while you're learning the basics. In Chapter 2, we help you find the right sailing course for any experience level.

Location, location, location

You can probably guess that the weather and water conditions in a given area affect the sailing possibilities and that most sailors put away their sailing clothes in wintertime in the snowy latitudes, while Southern Californians can sail year-round. But even snow and ice can't stop some die-hard enthusiasts who sail ice boats on frozen northern lakes. Not to be outdone, adventurous sailors in dry desert areas blast around on "land yachts" or "dirt boats" with wheels. Assuming that you plan to go sailing on regular, salt or fresh, nonfrozen water, your main concerns are twofold: the water conditions (waves, currents, depth, and water temperature) and the wind conditions (wind strength and changeability). Some areas have very consistent conditions during a particular season; in others, conditions are more variable. In some places, a typically windy spot and a calm location may be less than a mile apart due to some geographic feature.

REMEMBER

That's why knowing the local conditions can be invaluable to any sailor. We encourage new sailors to start, if possible, in steady light-to-medium winds and protected (calm) waters. A sailing school knows where and when to find those conditions in your area. But as you gain experience, you can enjoy boating in more challenging conditions, such as sailing in windy Chicago or San Francisco in midsummer, cruising in foggy Maine, or blasting down the Molokai Channel in Hawaii.

Feeling the wind

You probably know that a sailboat doesn't move unless it has wind. (Yes, you can start the engine, get a tow, get out a paddle, or swim along pulling your boat — but we're talking about "sailing" by using the power of the sails, right?) The wind rules a sailor's universe; it's the sailor's alpha and omega. To become a sailor, you need to raise your awareness of the weather, starting with the importance of feeling and finding the wind's direction.

Look around for a nearby flag, and use its direction as a clue. In Chapter 5, we show you how to develop your feel for sensing the wind direction and staying aware of any shifts. Knowing the wind's direction is crucial because you get your boat to move by adjusting the angle of the sails relative to the wind's direction. When the wind direction changes or you change course, you need to change your sail *trim*, or the angle of your sails to the wind, as you see in Chapter 5.

WARNING

No matter how constant the weather seems to be on shore, the wind is frequently shifting both speed and direction. Staying aware of these changes is important for your safety and comfort while sailing. Sensing the wind's speed is also important so that you avoid going sailing when the wind is too strong or blustery or getting *becalmed* — unable to sail when the wind dies. Check out the marine forecast (www.weather.gov) or study the forecast for your area on a marine weather app recommended in Chapter 8 before a day of sailing to avoid getting caught in unpleasant (and potentially dangerous) conditions on the water, such as thunderstorms or thick fog.

Considering safety

REMEMBER

Before going out on the water, you need to consider some safety issues and be prepared with basic safety gear, especially life jackets. In Chapter 3, we give you plenty of tips on what to wear and bring so that you're comfortable and safe on the water. Chapter 7 covers other essential safety information, such as safely recovering a person who falls overboard and getting a capsized dinghy upright and sailing again.

Looking at a Sailboat

Sailboats come in all sizes, shapes, and types. The beauty of sailing is that you can't help but find a boat (or two or three) that's just right for you. All sailing craft, big or small, have at least one (and sometimes more) of the following components, which we outline in the following sections: a hull, an underwater fin for steering control and stability, a mast to hold up the sail (or sails), a sail, and plenty of rope.

All sailboats have a hull

The hull is (ideally) the floating body of a boat and can be made of a wide variety of materials, including wood, fiberglass, metal, plastic, or even cement. The hull can be as small as a surfboard or more than 100 feet (30 meters) long.

You can get a good idea about how fast a boat is by how it looks. Just as you can tell that a sports car will be faster than a golf cart, you can tell that a big, heavy, wide boat with a short mast is a good cruiser but won't break any speed records on the water. Sailboats fall into three basic types based on their hull shape, as Figure 1-1 illustrates.

- **Windsurfers and kiteboards:** These boats are basically surfboards with a sail or kite. They come in many sizes and shapes, depending on their intended use and the skill level of the rider. Windsurfing and kiteboarding are great ways to enjoy the sport with equipment that you can put in or on top of your car. For more on this fun and fast part of the sport, check out Chapter 13.

WHAT FLOATS YOUR BOAT?

Have you ever sat in a boat and wondered how the heck it doesn't sink? Well, you don't have to wonder anymore.

Your boat floats because it's less dense than the water in which it sits. *Density* is expressed as mass per unit volume. The density of fresh water is 62.2 pounds per cubic foot (1 gram per cubic centimeter). Salt water is denser, at 64 pounds per cubic foot, so a given object can float better (or higher) in salt water than in fresh water. In salt water, a boat floats if it's less dense than 64 pounds per cubic foot, including everything on board: mast, sails, and people. If the density of a boat in salt water is 32 pounds per cubic foot (½ gram per cubic centimeter), the boat floats half in and half out of the water.

The weight of a boat is also called its *displacement,* because the boat displaces (pushes aside) a volume of water equal to its weight. An object with very light displacement, such as a surfboard, lies on top of the water like a leaf. A boat with heavy displacement sits lower in the water, displacing more water to stay afloat.

Here's the amazing part: You can build boats of nonbuoyant (denser-than-water) materials, such as steel or concrete, as long as you design them with enough volume that their total density is less than the density of the water. As proof of that principle, consider the fact that an empty aluminum soda can floats, but the same can sinks if you flatten it and decrease its volume. (Don't try this experiment on the water, of course; you'd be littering.)

- **Multihulls:** *Multihulls* are boats with more than one hull (makes sense, doesn't it?). A boat with two hulls is called a *catamaran;* a boat with three hulls is a *trimaran.* Multihulls, especially small, light ones, can be thrilling to sail. With a little wind, one hull lifts out of the water, and you feel like you're flying across the water. (You can find out more about sailing a small catamaran, often referred to as a *cat* [without the fur] in Chapter 11.) Bigger multihulls (more than 30 feet, or 9 meters) can be great cruising boats. Because of their width, they're very stable and have a tremendous amount of space for their length. Multihulls are fast, too, because they're very light and don't have heavy *keels,* or as much surface area underwater, as *monohulls* (boats with one hull) of the same size. Check out "All sailboats have an underwater fin" to find out more about the daggerboards used on most multihulls instead of a keel. Huge multihulls more than 120 feet (37 meters) long compete in races across oceans and hold most of the point-to-point, long-distance sailing speed records, including sailing nonstop around the world in 40 days! (For more on the fast world of offshore racing, see Chapter 14.)

FIGURE 1-1: Three types of sailboats: windsurfer, multihull, and monohull.

- **Monohulls:** These sailboats are the most common type of boat, and they have one hull (still makes sense, right?). Most of the world's sailing and racing takes place in monohulls, broadly classified as either dinghies or keelboats, as the next section explains. Most sailing schools teach their basic sailing classes in monohulls — dinghies or keelboats (although some specialty schools, often in tropical climes, teach windsurfing and kiteboarding too). For more information on learning how to sail, including types of boats and where to find a good school, check out Chapter 2.

All sailboats have an underwater fin

Hanging underneath the back end of most sailboats is a rotating fin called a *rudder.* The rudder does just what you think it does: steers the boat. Underneath the middle of most sailboats is a second, larger, fin called a *keel* or *centerboard*.

Comparing keelboats and dinghies

The primary purpose of both keels and centerboards is to keep the boat from skidding sideways from the force of the wind and to provide lift so that your boat can sail closer to the wind. (When you're sailing, your sails and the underwater fins act like wings.) Although a few exceptions exist, if the fin is fixed (not movable) and made of a heavy material such as lead, it's usually a keel; if the fin is lightweight and retractable, it's usually a centerboard.

- **Keelboats:** *Keelboats* have a *keel,* a fixed, heavy lead fin for ballast hanging under their hull, as Figure 1-2 shows, providing stability against the wind's force. The smallest keelboats are model (sometimes radio-controlled) sailboats, but keelboats that carry human passengers are usually more than 20 feet (6 meters) in length.

FIGURE 1-2: Keels and rudders come in different shapes and configurations. The photo on the left is common; the right photo has twin rudders and a canting ballast fin and bulb.

Photo courtesy of Sally Samins

Dinghies: *Dinghies* are small, nimble sailboats that are typically more responsive than their ballasted cousins sporting keels. But watch out — dinghies can *capsize,* or tip over. Instead of that ballast weight in the keel, they have a lighter fin called a centerboard that's retractable. The centerboard may also be called a *daggerboard* if it retracts vertically (see Figure 1-3), depending on its position and movement (or a *leeboard* if it's mounted on the side of the boat). Most dinghies range in length from 8 to 20 feet (2.5 to 6 meters).

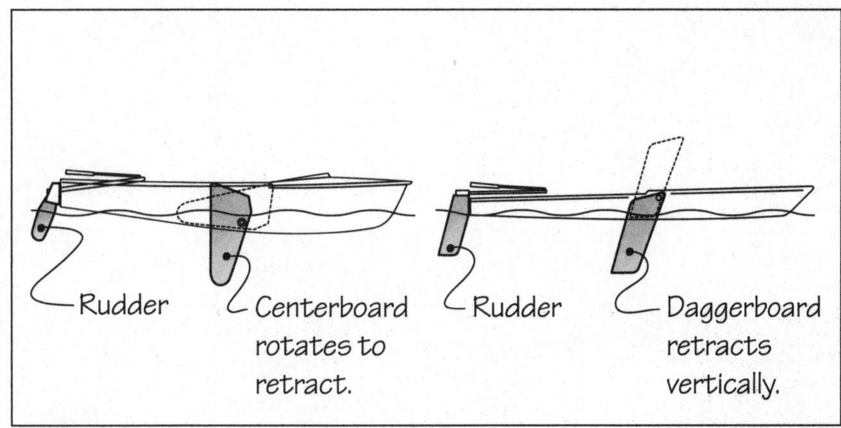

FIGURE 1-3: Two dinghies: (left) with a centerboard and (right) with a daggerboard.

© John Wiley & Sons, Inc.

Comparing tillers and wheels

So how do you drive (or *steer*, in sailor speak)? Well, those rudders shown in Figure 1-2 and Figure 1-3 are connected to either a *tiller,* a long lever arm that allows you to turn the rudder, or a *wheel,* which is attached to cables that turn the rudder. Generally, smaller boats have tillers, and bigger boats have wheels, because bigger boats have greater force on the rudder and would require an enormous lever arm.

A boat with a wheel steers just like your car: Turn left to go left and right to go right. But you push a tiller to the right to turn left and to the left to go to the right. (Check out Chapter 4 for more on steering.) Steering sounds trickier than it really is; a tiller is quite responsive, and you quickly develop a feel for the correct way to turn.

All sailboats have a mast

The *mast* is the vertical pole that supports the sails, as the dinghy in Figure 1-4 shows. Although most modern sailboats have one mast, some sailboats have several masts that can carry many sails. (Remember the pictures of the *Niña*, *Pinta*, and *Santa Maria* in your history textbook?) You may have heard of *square riggers*, *schooners*, or *yawls*. These types of sailing craft are named for the number and position of their masts and the profile of the sails. If you want to know how to identify these cool, vintage sailboats, check out the glossary.

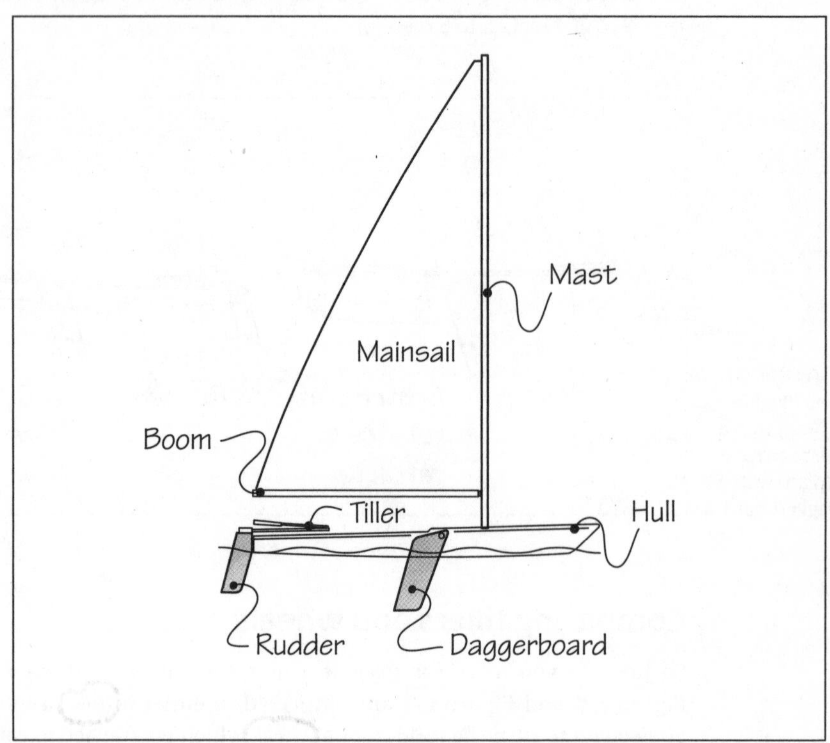

FIGURE 1-4: The basic parts of a dinghy.

Although older boats have wooden masts, most modern boats have masts made of aluminum, which is easier to mass-produce into a lighter and stronger pole. For the ultimate in strength and light weight, the fastest racing boats use carbon fiber. On bigger boats, an array of wires usually supports the mast. These wires are called the *standing rigging.* See the *forestay, backstay,* and *shrouds* on the keelboat in Figure 1-5.

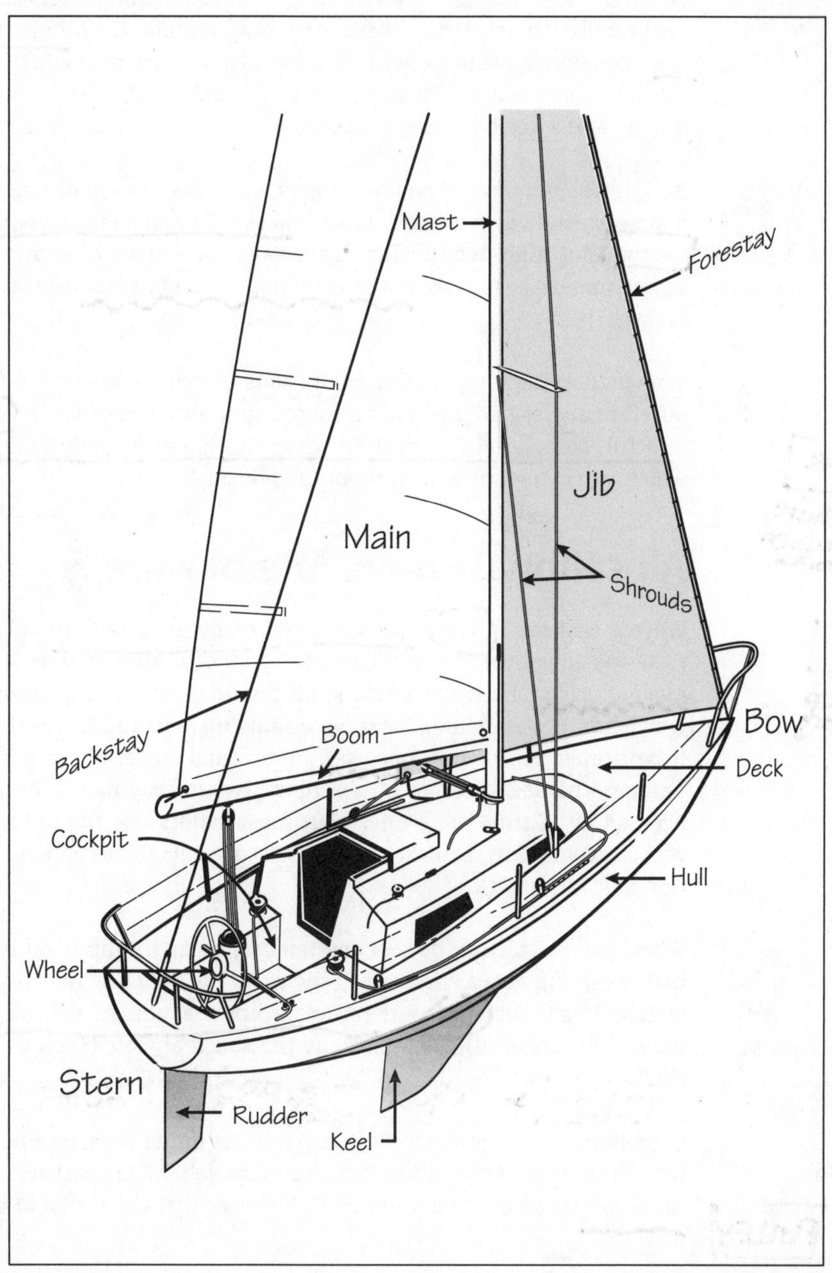

FIGURE 1-5: The basic parts of a keelboat.

© John Wiley & Sons, Inc.

All sailboats have sails

The mast (and standing rigging) supports the third and most common feature of sailboats: the sails. A *sail* is simply a big piece of fabric that catches the wind, enabling you to use its force to move the boat. The sails are your engines; their power or fuel comes from the wind. The *main*, or *mainsail*, sets along the back edge of the tallest mast. Some boats carry only a mainsail; others have a *headsail* as well. A headsail sits in front of the mast. Headsails come in different types, but the most common is a *jib*. (Refer to Figure 1-4 and Figure 1-5 for the basic parts of a dinghy and a keelboat, respectively.)

TECHNICAL STUFF

Back in the old days of square riggers, sails were made of flax or cotton canvas, and heavy and very stretchy. Today, most sails are made of a polyester fiber called Dacron. But high-tech racing boats have sails made of exotic, lightweight, yet strong materials such as Mylar, carbon fiber, and Kevlar (the fabric in bulletproof vests).

You can use many types of specialty sails to make a boat go as fast as possible at different angles to the wind. A common specialty headsail is the *spinnaker* — a big, colorful, parachutelike sail used when sailing *downwind* (going with the wind), which you can learn how to fly in Chapter 12.

All sailboats have lots of rope

When a sailboat is *rigged* (prepared and ready to go sailing), all the ropes used to raise and adjust the sails can look like spaghetti. All this pasta is part of the boat's *running rigging*. Even the simplest sailboat has several adjustment ropes, each of which has its own name. The rope running up mast that's used to pull the sails up, for example, is called the *halyard*. Just to make everything more confusing, the "proper" names for ropes on a sailboat, when they have a purpose and use, are *lines*, as in "Throw me a line." But most sailors use the terms interchangeably without confusing their crews, and both are equally acceptable (and we use both terms in this book).

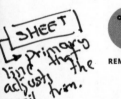

REMEMBER

When you're starting out, understanding what the lines do is more important than worrying about what to call them. So the only line that you need to know to start sailing is the *sheet* — the primary line that adjusts the sail *trim* (the angle of the sail to the wind), referred to by the sail it adjusts (such as *mainsheet* and *jib sheet*).

Depending on the wind strength and the size of the sails, pulling in the mainsheet (and most of the other lines) can be a tough job. Most boats use a system of *blocks* (pulleys) to make it easier to pull in the lines that carry a lot of load. So you don't have to hold that mainsheet with your teeth when your arms get tired; the typical mainsheet system also has a conveniently located cleat.

In a sailboat, the wind is your fuel, and the sail is your engine. So the gas pedal is the sheet (shown in Figure 1-6), the rope that pulls in the sail and harnesses the power of the wind.

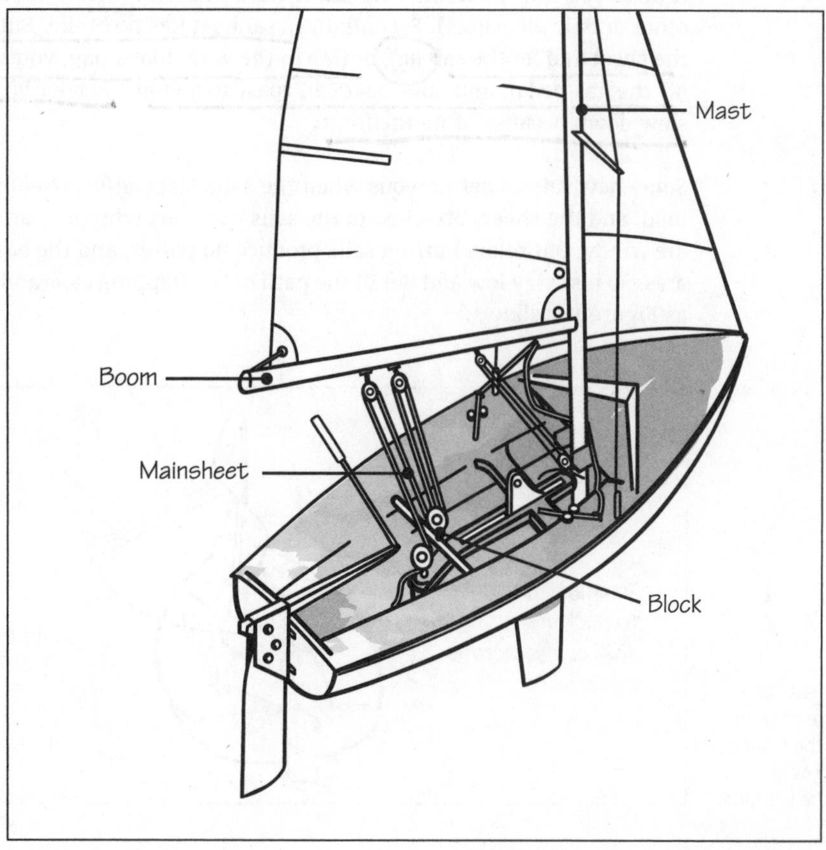

FIGURE 1-6: Mainsheet system on a dinghy.

Tackling Some Basic Sailing Maneuvers

Now that you know the basic components of a sailboat, you may have some basic questions. Earlier in this chapter, we cover how you drive this thing (with the wheel or tiller connected to the rudder) and show you the gas pedal, or mainsheet (see "All sailboats have lots of rope" earlier in this chapter). If you're a responsible driver, your next question may be "Where's the brake?" (or "How do you stop this %#$@ thing?"). In this section, we also answer a few other basic questions you may have, including "Can you sail anywhere?" and "Where do I go next?"

Coasting to a stop

So you want to find the brake pedal? Unfortunately, sailboats can't stop on a dime (unless you run them into something hard like land, throw out an anchor, or take other drastic measures). Essentially, a sailboat has no brake. But when you let out the sheet and let the sail *luff*, or flap in the wind like a flag, you've taken your foot off the gas pedal, and your boat can coast to a stop. Heavier boats take longer to slow down because of momentum.

Some new sailors get nervous when the sails start *luffing* (flapping); the sails are loud, and the sheets attached to the sails can start whipping around if conditions are windy. But relax. Luffing sails produce no power, and the boat gently decelerates. So just stay low and out of the path of the flapping sail (and that hard boom), as Figure 1-7 shows.

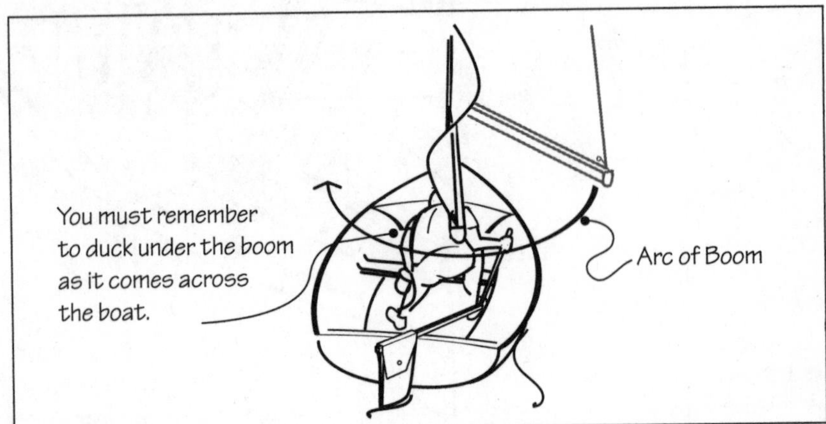
You must remember to duck under the boom as it comes across the boat.
Arc of Boom

FIGURE 1-7: Beware of getting hit in the head by the boom when the sail luffs.

Sailing into the wind

You may wonder whether you can sail anywhere. Our answer is yes, you *can* sail anywhere! You can even sail to a point directly into the wind, but not by just steering straight there. If you try steering your boat directly into the wind, your sails luff, and you slow and then come to a stop. So to sail to a point directly upwind, you must take an indirect zigzag route, as Figure 1-8 shows. First, the zig: Pull in your sails (with their sheets) as hard as you can and then steer a course as close as you can to the wind direction without having the sails flap. Halfway to your destination, the time comes to zag and perform the basic sailing maneuver of tacking. (Check out Chapter 5 for more about tacking and other basic maneuvers.)

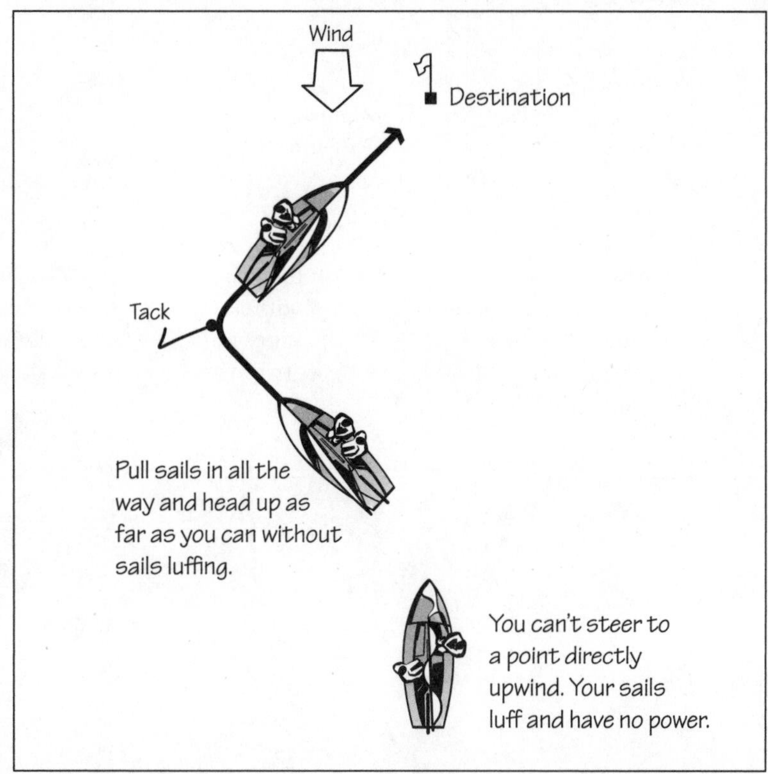

FIGURE 1-8: To sail to a destination directly upwind, you must take an indirect route.

A *tack* entails a course change of about 90 degrees. In a tack, as you begin the turn, your sails start to luff because you're steering directly toward the oncoming wind. But as you continue your turn, the sails refill, with the wind now blowing across the opposite side. If you time your tack correctly, you're steering directly toward your initial destination.

» Choosing the right type of boat

» Starting in ideal conditions

» Selecting a sailing school

» Practicing your new skills

» Moving on to higher education

Chapter 2
Where You Can Learn: Classes and Sailing Schools

There be three things which are too wonderful for me . . .

The way of an eagle in the air;

The way of a serpent upon a rock;

The way of a ship in the midst of the sea.

—OLD TESTAMENT, PROVERBS 30:18,19

Suppose that you don't know how to sail but want to learn. (A good guess, because you're reading this book, right?) Sailing is a very accessible sport if you know where to begin. Believe it or not, plenty of people would love to introduce you to the joys of sailing.

This chapter answers some key questions you may have, such as where you can go to get started in sailing and what type of boat to start on. We highly recommend attending sailing school, and we help you choose the right one for you. This chapter looks at all your options for finding out about this great sport.

Resources for Learning

The following list provides a few ways you can start discovering more about this great sport, but we strongly recommend that beginners take classes from a certified sailing school:

- **Through friends:** Your first sail may be aboard a friend's boat. But unless your friend is a certified sailing instructor with plenty of free time to dedicate to your education, you probably should just enjoy the ride and plan on getting your first formal training from a professional sailing instructor.
- **By reading this book:** Like many sports, sailing is part mental and part physical. You can study its theories, but you can discover some things only with the wind in your face and your hand on the tiller or ropes.
- **On your own:** Purchasing (or borrowing) a boat and teaching yourself to sail is entirely possible. But we don't recommend teaching yourself (in fact, we discourage it) because it may be downright dangerous. We devote an entire chapter of this book to safety afloat (Chapter 7) and provide safety tips throughout the other chapters too. Practice on your own, but learn the basics from a qualified instructor first.
- **In a formal class from a professional instructor:** Have an idea of where we're heading? We feel very strongly that despite all the options, you should get your education from a pro. See "Choosing a Sailing School" later in this chapter for detailed advice.

What Kind of Boat You Should Learn On

You can choose where and how to start your sailing studies, and you may also be able to choose what kind of boat to start on. We both started on dinghies, as do most racing sailors. But then again, we started as kids, and almost all junior sailing programs use dinghies. Dinghies are smaller boats (usually under 20 feet, or 6 meters, long) with a retractable centerboard; they can also tip over. Keelboats are usually longer than 20 feet, with fixed keels that provide extra stability.

TIP

The bottom line: Consider the pluses and minuses of dinghies and keelboats that we outline in this section; then go take lessons from the best instructor you can find!

Dinghies

Many sailing schools and junior programs instruct beginners in small (10- to 14-foot, or 3- to 4-meter, long) one-person boats; others use larger two- or three-person dinghies, as Figure 2-1 shows. Ideally, the boat has a relatively stable hull shape (not too tippy) and a conservative amount of sail area. You don't need to break any speed records on your first sail!

FIGURE 2-1: (Left) Kids on a 420 trainer dinghy. (Right) A single-handed Optimist dinghy next to an E-22 keelboat.

© J World, San Diego

Pros

Following are the advantages of using a dinghy for your training:

- **They're responsive.** Due to the boat's light weight, changes in helm, weight position, and sail trim provide instantaneous feedback. You can really feel the boat sail.
- **The skipper (driver) trims a sail.** On most dinghies (especially the single-person variety), the skipper must adjust the sails as well as steer, giving you a more complete understanding of how everything works.

- **They're inexpensive.** For this reason, dinghies are favored by many programs that have limited budgets.
- **Their smaller size makes them less intimidating.** Would you rather take your driver's-education class in a compact car or a truck?

Cons

Starting to sail on a dinghy does have the following disadvantages:

- **They can capsize.** You can argue that the possibility of capsizing is a "pro," especially because we think that everyone who sails a dinghy needs to know how to right a capsized boat. (We cover that subject in Chapter 7.) Finding out how to right a flipped boat, however, isn't a priority if you start on a keelboat.
- **They're wet.** Typically, you sit lower to the water in a dinghy than on a keelboat. But hey — if water hurt, sailors wouldn't go sailing (at least not as often). Check out Chapter 3 for some clothing ideas to help you stay more comfortable in the inevitable dampness of sailing.
- **The instructor doesn't ride with you.** Having the instructor with you is an option, but some small dinghies get pretty cramped with two people on board. Often, the instructor follows you in a motorboat, shouting advice as needed.

Keelboats

Most commercial sailing schools that cater primarily to adults use small (20- to 28-foot, or 6- to 9-meter) keelboats as their introductory training vessels. Ideally, the boat has a large, open cockpit area capable of holding a class of one to four students plus an instructor, as Figure 2-2 shows.

Pros

Advantages to starting off on a keelboat include the following:

- **The instructor and other students are on board.** Getting instant feedback is nice. Also, studying with other students on board can be fun.
- **You can focus on one skill at a time.** On a keelboat with several crew members, one person can drive while another adjusts the sail.

FIGURE 2-2: A good sailing-school boat has space for the instructor to observe and teach without getting in the students' way.

© J World, San Diego

- **You won't capsize.** Removing the constant distraction of possibly capsizing enables students to concentrate on sailing.
- **They're more comfortable to sail.** On a dinghy, you must pay constant attention to where you're sitting to keep the boat from tipping over too far. One decision you have to make when figuring out how to sail on any boat is where to sit (see Chapter 4). On a keelboat, however, you don't affect performance very much if you're a little slow to react or are out of position by a foot or two. Furthermore, keelboats are drier — although you don't get any guarantees that a big wave won't come right over the side and land on your lap!
- **They can use an engine.** If the wind dies, or if no wind is in the harbor, you can start the engine and make your way to good sailing water faster.

SAILING FOR EVERYONE

Thanks to developments in assistive technology, people with all kinds of disabilities get out on the water to go sailing and sailboat racing. Personal lifts can give wheelchair users a needed boost from the dock to the boats with special modifications. Counter-balanced swivel chairs are available for people with limited mobility, and talking compasses and Global Positioning System (GPS) devices allow the sight-impaired to navigate. US Sailing provides resources including instructor training and links to adaptive sailing centers around the country. The US Para Sailing Championships are held annually, and sailing crews with disabilities have competed in distance races like the big Transpac race from Los Angeles to Hawaii and internationally in the Paralympics and Para World Championships. With so many great organizations providing access to the water for the differently abled, when we say that sailing is for everyone and anyone, we really mean it!

Cons

If you choose to start your sailing career on a keelboat, remember the following disadvantages:

- **They're duller instruments.** Keelboats are heavier and less responsive to the subtle changes in sail trim and steering that are immediately apparent on dinghies. This fact can make it more difficult to "feel" the boat, which is an important part of sailing.
- **Everything pulls harder.** The heavier the boat, the bigger the sails and the more load on all the control ropes. So the boat may be rigged with devices like winches to provide mechanical advantage.
- **They may steer with a wheel.** Steering wheels are normally used on larger (more than 40 feet, or 12 meters, long) keelboats, and some smaller ones have them too. But tillers provide a much better feel of the boat and the water flowing past, so you'll probably have more fun sailing on a boat with a tiller.

Keeping It Easy the First Time

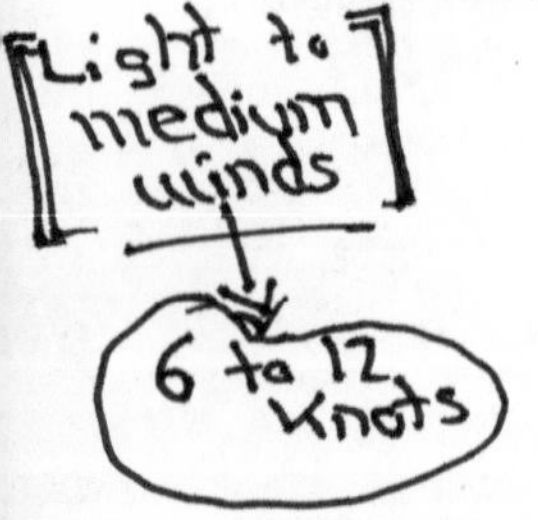

Here are the ideal conditions for learning to sail, in order of priority:

- **Light to medium winds (6 to 12 knots) that are very steady in direction:** For more on wind strength, see Chapter 8.

- **Smooth water:** Ideally, stay in an area protected from surf, swells, and wind-blown waves.
- **An uncrowded, open area with minimal obstructions and room to sail in any direction:** Not having to contend with other boats when you're learning can enable you to focus on the task at hand.
- **Warm air and water:** Air and water temperatures higher than 70 degrees Fahrenheit (21 degrees Celsius) are nice; temperatures in the 80s Fahrenheit (upper 20s to low 30s Celsius) are sheer paradise!

If you live in Stockholm, of course, you may have to wait a long time for the air and water temperatures to get that warm. So as long as you dress warmly (see Chapter 3 for ideas), the key conditions are the first three: light to medium winds, smooth water, and plenty of room to sail. If the wind is constantly shifting or so light that the sails don't fill, getting in the groove and feeling what's happening can be difficult. By contrast, too much wind is a bad thing for beginners. The waves throw the boat around, the sails flap so loudly that you can't hear your instructor, and everything happens way too fast. In short, you have a very difficult time understanding what's happening and why.

Choosing a Sailing School

Now that we've strongly recommended that you start your sailing career with some lessons, we want you to find the right school. Children and teens may have some options that aren't available for adults, such as summer camps and junior programs at clubs, so we discuss tips for them later in this section, in "Picking a sailing school for the kids."

Exploring your options

If your community has sailboats and sailors, you probably have a choice between a community sailing program and a commercial sailing school or two. Yacht clubs, universities, and some charter-boat rental companies may also offer instruction. You can always search online for sailing schools, of course. You can ask a sailor or someone at a marine business for recommendations, and a boat show can be a good source of information too.

In the United States, two organizations oversee national educational programs that certify instructors and provide schools curriculum and standards. You can contact each of them to receive a list of accredited schools:

- **US Sailing:** US Sailing (www.ussailing.org) is the national governing body for the sport of sailing, offering programs at schools around the country in dinghies, keelboats, powerboats, and windsurfers, as well as special courses in areas such as adaptive sailing, safety at sea, racing, and STEM education (see the nearby sidebar "Sailing to a STEM education"). US Sailing certifies instructors and coaches to the highest standards. The organization also oversees the racing side of the sport, including the U.S. Olympic sailing team, which JJ was on in 1992 and 2000. US Sailing is the U.S. representative to World Sailing, the organization that produces the racing rules and represents the sport of sailing for the International Olympic Committee.
- **American Sailing Association (ASA):** Founded in 1983 (Peter was one of the founders and remains on the board of directors), the ASA (https://asa.com) is affiliated with more than 400 sailing schools and has certified almost 600,000 students in Basic Sailing. Major charter-boat companies recognize ASA certification. The multilevel ASA program begins with Basic Keelboat Sailing through Offshore Passagemaking, and many accredited schools also offer instruction in dinghies.

Taking lessons while on vacation

Why not take sailing lessons during your vacation to an exotic (and warm) waterfront location? Such vacations are a great way to find time in your busy schedule to get out on the water and figure out which way the wind is blowing. You can use the sources we mention in "Exploring your options" earlier in this chapter to find sailing schools at your vacation destination. Our favorite sailing school in paradise is the Bitter End Yacht Club (https://beyc.com), a resort in the British Virgin Islands that was completely rebuilt after being destroyed by Hurricane Irma in 2017. The club offers sailing, windsurfing, and kiting lessons from well-qualified instructors.

SAILING TO A STEM EDUCATION

US Sailing's Reach Program uses the sport of sailing to teach science, technology, engineering and math (STEM) topics as well as environmental stewardship to youth sailors. The organization offers educator courses and lesson modules to help organizations add STEM educational opportunities to their sailing classes. For more information, check out www.ussailing.org/education/youth/reach.

Thousands of more experienced sailors take sailing vacations by chartering (renting) boats. We cover that sort of ultimate vacation in Chapter 18. Many sailboat charter companies offer advanced courses designed to introduce intermediate sailors to the joys of bareboat chartering (chartering a boat "bare" means without hiring a skipper or crew), and some offer beginning sailing courses as well.

Looking outside the United States

Many countries have a national authority like US Sailing that promotes a standardized educational system. World Sailing (`www.sailing.org`) provides a list of countries with national entry-level sailing programs (`www.sailing.org/about/members/mnas/index.php`). These national sailing organizations should be able to provide you a list of accredited schools. Otherwise, you can always do an Internet search or ask for recommendations from local marine businesses.

Interviewing a potential school

If you decide to go to a school, you need to pick the right one for you. Besides asking the obvious question (how much it costs), you want to find out as much about the prospective school as possible. This short section provides some factors to consider during your selection process:

- **Curriculum:** Does the introductory course offer certification to a national standard? Just because a school doesn't offer certification doesn't mean that its course is deficient; the course may be great, but if it doesn't comply with some standard other than its own, how do you know? Also ask how long the course is. The typical beginners' course at a commercial sailing school takes place over four days (often, two weekends) and combines classroom and on-the-water training.
- **Instructors:** Are the instructors certified, and to what level and which national standard?
- **Boats:** What kind of boat does the school use? Dinghy or keelboat? Wheel or tiller? (Check out Chapter 1 for more information on these boat specifics.)
- **Class size:** How many students will be on the boat? Can you take private lessons? Having other students on the boat with you has advantages and disadvantages. To get enough time at each position, you probably don't want more than four students (including yourself) on the average 25-foot (8-meter)

keelboat. The typical dinghy is sailed alone or with one other student while the instructor follows the group on a powerboat.

- **Bad weather/makeup days:** How much wind is too much for the entry-level course? What is the school's policy for making up blown-out days?
- **Safety:** Ask about the school's safety record and any special safety procedures. Does it have any swimming requirements?
- **Equipment:** What do you need to bring? Most schools provide life jackets but not foul-weather gear.
- **Post-class sailing:** Does the school have a boat (or boats) available for graduates of the basic sailing course to take out to build sailing experience? If so, do any special policies apply to its use?
- **Higher education:** Does the school have other classes that you can take after you build some experience?

Finding the right sailing instructor

In addition to selecting a potential school, you need to look for the following desirable features in a beginning sailing instructor. Look for someone who is

- **Certified:** With certification, you know that your instructor has made an effort to be trained and to measure their skills and knowledge against a national standard.
- **A good teacher:** No matter how good a sailor the instructor is, communication and teaching skills matter most.
- **Patient:** Instructors need this quality in spades the 50th time someone asks them to explain something.
- **Congenial:** After all, you're sailing, not doing something serious like tax preparation. The more fun the students have, the better they can grasp the key concepts.
- **Able to anticipate potential problems:** This quality has everything to do with experience. When the boat is all the way downwind in a narrow passage with rocks on each side, it's too late.
- **Able to communicate well:** Your instructor must be able to make complex things perfectly understandable — sort of like the *For Dummies* series of books!

Picking a sailing school for the kids

Many areas have specific programs for kids. These programs are most commonly offered at yacht clubs, sailing clubs, or camps, or through community organizations, and are conducted during the summer months. Don't be put off if you're not a club member, a student at the university, or whatever. Most private yacht clubs' junior programs welcome nonmembers. (Otherwise, Peter would still be playing baseball today.) Check out the registration process in the winter months to make sure that the class doesn't fill up before your child is on the list.

TIP

The best class is one that you take with friends. If it's fun, your child is more likely to stick with it!

Keep the following factors in mind when checking out a youth sailing program:

- **Schedule:** Some programs run for two months; others are in biweekly increments. Advanced groups may meet in the afternoon and beginners in the morning. Make sure that you know the number of hours your child will be sailing per day. What about lunch? Hungry kids don't learn as well as kids who have full stomachs.
- **Type and availability of boats:** Find out what type of boats beginners sail. Most clubs and programs have boats for beginners to use, and many have boats for intermediate-level and learn-to-race instruction too.
- **Grouping criteria:** Most programs divide students into groups by age, which can create a small problem if your child is starting a few years late, as Peter did. Ask the organizers how they solve this problem.
- **Curriculum:** Some programs (especially yacht clubs) may stress racing over recreational sailing. This approach is okay, but having a balance is nice, and the best programs have a high fun factor.
- **Instructors:** What is the ratio of instructors to students? What certifications do the instructors have? Often, instructors are college students; find out how many have teaching experience. Instructors should have US Sailing's Level I certification and SafeSport training in creating a safe, positive learning environment for minors (`www.ussailing.org/competition/resources/safesport-us-sailing`).
- **Safety:** What sort of special equipment, safety procedures, and insurance does the program have? What are the age and swimming requirements?
- **Equipment:** What equipment does your child need? Does the school provide life jackets, or must you provide your own?

SAILING AT SUMMER CAMP

The American Camping Association's website (www.aca-camps.org) includes a search feature to help you find camps that offer sailing instruction. Your child will probably have a great time keeping cool on the water, because any camps with sailboats are probably located on a beautiful lake or on a beach.

If you can't talk your child into a sailing camp, try finding a camp where your child is exposed to a wide range of water sports. An interest in swimming, kayaking, and canoeing this summer may lead to an interest in sailing next summer.

Practicing: The More, the Better

After you graduate from your first course in sailing, make sure that you find time to practice all those newfound skills and build your experience level. Although many schools offer classes in higher education, don't rush things. Spend a season or more just building your skills before you embark on the next level of education. Your new skills and knowledge will fade quickly if you don't keep practicing.

REMEMBER

We may discourage learning to sail from friends, but after you master the basic skills in a class, having friends who are sailors is great. Sailboat owners are often happy to find eager crew. You don't have to be a lifelong friend; just let people around the docks know that you're willing to help with sailing duties and make a few sandwiches. Crewing for someone more experienced is a great way to build your own knowledge.

You can also take advantage of the opportunity to try out other types of boats. If you learned in a keelboat, find someone to take you out on a dinghy, or vice versa. Sailing different boats can be a great way to expand your horizons, because each boat is different in the way it's rigged and handled.

Unless you live on a body of water where you just absolutely have to have your own boat, you probably should rent or borrow boats (if you have generous friends) for the next phase of your education in the sport.

Many commercial sailing schools also have sailing clubs or charter/rental operations, and they love to get repeat business from their recent graduates. Renting is a great way to get sailing time without the joys (and hassles) of owning a boat. You may even want to hire an instructor for an afternoon just to refine the basic skills that you're practicing.

If you're not one of its students, a boat rental company may want to see proof of your experience level before it lends you one of its boats, which is one reason why you want to take your course at a facility that offers national certification. The rental company may also require one of its staff members to check you out on a particular boat before renting to you, no matter how experienced you say you are.

REMEMBER

Just because you've taken one course in sailing doesn't mean that you're ready for a solo sail in the ocean. Avoid sailing in wind and sea conditions beyond your ability. These experiences come with time, and now is the time for gaining confidence in mild conditions.

Taking Advanced Classes

After you spend a season or so refining your basic sailing skills, you're ready to take the next step in your education.

The U.S. Coast Guard may offer classroom courses in your area on subjects such as safety, seamanship, basic rules of the road, navigation, knots, and weather. Some of these courses are oriented to powerboaters, but most of the classroom subjects pertain equally well to sailing. Check out `www.uscgboating.org` for details.

If you're interested in cruising, you should head to the next levels of certification, such as those that US Sailing and ASA offer, and read Chapter 18. If you're interested in racing, check out Chapter 14. How far you go depends on what kind of sailing you want to do and what other opportunities you have for gaining experience and practical education.

» Staying dry on a little boat

» Needing foul-weather gear

» Bringing the right safety gear

Chapter 3

Planning Ahead: What to Wear and What to Bring

Hoist up sail while gale doth last,

Tide and wind stay no man's pleasure.

—ROBERT SOUTHWELL

Face up to the fact that you're going to get wet on a sailboat. Maybe just a bit of innocuous spray will come aboard, but at some point, you're likely to face a big wave that will jump down your collar, soaking you and all your clothes. If the breeze is light, the water is warm, and the day is hot, that douse may be welcome. But on a blustery, cool day, you want to stay as warm and dry as possible — and staying dry means wearing some sort of waterproof outerwear.

Even more important than staying dry is staying safe. This chapter lists the essential safety gear to have on board: Item No. 1 is a life jacket. Even if you can swim the English Channel in your sleep, always make sure that each person aboard has a life jacket before going sailing. In addition to showing you how to select the right life jacket, this chapter recommends everything to take with you for a fun, safe sail.

Staying Safe with Life Jackets

Wearing a life jacket increases your chances for survival in the water; that's why they're called *life* jackets. About 75 percent of boating-related deaths are due to drowning. In the United States, life jackets approved by the U.S. Coast Guard (USCG), called *personal flotation devices* (PFDs), are required on board all boats. How many PFDs and what type depend on the size of your boat and the number of people on board. Keep in mind the following requirements for the number of life jackets you need:

- For boats shorter than 16 feet (5 meters), USCG regulations require one wearable life jacket for each person on board.
- For boats longer than 16 feet, you must have one life jacket for each person *plus* one throwable flotation device, which must be immediately accessible. Each life jacket must be USCG-approved, in good and serviceable condition, of appropriate size for the intended user, and readily accessible.

TIP

Most boat owners and sailing schools keep the required number of life jackets on board all the time, but you should double-check and ask before you leave the dock.

Many states have additional regulations. You can find information about all the federal and state requirements on the USCG website at `www.uscgboating.org`.

TECHNICAL STUFF

If you're sailing outside the United States, check with the local authorities to be certain that you're abiding by their laws. The USCG regulations, however, are highly respected standards in the international boating community.

Choosing the right jacket

To ensure safety, you need to wear the right life jacket for you. Life jackets are sized by the weight or chest size of the person who intends to wear them; size information should be clearly marked on the inside label. The Coast Guard classifies life jackets based on their use and performance but states that the best life-jacket is the one you'll wear.

On a large keelboat, the most comfortable option may be an inflatable life jacket, as shown in Figure 3-1. This harness-style life jacket has a compressed air canister that can be inflated manually or that will inflate automatically when immersed in water. For dinghy sailing, vest-style USCG-approved life jackets, like the ones shown in "Sizing up your sailing wardrobe" later in this chapter, are comfortable and not confining.

FIGURE 3-1: The inflatable life jackets shown here can be the most comfortable options on a big boat.

Photo courtesy of authors.

Using life jackets correctly

TIP

When wearing your life jacket, you want to ensure that it fits properly. You put on most life jackets like a vest. A snug fit is most comfortable and safest, so always zip up the jacket, and tighten any adjustment straps. The following list provides some important safety tips to help you:

- Always wear a life jacket on a dinghy, because the dinghy can capsize.
- Wear a life jacket on a keelboat any time you feel the conditions warrant wearing it.
- As with all safety equipment, make sure that everyone knows where the life jackets are stored before you set sail.
- Children, nonswimmers, and anyone who requires extra assistance should always wear a life jacket on any boat.
- If your life jacket is waterlogged or damaged, replace it.
- Make sure that the life jacket has a snug fit! Don't put an adult's jacket on a small child; the jacket may slip off in the water.

Children and life jackets

Life jackets don't guarantee your children's safety around the water; you still must watch them vigilantly and know where they are at all times. Making sure that the life jacket fits well and that the child feels comfortable wearing it are very important. Federal law requires children younger than 13 to wear a life jacket when under way unless they're in an enclosed cabin or below deck. For more on sailing with children, see Chapter 17.

Staying Warm + Dry = Having Fun

We recommend that you go sailing several times and find out your favorite aspect of sailing before you spend money on special sailing gear. Planning what to wear for a day on the water is similar to preparing for a long hike or going skiing. You need to consider whether you'll still be comfortable if you get damp or wet.

In this section, we assume that you're not going sailing right after the first thaw, and we take a look at what clothing you can bring for a typical day sail in light or moderate winds in the summer months.

Sizing up your sailing wardrobe

Although a wide range of sailing-specific clothing is available, you don't need to be in any rush to spend money. You can probably find clothing in your closet that works. After you identify the type of boat and sailing you prefer, you may consider heading to the marine store. For sailing a dinghy in colder water, a wet suit may be your big clothing purchase (see the left photo in Figure 3-2). Or you may find that your greatest love is keelboat sailing, and you want to invest in foul-weather gear for wet days (see the right photo in Figure 3-2).

Ultimately, your clothing depends on three factors:

- The weather
- The water temperature
- The size of the boat

Weather and water temperature considerations are fairly obvious: If you head out to sail on lovely (and chilly) Lake Ontario in the early springtime, you definitely need to bring more layers than your friends who decide to go to Key West for a "learn-to-sail" summer vacation (and will probably get by with a few T-shirts and swim trunks).

FIGURE 3-2: On the left, ready for a day of dinghy sailing on San Diego Bay; on the right, the proper outfit for a day sail in a keelboat on San Francisco Bay. Note that both sailors are wearing their life jackets.

Photos courtesy of authors.

REMEMBER

The boat's size plays a role in deciding what to wear and bring, too. Aboard a small boat with a centerboard (dinghies and catamarans), you're very close to the waves, and when the weather is windy, plenty of spray comes aboard. Also, you always have the chance of capsizing and taking an unexpected swim, so you want to dress to stay warm even if you get wet. On a larger boat, you sit higher off the water, with the benefit being a drier ride. What's more, bigger sailboats (keelboats) don't capsize, so your clothing needs are different.

Layering

When you're getting dressed to go sailing, keep in mind that the temperature on the water can vary much more than it does on shore. One minute, the wind is light, and you're basking in the sun with your shirt off; the next minute, the wind comes up across the cool water, and you want your jacket in a hurry.

TIP

Bring clothes that you can wear in layers so that you can vary your attire depending on your comfort needs. Layering is an efficient way to stay toasty when the air is cold, because the air trapped between the layers warms up and acts as extra insulation. When the temperature rises, you can strip off layers until you reach your comfort zone.

Staying dry on top

The best way to keep warm on the water is to stay dry. This advice may sound pretty basic, but staying dry on the water requires a little forethought — especially about your top layer. We recommend that your outside layer be a windbreaker-style jacket.

You probably already have a windbreaker in your closet. Most any nylon-shell jacket works just fine for 90 percent of your sailing requirements. A windbreaker that's a little oversize is nice so that you can wear a sweater or a couple of layers underneath. Good pockets that keep your hands warm (and that you can zip closed so you can store stuff) are nice features too.

Preparing Yourself for Getting Wet

Any time you're sailing a dinghy in summertime conditions, expect to get wet. You have more fun when you aren't too concerned about staying dry. This section contains some important clothing tips for dinghy sailing, and many also apply to keelboat sailing on windy, wet days:

- **Bring a towel and a change of clothes, and leave them on shore.** Nothing's worse than having to drive home in wet, salty clothes.
- **Consider leaving the gear bag on shore and wearing a bathing suit underneath your clothes.** You probably have only enough room on board a dinghy for a bottle of water and a tube of sunscreen.
- **Leave your car keys and wallet in a safe place on shore too.** Assume that everything on a dinghy will get wet.
- **Choose wool or modern fleece instead of cotton.** Cotton is great for keeping you cool on hot days, but it doesn't retain heat when it's soaking wet. Wool does a much better job of retaining heat while wet, but polyester fleece materials are the best underlayers when conditions are really wet and chilly; they wick water away from the innermost layer, so your skin stays drier.
- **Wear the appropriate shoes.** Check out "Picking the Right Shoes" later in this chapter.
- **Reapply sunscreen often if you're getting wet.** Even supposedly "waterproof" sunscreens need to be reapplied. While sailing, you can easily get sunburned because of the double whammy of the sun's reflected rays off the water.
- **Don't forget to wear a life jacket!** See "Staying Safe with Life Jackets" earlier in this chapter for details on why wearing a life jacket is so important.

Choosing Foul-Weather Gear

Whether you're on a dinghy or a keelboat, if you decide that you really don't want to get wet (even in nice weather), you want to make sure to choose the appropriate foul-weather gear. When looking for *foulies* (foul-weather gear), keep the following points in mind:

- **Style:** Separate chest-height overalls and a jacket are the most versatile and warmest combination, as shown in Figure 3-2 earlier in this chapter. Paddling or kayaking tops with neck seals that keep water from going down your neck are popular with small-boat (dinghy and catamaran) sailors, and you can even wear them in combination with a wet suit. In colder weather, dinghy sailors favor one-piece dry suits with elastic cuffs at the neck and wrists.
- **Material:** Many manufacturers offer several lines of foul-weather gear. Lighter weight is for active, small-boat racers in temperate conditions, and heavier gear is for cold-weather offshore sailing. If you have to have the best, invest in breathable gear made from a high-tech fabric that allows water vapor to escape from the inside, minimizing the clammy feeling you get from most waterproof clothing.
- **Room to move:** Make sure that you still have a full range of motion, even with your warmest layers underneath and your life jacket on top.
- **Construction:** To minimize leakage, make sure that tape seals the seams on the inside. Look for extra fabric on the seat and knees; these areas can wear out from the rough deck surfaces on a boat.
- **Hood:** A built-in hood that you can fold away under the collar is invaluable when it starts to rain.
- **Pockets:** Make sure that the overalls and the jacket have pockets. Bigger and more are better.
- **Color:** Choose bright colors so someone can see you if you fall overboard. Avoid white or blue outerwear, because you may be hard to find in the water.
- **Safety:** With all this cool gear, don't forget that you might be wearing it in the water. Give your attire the float test: Jump in a swimming pool while wearing the maximum cold-weather layered look. The float test should further encourage you to wear your life jacket.

TIP

Picking the Right Shoes

Sailing barefoot may seem like a good way to get in touch with nature, but running around without shoes is an open invitation for a stubbed toe — or worse. On any bigger boat where you're going to walk on a wet, slippery deck, nonslip shoes are required equipment. You probably own a pair of sneakers that are fine; look for ones in your closet that have soft, nonmarking soles and plenty of grooves to grip the deck.

On a dinghy, because you're always sitting down, the nonskid tread on your shoes is less important than on a keelboat. Wet-suit booties may be the most comfortable.

Packing What You Need

When you're going out on the water, you want to make sure you're prepared. Nothing is worse than leaving the dock and then having to turn around because you've forgotten something important. On a small dinghy, you may not have a secure space for any gear besides what you can put in your pocket. But on a bigger boat, here's a checklist of clothing essentials:

WARNING

- **A life jacket for each person:** Check out "Staying Safe with Life Jackets," earlier in this chapter, for more information.
- **Jacket or foul-weather gear and/or a bathing suit and wool cap:** Now you have all weather extremes covered.
- **Nonslip, rubber-soled shoes:** Don't go offshore without them.
- **Sun stuff (sunglasses, hat, and sunscreen):** The glare of sunlight (even on an overcast day) reflecting off the water and sails makes sun stuff essential. Make sure that you have a string or some sort of retainer for your sunglasses and your hat. We've proved beyond a doubt that sunglasses sink.

  TIP

  When we're going to be on the water all day, we apply good sunscreen (SPF 30 or higher) first thing in the morning and reapply it several times during the day. Chemicals in certain sunscreens can be harmful to coral reefs and marine life, so make sure to use reef-safe sunscreen.
- **Long-sleeve shirt, neck gaiter, and long pants:** Especially in the tropics, this attire is the best way to protect your skin from the sun. Look for fabric with extra UV protection.

WHEN TO BREAK OUT THE BLUE BLAZER

The only times we've ever worn blazers and cocktail-party attire on the water were at weddings and formal parties on large powerboats, not sailboats. But if someone invites you to go sailing on a fancy yacht, especially an antique wooden boat, be forewarned that you may be asked to take off your shoes to prevent damage to the wooden decks. Make sure that you trimmed your toenails and that your socks aren't holey!

- **Gloves:** Sailing gloves are a good investment unless your other hobby is rock climbing and your hands are well calloused.
- **Hair band:** Keep long hair in a ponytail or a braid. Loose hair can get caught in the lines and blocks. (That's painful even to think about. Ouch!)

Knowing what to leave on shore

Leave the jewelry at home; you don't want to lose your favorite necklace overboard. Take off your rings too, because you have to grip ropes with your hands, and rings can pinch your fingers (or worse). Any item of clothing or equipment that water can ruin should stay on shore. (If you must bring it, at least put it in a sealed plastic bag.) We'll say it again: Sailing is a wet sport, and even a big boat can get wet down below.

Stowing your stuff

REMEMBER

If you need to bring extra gear, use a small duffel bag or backpack that closes securely. Ideally, your bag should be waterproof or at least water-resistant. Leave your nice leather bag or suitcase at home, and bring only what you need; most boats are tight on space. If the boat is big enough to have a cabin down below deck, put your gear bag there, preferably off to the side on a bunk or in a cubbyhole so that people don't step on it. Make sure your bag is securely wedged in and won't fall on the floor (where it can get wet) when the boat *heels* (leans or tips to one side).

TIP

Our final answer to the eternal question "What should I wear?" is to ask the people with whom you're going sailing. They have the best idea of what gear works well on their boat.

Checking Your Safety List

The following checklist of boating safety equipment is for a typical big keelboat around 30 to 50 feet (9 to 15 meters) in length, sailing in coastal waters (not across the ocean, but along it). We also recommend the starred (*) items for a smaller keelboat or dinghy:

- ❑ Life jackets*

  In case you forgot, they're USCG–required equipment.

- ❑ Drinking water and food*

  Always take more water than you think you'll need, and throw in a few extra energy bars in case that short sail turns into a three-hour tour.

- ❑ Sunscreen*
- ❑ Sunglasses, hats, and extra clothing*
- ❑ Paddle* (smaller boats only)
- ❑ Sufficient engine fuel and spare parts
- ❑ Binoculars
- ❑ Chart
- ❑ Compass*
- ❑ Bucket with a retrieval line (for bailing water or using as an impromptu toilet)

  Be careful when trying to fill a bucket by dunking it over the side while the boat is under way. The force of the water can pull the bucket out of your hand.

- ❑ Boat hook
- ❑ All USCG–required equipment for the boat*
- ❑ Sound signals (usually a whistle* and/or foghorn for larger boats)
- ❑ Fire extinguisher

  See Chapter 15 for details on fighting fire on board.

- ❑ Visual distress signals

  You can also use signals such as flares or a flashlight* at night to signal distress by using the international Morse code SOS distress signal (••• — — — •••). And remember spare batteries.

- [ ] Navigation lights

  All boats are required to display navigation lights (also called *running lights*) at night, including dusk and dawn, and whenever visibility is reduced, such as in fog, heavy rain, or haze). See Chapter 9 for information on navigation lights and sailing at night.
- [ ] Anchor and anchor rode (chain and line)
- [ ] Extra line (for repairs, heaving, mooring, and anchoring)
- [ ] Fenders
- [ ] VHF radio (see Chapter 7 for details) and cellphone
- [ ] First-aid kit and manual

  See Appendix B, and don't forget any personal medicines.
- [ ] Tool kit (or a multipurpose tool for a dinghy)*
- [ ] Knife*
- [ ] Lifesling or other person-overboard recovery equipment (see Chapter 7)
- [ ] Spare parts for the boat
- [ ] Adequate bilge pump(s)
- [ ] Radar reflector

REMEMBER

The USCG website (`www.uscgboating.org`) can provide all sorts of boating-safety information, including courses in your area, and can link you to the Coast Guard Auxiliary and the U.S. Power Squadron, which provides free vessel safety checks.

US Sailing's website (`https://www.ussailing.org`) has lots of information as well and offers excellent Safety at Sea courses for coastal and offshore sailors around the country.

PROS AND CONS OF BRINGING YOUR CELLPHONE

Your cellphone can be an important safety item, allowing you to call for help in an emergency on the water, and you can document the fun day on the water by taking lots of photos. But watching your cellphone sink after you accidently drop it overboard is both depressing and expensive. So it's your call!

» Getting on the boat

» Preparing the boat for sailing

» Driving (and riding in) the boat

» Staying clear of collisions

Chapter 4

Before You Leave the Dock

And biased by full sails, meridians reel

Thy purpose — still one shore beyond desire!

The sea's green crying towers a-sway, Beyond.

—HART CRANE

Climbing aboard a sailboat can be trickier than you think, especially on a small boat. Because you want to maintain your cool image with the crew, pay close attention to this chapter. When you're safely aboard (and, we hope, still dry), you need to prepare the boat for sailing. When you complete this process of *rigging* the boat, you're probably ready to *hoist* (pull up) the sails and sail away from the dock. But in some places, such as marinas with many boats around, you may have to use the engine (if you have one) to motor your boat out into open water before hoisting the sails and having fun.

Most first-time sailors have a sailing instructor or experienced friend put the mast up and *launch the boat* (get it in the water). In this chapter, we assume that your boat is already launched and tied to a dock or *mooring* (a permanently anchored buoy). If you have to put up the mast or launch the boat, see Chapter 6.

In this chapter, we focus primarily on the rigging systems common to a small (20- to 25-foot or 6- to 8-meter) keelboat — an approach that provides an excellent general introduction to the different components involved in the rigging process, no matter what boat you sail. Every boat is different, however, and yours may have some steps to rigging that are peculiar to its type. That's why we recommend that you rig the boat with an instructor or someone who knows the boat.

Dissecting a Sailboat: This Part and That Part

Before you climb aboard and rig your boat, we need to briefly introduce you to the names of the parts of a sailboat. Take a closer look at the two basic types of sailboats we discuss in this book — keelboats and dinghies — in Figure 4-1 and Figure 4-2 to see most of these parts (many of them common to both keelboats and dinghies).

REMEMBER

All sailboats are different, so we can't guarantee that your boat has all (or only) the following parts, but this list is a start. This section isn't one of those mission descriptions on *Mission: Impossible* that self-destructs after the first reading. You can always come back and brush up on your terminology.

Following are the parts of a dinghy:

- **Mast:** The vertical pole that supports the sails.
- **Boom:** The horizontal pole that supports the bottom edge of the mainsail. The boom swings from side to side as the boat turns, so be careful not to get in the boom's way as it swings, or else . . . boom!
- **Tiller:** A lever arm that turns the rudder (thereby steering the boat); commonly found on smaller boats (instead of a steering wheel).
- **Wheel:** On larger boats, the steering wheel that controls the position of the rudder.
- **Bow:** The front of the boat. The direction toward the bow is *forward.*
- **Stern:** The back of the boat. The direction toward the stern (the opposite of forward) is *aft.*
- **Cockpit:** The area where the crew sits to operate the boat.
- **Deck:** The top of the hull.
- **Hull:** The floating part or body of the boat.

» **Lifelines:** Safety line or coated wire that runs around the deck.

» **Stanchion:** Metal poles around the perimeter of the deck that support the lifelines.

» **Backstay:** The support wire that runs from the mast down to the stern.

» **Forestay:** The support wire that runs from the mast down to the bow, also called the *headstay.*

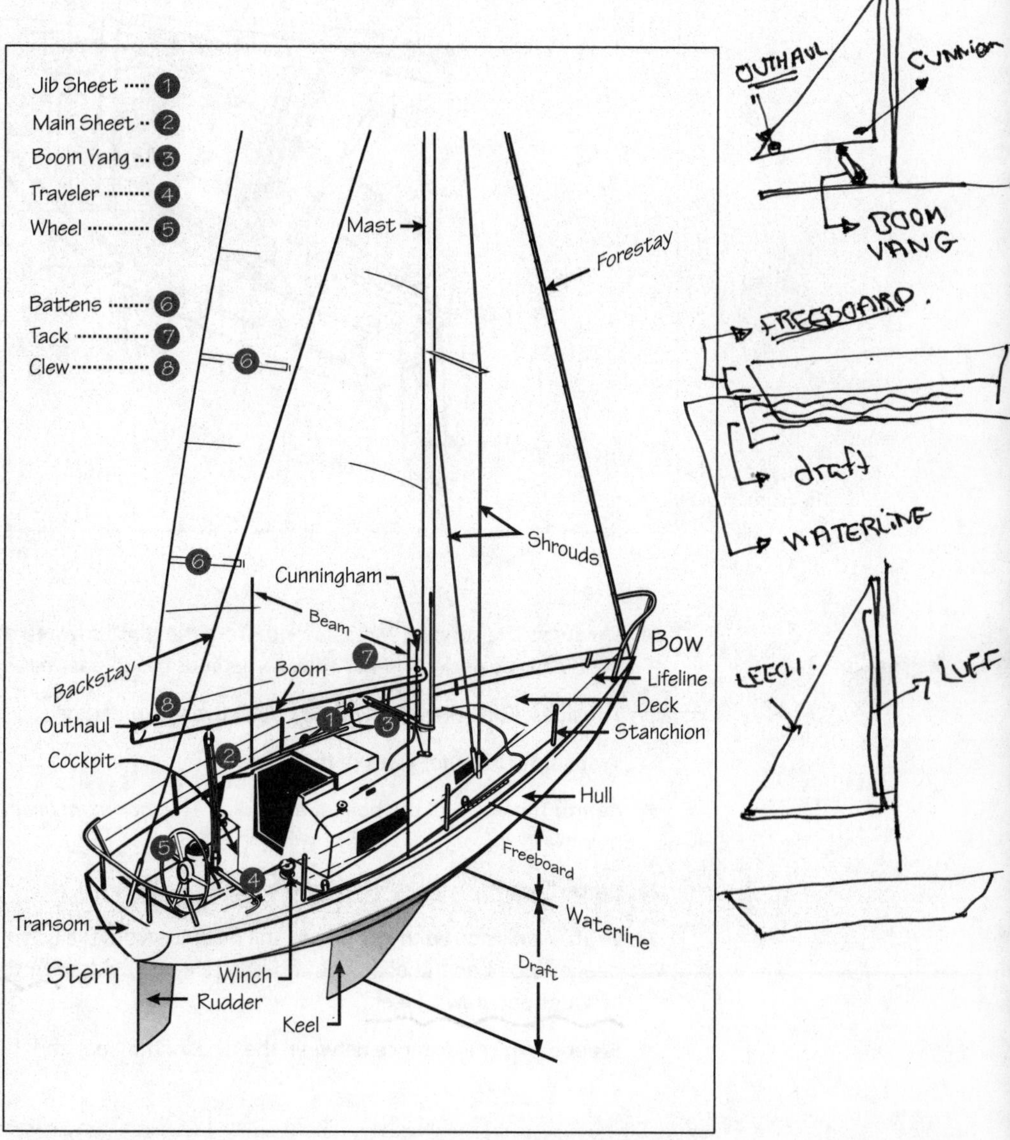

FIGURE 4-1: The parts of a keelboat.

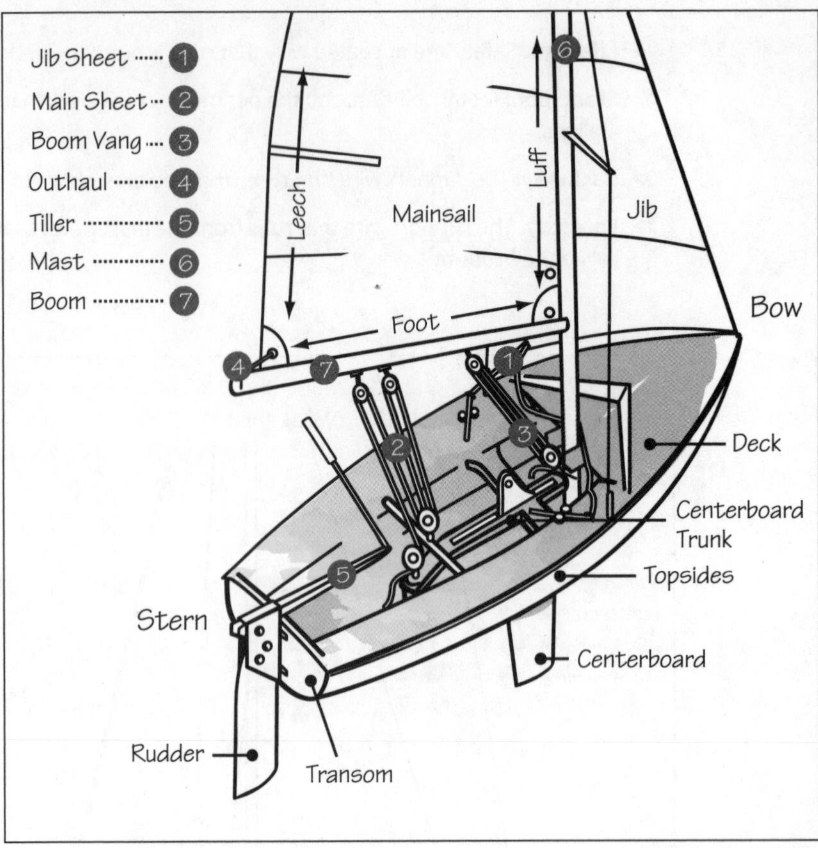

FIGURE 4-2: The parts of a dinghy.

- **Shrouds:** The support wires that run from the mast down to the edge of the middle of the deck on either side, sometimes called *sidestays.*
- **Topsides:** The outer sides of the hull above the waterline.
- **Transom:** The outer sides of the stern.
- **Beam:** The width of the boat at any point. The *maximum beam* is the widest point.
- **Waterline:** The water level on the hull.
- **Draft:** Also referred to as *draught,* the distance from the water's surface to the deepest point on the boat. You can also refer to the draft by the verb *draw,* as in "Our boat draws 7 feet."
- **Freeboard:** The distance between the deck of the boat and the water.

Climbing Aboard

Just as different boats can have different parts, how you climb aboard differs depending on the boat type. This section has tips for boarding all kinds of boats. We start with the tippier boats — dinghies — and then cover how to climb on a bigger keelboat.

Climbing aboard a dinghy

Dinghies, as we explain in Chapter 1, are smaller boats (usually under 20 feet, or 6 meters) that carry no *ballast* (weight) in their movable *centerboard* (underwater fin). Dinghies can also tip over. Because we want this book to help you master sailing, not swimming, make sure that your first step into a dinghy is as near to its *centerline* (an imaginary line that runs down the center of the boat from end to end) as possible, near the midpoint from *bow* to *stern* (front to back). If you're not careful, you may tip the boat and end up in the water.

TIP

If the dinghy has wire rigging *(shrouds)* connecting the mast (near or at its top) to the right and left sides of the boat for support, you may want to gently hold on for balance and to keep the boat near you as you step on board. You may also want to consider starting from a sitting or crouching position on the dock. In any case, keep your weight as low and close to the centerline as possible as you step aboard, as Figure 4-3 shows.

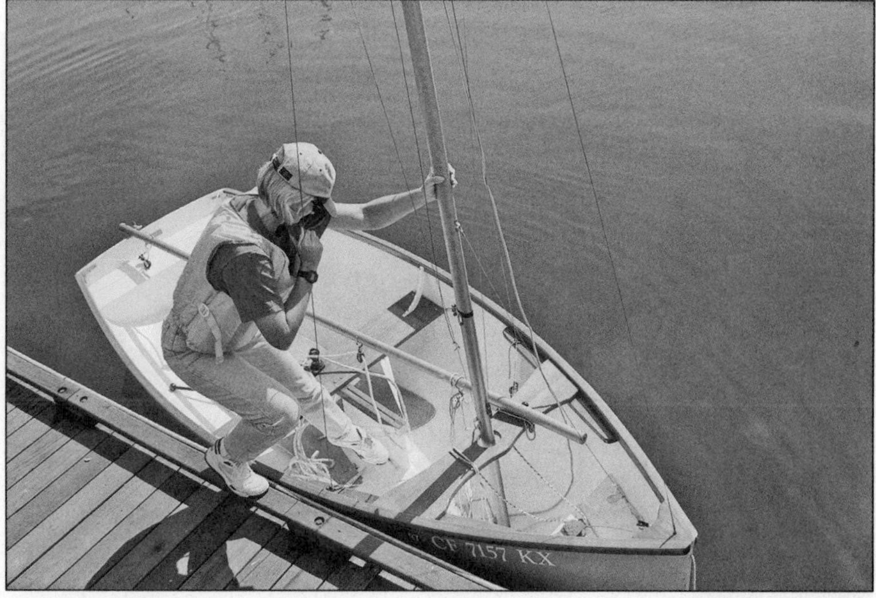

FIGURE 4-3: JJ shows how to stay dry while climbing into a dinghy.

Photo courtesy of Sally Samins.

TIP

Putting the centerboard, daggerboard, or leeboard down all the way increases the boat's stability, which makes moving around the boat much easier. Therefore, putting down the fin is the first thing you should do after you climb aboard.

The boat becomes much more stable when it's moving and the pressure of the wind is in the sails. But until you're sailing, keep your weight as low and near the centerline as possible as you rig the boat.

Climbing onto a keelboat

REMEMBER

Although keelboats have more stability than dinghies, due to their ballasted keel fin, keelboats can be tricky to board too. The bigger the boat, the higher the *free-board,* or distance between the boat's deck and the water. Bigger (more than 25 feet, or 8 meters) keelboats usually have *lifelines,* a wire perimeter around the deck supported by metal poles called *stanchions.* Lifelines help the crew stay on board, but they can be tricky to climb over when boarding.

Some small keelboats don't have lifelines, so you can use the same techniques that we outline for dinghies to climb aboard small keelboats. But boarding a larger keelboat with lifelines from a dock near water level requires different methods. Maybe some stairs lead from the dock to an open gate in the lifelines, making you feel like you're boarding the *Queen Mary.* Or on some boats, an open *transom* (back end) makes boarding a breeze. But if you must navigate up and over lifelines, try to grab a shroud with one hand and then step up on deck and swing one leg over the lifelines, sort of like mounting a horse, as Figure 4-4 shows.

FIGURE 4-4: Peter climbs over the lifelines on a keelboat.

Photo courtesy of Sally Samins

Now you know why we suggest in Chapter 3 that you carry your gear in a bag: so that you can easily hand it to someone on board or throw it into the *cockpit* (the inside of the boat, where the crew sits). You need both hands free for climbing onto the boat.

TIP

Grab the shroud (if you can reach it) for support; a lifeline or stanchion may not be strong enough to support your weight.

If you're not so athletically inclined, and if the lifelines don't have a gate or the transom doesn't have an opening to facilitate your entrance, you can always crawl through the lifelines. Your ego can survive having to crawl on board better than being left at the dock.

Rigging the Boat

You *rig*, or prepare, the boat for sailing by attaching all the necessary parts, including the sails. The best way to find out how to rig a boat is to watch someone else rig it and then try to do it yourself next time.

TIP

Until you're more experienced, always check with your instructor or a knowledgeable sailor to make sure that you rigged everything properly before hoisting the sails.

Preparing the sails

As we discuss the process of rigging sails, keep in mind that many variations are possible. On some boats, for example, you store the mainsail (folded, or *furled*) on the boom, under a cover to protect it from the sun. In this case, take the cover off and skip to the "Preparing the mainsail" section later in this chapter.

Each part of a sail has a name too. Check out the following list for a brief definition of the terms in Figure 4-5:

- **Head:** The top corner of a sail
- **Tack:** The front-bottom corner of a sail
- **Clew:** The back-bottom corner of a sail
- **Foot:** The bottom edge of a sail
- **Leech:** The back edge of a sail

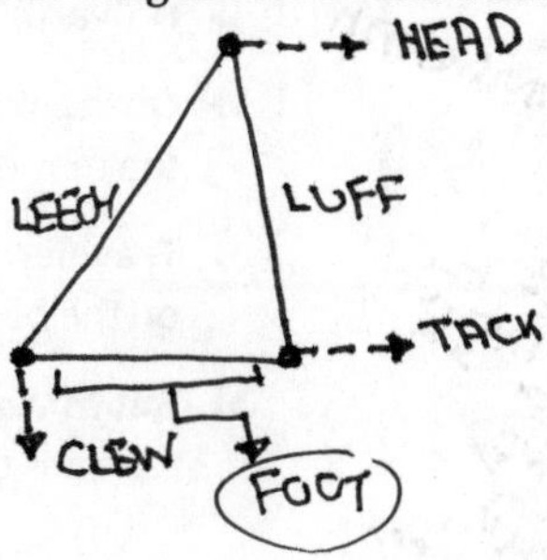

» **Luff:** The front edge of a sail

» **Battens:** Solid slats inserted into pockets along a sail's leech to help maintain its shape

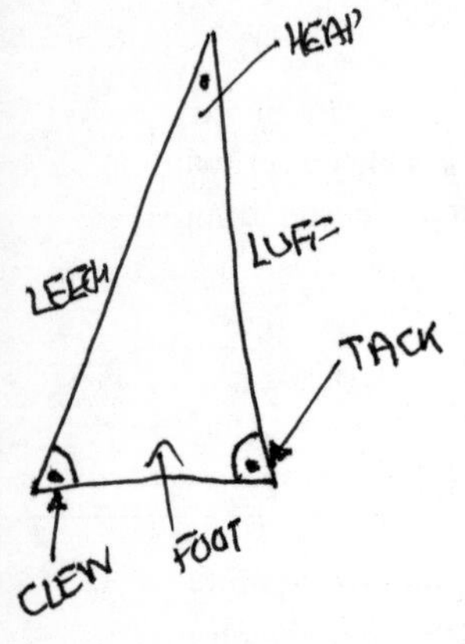

FIGURE 4-5: The parts of a sail.

© John Wiley & Sons, Inc.

Sailors also use specific names for the *lines* (ropes with a purpose) used to control the sails. Here are the most common sail controls, shown in Figure 4-6:

» **Cunningham:** The control line system near the tack of a sail used to adjust luff tension

» **Halyard:** The rope running up the mast used to pull the sail up

» **Outhaul:** The control line system (mounted on the boom) used for controlling the tension of the foot of the mainsail

» **Traveler:** A sail control system that can move the mainsheet attachment point on the boat from side to side

» **Boom vang:** The control line system running from the boom to the mast that tensions the leech of the mainsail

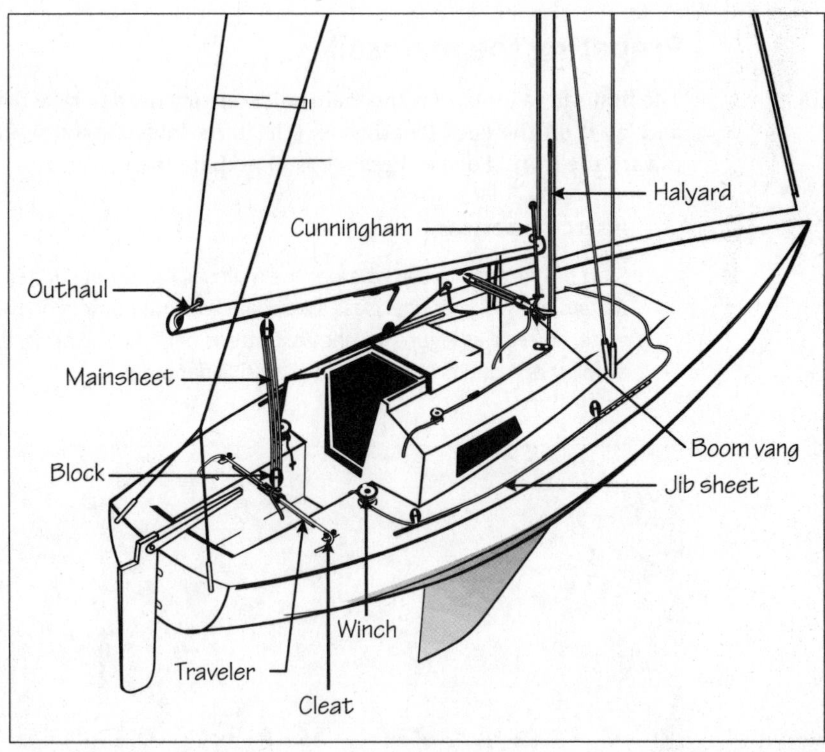

FIGURE 4-6: The primary control lines (and some of their fittings) that adjust the sail trim and shape.

To adjust those ropes, your boat has the following equipment:

- **Block:** A pulley that provides a mechanical advantage to make it easier to pull a rope.
- **Cleat:** A fitting used to tie off or secure a line so that it doesn't slip.
- **Winch:** Larger boats have at least one *winch,* a revolving drum that increases the sailor's power to pull on a rope. (See more about pulling pulleys and using winches at the end of Chapter 5.)

Don't think that you have to memorize all these terms before stepping on a sailboat. Just look them over and acquaint yourself with them; then put on your sunscreen and get your sails ready.

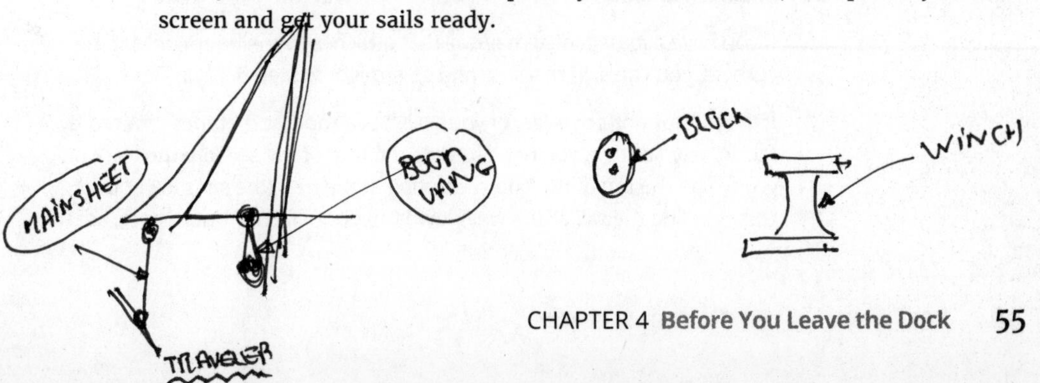

Preparing the mainsail

The first sail to prepare is the mainsail. You may need to take the sail out of its bag and lay it on the deck lengthwise, still in its folded state, with the leading edge toward the front. Follow these steps to prepare the mainsail:

1. **Insert the battens.**

   Start by checking to see whether the mainsail has empty batten pockets. *Battens* are wood or fiberglass slats that slide into pockets on the sail's back edge, or *leech,* as Figure 4-7 shows. Battens help the sail project its designed airfoil shape and protect it from excessive flapping.

FIGURE 4-7: Insert battens into the pockets along the sail's leech.

Photo courtesy of Sally Samins

TIP

   If one end of the batten is more flexible, insert that end first.

   Make sure that the battens are secure so that they don't slide out of their pockets when the sails *luff* (flap). Sailmakers use many systems, such as ties or Velcro, to keep the battens in place.

2. **Slide in the foot.**

   If you have a *loose-footed* mainsail that attaches to the boom only at the corners, you can skip this step and go straight to step 3.

   If the *foot,* or bottom edge, of your sail has a rope (sometimes covered by fabric) sewn onto it, you need to slide the foot of the sail into the track or groove on the top of the boom. Starting at the *clew* (the sail's lower back corner), slide the sail all the way down the boom from front to back, as

Figure 4-8 shows. This process usually takes two people: one to feed the rope into the track and the other to hold the sail and help slide it along. Instead of a foot rope, some mainsails have many small plastic or metal slides attached along the foot that you insert into the groove on the boom, similar to the foot rope.

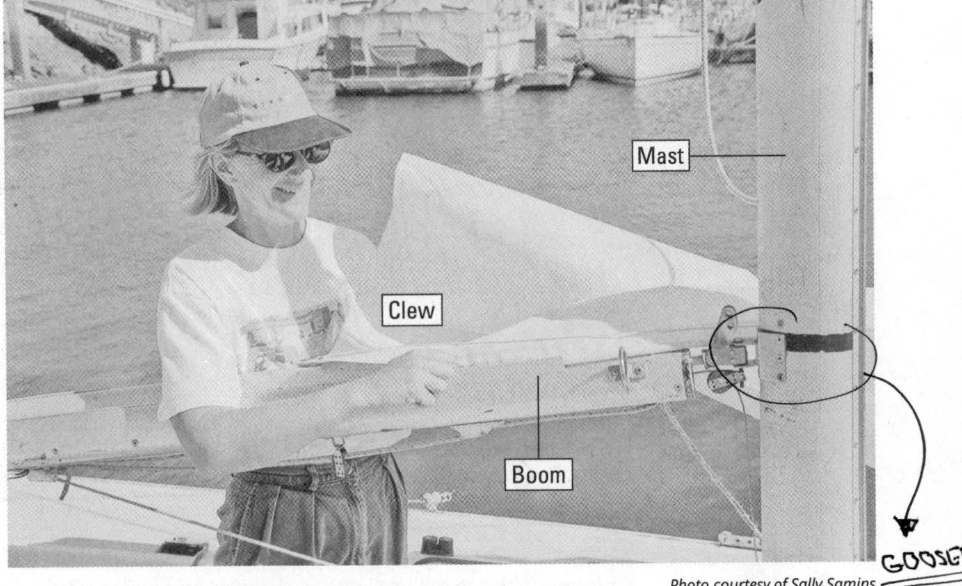

FIGURE 4-8: Sliding the mainsail foot rope into the track on the bottom.

Photo courtesy of Sally Samins

3. Attach the tack.

The *tack* (front-bottom corner) of the mainsail usually attaches to a fitting at the front of the boom or to the *gooseneck* (the fitting that attaches the boom to the mast), as Figure 4-9 shows. Preparing the mainsail is starting to sound like ". . . your hip bone attaches to your thigh bone. . . ." But stay with us; it all makes sense when you put it together.

All three corners of the sail have a grommet or strap loop that enables you to attach them to the proper control lines or fittings. A *grommet* is a plastic or metal ring built into a sail (refer to Figure 4-9). Quite commonly, you use a *shackle* (a closed metal hook) to connect one or more of the corners to the appropriate fitting. (See Chapter 19 to find out how to tie a *bowline,* the best knot to use when tying a line to a sail.)

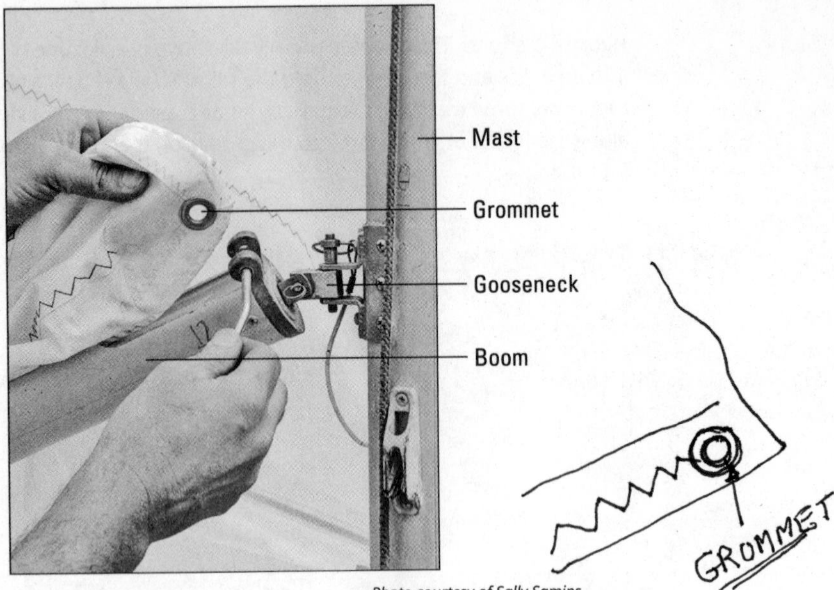

FIGURE 4-9: Attach the mainsail tack to the fitting near the front of the boom.

Photo courtesy of Sally Samins

4. **Attach the clew.**

   Next, attach (usually with a shackle) the clew to the outhaul at the end of the boom. The *outhaul* is the control line system, located at the back of the boom, that tensions the mainsail's foot.

   REMEMBER

   You can launch some smaller dinghies (usually shorter than 16 feet, or 5 meters) with the mainsail already hoisted and luffing (flapping). With these boats, attaching the clew is the last thing you do before leaving the dock. But on most boats, attaching the bottom corners of the mainsail (the tack and the clew) before you hoist is easiest. After you attach the clew to the outhaul, pull the outhaul rope snug, and secure it.

5. **Attach the halyard.**

   To hoist the sail to the top of the mast, you use a halyard. A *halyard* is a rope or wire attached to the top corner *(head)* of the sail that's rigged to let you raise the sail to the top of the mast from cockpit level.

   Before attaching the halyard, pull it taut and then look up, following the line all the way to the top of the mast. Unwind any wraps or tangles before attaching the halyard to the sail. The halyard attaches to the head of the sail by a shackle or a rope knot, preferably a bowline. You can read all about knots in Chapter 19.

   WARNING

   Always make sure that the halyard is securely attached. Use pliers to tighten a shackle with a screw pin or make sure your bowline is secure.

6. **Prefeed the luff of the main.**

   No, the *luff* (the front edge of the sail) isn't a hungry animal. To *feed the luff* means to slide the top end of the luff (usually a rope) into the groove in the back edge of the mast just above the boom — just as we explain for the foot of the sail. On some boats, you feed the first foot or two of the top of the sail into the mast well before hoisting. On other boats, you leave the halyard off, keeping the head of the sail down on deck or tied up on the boom, and wait until it's time to hoist.

Preparing the jib

If your boat has a jib, this section can help you prepare to hoist this forwardmost sail. (A *genoa* is a large jib. To be perfectly accurate, calling a genoa a jib is okay, but calling a small jib — one that doesn't overlap the mast — a genoa is wrong. For simplicity, we always use the term *jib.*) Follow these steps when preparing your jib:

1. **Take the jib out of its bag.**

   Set it down on the foredeck lengthwise, with the front edge toward the bow.

   Jibs are attached at the three corners (fortunately, they share the names *head, tack,* and *clew* with the mainsail), as well as along the front edge *(luff).*

2. **Attach the tack to the fitting near the bow.**

   Usually, you use a *shackle* for this job.

3. **Prepare the luff for hoisting.**

   The system for attaching the jib to the *forestay* (a support wire from the mast running down to the bow, also called the *headstay*) can vary. Some sails attach with snaps or clips *(hanks)* located at intervals along the luff of the sail. Other sails have a *luff tape,* similar to the foot and luff ropes in a mainsail, which slides into a special, grooved channel built into or attached to the forestay. With this system, one person must feed the tape as another hoists the sail. On a jib with hanks, you clip them onto the forestay (starting at the bottom and working upward) without hoisting the sail, as Figure 4-10 shows.

4. **Attach the halyard to the top of the jib.**

   As with the main halyard, pull the jib halyard taut and then look up to ensure that it isn't twisted.

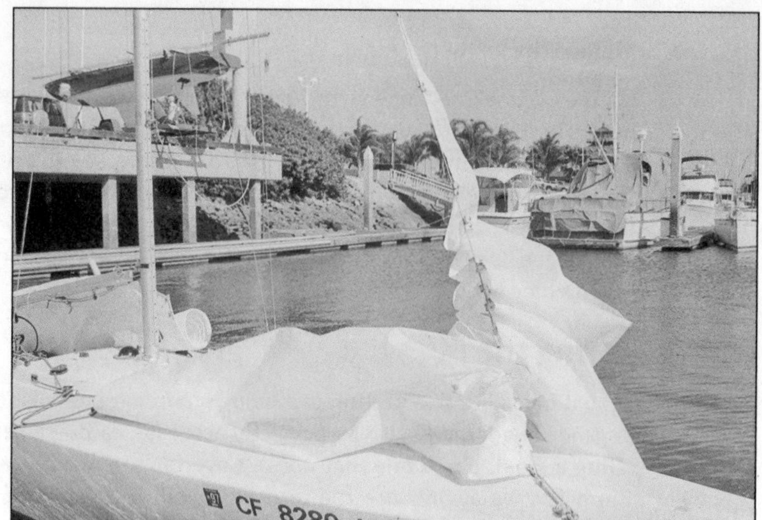

FIGURE 4-10: This jib is ready to hoist, with the snaps attached to the forestay.

Photo courtesy of Sally Samins

5. **Attach the jib sheets, ensuring that they're fed through the proper *blocks* (pulleys) and cleats on each side of the boat.**

   Many jib-sheet systems are available. A bowline (there's that knot again; check out Chapter 19) or a shackle may attach the sheets (there are two — one for each side) to the sail. Then the sheets are run back to the cockpit, where the crew controls them. You must rig jib sheets through a specific path that may include passing through several pulleys. Figure 4-11 shows the jib-sheet system on a typical dinghy.

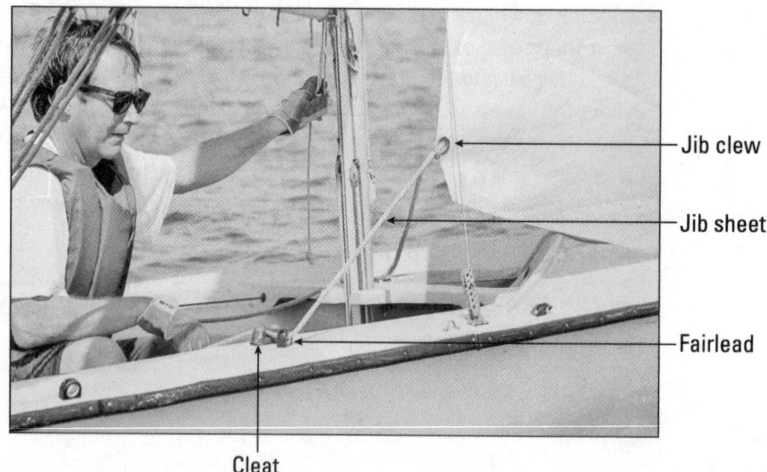

FIGURE 4-11: Jib-sheet system on a typical dinghy.

Photo courtesy of Sally Samins

6. **Secure the jib.**

   You don't want it to blow into the water before hoisting, but you must keep it out of the way on deck so you don't slip on it. So do whatever works best. You might just pull it tightly along one side of the deck with a jib sheet or lash it down, but try to avoid crumpling the sailcloth, which would shorten the life of the sail.

Double-checking before hoisting the sails

Before you hoist the sails, check that everything is ready for you to leave the dock. When you hoist the sails, they begin to flap in the wind — which, although safe, isn't very seamanlike, because the flapping puts extra wear on the sails. Therefore, you want to get sailing as quickly as possible after hoisting. Use the following list to make sure that you're ready to go:

REMEMBER

- **The boat is in a good position to depart and is pointing "into" the wind.** Trying to raise the mainsail before pointing the bow of the boat toward the wind is a common mistake of new sailors. If the boat isn't pointed into the wind, raising the mainsail may be impossible, because the wind fills the sail when it's partway up, putting too much load on the halyard. After you determine where the wind is coming from (see Chapter 5), think about where you can put your boat so that it points into the wind. A boat secured only at the bow naturally points into the wind (unless affected by strong current). Also look around and plan the path you'll take to sail away from the dock.
- **The control lines — especially the main and jib sheets — are properly rigged and have plenty of slack.** Make sure that the main and jib sheets are uncleated too.
- **Everybody is on board.** Also ensure that everyone knows where to be for getting under way (check out "Knowing where the crew should sit" later in this chapter) and what their special tasks are (trimming sails, storing fenders and dock lines, getting the skipper a cold drink, and so on).
- **Life jackets and safety gear are handy.** Check out Chapter 3 for more on the importance of life jackets.
- **Loose gear is stowed.** Make sure that all bags are put below out of the way and where they will (ideally) stay dry. Extra hats or jackets should be put away so that they don't blow overboard.
- **Main and jib are properly rigged and ready to hoist.** Take an extra look to make sure that the halyard isn't twisted.

REMEMBER

- **The rudder (and centerboard if your boat has one) is down and secured.** Secure the rudder so that it stays with the boat if you capsize. Most dinghy rudders have a spring clip or tie-down line to keep them from sliding out if the boat flips. For dinghies with daggerboards, use a restraining line (a shock cord works well) that lets you adjust the daggerboard up and down but keeps it attached to the boat in case of a capsize.
- **You have proper clothing and sunscreen on.** Even if you applied sunscreen in the morning, reapply it now.

WARNING

Before hoisting, make sure that enough open water is around for you to sail away easily. Nothing's more embarrassing than casting off from the dock only to smash right into an adjacent boat. With this warning in mind, you may want to walk your boat down the dock or beach to a less crowded location before hoisting — or if your boat has an engine, you may want to power to an open area before hoisting sails.

Raising the Sails

Now you're ready to raise the sails. The general rule is to hoist the mainsail first, although there are some definite exceptions:

- If the dock is oriented in such a way that you can't point the boat into the wind, you may want to hoist the jib first and then sail downwind to an area where you can point the bow toward the wind and raise the mainsail. This maneuver is tricky, though, so don't try it without an instructor or experienced sailor on board.
- On some dinghies, you must hoist the jib first, because the tension of the jib halyard keeps the mast secure in the boat.

Most of the time, you can get under way with just the mainsail, saving the excitement and extra responsibility involved with using the jib for later.

Hoisting the mainsail

As we say earlier in the "Preparing the mainsail" section, you must feed the mainsail luff (usually a covered rope or slides) into the mast for hoisting. Unless you're vigilant, the luff invariably gets pinched and stuck as you hoist. On a dinghy, you may have to feed the luff in yourself as you hoist. On a bigger keelboat, assign one person to stand next to the mast to feed the luff into the groove, as

Figure 4-12 shows. Then someone else (and, if need be, a third person) can slowly and steadily pull up the halyard.

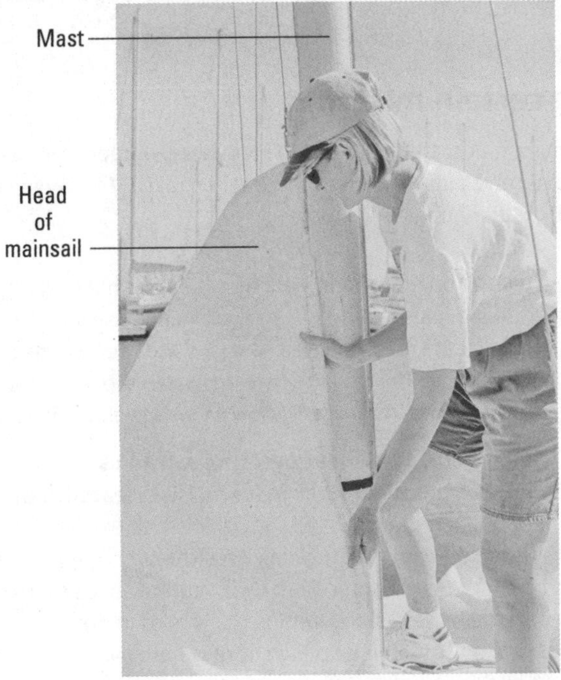

FIGURE 4-12: Feeding the mainsail luff into the groove in the mast during hoisting.

Photo courtesy of Sally Samins

Hoisting the mainsail with a winch

Boats more than 25 feet (8 meters) long may have a winch to help pull up the halyards. A *winch* is a revolving drum that mechanically increases the sailor's power to pull on a rope. See Chapter 5 for how to use a winch.

To raise the main halyard by using a winch, start by putting a couple wraps of the halyard line in a clockwise direction around the winch drum. You want just enough wraps to enable you to hold the line without its slipping. As the load increases (when the sail is partway up), you need to add a wrap or two.

REMEMBER

Even with a winch, the easiest way to hoist a sail on a bigger boat is usually by *jumping* (pulling on) the halyard at the mast. Have a crew member (the jumper) stand at the mast where the halyard exits (presumably above the jumper's head; otherwise, jumping won't work). Now they have great mechanical advantage to pull downward on the halyard. As they pull, another person in the cockpit takes up the slack in the halyard by pulling the halyard that's wrapped around the winch.

When the sail nears the top, the load may increase so much that jumping is inefficient. Then you must *grind* (rotate) the winch by turning the *winch handle* (a metal arm placed in the top of the winch) until the sail is up to the top. Pulling the halyard away from the mast like a bowstring can also increase your mechanical advantage.

Avoiding certain mistakes

When hoisting a mainsail, you want to stay clear of a few important mistakes that can cause havoc and put a damper on your day at sea. The most common problems when hoisting sails include

- **Getting the luff rope jammed, which makes the halyard impossible to pull:** If the luff jams, stop pulling the halyard, and ease it until the person feeding the sail at the mast can clear the jam and prepare the sail to slide up cleanly again. If you're hoisting the halyard, watch the area where the sail is feeding into the mast so that you'll know when a problem is about to happen.
- **Failing to ensure that the *mainsheet* (the sail adjustment rope attached to the boom) has plenty of slack in it and isn't cleated:** If the mainsheet doesn't have enough slack, the sail can fill when it's partway up, which is a real drag for the person doing the hoisting. Free the *cunningham* and *boom vang* to facilitate hoisting. (See Chapter 12 to discover how these control lines affect sail shape.) If the halyard starts getting really hard to pull, stop and look up; it may be caught on something up high or may not have been led correctly.
- **Forgetting a step such as attaching the halyard to the head of the sail:** This common (and embarrassing) mistake is sometimes tough to remedy. On small dinghies, you can tip the boat over at the dock to retrieve the errant halyard, but on big boats, you have to climb or hoist someone up the mast to retrieve the lost halyard. (For more on doing the high-wire act up in the rigging, see Chapter 15.)

How high is high enough?

TIP

How high should you pull the sail? All the way! The amount of tension you need for optimum sail shape varies (see Chapter 12), but in general, pull the sail up until the sailcloth is taut and just barely begins to show vertical lines of tension when luffing. The windier it is, the more tension you want. The visual aid is the tension in the luff, as Figure 4-13 shows. In the photo on the right, the mainsail is too low; note all the wrinkles along the luff and the gap at the bottom of the mast. In the left photo, the mainsail halyard tension is too tight; note the vertical strain marks just behind the mast.

FIGURE 4-13: Mainsail luff tension: too tight (left) and too loose (right).

Photo courtesy of Sally Samins

Cleating off the halyard

After you have the mainsail hoisted properly, you need to make sure that your halyard doesn't slip. Secure it with one of the following fittings:

- **Horn cleat (also called a *t-cleat*):** A common *cleat* (fitting that firmly holds a rope under load) for halyards on dinghies and smaller keelboats. These fittings are simple ones, with no moving parts to break or malfunction. To secure a line around one of these cleats, put one complete wrap of rope around the base. This wrap provides friction to keep the line from slipping when cleating or uncleating. Then make a figure eight and finish by twisting to create a *hitch* on the final turn so that the end is underneath. (See Chapter 19 for details on tying a cleat knot.)
- **Jammer or rope clutches:** Mechanical fittings with a lever arm that "squish" a rope so tight that it can't slip, even under an intense load. (Check out Figure 4-14.) They're especially common on larger boats, where the loads on ropes are higher. Most jammers enable you to pull the line in when it's closed, but you can't ease it out. Keep the jammer open as you hoist the mainsail so that you can quickly ease the halyard if the sail gets pinched at the feeding point. When the sail is up and the luff is properly tensioned, you simply pull the jammer's lever down to cleat the halyard in position.

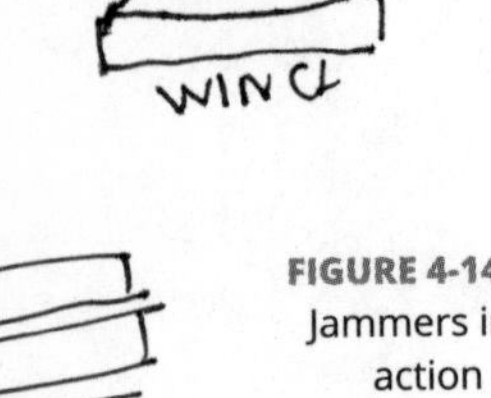

FIGURE 4-14: Jammers in action – "jammin'."

Photo courtesy of Sally Samins

WARNING

Before opening a jammer holding a rope under load, be very careful. Put a few wraps around a winch and then pull snug to take up the tension on the rope behind the jammer so that the rope doesn't burn your hands when it eases out.

Hoisting the jib

TIP

Hoisting the jib is similar in many ways to hoisting the main. On small boats, you can hoist the jib while your boat is still tied to the dock and pointed into the wind. Make sure that the jib sheets are fully slackened so that the sail can luff freely (and doesn't fill) while being hoisted. You can also hoist your jib while sailing; just ensure that the jib sheets are free to run so the sail doesn't fill.

Hoisting a big, overlapping jib (called a *genoa*) on a keelboat is best done while sailing downwind (see Chapter 5 for the *points of sail* diagram), because if you hoist it while pointing into the wind, it flaps against the mast as you hoist. Also, by hoisting a genoa while going away from the wind direction, as Figure 4-15 shows, the mainsail protects it from the force of the wind. This system works equally well even if you have only a smaller jib. After the sail is hoisted, save your crew's strength by letting them pull the jib sheet in and cleat it before you turn to your course.

WARNING

Any time you sail downwind, be careful not to jibe by mistake. If you do, someone could get hurt by the boom. See the "Avoiding danger areas" section near the end of this chapter, and find out more about jibing in Chapter 5.

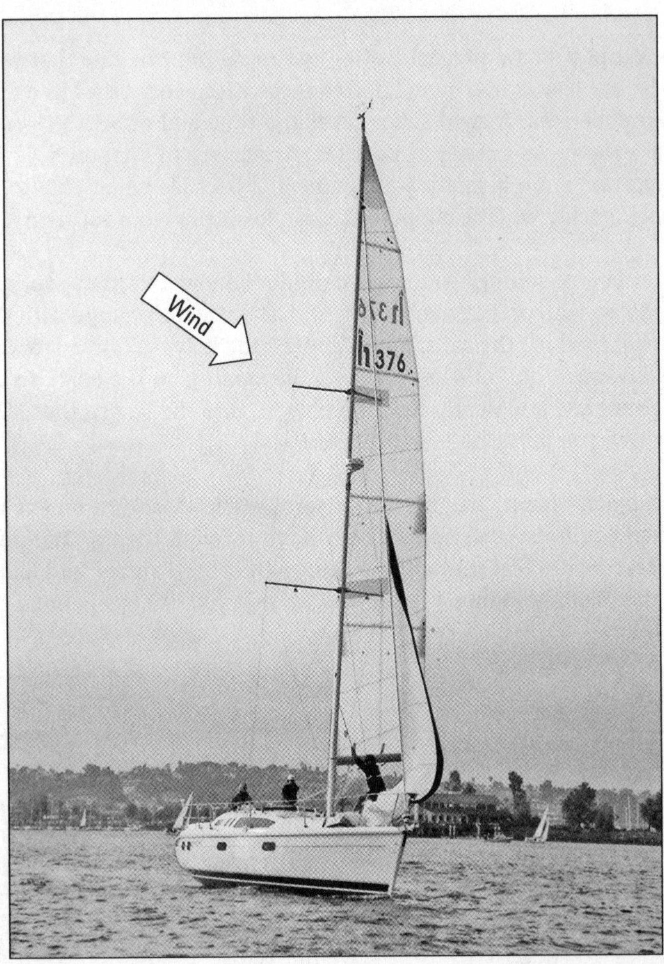

FIGURE 4-15: Hoisting the jib while under way and pointing downwind.

Photo courtesy of Sally Samins

If your jib has a luff rope or tape, a crew member may need to stand on the bow to feed the luff tape into the groove of the headstay. If your jib has hanks (metal clips) or snaps, you don't need anyone on the bow, because those clips are attached during the rigging process.

Cleaning up all that rope

After you've *hoisted* (raised) your sails, you need to clean up all that spaghetti of rope you created while rigging. Some sailboats have a daunting number of sail control ropes, and ropes left to their own devices have an amazing capability to knot themselves.

As Murphy's Law suggests, after you're sailing, the line that you absolutely have to let out *now* is in a huge knotted mess with every other line on board, including your shoelaces. A good sailor takes the time and effort to clean up the mess and make the ropes as neat as possible. As you see in Chapter 5, keeping lines neat is important from a safety standpoint too, because being able to let out the mainsheet quickly when a big puff hits can keep you from capsizing.

After you're sailing, you don't commonly adjust certain ropes, such as the halyards, so you can put them away so that they don't tangle with the ropes you need to *trim* (pull in) the sails. You may feed the halyard into a storage bag or coil it in a convenient out-of-the-way area, depending on the boat. To use a bag, start at the very end and neatly feed the halyard into the bag so that it can come out just the way you put it in — with no tangles!

If you don't have a bag for the halyard, coil it, starting a foot or two from its cleat. When you finish coiling, put your hand through the coil and pull part of the line closest to the cleat through the coil, twist it a few times, and loop it over the cleat, as the photo in Figure 4-16 shows, so that you can easily undo the coil.

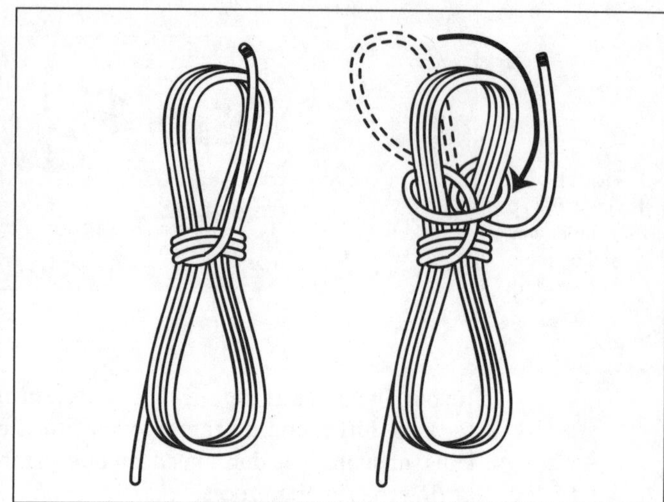

FIGURE 4-16: Left: Storing an active halyard for easy release. Right: Ropes coiled and finished off securely for storage.

Photo courtesy of Sally Samins; illustration © John Wiley & Sons, Inc.

WARNING

Never tie off a coiled halyard in such a way that you can't immediately release it to run freely; you never know when you'll want to lower a sail quickly in an emergency.

Other lines (such as dock lines) that should be put away before sailing are coiled by a different method. Start at one end and make loops of equal size (usually about

3 feet, or 1 meter, in diameter) until you get near the other end. When you have about 5 feet (1½ meters) left, make three or four tight loops around the "throat" at one end of the coils. Then take the doubled end through the top of the coil and pass it over the top, as the right drawing in Figure 4-16 shows.

Sitting at the Dock on the Bay

After you hoist the sails, but before you leave the dock, the sails *luff* (flap) in the wind. This flapping is noisy, the boom is swinging back and forth just above your head, and you don't have a clue what to do next. Don't panic. Just sit low enough that the boom doesn't hit you as it swings through its arc, and take a deep breath. You need to feel comfortable with luffing, because you'll find yourself in this position quite often when you're beginning to sail.

A *luffing* sail flaps because the wind is blowing straight along its surface from front to back. Just like a flag, a luffing sail shows you the wind direction. After you read Chapter 5, you'll know how to *trim in* a sail (by pulling on the mainsheet rope — or the jib-sheet rope, as the case may be) to make it stop luffing. You're forcing the sail to lie at an angle to the wind and therefore "fill" with wind. (But if you're in the no-sail zone, your sails luff even if you trim them in.)

When your sails are fully luffing, they don't have any power, so the boat slows and ultimately coasts to a stop. Luffing sails, then, are your brakes. You apply your "sea brake" simply by letting the sheet out.

Steering (And Riding in) the Boat

All sailboats have a *rudder,* an underwater movable fin that turns the boat. This rudder is attached to either a long stick *(tiller)* or a wheel that you use to steer. In this section, we explain the differences between tiller and wheel steering systems. We also cover where to sit when you drive or crew (on a sailboat, the driver's seat isn't always obvious and can change when the wind changes), as well as areas to steer clear of on a sailboat.

Tiller or wheel?

Most sailboats longer than 30 feet (9 meters) are steered with a wheel, just like a car. Through a mechanical linkage, the wheel controls the position of your rudder. When moving forward, turn the wheel left, and the boat goes to the left — and vice versa. You may think that we're stating the obvious, but you see why when you compare turning the wheel with the other way of steering a sailboat: with a tiller.

You steer most smaller sailboats by using a tiller. Using a tiller for the first time takes a bit of getting used to, because the boat turns in the opposite direction of the tiller. If you move the tiller to the left, the boat turns right; move the tiller right, and the boat goes left, as Figure 4-17 shows.

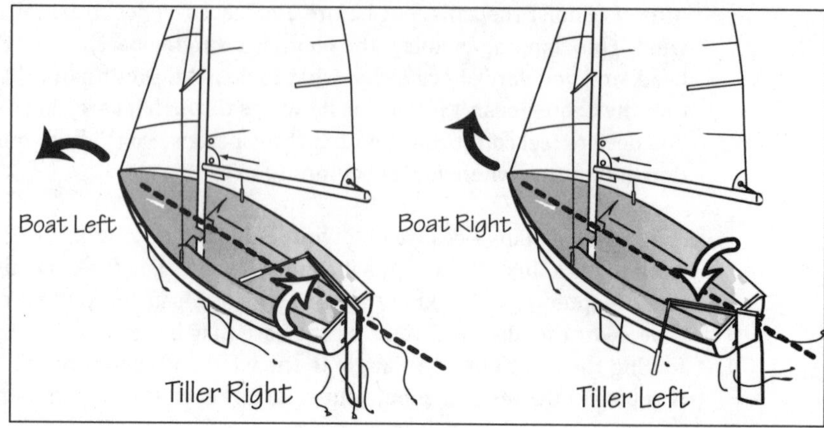

FIGURE 4-17: Move the tiller to one side to turn the boat the opposite way.

TIP

Steering a sailboat is also like driving a car in that turning becomes more efficient the faster the boat is going (and in that you can't steer when stopped). So when you're going fast, you can turn the tiller or wheel less to achieve the same turning arc. To turn when you're going slow, turn harder, and keep the rudder over for a longer time.

"TAKE THE HELM, MR. SULU"

Although you can refer to the person steering a boat as the *driver,* you also hear terms like *skipper* and *helm* (short for the old-fashioned terms *helmsman/woman). Helm* is another sailing term with multiple meanings. The helm is the rudder or tiller — the steering device. It's also the role of the driver on the boat. And *helm* is also a technical word (refer to Chapter 11) describing the balance of your boat's rudder when sailing.

Knowing where to sit when you drive

One of the easiest ways to spot nonsailors is to see where they sit on a boat. If you're driving, you want not only to steer well, but also to look good. The following tips can help:

REMEMBER

- **When steering a dinghy, keep in mind the effect your weight has on the balance of the boat.** Not only should you sit down, but also, the *windward* side (the side the wind blows on) most likely needs your weight to counteract the *heeling* (tipping) forces of the sails. (In chapters 11 and 12, we discuss techniques for limiting heel.)
- **Sit just forward of the end of the tiller so that you can move it freely from side to side.** Most boats have a *tiller extension* or *hiking stick* attached to the end of the tiller that enables you to sit farther out to the side of the boat while steering. Using this extension all the time enables you to sit comfortably while steering — and look cool. Hold the tiller extension in your aft hand so that your forward hand is free to adjust the mainsheet, as Figure 4-18 shows. You also have a better view of the sails on a boat with a jib if you sit farther forward.

Skipper holds tiller extension in "back" hand and mainsheet in "front" hand.

FIGURE 4-18: Proper steering position on a dinghy.

- **On keelboats with a wheel, stand or sit behind or to either side of the wheel.** On keelboats with a tiller, sit on either side, wherever you have the most visibility and feel most comfortable — although keeping your weight on the high side to counteract heeling is important on a smaller keelboat.
- **If your boat has a blind spot because of a cabin top or the sails, move around occasionally to peek into the blind spot.** Periodically asking a crew member to look for obstructions and other boats never hurts either. It's your responsibility to be aware of everything that may pose a danger to your boat at all times.

Knowing where the crew should sit

REMEMBER

On most boats, the crew sits forward of the skipper. The crew members often are responsible for trimming the sails and moving their weight outboard *(hiking)* to keep the boat from heeling. In most conditions, they can sit on the windward side. But if the wind is very light or the boat's sailing downwind, they may need to sit on the side opposite the skipper to help balance the boat.

On larger boats with several crew members, divide up the jobs so that everyone can feel useful. The skipper usually steers (although nothing says you can't trade around and share the joys of being at the helm). In Chapter 12, you find out about other sail-handling jobs for the crew. As the boats get bigger, your individual weight makes less of a difference in counteracting the heeling forces, but you'll still find staying on the windward side to be the most comfortable, whether you're operating the boat or just hanging out.

Avoiding danger areas

WARNING

Certain spots on a boat are safer than others. Before you leave the dock, make sure that you know what spots to avoid (or at least be extra careful in) after you're under way. These danger areas include

- **Anywhere in the plane of the boom when it swings across in a jibe or tack:** Don't forget to duck! Along with the boom, be aware of all the associated rigging, including the boom vang and the mainsheet.
- **Anywhere outside of the cockpit where you walk or stand:** Many boats have handrails that make it easier to hold on if you must leave the cockpit.
- **At the bow and the stern:** If you must go to these places, hold on tight, because the motion of the boat is accentuated at the ends.
- **In the path of the jib and jib sheets during a tacking maneuver:** This path runs from the foredeck all the way back on either side to where the jib sheets go through pulleys heading for the cockpit. During a tack (or jibe), when the headsail flaps in the wind, the sailcloth and ropes are like whips.
- **In the "slingshot target zone" of pulleys under high load:** If the block were to break loose, it would go flying.
- **On the leeward side of the boat:** The *leeward,* or downwind, side is especially dangerous if the boat is *heeling* (leaning from the wind); the leeward side is closer to the water, and gravity is pushing you that way.

- **Shiny areas, such as varnished wood or plastic hatch covers:** Shiny areas are probably as slippery as they look. Most bigger boats have a *nonskid* (textured) surface on deck to help keep you steady, but look where you step, and hold onto something if you can. Sails on deck are also very slippery.

Yes, you figured it out — the safest place in most boats is the cockpit (as long as you stay low and watch out for the darn boom). Check out Figure 4-1 early in this chapter to identify where the cockpit is on a basic keelboat. The deck can be dangerous during maneuvers or in rough seas at any time.

Avoiding Collisions: Rules of the Road

Before you actually set sail and leave the dock, you need to know how to avoid collisions with other boats. Hey, your driver's-education teacher didn't let you drive before you knew the basic rules of the road! In bigger harbors, your main concern is staying out of the way of commercial vessels: barges, tugboats, and big ships.

Following are some basic concepts to help you when your course takes you near large vessels:

WARNING

- **Be very careful around tugboats and barges.** Sometimes the towing cable (which can be several hundred yards long) between a tug and a barge submerges, creating the false appearance of a safe passageway.
- **Large ships and tugboats pushing barges can have a blind spot that extends for hundreds of feet in front of them.** If you can't see the pilot house, the pilot or captain probably can't see you.
- **Large ships are difficult to maneuver and can't turn at all when stopped.** Stay out of their path. Avoid them; don't make them avoid you. Furthermore, the speed of large ships is very deceptive, and stopping can take them more than a mile.
- **Large ships can block your wind from a long way away.** This interference can slow you down and make avoiding them difficult.
- **Large ships must stay in the channel to avoid running aground.** In confined waters, aids to navigation (usually buoys) mark the channel. You may need to consult a chart to find the channel. (For more information on reading a chart, see Chapter 9.)

» **The turbulence in a large ship's wake can throw your boat around.** A heavy ship's wake can create big waves that *swamp* (flood) your little boat.

» **Understand the whistle blasts.** Five or more short blasts is the danger signal. Get out of the way now!

» **Stay away from U.S. Navy ships.** You must stay more than 100 yards (91 meters) from any U.S. Navy ship, and you must slow down to minimum speed within 500 yards (457 meters) under U.S. Department of Homeland Security regulations.

If two boats meet, follow these basic rules:

» Moving boats must avoid stopped boats.

» Sailboats have right-of-way over powerboats, except for fishing vessels and large commercial vessels with restricted maneuverability (which means all big ships, especially in channels).

TIP

If you find yourself on a collision course with another boat, even if you have right-of-way, make an early and obvious course change away from the boat. Don't assume that the other boat sees you or that it will change course. Don't play a game of chicken. Alter your course early to clearly show the other boat your intended new heading to stay out of its way. For tips on steering straight, see Chapter 11. For the basic rules to follow when any two sailboats meet, see Chapter 14.

2 Casting Off and Sailing Away

IN THIS PART . . .

Take a quick tour of the basics of sailing.

Understand what you need to do to stay safe on the water.

Stay apprised of the weather.

Navigate using the latest technology.

Anchor your boat (which is more involved than you might think).

IN THIS CHAPTER

» Feeling the wind

» Understanding the points of sail: Close-hauled, reaching, and running

» Knowing port from starboard

» Tacking, jibing, and getting out of irons

» Pulling in the ropes

Chapter 5

Going Sailing: Just the Basics, Please

It was with a happy heart that the good Odysseus spread his sail to catch the wind and used his seamanship to keep his boat straight with the steering-oar.

—HOMER

Understanding the important relationship between the wind and your boat and getting yourself, your boat, and your crew ready all lead up to the best part: going sailing! If you have time to read only one chapter of this book before heading out on the water, this is the one.

This chapter covers the basics of sailing and seamanship. *Webster's Dictionary* defines *seamanship* as "the art or skill of handling, working, and navigating a ship." This definition is purposefully vague regarding the size of boat or the wind and sea conditions. This chapter focuses on the skills you need to handle your boat in moderate conditions — which we hope describes the weather for your beginning sailing trips.

The first part of this chapter shows you *when* to pull in the sails, and the last part shows you *how* to pull in the sails safely. So hoist your sails (refer to Chapter 4 for help), and get out on the water!

Finding the Wind's Direction

The world of sailing revolves around the wind. Your boat can't go anywhere without wind (unless you fire up the engine, which at this point would be cheating).

REMEMBER

But before you head out to sea, keep safety in mind. Whether you're an old salt or a beginning sailor, being safe on your boat is integral to enjoying the sport. In Chapter 7, we review various safety issues in detail. But remember that no sailor should go out in conditions that exceed their ability. A beginner's first sail should be in light to moderate wind conditions in protected waters. Furthermore, as we explain in Chapter 2, the best and safest way to start sailing is to take instruction from an experienced and qualified person. As you grow in experience, you can expand your limits.

Assessing the wind's direction is of utmost importance to sailors. The wind's direction is our North Star. Where we go, how we trim our sails, whether the ride is wet or dry, fast or slow — all these elements depend on the wind and its direction.

The wind changes all the time, and your ability to accurately sense changes in the wind speed and direction is the single most valuable skill you bring aboard a sailboat. Increasing your sensitivity and awareness of the wind is the first step in becoming a sailor.

Feeling the wind

The best way to track the wind is simply to feel it. Your body, especially your face, can feel the exact direction of the wind if you just let it. Here's how:

TIP

Close your eyes and turn your face until you think that the wind is blowing straight at you. Rotate your head back and forth slightly until you sense that the wind is blowing equally hard across each side of your face and the sound of the wind is the same in each ear.

Practice feeling the wind whenever you can. The wind can keep shifting direction and strength. A key to sailing is staying aware of the wind's changes.

Using other clues to find the wind

Besides feeling the wind, you can look around and see clues to the wind's direction. A flag or wind vane on top of a mast can show the wind direction, and so can a flapping sail, which waves in the wind like a flag. On your own boat, short pieces of yarn tied to the *shrouds* (the wire rigging supporting the mast) can provide crucial information about the wind's direction. Also look for sailboats under way. Another way to see the wind direction is to look at the wind ripples on the water. Watch the movement of a darker patch of water caused by a puff of wind.

After you gain more experience, you'll also be able to assess the wind speed by looking at the water. Whitecaps generally begin to form on waves at 12 knots of wind speed, for example. (See Chapter 8 for more on wind speed.) Being able to gauge the wind strength is important for safety, because beginning sailors should head for shore if the wind is above 12 knots (unless you have an instructor on board).

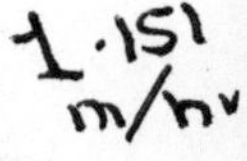

REMEMBER

If you find yourself getting overwhelmed by which rope to pull and what to call a piece of equipment, *relax,* and just feel the wind on your face. A sailor's world revolves around the wind, and you're becoming a sailor.

Identifying the Points of Sail

Figure 5-1 is the Rosetta Stone of sailing: the *points of sail* diagram. As you become a sailor, you can get away with forgetting which side is starboard or which corner of the sail is the tack, but you can't sail without understanding the information in this diagram.

The points of sail diagram looks like the face of a clock, with the wind blowing from 12:00. At the top of the clock face, from about 10:30 to 1:30, is the sector called the *no-sail zone.* It gets its name from the fact that it's physically impossible to sail a boat in this zone. You can call the no-sail zone whatever you like — the *can't-sail zone* or the *antisail zone* or (if the sun is setting and strange things are happening) the *Twilight Zone.*

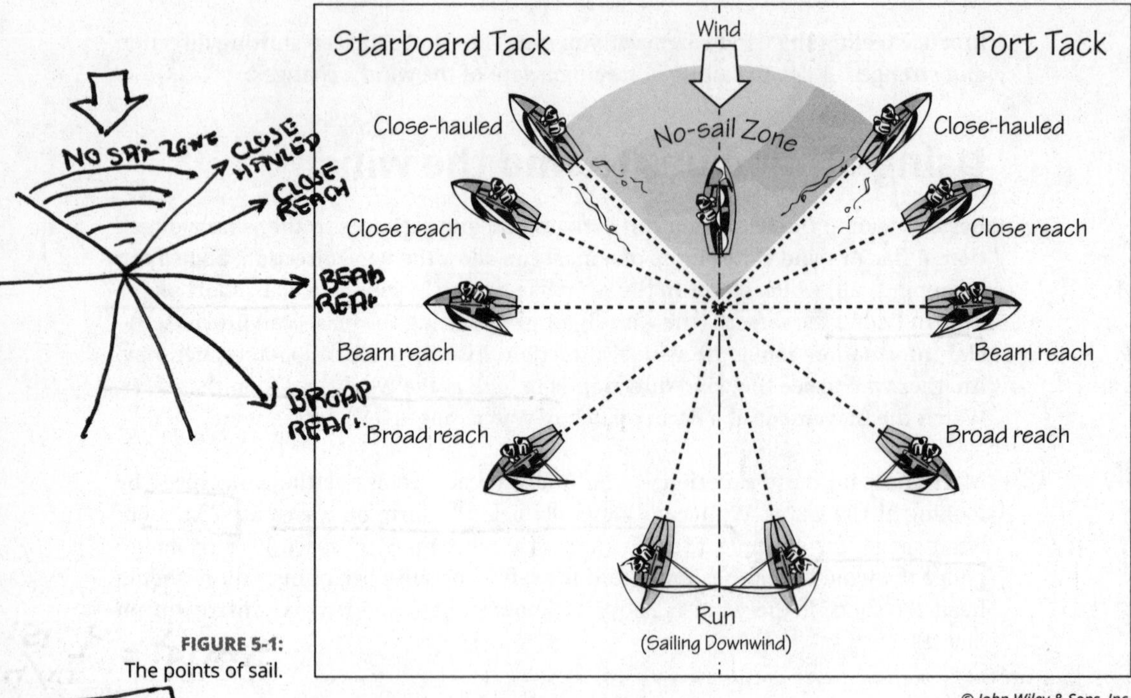

FIGURE 5-1: The points of sail.

© John Wiley & Sons, Inc.

If you point your boat anywhere else around the clock face and trim your sails properly, you'll move forward. This sail zone further divides into three basic points of sail:

- **Close-hauled:** Also called *beating, sailing upwind,* or *sailing to windward,* the closest course to the wind that you can effectively sail on the very edge of the dreaded no-sail zone. So close-hauled is right at 10:30 and 1:30.
- **Reaching:** Anywhere between close-hauled and running.
- **Running:** The course you're steering when the wind is dead behind, exactly 6:00 on the clock face if you're a stickler. But 5:30 to 6:30 is close enough.

More about that darn no-sail zone

The no-sail zone is about 90 degrees wide — about 45 degrees on either side of the wind direction, or from 10:30 to 1:30, if you like the clock. In this zone, a sailboat can't generate power from its sails and will coast to a stop. The problem is that your sails *luff* (flap) even when you pull them in all the way.

As you enter the no-sail zone from the sail zone, the front edge *(luff)* of your sails start luffing a little bit (looking like the front of the sail is bubbling), and you start to slow down. If you turn to the very middle of the no-sail zone, your sails flap like flags, and your boat quickly coasts to a stop. In fact, if you stay in the no-sail zone too long, the wind blows your boat backward, which is called being *in irons.* Getting *in* irons happens to every first-time sailor. Find out all about getting *out* of irons in the "Ironing out those irons" section later in this chapter.

But the beauty of sailing is that you have a way around this apparently forbidden territory. To get to a destination directly *upwind* in the no-sail zone (say, 12:00), you can take a zigzag route (see Figure 5-2), like switchbacks on a hiking trail up a very steep mountain. This technique involves sailing close-hauled and periodically *tacking* (a maneuver in which you turn the boat from 1:30 to 10:30, or vice versa). With this knowledge, you can literally sail wherever you want! (We explain the wonders of tacking in "Tacking: Turning toward the wind" later in this chapter.)

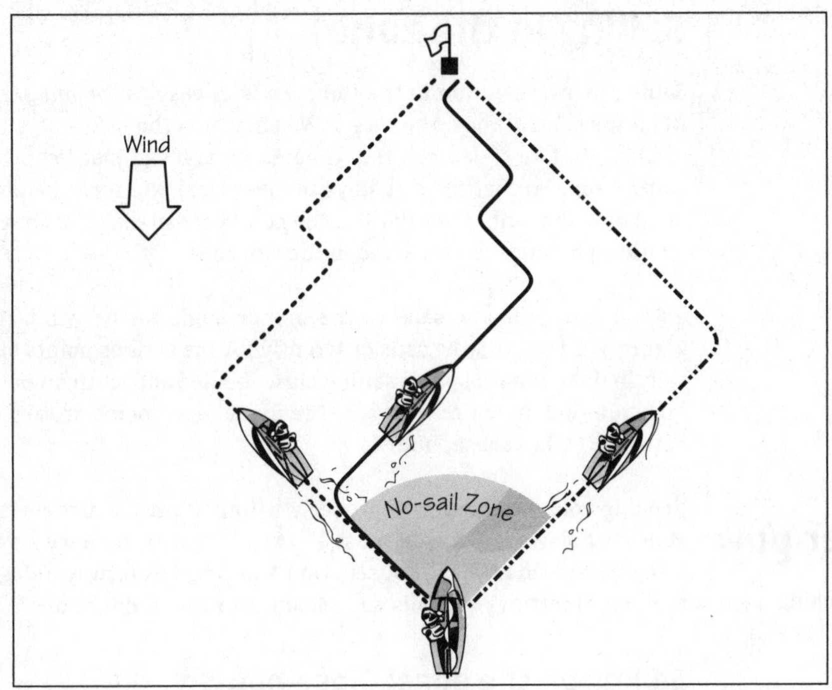

FIGURE 5-2: To sail directly upwind, you must take a zigzag route to avoid the no-sail zone. The choice of the exact route is up to you.

WHY IS THE NO-SAIL ZONE 90 DEGREES?

The size of the no-sail zone is slightly different for each boat. Some racing boats with very efficient sails and keels can sail as close as 30 degrees to the wind. For those boats, the no-sail zone is around 60 degrees wide (the angle from close-hauled on one side of the zone to close-hauled on the other). The wind strength also affects the size of the no-sail zone. In very light air, all boats go slower, and the *foils* (keel, rudder, and sails) are less efficient, so you sail a wider angle to the wind than you do in stronger winds.

You must be very clear on one point: No boat can sail a course directly into (toward) the wind. If you try to do so, the sails start luffing, no matter how tight you try to trim them — as they do when the bow is pointed into the wind at the dock. The boat glides to a stop and eventually blows backward, like any other object floating on the water.

Sailing in the zone

Sailing in any direction in the sail zone is as easy as *trimming* the sail (by pulling in on the control rope: the *sheet*). We show you the safest way to pull in ropes in "Pulling In Lines" later in this chapter. Or you can just *cleat* the sail (tie off the control rope so that the sail stays in one place) and turn the boat away from the wind direction until the sail fills. The points of sail diagram shows boats sailing at all different angles to the wind in the sail zone.

To sail fast, trim the sails to the proper angle to the wind. As you can see in Figure 5-1, you trim the sails differently for the various points of sail. You pull the sails in tight when a boat is sailing close-hauled and let them out all the way when on a run. When you're *reaching* (the in-between point of sail), trim the sails in between. Makes sense, huh?

Keeping your sails trimmed properly is important for maneuverability. Any time your boat slows down, you must be extra-vigilant, because a very slow boat can lose steerage on any point of sail. Don't stop in a waterway unless you have plenty of room to retrim your sails and regain your forward motion.

Sailing on the edge: Close-hauled

The key to sailing upwind is steering a course just on the edge of the no-sail zone, as physically close to the wind as possible — at about 10:30 or 1:30 on the clock face, depending on which side you're sailing on. Because the wind is never perfectly steady, continuous attention and subtle steering adjustments are required to stay right on the edge. When sailing close-hauled, you must trim your sails in very tight, as Figure 5-3 shows. When the sails begin to luff, you can't trim them in anymore, so you must turn (with the rudder) away from the wind just a tiny bit until they stop luffing.

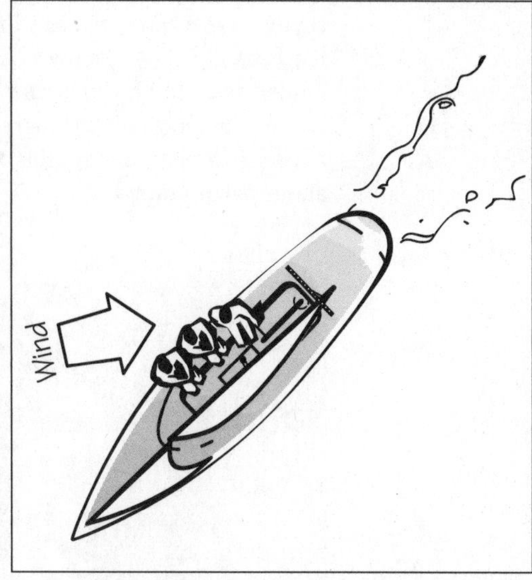

FIGURE 5-3: Sailing close-hauled with sails trimmed in tight.

Photo courtesy of Sally Samins; illustration © John Wiley & Sons, Inc.

TIP

When your sails are full, try to turn the boat a little bit toward the wind to see whether you can sail closer to the wind without luffing the sails. See, it really is like sailing on the edge!

Sailing upwind is a modern feat. Columbus sailed across the ocean blue by letting the sails on his square rigger act like a parachute and push the boat along on a reaching or running course. But your boat can sail upwind by efficiently harnessing the lift generated by the sail and the keel or centerboard and rudder. Therefore, you can sail much closer to the wind than Columbus ever could.

Reaching for the gusto

Reaching is a catch-all phrase for all points of sail between close-hauled and running. Because it spans such a large range of wind angles, reaching is the easiest place to start sailing. Reaching is also the fastest point of sail.

TIP

For your first time on a reach, steer the boat so that the wind is coming from a direction roughly 90 degrees off the bow (blowing across your boat), and trim your sails in until they just stop flapping. Reaching is the easiest point of sail for a new sailor, so try it first, steering the boat to the right and left a little bit to get the feel of how it responds to the tiller or wheel.

If you're reaching on a heading 90 degrees to the wind direction, you're on a *beam reach,* as Figure 5-4 shows. A reach at any heading between 90 degrees and close-hauled is called a *close reach.* If you're reaching at a wider angle to the wind (an angle greater than 90 degrees), you're on a *broad reach.* The expression *broad-reaching through life* applies to happy-go-lucky people who never have to worry about getting upwind.

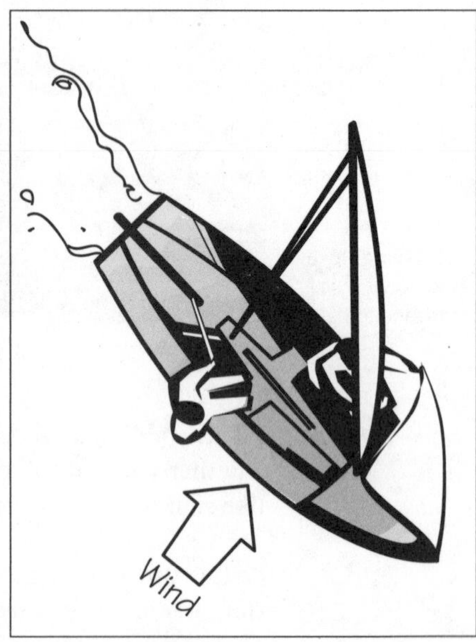

FIGURE 5-4: Beam-reaching: one of the fastest points of sail.

Photo courtesy of Sally Samins; illustration © John Wiley & Sons, Inc.

On a reach, the sails are pulled in just to the point where they're no longer luffing. Although the sails still look full if you trim them farther in, you give up valuable power when you overtrim them.

REMEMBER

An important rule for sail trim is *When in doubt, ease it out!* Check the trim of your sails by *easing* (letting out) their respective sheets slightly. If they begin to luff, you were set perfectly, so pull your sails back in to where they were. If they stay full, you were overtrimmed. Check the trim by easing and then pulling back in periodically, as Figure 5-5 shows.

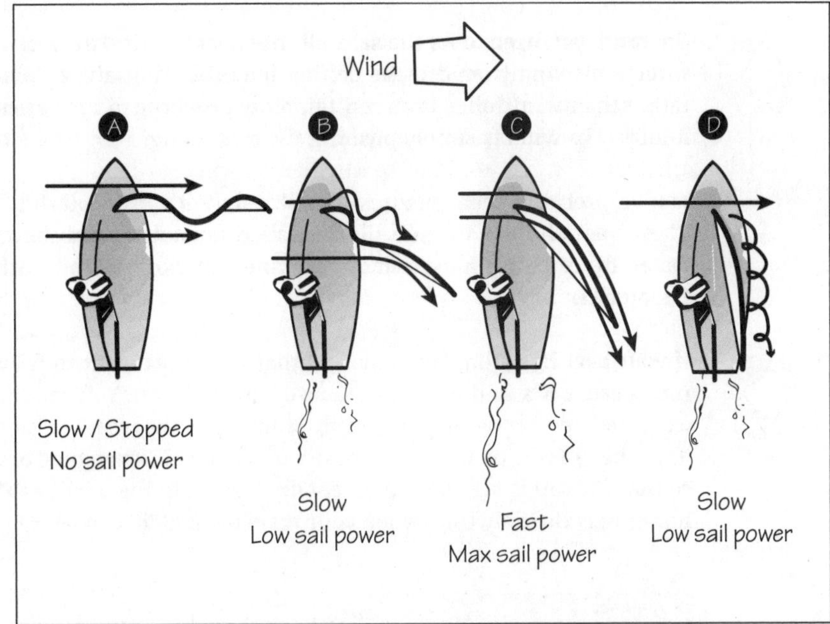

FIGURE 5-5: Stages of sail trim, from left to right: (A) fully luffing; (B) undertrimmed, just luffing in front; (C) optimum trim; and (D) overtrimmed (stalled).

Running with the wind

Sailing with the wind behind you (going the same direction as the wind is blowing) is called *running* (or sailing *downwind*). Sailing with the wind at your back is great; the boat doesn't heel, and because your forward motion reduces the wind blowing across the deck and no spray comes on board, you're warmer. Naturally, you'd like to sail on a run all the time. But unless you're going on a one-way trip, you must at some point pay the price by sailing back upwind.

SAILING WITH A NOT-SO-PATIENT JOE

One of the great collegiate sailing coaches was longtime Tufts University sailing coach Joe Duplin. Joe was a world-renowned racer, famous for his creativity on the race course and his New England accent, but not for his patience in teaching beginning sailing to inexperienced pupils. Joe would sum up all the information in the previous two chapters in two sentences. Pointing to the tiller, he'd say, "This is the steering wheel; pull it this way to turn right and this way to turn left." Then, grabbing the mainsheet rope, he would finish the lesson by saying, "This is the accelerator. To speed up, pull it in; to slow down, let it out!" Then he'd push his student's boat off the dock and hope for the best.

On a run, you need to let the sails all the way out — 90 degrees to the wind so the wind is blowing from directly behind the boat. The sails act like a big barn door rather than an airfoil, so you can't find the proper trim by overeasing the sail until it luffs. The wind is simply pushing the boat along.

You've probably seen pictures of sailboats with big, colorful, balloonlike sails. These specialty downwind sails are called *spinnakers*, and they help you go even faster by catching more wind. You find out how to sail with a spinnaker in Chapter 12.

TIP

If your boat has a jib, you may find that it doesn't want to fill when you're on a run because it's in the wind shadow of the mainsail. You can, however, get some extra horsepower by *winging* the jib. Simply pull the weather-side jib sheet around until the sail fills on the side opposite the mainsail. Then hold or cleat the jib sheet so that the sail is set approximately 90 degrees to the wind, as Figure 5-6 shows. Running is the only time when your mainsail and jib can be set on opposite sides.

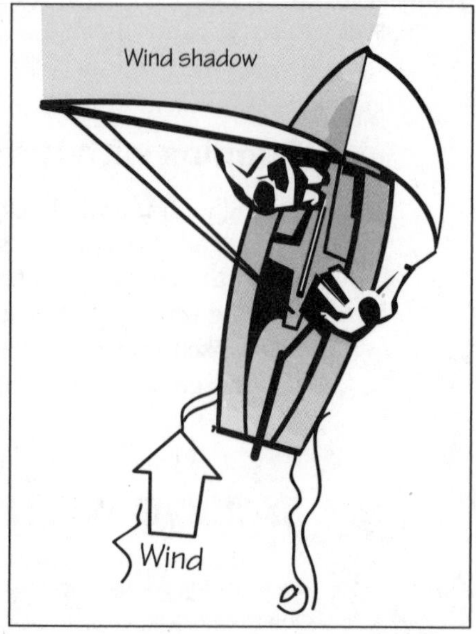

FIGURE 5-6: Winging the jib creates extra speed when running; the jib is out of the mainsail's wind shadow.

Photo courtesy of authors; illustration © John Wiley & Sons, Inc.

Avoiding sailing by the lee

WARNING

If you're running close to dead downwind (or 6:00), you must be careful that you don't turn a little farther and end up sailing *by the lee* (with the wind coming across the same side of the boat as the boom is on, as Figure 5-7 shows). Changes in wind direction can be tougher to feel when you're sailing on a run; also, a wind shift can force you suddenly by the lee.

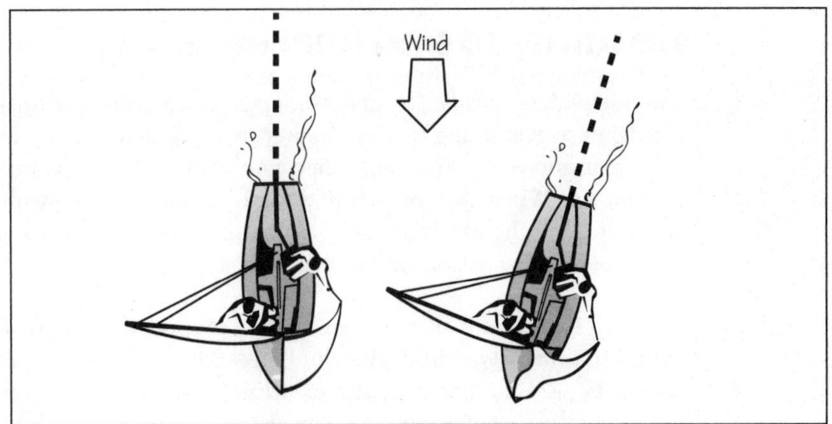

FIGURE 5-7: Left: Running. Right: Sailing by the lee. Danger!

© John Wiley & Sons, Inc.

Sailing by the lee can be very dangerous, especially in stronger winds, because as soon as the wind pushes on the "back" side of the mainsail, it can force the boom across the deck very suddenly and make you jibe accidentally.

You can usually sail 5 or 10 degrees by the lee (compared with dead downwind) without having the boom fly across. But depending on the setting of your mainsail, as you sail farther and farther away from dead downwind on the wrong heading, at some point that wind is going to send your mainsail and boom whizzing across via special delivery.

REMEMBER

You can prevent sailing by the lee by watching your sails and the wind direction. Some boats have an arrowlike wind indicator at the top of the mast that can help. Also watch the battens; if they're trying to flip over, you're in a trouble zone. Another good indicator that you're close to this trouble zone is when your jib collapses because the main is blocking it. Keep asking yourself, "Where is the wind coming from now?"

WARNING

If the boom does start to come over unexpectedly, be sure to yell "Duck!" as loudly as you can to warn your crew. Many sailors have suffered bruises or worse from getting whacked in the head by the boom.

Pointing Out the Basic Sailing Terms

You need to be familiar with some basic sailing terminology before getting into sailing maneuvers. The following section covers *heading up* and *bearing away*, *port* and *starboard*, and *windward* and *leeward*.

Heading up and bearing away

The two phrases *heading up* and *bearing away* describe any turn on a sailboat. As with almost everything in this chapter, their definitions are also relative to the all-important wind direction. When you make a turn toward the wind, you're *heading up*. When you're steering with a tiller (and sitting in the proper position — on the windward side, facing the sails, as we show in Chapter 4), you push the tiller away from you to head up.

The term *bearing away* is more common than *heading down* or *bearing off*, but they all mean a turn away from the wind direction. You pull the tiller toward you to bear away — assuming that you're sitting in the proper position. If you were to sail in a complete circle, you would by definition be bearing away half the time and heading up half the time. Figure 5-8 shows both heading up and bearing away.

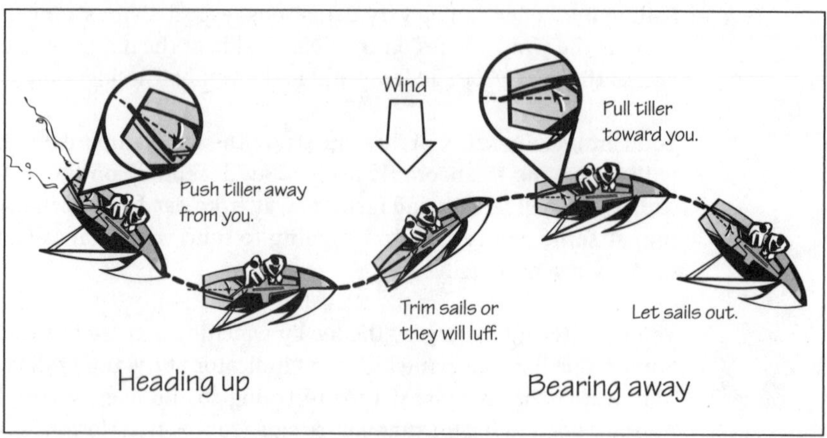

Wind
Push tiller away from you.
Pull tiller toward you.
Trim sails or they will luff.
Let sails out.
Heading up
Bearing away

FIGURE 5-8: Heading up and bearing away.

Port and starboard tack

REMEMBER

Port is left, and *starboard* is right (when you're facing the *bow*, the front of the boat). The easiest way to keep these new terms straight is to remember that both *left* and *port* are shorter than *right* and *starboard*. These nautical words for left and right are optional much of the time, because their land-based cousins are equally clear, but using them is important when you're describing whether a boat is on port or starboard tack.

When you're sailing with the wind coming over the left side of your boat, you're on *port tack*. When the wind is coming over the boat's right side, you're on *starboard tack*. Whether you're close-hauled, reaching, or running doesn't matter; the determining factor is which side of the boat the wind is hitting first (except if you're sailing by the lee, as described in "Avoiding sailing by the lee" earlier in this chapter).

Windward and leeward

The left side of your boat is always the port side, but which is the *windward* and which is the *leeward* side changes depending on the angle of the wind to your boat. The wind always hits the windward side of the boat first. The leeward side, then, is the other side of the boat. You can remember *leeward* because the word comes from *in the lee,* which means "out of the wind." The wind pushes your sails onto the leeward side. If your sails are in the center, they're luffing, and you're *in irons.* (See "Ironing out those irons" later in this chapter.)

REMEMBER

Except when you're winging out the jib on a run, you always set your sails on the leeward side. If you get confused about which side is windward and which is leeward, simply let the jib or mainsail luff so that the sail flaps like a flag as Figure 5-9 shows. Whichever side the sail is flapping toward is the leeward side.

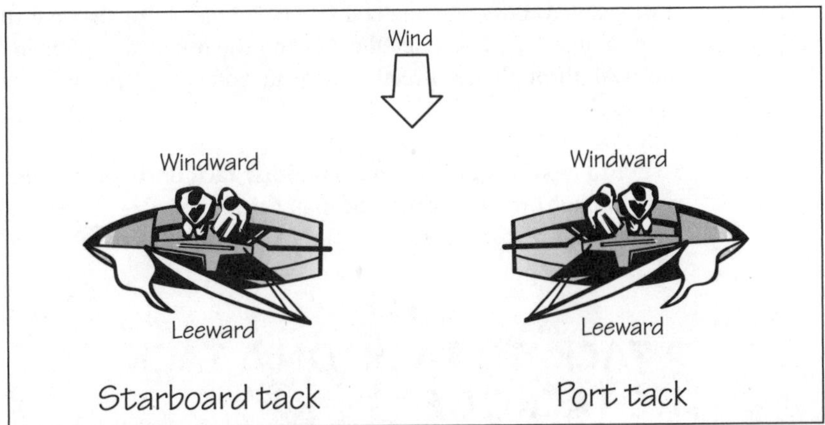

FIGURE 5-9: The wind pushes the sails onto the leeward side.

When the wind's blowing, docks, buoys, and land also have two sides relative to the wind. The side closer to the wind is called *windward,* and the side farther away from the wind is called *leeward.* The windward side of an island can be much wetter, as storms hit that side first; the leeward side is calm and protected.

Making the Basic Sailing Maneuvers

Imagine that you're sailing along on a nice beam reach, but a long shoreline looms in front of your bow. You can avoid this obstruction by choosing one of the two basic sailing maneuvers:

- **Tacking**, or changing tacks by turning the boat from one side of the no-sail zone to the other
- **Jibing**, or changing tacks by turning the boat away from the wind until the wind blows on the opposite side

This section also delves into the most common mistake in tacking: getting *in irons* (getting stuck pointing into the wind).

Tacking: Turning toward the wind

Earlier, in the "More about that darn no-sail zone" section, we point out that you must take a zigzag route to reach an upwind destination. First, you sail on a close-hauled course on one tack; then you *tack* (turn the boat through the no-sail zone) and sail a close-hauled course on the other tack. This maneuver of turning the boat through the dreaded no-sail zone, or "through the wind," is called *tacking*.

To get to a point upwind, you can either tack once (assuming that the harbor is wide enough), or you can tack many times. You're the skipper, so you decide! Refer to Figure 5-2 to see examples of several upwind tacks.

A TACK, TO TACK, ON A TACK, TIC-TACK-TOE

The word *tack* has many meanings in sailing. The front-bottom corner of a sail is the *tack*. The noun *tack* also refers to the boat's heading in relation to the wind (that is, on *starboard* or *port tack*). *Tacking* is the act of changing tacks by turning through the wind, entering the no-sail zone from one side and exiting the other.

Here are the steps in tacking (see Figure 5-10).

1. **Prepare your crew by calling out "Ready to tack!"**

   Make sure that your crew members are ready and in their positions.

2. **Call out "Tacking!" and begin turning the boat toward the wind (heading up), as shown in photo C in Figure 5-10.**

   REMEMBER

   Instead of using the word *tacking,* some sailors say *helm's alee* or *hard alee,* meaning that their helm (the rudder) has been put hard over to the leeward side to initiate the turn. As with most sailing terms, any hail will do, as long as everyone on board understands it.

   As you begin to turn, the sail begins to luff wildly. This step is when most beginners have problems, because if you stop turning at this point, you get stuck in the no-sail zone.

   WARNING

   Don't forget to duck your head as the boom swings across.

3. **Release the old jib sheet and trim the new one as the boat rotates through the no-sail zone.**

   Your crew can omit this step if you don't have a jib.

4. **Switch sides (see the middle photo in Figure 5-10).**

   You (and your crew, if necessary) switch sides to retain visibility and to get your weight to the new windward side. You may find moving across to be easiest when the boat turns through the no-sail zone — especially on a dinghy, where your weight is needed as ballast when the sails fill on the new close-hauled course.

5. **Keep turning the boat until you exit the no-sail zone.**

   Slow your turn as the sails begin to fill on the new side. When you're safely out of the no-sail zone, begin steering straight.

6. **Check the trim of the sails on the new tack (see the top photo of Figure 5-10).**

   Now the wind is blowing across the other side of the boat. Congratulations! You've changed tacks successfully. As you settle in on a close-hauled course and confirm the proper trim of your sails, you may want to cleat the sheets if they're pulling so hard that holding them is uncomfortable.

WARNING

When you're tacking, turning all the way through the no-sail zone is important. As the boat turns and the sails flap, your boat is losing momentum. Dally too long in this zone, and you risk losing headway and getting stuck *in irons*, as we discuss in the next section. Make sure that you keep turning until the boat is turned far enough on the other tack that you can trim the sails in without any luffing, and start accelerating. The entire maneuver should take about 5 seconds on a small keelboat or dinghy.

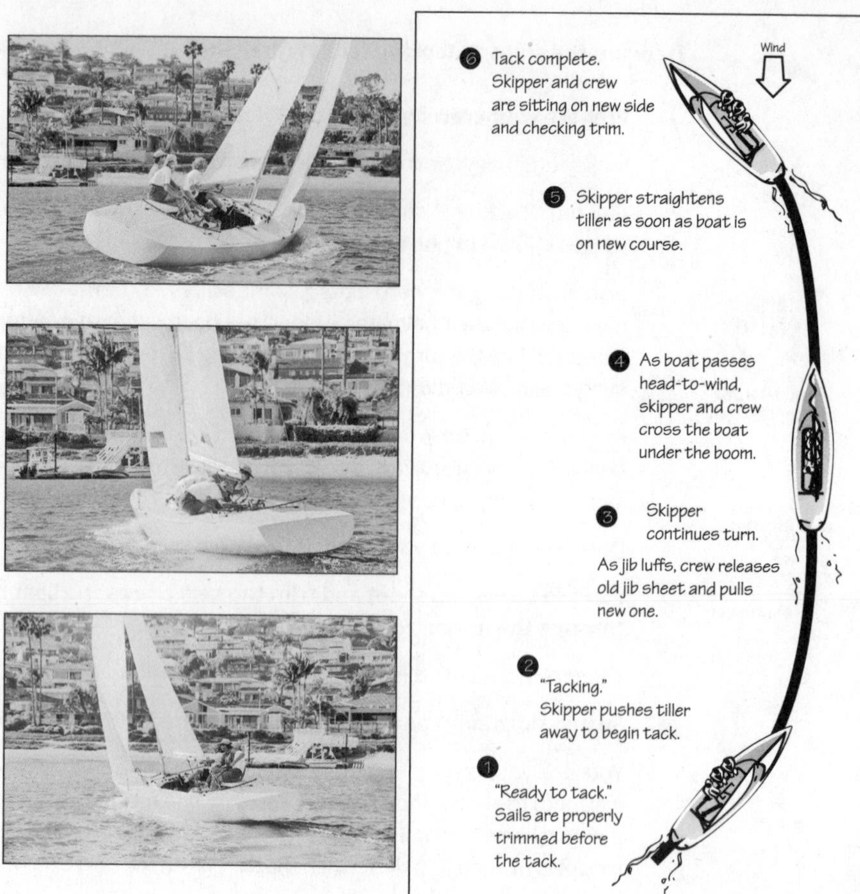

Wind
6 Tack complete. Skipper and crew are sitting on new side and checking trim.
5 Skipper straightens tiller as soon as boat is on new course.
4 As boat passes head-to-wind, skipper and crew cross the boat under the boom.
3 Skipper continues turn.
As jib luffs, crew releases old jib sheet and pulls new one.
2 "Tacking." Skipper pushes tiller away to begin tack.
1 "Ready to tack." Sails are properly trimmed before the tack.

FIGURE 5-10: The steps in tacking.

Photos courtesy of Sally Samins; illustration © John Wiley & Sons, Inc.

Ironing out those irons

REMEMBER

The most common mistake beginners make when trying to tack is getting the boat stuck in the no-sail zone — dead in the water, with no maneuverability. Just like the steering wheel on a car, the tiller has no effect if your boat isn't moving. Being stuck *head-to-wind* in the no-sail zone is called being *in irons.* (Some interesting reason going back to the days of the square riggers must explain why this situation is called "in irons," but that's a story for another day.) You get in irons when you don't turn the boat all the way through the no-sail zone during a tack, if you turn too slowly during a tack, or when you try to sail too close to the wind direction.

To get out of irons and moving again on a boat without a jib, follow these steps:

1. **Uncleat or release the mainsheet.**

   Keep it released until your boat has turned all the way to a close reach. Your boat needs the mainsheet eased to be able to rotate out of the no-sail zone.

2. **Push the tiller (or turn the wheel) to one side.**

   Keep the helm hard over until the boat backs away to a close-reaching position. Be patient; the boat turns as it starts to go backward. Basically, you're doing the sailing equivalent of a three-point turn. To speed the process, you can push on the boom to *back* the mainsail (fill it backward) and help the boat go in reverse.

3. **Trim the sails, and steer straight (don't pinch!).**

   You're off!

Sounds easy, right? But beginning sailors are impatient; they tend to steer back and forth as they go backward, remaining stuck in irons. Just leave the helm hard over to one side or the other until you're on a reaching heading.

TIP

If your boat has a jib, you have an additional — and powerful — tool for escaping the clutches of the no-sail zone. To get out of irons on a boat with a jib, follow these steps:

1. **Pull the jib sheet taut on one side, and put the tiller to the opposite side.**

   If you're pointed head to wind, either side works equally well. The jib fills backward and pushes the bow, as Figure 5-11 shows.

2. **Keep your mainsheet loose so that the main doesn't fill until the boat rotates around and is pointed on a reaching course.**

   Keep the tiller hard over on the side opposite the jib. With a wheel, you turn toward the jib.

3. **Release the jib sheet, and trim both sails in on the "proper" side as the boat accelerates.**

4. **Straighten the tiller or wheel to avoid turning back up into the wind when the boat begins to move forward again.**

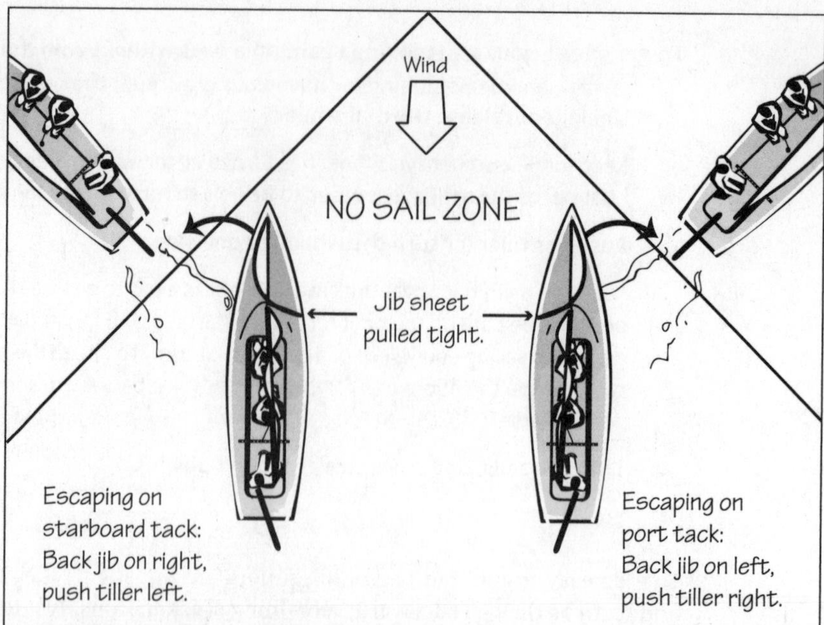
Wind
NO SAIL ZONE
Jib sheet
pulled tight.
Escaping on
starboard tack:
Back jib on right,
push tiller left.
Escaping on
port tack:
Back jib on left,
push tiller right.

FIGURE 5-11: Get out of irons by pushing the tiller to one side and the jib to the other.

Jibing: Turning away from the wind

The other method of changing tacks (changing your direction so that the wind is blowing over the other side of the boat) is turning away from the wind and *jibing*. (Some books spell the term *gybing* — the British style. We stick with *jibing*, in which *ji* is pronounced as in *giant*.)

WARNING

Because the downwind side of the points of sail diagram doesn't have a no-sail zone, jibing should be easier than tacking, and in some ways, jibing *is* easier, because you need to change course by only a few degrees instead of the 90 degrees required when tacking. But jibing is inherently more dangerous than tacking because of the force with which the boom swings across the cockpit. Keep in mind that you're on a broad reach or a run before you jibe, so the sails are eased a long way out; therefore, that boom has a long way to travel across the boat. You can also start jibing from a reach, but doing so requires a bigger turn.

The following steps and Figure 5-12 explain in detail how to jibe:

1. **Prepare your crew for the jibe by calling out "Ready to jibe!"**

   Reminding them to duck never hurts. Given the force with which the boom can swing across, you need to make sure that your crew members are ready and in position for this maneuver.

2. **Call out "Jibing!"; then start turning the boat away from the wind (bearing away), and begin pulling (or have your crew pull) the main to the other side.**

   The traditional term is "Jibe-ho!" Feel free to add "Boom coming across!" or "Duck!" if you see that someone is in danger of getting hit by the boom.

   TIP

   You don't need a big or a fast turn, because there's no equivalent to being stuck in irons on this side of the points of sail diagram. Unlike tacking, in which you have to keep turning the boat so that you don't get stuck head-to-wind, jibing may not require you to turn the boat at all if you're already heading straight downwind.

   On bigger boats with several crew members, having a person other than the skipper pull in the mainsheet is safer because of the amount of line to pull in and then release after the boom crosses the boat. (Make sure that crew members keep their feet clear of all that mainsheet line.)

3. **Make sure every crew is attentive as the boom comes across the boat.**

   As you turn and the wind shifts from one side of the boat to the other, the wind wants to push the mainsail to the other side with tremendous force. If you didn't pull the boom across in a controlled manner (in step 2), at this point it will come flying across, taking with it everything in its path — so use extreme care not to let this force pull the line through your hands. And keep your head low.

4. **Stop turning, and steer straight as you trim the sails on the new jibe.**

   If you have a jib, you can pull it across to the opposite side now.

5. **Switch sides of the boat.**

   On a keelboat, you can perform this step whenever you're most comfortable. On a dinghy, you need to switch sides as soon as the boom flies overhead or immediately afterward so that your weight keeps the boat from tipping. The entire jibing maneuver takes about 4 seconds on a small keelboat or dinghy.

WARNING

In windy conditions, you may choose to change tacks without jibing. Instead, just turn toward the wind, tack around, and then head down to your new course. Equipment breaks easily when you're jibing in strong winds because of the sudden load on the mainsail after it swings across.

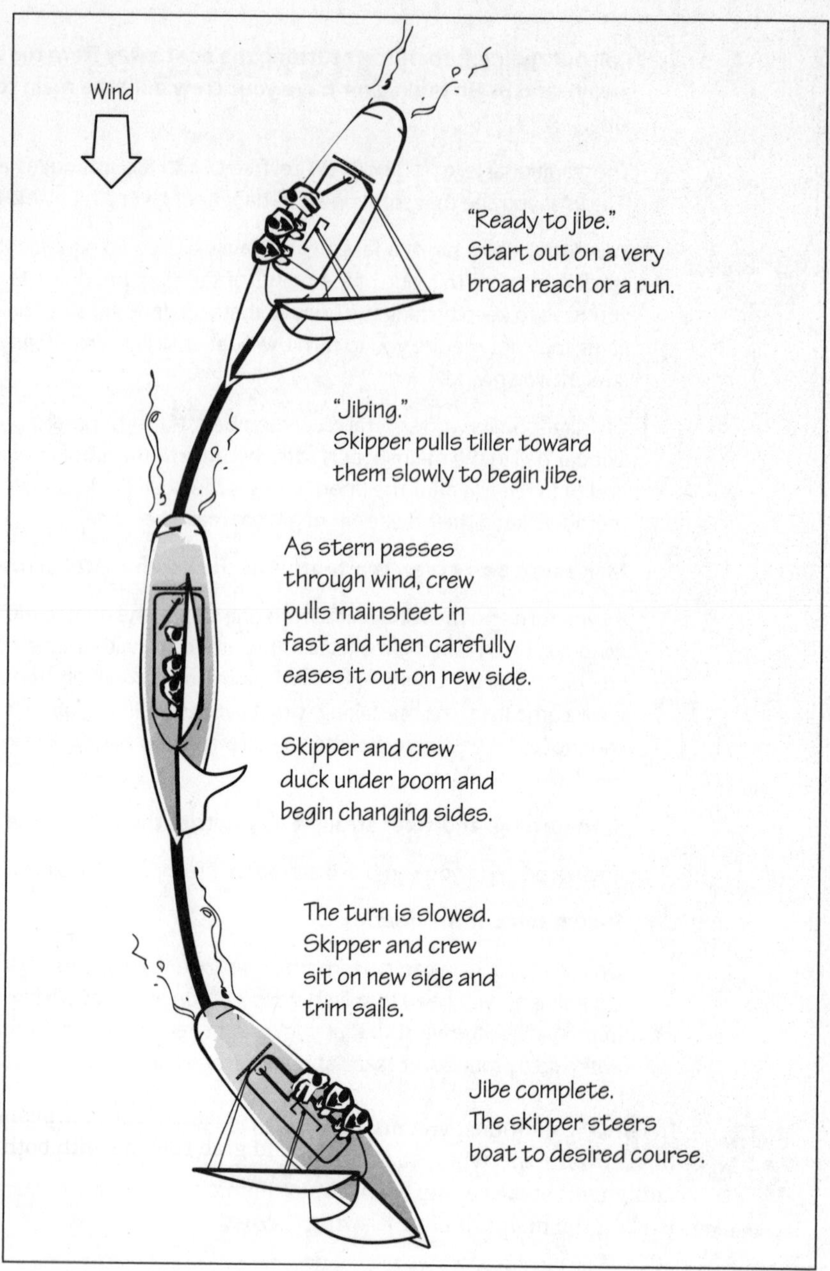

Wind
"Ready to jibe."
Start out on a very
broad reach or a run.
"Jibing."
Skipper pulls tiller toward
them slowly to begin jibe.
As stern passes
through wind, crew
pulls mainsheet in
fast and then carefully
eases it out on new side.
Skipper and crew
duck under boom and
begin changing sides.
The turn is slowed.
Skipper and crew
sit on new side and
trim sails.
Jibe complete.
The skipper steers
boat to desired course.

FIGURE 5-12: The steps in jibing.

WHAT TO SAY TO YOUR CREW

As you can probably guess, sailors have many terms for the person who steers the boat: *skipper, driver,* and *helm*, to name a few. The one name you don't want to be called is Captain Bligh — the horrible captain from *Mutiny on the Bounty*. If you don't want a rebellion on board your boat, make sure that you treat your crew the way you'd want to be treated.

"Tacking!" and "jibing!" are important commands, but the "Ready to tack/jibe!" command is equally important. Your crew needs some time (30 seconds or so) to get in position before you start the turn. If conditions are windy, you may have to yell (nicely) to get them to hear you.

Planning your maneuvers to give your crew time to get ready is a skipper's responsibility. For safety's sake, the skipper should always look to make sure that everyone is prepared and in a safe spot *before* turning the boat. If someone gets hit by the boom, most often, the skipper is at fault.

Pulling In Lines

REMEMBER

On a windy day, pulling in the boom on a jibe or trimming the sails when close-hauled can be tough work. Some lines on sailboats are lightly loaded, and adjusting them is easy, but others carry tremendous load, especially in strong winds. Trying to pull these lines can result in strained muscles or burned hands. Consider the forces on a line before uncleating it and trying to hold it. "Plucking" the line like a guitar string gives you an indication of the load on it. If the line feels like a steel rod, don't uncleat it or try to pull it without the help of a mechanical device like a winch, which we cover in this section.

To use all your strength, make sure that you're in the correct position to pull. You may need to sit down across from the line with your feet pushing against some solid object. Fully extend your arms and grab the line with both hands for maximum pulling power, as Figure 5-13 shows.

If you can't pull the line even when you're in the correct position, don't give up. Sailors of all ages and sizes can operate any boat, because various combinations of pulleys and winches (including electric winches) can provide the necessary mechanical advantage.

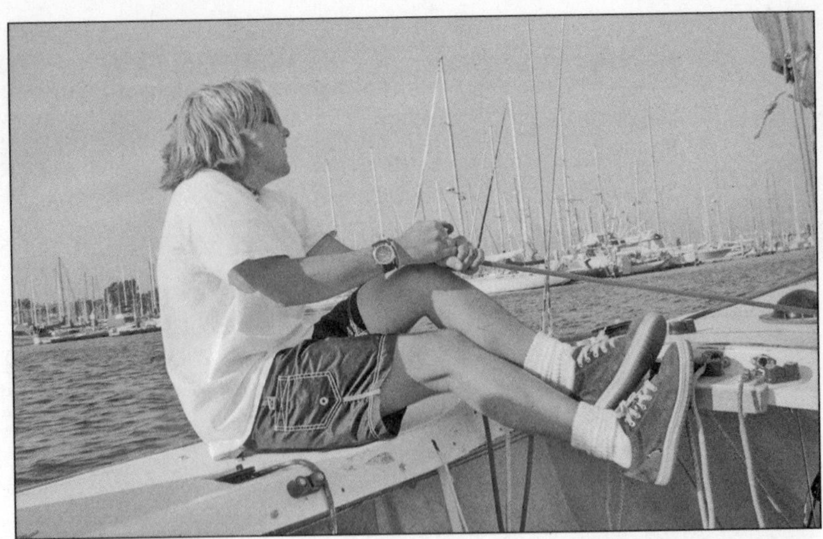

FIGURE 5-13: Using your whole body (including your legs) to pull can improve your power.

Photo courtesy of Sally Samins

TIP

This may be the most valuable sailing tip in this book: You can make pulling in the lines easier through clever driving and by relying on teamwork. Grinding in the jib sheet on a big cruising boat in strong winds, for example, can be a real chore. But if the skipper simply heads up slightly toward the wind, the sail begins to luff, and the load decreases. You may even be able to pull in the sheet by hand. Another way to substantially decrease the load on most of the sail control ropes is to turn the boat downwind (bear away) onto a broad reach or run. If your crew has a job to do on the bow, turn the boat downwind. Then the crew can safely go forward and have a flat, dry work space. (Careful — no accidental jibes, please!)

Next time you face a really difficult physical task on a sailboat, ask yourself whether you can do the job more easily by steering the boat at a certain angle. Usually, the answer is yes.

Using blocks

Mainsheets and most of the other lines on a sailboat run through *blocks* (pulleys). Some blocks just change the direction in which the line travels, but when you use several blocks in combination — block-and-tackle systems — they make the line easier to hold and pull. The amount of extra lifting power, called *purchase*, depends on the number of pulleys used and the arrangement. Without delving into the mechanics involved, a *four-part* mainsheet system (also referred to as a *4:1* system) requires only one-fourth the effort to pull in the sail compared with a single rope hanging from the boom (a 1:1 system). The disadvantage of a four-part mainsheet system is that you have to pull in four times as much line to bring in the sail.

A *cascading* arrangement multiplies the benefits, so a 2:1 system used with a 4:1 system provides an 8:1 mechanical advantage, as Figure 5-14 shows. (We talk about the care and selection of blocks in Chapter 16.) No matter what style they are, all purchase systems have the same purpose: to optimize mechanical advantage so that the average person can pull the line and sail the boat easily.

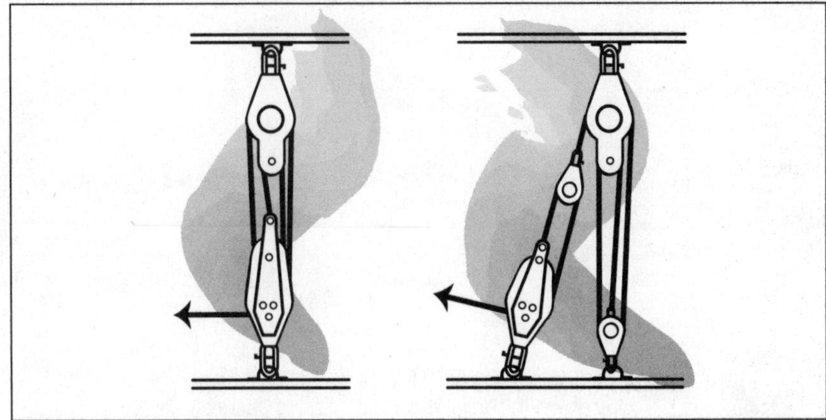

FIGURE 5-14: Left: A simple 4:1 purchase system. Right: An 8:1 cascading system.

Regardless of the block-and-tackle system you use, you need to keep the line from slipping when you have the rope trimmed where you want it. To prevent slipping, you have two options: Hold on to the rope, or cleat it.

Ratchet blocks

Some blocks *ratchet*, which means that they turn freely when you pull the line but don't turn at all in the other direction. This extra friction makes the line easier to hold. Ratchet blocks are common on the mainsheets and jib sheets of smaller keelboats and dinghies. They usually have a button or lever to turn the ratchet action off and let the block turn freely in both directions, which is useful in light wind. The extra holding power of a ratchet block makes hanging on to the mainsheet on a windy day much easier.

Cleats

Most sailboats have more control lines than you have hands. Although certain creative sailors have been known to use their mouths to hold a rope or two (which the American Dental Association doesn't recommend), most control lines have some sort of cleat to hold them:

- **Horn cleats and jammers:** These very secure cleats are best for lines such as halyards that you don't adjust often. (See Chapter 4 for more on hoisting sails.)

- **Clam cleats and cam cleats:** Easier to uncleat, these two cleats are well suited to mainsheets, jib sheets, and other lines that you need to adjust regularly. As you see in Figure 5-15, a *clam cleat* has grooves that make it look like the two sides of a clamshell. These grooves help hold a line that's under load. A *cam cleat* has two movable, notched jaws that use spring action to open and to grasp the line. To uncleat the line, you pull up and toward yourself (sometimes forcefully) to lift it out of the jaws.

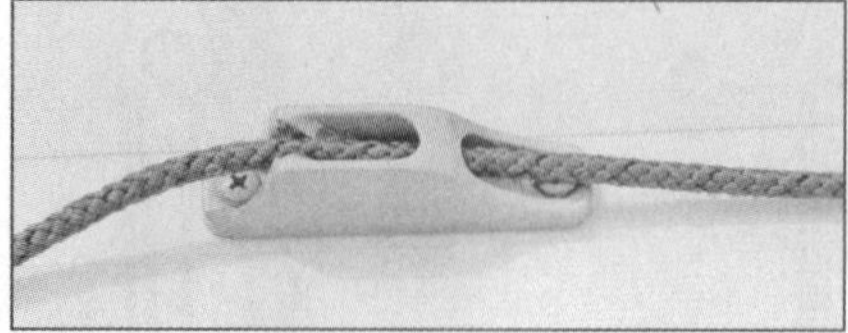

FIGURE 5-15: Clam cleat (left) and cam cleat (right).

Photos courtesy of Sally Samins

TIP

If your boat uses cam cleats or clam cleats, make sure that the line is all the way down in the jaws so that it stays securely cleated.

Using winches

In old pirate movies, sweaty sailors pulled in ropes and grunted "Heave, ho!" while a barbaric foreman cracked a whip. Nowadays, you can use a *winch* to pull in that line (and leave the whip at home). You use winches to provide mechanical advantage to adjust ropes under load, mainly on bigger boats, where loads on lines can get really heavy.

REMEMBER

Winches use a system of gears inside a round cylinder called a *drum* to give you the necessary pulling power. Always wrap the line clockwise around the drum, using more wraps as the load on the line increases. Put as many wraps around the drum as you need; the wraps provide the friction so that you can hold a heavily loaded line in your hand.

The winch drum spins as you pull the rope wrapped around it if the rope isn't under load. But when the load builds (such as on a jib sheet when the sail fills during a tack), you need to turn the drum with a removable handle called a *winch handle.* This process is called *grinding* (and the folks who do it on big racing boats are called *grinders*).

Grinding

While one person grinds, the other person pulls in (or *tails*) the line that feeds off the drum. One person can do both jobs, but doing so is less efficient. Some winches are *self-tailing*, meaning that they have a built-in mechanism that grips the line and holds it in place so that one person can grind without needing anyone to pull the rope. But grinding is often a two-person process, as Figure 5-16 shows.

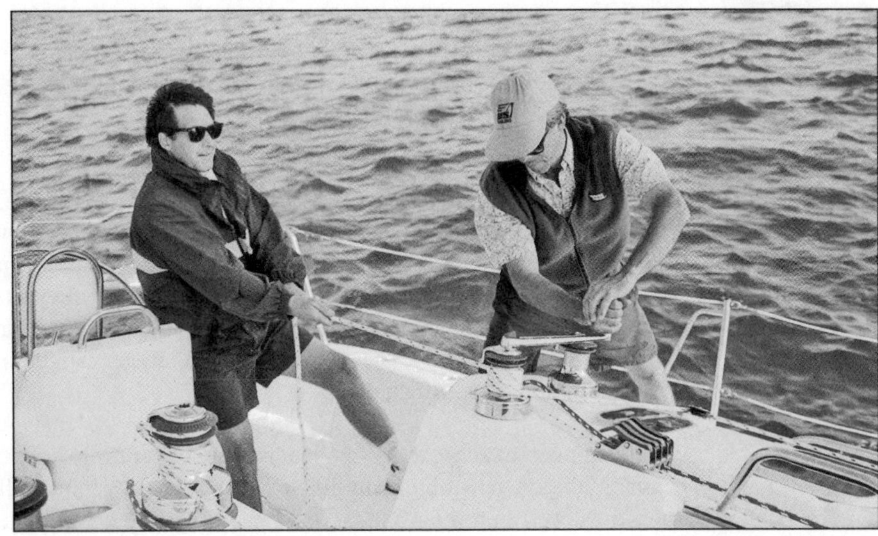

FIGURE 5-16: Sharing the workload: One person grinds the winch while the other pulls in the line.

Photo courtesy of Sally Samins

Here are some tips for grinding and tailing properly:

- **Choose the right speed.** Many winches have two or more speeds or gears. You change gears by changing the direction in which you turn the handle so that you can shift speeds if the grinding gets harder.
- **Grind in a full circle, using two hands if necessary.** If you can't complete a circle, turn as far as you can and then ratchet the winch handle back to your starting point.
- **If you feel the rope slipping, you aren't pulling hard enough, or you need to add a wrap on the drum.** When you're pulling in a slack or lightly loaded rope by hand, you usually need only one or two wraps. But after the line becomes so loaded that you can no longer pull it by hand and need to grind with the winch handle, you need about four wraps. When you're rapidly pulling in the slack out of a lightly loaded rope, you should add enough wraps for grinding just before the line gets loaded up because when you're rapidly pulling in a lightly loaded line spinning around a winch, having too many

wraps may cause a tangle called an *override*. In the next section, we discuss adding a wrap to a loaded winch and avoiding overrides.

» **Stand in a comfortable position over the winch.** You can grind a winch sitting beside it (some winches are placed where standing over them is impractical), but you won't be able to grind as hard.

TIP

» **When you're not grinding the winch, remove the handle, and place it in its holder.** These expensive items have never passed the float test, and having the handle already removed is safer if you must quickly release the rope on the winch. You never find winches on dinghies, so you don't have to worry about losing that handle in a capsize.

Adjusting lines safely on a loaded winch

WARNING

A line under tremendous load can be dangerous to *ease* (let out) or trim. Think first. The last thing you want is to burn your hands as a rope goes whizzing through them. Don't sail with any finger rings, because they can get caught on a line. Be especially careful with winches when you're wearing gloves. Make sure that your gloves fit snugly, because extra fabric can get caught and pinched by the line spooling onto the winch drum.

When you need to add a wrap to a loaded winch, carefully hold the line with both hands. Maintain tension on the line as you take both hands all the way around the winch, turning your hands to keep your fingers from getting caught, as Figure 5-17 shows.

To ease a line slowly and safely, hold on to the line with your right hand, and put your left hand on the wraps on the winch. Slowly let the line out counterclockwise, a couple of inches at a time, keeping some pressure on the line and varying the pressure your left hand applies to the coil of line on the winch.

To take all the wraps off a winch quickly (common in a tacking maneuver on bigger boats that use winches for their jib sheets), pull up on the line with a slight counterclockwise rotating motion. Before you take off the wraps, make sure that the long tail of the jib sheet is free to run, not tangled around your foot (or a crew member's body part!).

WARNING

When releasing a jib sheet on a winch during a tacking maneuver, wait until the load has just eased on the sheet before removing all the wraps on the winch drum. Watch for the jib to begin luffing as an indication that the helmsperson has begun turning the boat. If you cast all the wraps off the winch drum too early, you risk burning your hands as the highly loaded rope runs out. If you wait too late, the jib fills backward, and your hands could suffer the same abuse.

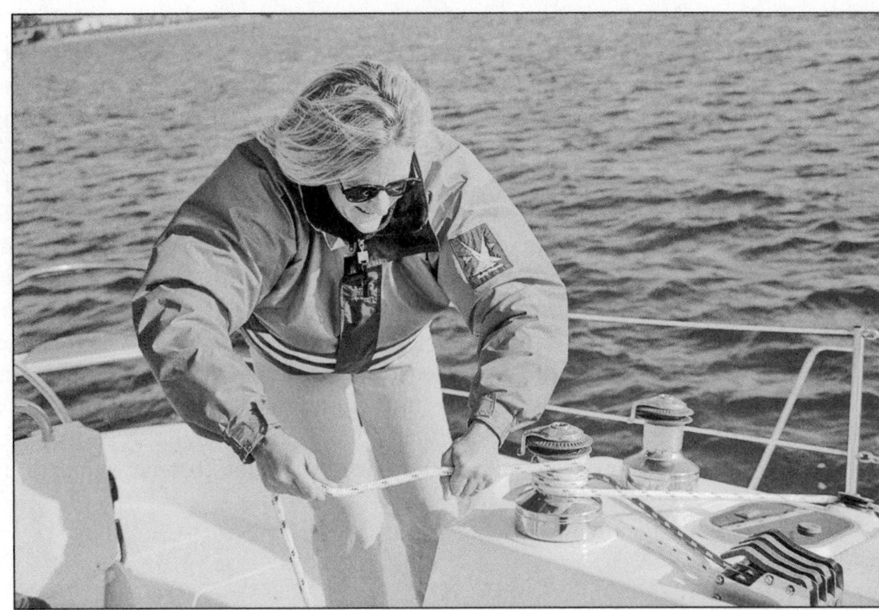

FIGURE 5-17: Keep pulling on the line as you use both hands to add a wrap on a highly loaded winch.

Photo courtesy of Sally Samins

At some point, probably when you're already having a bad day, you're going to get an *override* — a misfed line that effectively creates a knot around the winch, as shown in Figure 5-18. Overrides can be caused by improper winch placement so that the rope feeds on it incorrectly or by having too many wraps when you pull in a slack line.

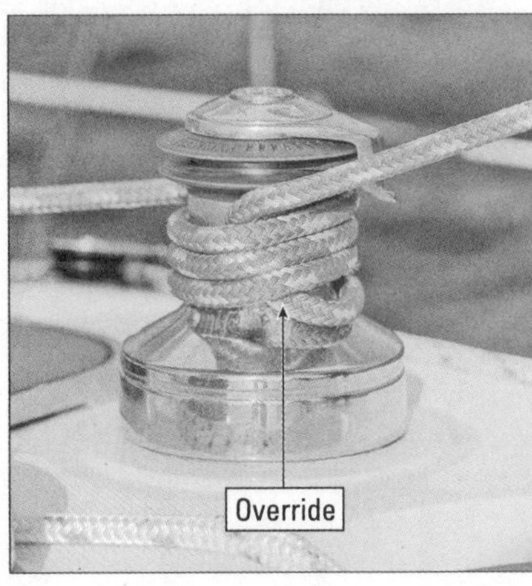

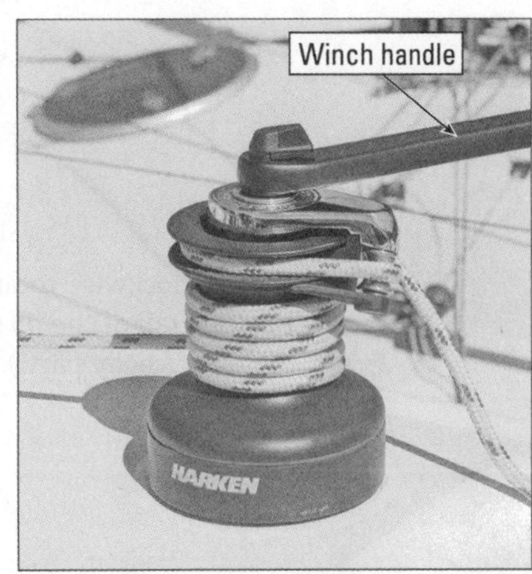

FIGURE 5-18: An override (left) and a properly wrapped winch (right).

Photo courtesy of Sally Samins

In light air, you may be able to untangle the mess by pulling the rope's end up and around the winch the "wrong" way (counterclockwise). In stronger winds, taking the load off the rope going to the winch and then untangling the mess is usually best.

Before the sail is sheeted hard, you may be able to head up, take the load off the sheet, and untangle it manually. Otherwise, to take the load off the override, rig another line to do the same job. Or you can tie another line to the tangled line (forward of the tangle) with a rolling hitch (see Chapter 19) and then tighten the new line so that you have slack in the tangled part. When danger is imminent or none of the other methods work, the final option is cutting the infringing rope with a knife. Be sure to cut the line near its end (near the clew of the jib on a jib sheet, for example) so that it's still usable and only a little bit shorter. If at all possible, avoid cutting a halyard, because that act requires a major rerigging exercise.

- » **Returning to docks and moorings**
- » **Putting up a mast**
- » **Leaving a boat secure**
- » **Launching a boat**

Chapter **6**

Leaving the Dock (And Coming Back)

I find the great thing in this world is not so much where we stand, as in what direction we are moving: To reach the port of heaven, we must sail sometimes with the wind and sometimes against it — but we must sail, and not drift, nor lie at anchor.

—OLIVER WENDELL HOLMES

Getting under way and getting back safely can be the trickiest part of your day on the water. You're often in a confined area with many other boats (not to mention the shore) nearby, and the rudder doesn't provide much maneuverability while you're at slow speeds and getting the boat going. What's more, all the sailors on the other boats are watching and waiting for you to mess up (not really, but it always feels like that).

We strongly encourage you to get some lessons before sailing (check out Chapter 2). Try to have an instructor or at least a knowledgeable friend along on your first few sails to help you get under way and back safely. Most novice sailors practice on boats that already have the mast up and are tied to a dock or a mooring (a permanently anchored buoy). But in case you need to know, the end of this chapter covers a variety of ways to put up the mast and get your boat from land to sea.

Leaving the Mooring or Dock

Casting off means untying and getting under way from a dock or mooring. If your boat has an engine (an *iron headsail*, in sailor slang), you can motor away and put the sails up after you're in open water. But knowing how to sail away from a dock or mooring (and back again) under sail is a good idea in case your engine decides not to cooperate some day.

Using an engine

The biggest concern when using the engine (besides polluting the environment) is keeping lines from getting tangled in the propeller. We discuss that problem and other mishaps in Chapter 15. Make sure that no loose lines are dangling off the side of the boat. And always let go of the *mooring line* (the line permanently attached to a mooring buoy) on the windward side so that you don't run over it as the boat sideslips while building speed.

Some moorings have stern anchors attached so that all the boats face one uniform direction. If so, let go of the stern anchor line (which usually has weights attached), and make sure it sinks out of the way before proceeding.

Leaving the mooring under sail

Leaving a mooring is usually easier than leaving a dock because the boat is already in relatively open water, but getting the boat turned to an angle out of the no-sail zone is trickier. We're assuming that your boat is tied by the bow with sails already hoisted and pointed into the wind. Take the following steps to sail away from a mooring buoy, as Figure 6-1 shows:

1. **Before casting off a dock or mooring, plan your best escape route.**

   Plan a course to sail away on a reach (which gets you up to speed quickly). Make sure that the whole crew knows the plan.

2. **Have the forward crew uncleat the mooring line but continue to hold it.**

   REMEMBER

   On bigger boats and in strong winds or current, one person won't have the strength to win the tug of war on the mooring line. So have your crew keep one full wrap of the line around the base of the horn cleat on the bow (if available) so they can hold on, yet be ready to cast off quickly.

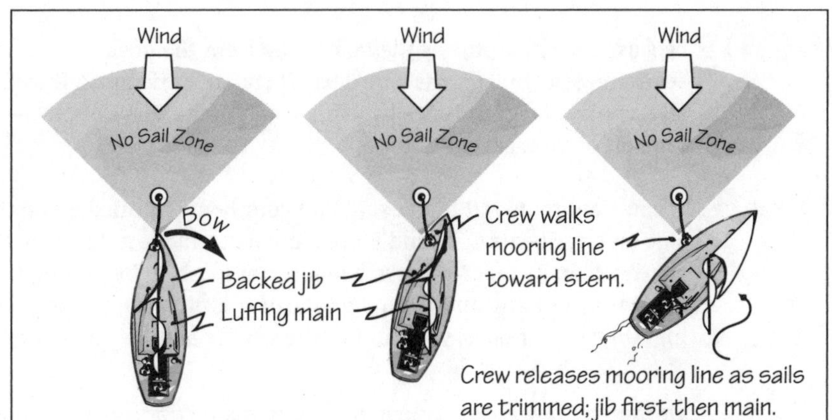

FIGURE 6-1: Getting the boat sailing from a mooring.

© John Wiley & Sons, Inc.

3. **With the mainsail luffing, back the jib.**

   Trim (or have a crew member trim) the jib on the side opposite the direction in which you intend to sail so that the jib *backwinds* (fills with wind backward) and pushes the bow away from the no-sail zone. Make sure that the mainsheet has plenty of slack so that the main can fully luff and won't fill. See Chapter 5 for details on getting your boat out of irons; the technique is the same.

4. **Have the crew walk the mooring line back along the windward side to shoot the boat forward.**

   The crew holding the mooring line walks with it toward the stern — on the windward side, so that the line doesn't get caught under the boat. As your crew moves back, your boat is pulled forward, especially on a smaller boat, helping you gain speed and control. On bigger boats, if holding the mooring line is too difficult after it's uncleated, just have your crew give it a good heave away from the boat when you give the command.

5. **Have the crew let go of the mooring and trim in the sails.**

   Wait until the combination of your steering and the force of the backed jib and fully luffing mainsail rotates your boat onto a reaching course. Then release the backed jib, and trim it on the correct side. As the boat begins to gain speed, trim the luffing main, and sail away on your desired course.

Leaving the dock under sail

REMEMBER

The key to easy arrival and departure from docks is to avoid tying up on the windward (upwind) side of the dock. If you try to leave the windward side of the dock under sail, the boat slips sideways as it gains speed and drags along the dock — not good form! Also, tying your boat to the leeward side of the dock is better because the wind pushes the boat away from the dock, minimizing the chance of scratching the hull against the dock. If you must tie up on the windward side, ideally, you can leave the dock by using your engine. Have extra crew on board to help fend off as you leave.

If you want to depart under sail, and your boat isn't tied up on the dock's leeward side (such as boats C, D, and E in Figure 6-2), move it. You can usually move boats shorter than 25 feet (8 meters) to a better location by pulling them with the dock lines or by holding onto a *shroud* (one of the wires supporting the mast) and pulling. On a bigger boat, you can use the engine and put the sails up in open water.

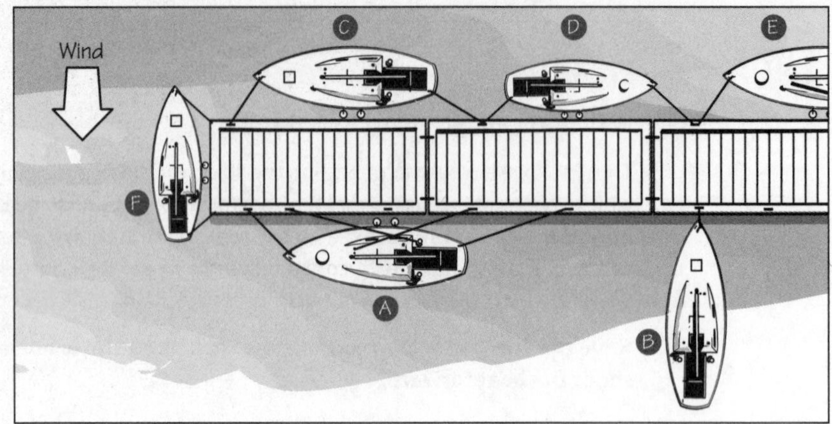

FIGURE 6-2: In this wind direction, boats A, B, and F are easiest to sail away from the dock.

© John Wiley & Sons, Inc.

Just like when you leave a mooring, you don't want to let go of the dock until you have the boat turning so that you'll be safely out of the no-sail zone. If you have room at a dock, you can begin to turn the boat by pulling in on the bow line and walking the boat along to generate forward motion so that the rudder is effective. Usually, you want to keep the mainsail fully luffing until you're safely into the sail zone; if necessary, back your jib as described in "Leaving the mooring under sail" earlier in this chapter to help turn the boat onto the desired course.

TIP

If you have plenty of space, you may be able to gain speed (and thus *steerageway* — the speed needed to steer) by having your crew members give a push as they jump on board or by sailing close enough to a nearby boat or dock to push off and get some extra speed.

REMEMBER

After you're safely away from the dock, remove any *fenders* (the rubber cushions tied to the side of the boat to keep it from hitting the dock), and store them down below, out of the way. Also untie any dock lines, coil them up, and store them out of the way too.

Getting Back to the Dock or Mooring

Leaving the subject of launching your boat without discussing how to get back to the dock or mooring would be like teaching you to ski and sending you down the mountain without telling you how to stop. In skiing, you can always stop by running into a tree or a big snowbank. The same technique works in sailing: You can always run the boat aground or into the dock. But considering how expensive insurance is, we want to give you cheaper and less painful alternatives.

The key to docking or mooring is slowing at a controlled rate before you get there. You slow down by luffing the sails (see Chapter 5) and letting the boat glide to a stop. The trick is knowing when to start luffing so that you keep enough steerageway to reach the dock without having so much speed that the phrase *ramming speed* becomes applicable.

TIP

When in doubt, err on the slow side. If you find that you aren't going to reach your destination, you can always accelerate by retrimming your sails. But there's a catch: If you slow so much that the boat is pointed in the dreaded no-sail zone, you're out of luck and in irons, as we describe in Chapter 5. Getting in irons is a big problem when you're in a confined area. So please don't go too slow or too fast!

What if you're approaching too fast and can't kill enough speed? The best solution is to turn the boat around and try the approach again. (There's nothing like a practice run to help you judge when to begin luffing your sails on the second try!) In fact, a wise sailor on a new boat always does some practice runs out in the open, next to a buoy or some other floating object, to help judge how the boat maneuvers as it decelerates.

Here are some other tricks that you can use to slow the boat:

- **On smaller boats, you can kill speed by *backing the main*.** Backing the main is like having a huge air brake. To back the main, push the boom toward the wind; the sail fills backward. Don't try this technique unless you're strong enough to control the boom and smart enough to let it go (and duck) if the boom begins winning the pushing contest.
- **You can kill speed with the rudder.** If you think you're coming in too fast, make some big turns instead of steering straight so that the boat has more distance to slow down. Make sure that your crew members are ready for this maneuver and are holding on.

Coming back to the mooring

Always make a plan before you attempt to make a landing on any object. In the case of a return to a mooring buoy, make sure that the whole crew knows which mooring you plan to pick up. Designate one person to pick up the line attached to the mooring buoy. Grabbing this mooring line may require a *boat hook* (a pole with a hook on the end) to help extend a person's reach. Some mooring lines have a tall stick attached to a float so you can grab the stick to pick up the mooring line. Other crew members should be ready to luff the sails on your command.

Follow these steps when picking up a mooring:

1. **Approach the buoy on a close reach, and steer at an imaginary point two to three boat lengths directly downwind from the buoy.**

REMEMBER

   Adjust this offset distance based on the coasting or stopping characteristics of your boat. Lighter dinghies slow very quickly. On heavier boats, the extra momentum makes slowing take longer.

2. **Depending on the wind strength and your boat speed (and other factors, such as current, which we discuss in Chapter 8), use your best judgment to decide when to luff the sails to begin to kill speed.**

   You may want to luff the jib first and then the main to have more flexibility in adjusting your final speed.

3. **When you're almost directly downwind of the buoy, and if your rate of deceleration appears to be correct, turn in a smooth arc toward the wind, and coast up to the mooring, pointed directly toward the wind.**

REMEMBER

   If you're approaching too quickly, abort the landing and make another try. If you're approaching too slowly, retrim the sails and build more speed. If you can't see the buoy, have a crew member point at it for you. As the bow reaches the buoy, the boat (ideally) comes to a dead stop. On a bigger boat, a boat hook helps the foredeck crew grab the buoy.

4. **Have the crew attach the boat to the mooring buoy.**

   Use a strong line, and securely attach it to both the buoy and the boat (a cleat or some other strong object on the bow). Make sure that the crew informs you when the boat is secure.

5. **Now you can lower the sails to stop their incessant flapping!**

TIP

On a boat with main and jib, dropping the jib (and maybe even clearing it away from the foredeck) before making the approach may be best. Doing so gives the crew more room to work up forward, reduces your sail power, and gives you more visibility. The downside is that without a jib, you have less control and ability to get out of irons, so be very careful to keep steerageway.

Coming back to the dock

Docking under sail is often trickier than sailing up to a mooring because the dock is usually in a more confined space. But the same basic rules apply:

- Plan your approach so that your crew knows what to expect.
- Have your fenders and dock lines tied and ready to go well before you begin your final approach.
- Approach the leeward side of the dock or a side parallel to the wind (any side except the dreaded windward side).
- Approaching slower is better, but don't go too slow. If you stop, you lose steerageway.

An ideal situation is a long, uncrowded dock with the wind blowing almost parallel to it. As with the mooring buoy, plan your approach so that the boat has room to coast into position as it decelerates (see Figure 6-3). When the boat is close enough (and going slow enough), have a crew member step from the middle of the boat onto the dock so that they can begin securing the dock line(s). Never yell for someone to jump; let the person who's going to get off judge when the boat is close enough to make their move. With this type of approach (in which the sails are still up), the first line to be secured is the bow line; then you can begin lowering the sails and further securing the boat as necessary.

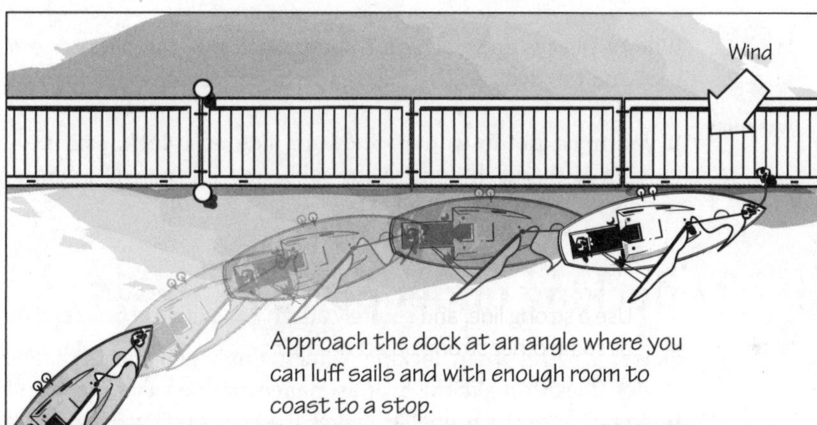

Wind
Approach the dock at an angle where you can luff sails and with enough room to coast to a stop.

FIGURE 6-3: Docking under sail.

REMEMBER

So what do you do if you don't have the ideal long runway? If you're bringing the boat alongside a dock, but you don't have as much space, tie a *spring line* (a line secured at the widest point in the middle of the boat; see "Spring lines" later in this chapter). You still need a bow line, stern line, and fenders all in place and ready to go, but the most important line to secure first is the spring line, because it helps stop the boat, followed quickly by the bow and stern line. When approaching *side on* (as in Figure 6-3), if your crew pulls in on the bow line while you're coasting forward, this action pulls your bow in and swings your stern out. A spring line just stops the boat without turning it because it's pulling from the middle, widest point.

As soon as your crew is safely on the dock with the bow line secured (see Chapter 19 for the proper knots), you can begin lowering the sails. Depending on the angle of the wind to the dock, you may want to use more lines to tie the boat alongside the dock (see "Tying Up a Boat: Leaving It Secure" later in this chapter). If there's enough space on the dock, you may want to concentrate on dropping the sails and cleaning up the boat before putting the boat in its final resting place.

TIP

When helping to stop an incoming boat, the crew member with the dock line should loop their line around the horn cleat on the dock (or around a piling or other secure object) so they have some friction to give them more stopping power than just their body weight. After the line is around the cleat, they can ease it out slightly as the boat's weight tugs on it rather than securing it and causing the boat to stop short.

WARNING

When a boat is approaching a dock, never put any part of your body between the boat and the dock. Repairing a little fiberglass is easier than repairing your body.

If you must tie up to the windward side of a dock, sail into a position directly upwind of the dock, lower your sails, and let the wind gently push you down to the dock.

Docking under power

Slower is better when docking — including when docking under power. Having an engine doesn't make the boat as maneuverable as your car. In fact, at low speeds, the rotation of the propeller makes the boat pull (turn easier) to one side. In open water, practice slowing the boat to see how much the propeller torque turns the boat and in what direction, especially in reverse gear. As with docking under sail, the boat's momentum, the wind pushing the hull, and other factors (such as current) also affect your maneuverability. When you discover the maneuvering characteristics of your boat under power, the principles of docking remain the same as those that we outline in the preceding section.

TIP

Make sure that all lines are out of the water before starting your engine. If you're approaching from upwind (or from an angle at which you can't fully luff the sails), you should drop the sails before docking a sailboat under power. Always approach slowly; never rely solely on reverse to slow the boat. Instead, use a spring line, which we describe later in this chapter in the "Spring lines" section.

Docking between pilings

In many parts of the world, you won't have a nice, protected dock to tie alongside. Often, the sailor's best friends are *pilings* (large wooden poles driven solidly into the bottom. Your array of dock lines depends on the position and orientation of the pilings, and you have to be creative as you plan your strategy to keep the boat from getting banged up no matter which direction the wind or current flows.

One of the most common dock arrangements is a short dock on one side and pilings on the other side. Tie the dock lines from each corner (as well as spring lines) so the boat hangs in the slot without banging into the dock or pilings, as Figure 6-4 shows.

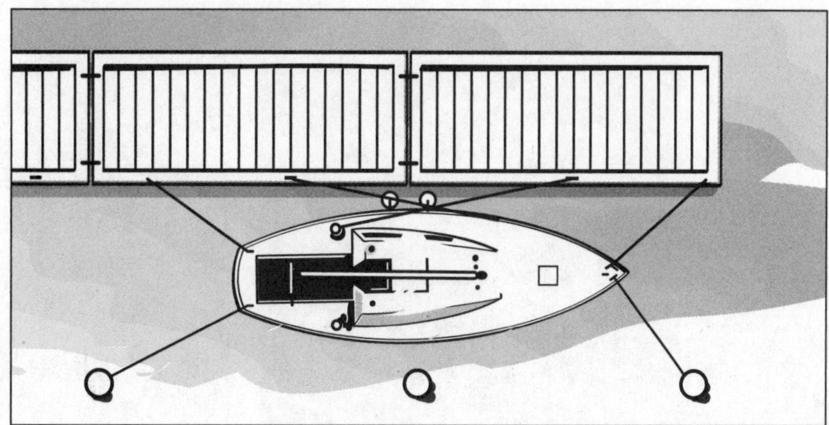

FIGURE 6-4: A boat properly secured between pilings and dock.

© John Wiley & Sons, Inc.

REMEMBER

To keep your boat from getting scratched on pilings or on a rough dock, the marina may use fender boards (long planks of wood with lines at regular intervals). Attaching the fender board to your boat outside your fenders keeps your boat off the pilings as the tide rises and falls.

If you fear that the wind is going to blow really hard, pushing the side of your boat directly into the dock, consider alternative locations to park. If no other locations are available, and no objects such as pilings are on hand to tie off to, you can ease the force of the boat against the dock (and ease your mind) by sending your dinghy out with an anchor directly *abeam* (perpendicular to the centerline of the boat). If this anchor extends into a waterway, do your best to mark it with a fender or other float to tell other boats to keep clear. Chapter 10 shows you how to anchor safely in all situations.

Throwing a Line

Sailing etiquette says that if sailors see a boat approach a dock, they should walk over and offer to help catch a line, so you need to know how to throw a line accurately and far. If you miss your target, you have to pull the soggy line back on board, coil it, and quickly try again.

The key to proper throwing is starting with a well-coiled line. Put a few coils (up to about 15 feet or 4½ meters) in your throwing hand, as shown in Figure 6-5, and hold your other hand (with the rest of the coils) open and pointed at the target so any extra coils can feed out as needed. Then throw (underhand) the coils, aiming slightly above the target.

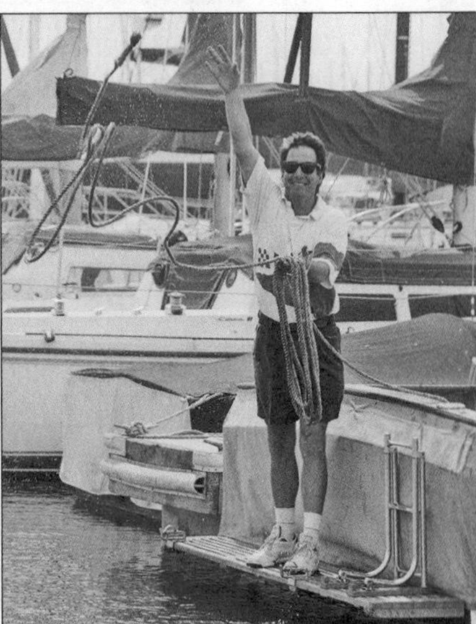

FIGURE 6-5: To throw a line, heave a few coils of rope with a good underhand toss.

Tying Up a Boat: Leaving It Secure

When your sailing day is done, and the time has come to return to the rigors of your shoreside life, you want to make sure that your boat is happy until you next get an opportunity to visit it. Temporarily, your boat may be happy to hang from a single bow line (while you're nearby). For more permanent storage, you need several lines. This section discusses how to tie your boat to a dock securely and safely. The following principles apply to all boats, but they're most useful when you're securing a larger keelboat alongside a dock:

- Always check for *chafed* (damaged) parts of the line.
- Always use fenders between the boat and the dock or pilings.
- Always use spring lines. (See the "Spring lines" section for more info.)
- Make sure that your docking lines are amply strong and thick — at least ⅜ of an inch (1 centimeter) for a 20-foot (6-meter) boat. Nylon line works well because it's designed to stretch.
- Don't pull the stern and bow lines too tight. Ideally, the boat lies just off the dock so that it doesn't rub.
- Tie bow and stern lines at about a 45-degree angle from the boat to hold it secure.

Spring lines

Spring lines are incredibly effective. Tied from the middle of the boat, they prevent the boat from surging forward or backward and keep it securely positioned so that the few fenders in the middle of the boat are always in the right place. Figure 6-6 shows a boat tied up by a bow line, a forward spring line, an aft spring line, and the stern line. In very rough conditions, you can add spring lines and double all the lines.

REMEMBER

Make sure that you secure dock lines at both ends. To tie off a line on a cleat or tie off to a piling (using a bowline knot or a clove hitch), see the nautical knots in Chapter 19.

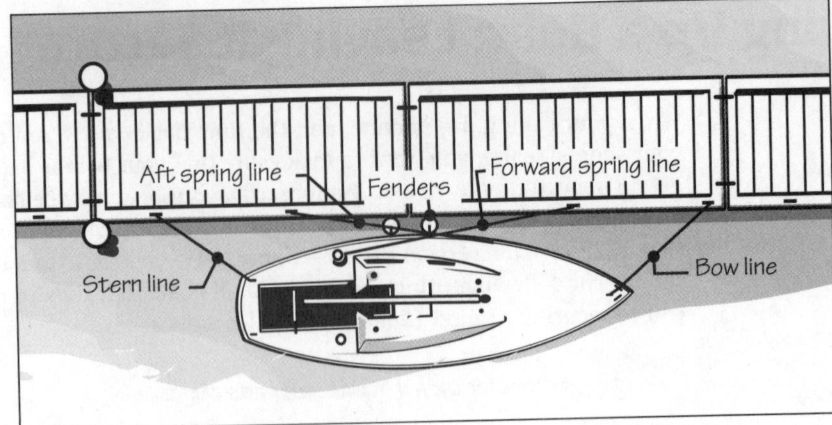

FIGURE 6-6: Spring lines help keep this boat securely cushioned by the fenders.

Watch out for that tide!

As you discover in Chapter 8, most large bodies of water have *tidal flow*, thanks to the moon. When tying up your boat, use some common sense. If your boat is going to float up and down on the tide, avoid tying it to something that doesn't float, such as a piling. If you tie your boat incorrectly to a piling or fixed dock at high tide, you may come back to find your boat suspended out of the water at low tide.

TIP

If you must leave your boat tied up to a fixed piling or dock in tidal waters, add more angle (and therefore more length) to all your dock lines by tying them to points farther away than the closest part of the dock.

Getting Your Boat into the Water

As we mention at the beginning of this chapter, when you first begin to sail, you probably don't have to worry about launching the boat; the school or the boat's owner more than likely takes care of that task. At some point, however, you may find yourself ready to sail, but with a boat that's high and dry. This section goes over how to launch both keelboats and dinghies in the most common situations.

WARNING

Whether you're launching from a trailer or a dolly, or carrying a smaller boat by hand, make sure you're aware of any power lines between the point where the mast is raised and the point where the boat is launched. Fortunately, most yacht and sailing clubs, launching areas, and marinas remove overhead power lines, but we want you to be vigilant.

TIP

Most boats stored on land have drain plugs. Leaving the drain plug out keeps rainwater from collecting in it. More than a few sailing trips have been ruined by neglecting to put the plug back in before launching, so be sure to check the plug — and note that some boats have several plugs!

Launching a trailerable sailboat

Getting your boat into the water can be an involved process — one that sometimes even includes putting up the mast. Many small keelboats (shorter than 25 feet, or 8 meters) and dinghies are *dry-sailed* — that is, stored on dry land on a trailer or dolly. Storing a boat on dry land means less maintenance (no barnacles or weeds to scrape off the bottom) and no docking fees. Storing your boat on a trailer makes sailing in many different places quite easy.

Two common methods of launching a keelboat or larger dinghy are using a *hoist* (crane) or a trailer off a ramp.

Using a hoist or crane

Launching a boat by using a hoist or crane is easy — as long as you have someone to help, the proper lifting bridle, and a boat that weighs less than the maximum allowable weight for the crane. Follow these steps when using a hoist to launch your boat:

1. **Move the boat so that it's underneath the crane.**

   Many cranes have an arc painted on the ground to help guide you in placing your boat. Place the boat so the crane pulls the boat straight up and off the trailer. On boats with a *backstay* (a wire extending from the top of the mast to the back of the boat), you may have to swing the crane's arm over the boat as it's wheeled into place, as Figure 6-7 shows.

2. **Attach the *lifting bridle* — the wire or rope sling arrangement that balances and lifts the boat.**

   WARNING

   Check the lifting bridle (or other lifting device) and attachment points for wear. And never let anyone stand or walk underneath a boat on a hoist.

3. **Attach the bow and stern lines so that the boat can be rotated into position as you lower it into the water.**

4. **Have one person operate the hoist and one hold the lines.**

   Don't try to put your boat in alone; make sure that you have a buddy.

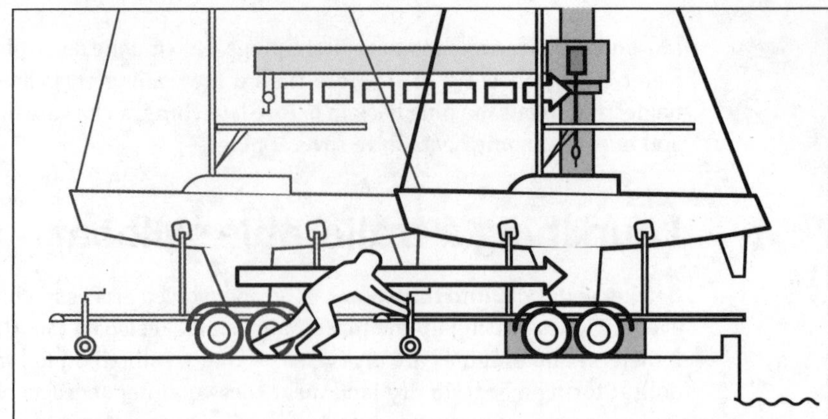

FIGURE 6-7: As the trailer is pushed under the crane, swing the crane's arm past the backstay.

© John Wiley & Sons, Inc.

5. **Begin lifting, making sure that the mast and shrouds are clear of the crane's arm.**

   TIP

   Try to keep the boat perpendicular to the arm as you swing the boat out over the water and begin lowering.

6. **When the boat is in the water, one person unhooks the lifting bridle while the other secures the bow line.**
7. **Before rigging, move the boat and trailer away so that others can use the crane.**
8. **Swing the arm back over shoreside.**

TIP

Because the greasy chain or cable from the hoist can mess up your sails (and your hands, and anything else), always rig the sails after the boat is in the water and away from the crane.

Launching from a trailer off a ramp

Our two main rules for successfully launching off a ramp are

- Accept that you're going to get your feet wet.
- Plan ahead. Stop, get out of your car, and check out the ramp before you back the trailer down. Look at its angle, check for a big drop-off at the end, and plan where you want to position your trailer. Then look at the dock space. When the boat is launched, where are you going to tie up so that you can hoist the sails? How are you going to get to the dock?

When you have a good plan in mind, get in your car, and go for it. Backing up a car and trailer is sort of like patting your head and rubbing your stomach at the same time; it can be difficult. Oversteering in reverse causes the most common malady, jackknifing the trailer. If your boat and trailer are light enough for one person to handle, carefully walk the trailer into the water. But do be careful: Ramps can be steep and slippery.

Follow these steps to launch your boat from a trailer on a ramp by using a car:

1. **Put the mast up.**

   See the section "Putting up a mast" later in this chapter.

2. **Position your car and trailer parallel to the ramp.**

   Going backward is much easier when you don't have to turn.

3. **Remove all the various lines and straps used to secure the boat, except for a line or cable that attaches the boat to the trailer and a bow line you'll need later to guide the boat to the dock.**

4. **Go slowly down the ramp, correcting any tendency to jackknife by turning the back of your car in the same direction in which the back of the trailer is turning.**

   Make sure that you can see or have a person outside your car directing you.

5. **Back up until the boat is just floating off the trailer before the wheels (or at least the brakes and wheel bearings) of your car touch the water.**

6. **Make sure that your parking brake is set before getting out of your car to disconnect the boat from the trailer.**

   Saltwater is highly corrosive (as you know from the salt put on the roads after a snowstorm), and even in freshwater, cars can't swim, so it goes without saying that you can't put your car in the water. You don't want to be featured in a "boat ramp fail" video on YouTube.

   WARNING

   If the bottom of the ramp has slimy algae, be careful! This stuff is as slippery as ice.

7. **When the boat is afloat, unhook or untie the bow from the trailer.**

   This part is where you get your feet (and maybe your legs) wet. If a dock is nearby, you may be able to take the bow line, walk around to the dock, and pull the boat to you while staying dry, but don't count on it.

   TIP

   If no dock is available, you may want to consider rigging the sails (but not hoisting them) before you launch, because you probably have to climb in the boat from the water — similar to launching and sailing away from a beach, which we describe in "Starting from the beach" later in this chapter.

8. **After you launch your boat and tie it to the dock, go back to move your car and trailer.**

Launching without a trailer

Dinghies are commonly dry-sailed. Because most are lighter than keelboats, you can often launch smaller dinghies off a dock or ramp or even off a beach without a hoist or a trailer.

You may be able to transport a small dinghy on roof racks on top of your car (assuming you drive something bigger than a convertible). To get the boat down without damaging it, find several friends and then follow these steps:

1. **Find a *dolly* (lightweight trailer for movement by hand) or padding to put the boat on.**
2. **Find enough people to make lifting the boat easy.**
3. **Slide or lift the boat off the roof and lower it, carefully setting the edge of the boat (at its widest point) on the padding or on the dolly, as Figure 6-8 shows.**

WARNING

Never set your dinghy on the ground; you could scratch the hull.

FIGURE 6-8: As you flip your boat, always make sure to set it on padding to protect the hull.

Photo courtesy of Sally Samins

4. **With most of the weight supported on its edge, flip the boat over in the air so that it's right-side up.**

5. **Lift and set the boat on the dolly or padded area for rigging.**

   Now, depending on how you're going to launch, you can prepare the boat to go sailing. (See Chapter 4 for more about rigging.)

Sliding a dinghy off a dock

Even without a dolly, you can launch lightweight dinghies off the dock; you just need the lifting skills of some friends to get the boat into position at the edge of the dock.

When you have the boat set at the side of the dock, get all the gear ready to sail (see Chapter 4), if you haven't already. Lift the boat on each side, and slide it into the water (see Figure 6-9). If the dock doesn't have padding at the edge, place some padding to cushion the hull as you slide it in, or keep lifting so that the boat doesn't touch the dock. Then grab the bow line, tie the boat to the dock to further rig it, and hoist sails.

FIGURE 6-9: Lift on either side of the boat, and slide it into the water.

Photo courtesy of Sally Samins

REMEMBER

Any time you must lift a boat, always ask for plenty of help. Bend your legs, and keep your back vertical to avoid injury.

REMEMBER

If the wind is very light or is blowing from the dock toward the water, you might consider hoisting the sails before you launch, but you usually hoist the sails afterward. Just remember to put the centerboard down when you first get in the boat; otherwise, the boat will be very tippy.

Starting from the beach

Launching off a beach is tricky unless the wind and wave conditions are really mild. Ideally, there are no waves and only a soft *offshore breeze* (wind blowing from shore to water) or *sideshore breeze* (wind blowing parallel to the shore), making it easy to sail straight off the beach.

You can rig boats in any number of ways, so don't be afraid to ask your instructor or the owner for assistance (and see Chapter 4 for details on rigging a typical boat). Most beach-launched boats require one or more of these tasks to be done before you put them in the water:

- Consider hoisting one or both sails while the boat is still on the beach, because hoisting them may be difficult after you launch the boat. Doing this makes carrying the boat into the water harder, however.
- If your boat has a *kick-up* rudder (one that rotates up and out of the water), rig it in the kicked-up position before launching.
- Rig the boat, and store all your gear on board.

Now you're ready to launch the boat off the beach:

1. **Grab as many people as you can to carry the boat into the water.**

   You can't avoid getting your legs wet here! Keep the bow pointed toward the wind if the sails are hoisted. If you have a dolly, you won't need a big gang to get the boat floating in shallow water.

2. **When the boat is floating in knee- to waist-deep water, have someone hold the bow while at least one crew member climbs into the boat to prepare it for sailing.**

   The boat is incredibly tippy at this point because you can't put your centerboard down very far until you're in deeper water — but do put it down partway.

3. **Hoist the sails and lower the rudder (if it's the kick-up variety) at least partway (if the water is very shallow) while someone holds on to the *bow* (front) of the boat.**
4. **Have the last person push the boat off on a reaching course and climb into the boat.**

   You're sailing!

REMEMBER

When you're the someone in step 2 who's holding on to the boat in the water, keep these safety tips in mind:

- Consider wearing shoes; there may be sharp objects underwater.
- If the waves are big, try to keep the boat pointed perpendicular to the waves, just like a surfboard going out through the surf. This way, the waves have less chance of grabbing your boat and throwing it — and you — back on the beach. This task may be difficult if the sails are up.
- In waves, never stand between the boat and shore. Otherwise, a wave could squish you between the boat and the beach. Always stand on the seaward side of the boat (although doing so may be difficult if the sails are hoisted).

WARNING

Never leave a boat halfway in the water with the bow pulled up on the beach. Even small waves (or wakes from powerboats) can hurt the boat or cause it to float away.

Returning to the beach

Coming back to the beach can be even more difficult than launching. Again, you can't avoid getting wet. Here are the basic steps for bringing a sailboat onto the beach:

1. **Luff your sails and kill your speed a long way out, and approach the beach slowly, with the sails fully eased.**

   You have to adjust the angle of approach to accommodate the wind direction. If the beach is dead downwind, you may have to briefly turn *head-to-wind* (away from the shore) when you get close and drop your mainsail.

2. **If the water is shallow, pull up your rudder and centerboard partway before the approach.**
3. **When you're close to shore, turn the boat head-to-wind, and stop.**
4. **Have your crew jump overboard (you should be close enough to shore that they can stand on the bottom) and hold the boat's bow while you drop sails, fully pull up the centerboard, and remove or kick up the rudder.**
5. **Jump in the water, and get the dolly or additional people to help you carry the boat onto the beach.**

   Dragging the boat on the sand scratches the bottom, so always carry your boat.

REMEMBER

When you've been sailing in saltwater, whether you return from sailing to the beach or to a dock, always hose off that salt. For more tips on caring for your boat, see Chapter 16.

Putting up a mast

Some boats are stored with the mast up. Other boats (usually dinghies) require the crew to *step* (put up) the mast before every sail. You can use several techniques to step a mast, depending on the boat's equipment. Some masts on bigger dinghies and keelboats are so heavy that they require a crane (or some other special lifting device) to help. If you're stepping the mast for the first time, make sure that you have experienced help. On smaller boats (up to about 14 feet, or 4 meters, in length), one person can usually lift the mast up and into position in the boat, but having help never hurts.

WARNING

We need to say it again: If you're putting up a mast on land, first take a good look around (and up) for overhead power lines.

To get the mast from horizontal to vertical, follow these steps:

1. **Have someone push the tip of the mast upward while the base is secure against your foot or other object.**
2. **When the mast is vertical, lift it into position in the boat.**

   You may find that handing the vertical mast to someone sitting in the boat is easier.

   TIP

   If you get uncomfortable, be sure to ask for help. Few sounds are louder than a mast falling over into the parking lot (especially on somebody else's car)!
3. **When the mast is set into its mast step, begin to attach all the standing rigging *(shrouds, forestay,* and *backstay).***

   Often, attaching the standing rigging is a two-person job to ensure that the mast remains vertical during the process (see Figure 6-10).
4. **As you attach the standing rigging, carefully inspect all the fittings that support the mast.**

   Tighten any shackles with pliers, and make sure that the fittings are secure. (Check out Chapter 16 for details on shackles and other rigging gear.)

Some small dinghies have freestanding masts without any standing rigging. On these boats, you can slide the sleeve on the mainsail luff (the front edge of the sail) over the mast before putting it up, as Figure 6-11 shows.

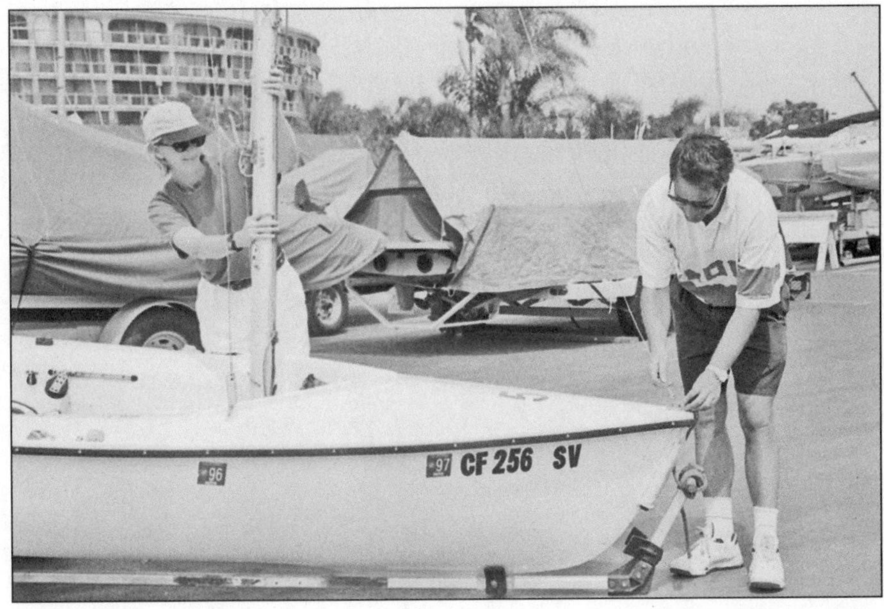

FIGURE 6-10: One person holds the mast while the second person secures the shrouds and forestay.

Photo courtesy of Sally Samins

FIGURE 6-11: Slide the mast into the sleeve to rig this sail.

Photo courtesy of Sally Samins

IN THIS CHAPTER

» Preparing for and managing in strong winds

» Recovering from a capsize

» Staying safe on board

» Handling a man-overboard emergency

» Calling for help by using the VHF radio and satellite devices

Chapter 7
Safety: One Hand for the Boat, One Hand for Yourself

There isn't no call to go talking of pushing and pulling. Boats are quite tricky enough for those that sit still without looking further for the cause of trouble.

—J.R.R. TOLKIEN

Never underestimate the power of Mother Nature! When you sail on the water, you're her guest, and even on the most relaxing of sailing days, you need to respect her capacity for pure brute strength. Safety on the water comes in many forms and at many levels. On a hot summer day, reapplying sunscreen and remembering to drink enough water may be your primary concerns. If you're out in the open ocean in strong winds, being tossed about by waves that make your boat seem like a toy, the concept of safety takes on a very real meaning of survival.

As you progress into the sport, we strongly recommend that you hone your skills with practice — and that you *never* go sailing on a boat or in conditions that exceed your experience and comfort level. Making sure that you have the requisite skills and equipment to handle whatever happens on your sailboat is the only safe way to approach a day on the water. But as a sailor, you'll learn to expect the unexpected any time you head out on the water.

Having fun when you sail is easy. In this chapter, we also help you prepare for the not-so-fun situations that can arise, such as handling bad weather, recovering from a capsize, and rescuing someone who's fallen overboard.

Preparing for Heavy Weather

When the sheep are in the pasture (that is, whitecaps are all covering the water), sailing can be fun or terrifying, depending on your boat, your and your crew's level of competence, where you are, and how fresh the weather really is.

Heavy weather and *heavy air* are sailors' terms for a strong breeze, often paired with rough waves. As you find out in Chapter 8, sailors measure wind velocity in units called *knots* and can estimate the speed of the wind by looking at the water's surface. We recommend that a beginning sailor head for home when *whitecaps* (foamy wave crests) become commonplace, at about 15 knots. But for an experienced sailor, especially on a high-performance dinghy or catamaran, this is when sailing gets fun, and wet!

Sailing in strong winds can be exhilarating. You get to blast around at high speeds. Pushing your limits and conquering your fears can boost your self-confidence. When you make it back to shore, you have a new appreciation for the simple things in life, such as a hot shower and dry clothes.

This section enables you to raise your wind threshold so that you can enjoy and stay safe on those blustery days. We concentrate on windy but sailable conditions because they're by far the most common. Look at Chapter 15 for tips on surviving a storm — when every sailor should be on shore.

Preparing for a blow

The following list includes some important safety rules you need to remember before you head out on a windy day:

» **Don't jump too far too fast.** If your limit has been 10 knots, try 12 or 15 knots before going out when the forecast calls for gusts up to 25 knots.

- **Go out in familiar waters.** If you're in a new area, check the chart to ensure that there's plenty of deep water and you know the shallow spots to avoid. The last thing you want to worry about is going aground.
- **Go on a familiar boat.** You'll better know its limitations and how it handles.
- **Have someone with more experience than you on board.** If you're sailing a one-person dinghy, make sure that a potential rescue boat is nearby, with experienced boaters watching you.
- **Put on a life jacket (if it's not already on).** And check the safety list in Chapter 3.

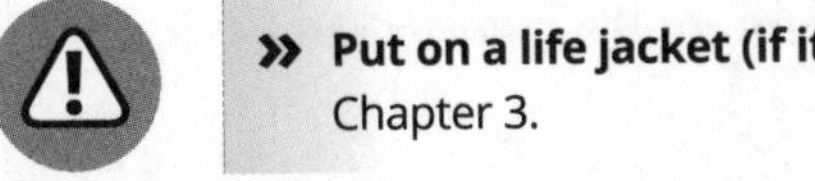

WARNING

We don't want to scare you away from sailing in heavy weather; we just want to tell you a few reasons why you shouldn't exceed your limits. Following are a few of the potential hazards you may face:

- **The boat may become much harder to handle.** In really heavy conditions, the force of the wind and waves can throw the boat around and change the way it sails. Being out of control isn't fun or safe.
- **You may capsize (on a dinghy or small cat).** Practice righting your boat (check out "Recovering from a Capsize on a Dinghy" later in this chapter) until it's routine. In really extreme weather, however, you may not be able to right the boat against the force of the wind.
- **You may lose someone overboard.** The bigger the waves and the more the boat is heeling, the harder it is to stay on deck. Practice the man-overboard rescue we describe in the "Rescuing a Man Overboard" section later in this chapter. But remember that in big waves and strong winds, returning and picking up a swimmer can be very difficult.
- **Gear may break.** If your boat isn't fully prepared (and sometimes even when it is), things can and do begin to blow apart as Mother Nature's forces increase. We discuss how to deal with potential accidents in Chapter 15 and boat maintenance in Chapter 16.

Preparing when you're already at sea

The wind strength and direction can change quickly, even on cloudless days. So even if you have the best intentions to follow the advice to not jump too far too fast, chances are that someday, you'll find yourself out on the water with the breeze building quickly.

When the sky starts looking ominous (or your weather app shows storms coming), your first plan should be to hurry back to shore. This may mean catching a tow (see the "Catching a Tow" section later in this chapter) or firing up the engine and dropping all your sails (see "Using an engine," later in this chapter). If sailing is your only option, adjust your sails and trim to reduce power (see Chapter 12), and run through the following list while making haste for home.

Getting your crew and boat ready for strong winds

When strong winds are imminent, perform the following tasks right away to get your boat and crew ready:

- **Point your boat toward the closest harbor.** Ideally, this harbor is your home; otherwise, remember the old saying "Any port in a storm."
- **Put on life jackets and warmer clothes.** If you're on a dinghy or small cat, you should already have your life jacket on, but even on a larger keelboat, it's time to be proactively safe. In Chapter 3, we cover your clothing options for various conditions. Bottom line: Conditions are going to get much wetter (waves and spray) and colder (wind chill), so put on warm, water-resistant clothes now.
- **Make sure everything is shipshape.** When the wind comes up, the boat *heels* (tips) more; on a dinghy, you may even capsize. Stow all loose gear securely. On a dinghy, your key equipment (such as your rudder and daggerboard) should always be secured to the boat. Now is the time to double-check.
- **Make the boat as watertight as possible.** Batten down the hatches! Close any windows or hatches, especially the ones up forward, where the first spray comes on board. Bail out the boat; if it's bound to get wet outside, it's nice to start out dry inside.
- **Review safety procedures.** It's time for a quick review of the info in this chapter. Also review the location of safety equipment. (See Chapter 3 for a checklist.)
- **Reduce your sail power.** Reducing your sail power is important, because your boat will be easier and safer to handle. Check out "Reducing your sail power" later in this chapter for more information.

Picking the right course

As the weather gets nasty, you can try to make that trip home easier by picking the safest course: a course that avoids the worst waves, shallow water, the lee shore, and accidental jibes.

GETTING OUT OF THE WAVES

Often, the big problem with heavy weather isn't so much the wind as the waves. We've sailed in the Gulf Stream in waves that are so big and steep that the crew called sailing upwind "condo-jumping." Because wave size (and shape) is a function of wind velocity, *fetch* (the distance of the wave travels over open water, gaining height along the way), current, and water depth, you can sometimes plot a course that minimizes condo-jumping. Here's how:

- **Plot a course that makes use of the natural breakwater created by land.** If you have a choice of sailing along the windward or the leeward side of the island, for example, go to leeward to get out of the waves.
- **Avoid shallow water.** Unlike sailing in smooth conditions, when you sail in rough water, the effective water depth changes with every rise and fall of the waves. And in shallow water, waves change their characteristics, from smaller, longer swells to larger, breaking crests that add to the discomfort and danger.
- **Avoid an upwind destination.** Hey, that sounds pretty simple, but it's easier said than done. A savvy sailor will study the weather before they depart so that they don't find themselves having to claw their way back upwind in big waves and wind.

TIP

Sailing upwind in big waves can be fun, like offroading, except that the road is moving. If the waves are so big that you feel them pushing your boat backward, turn a little bit toward the wave — more perpendicular to the crest just as it reaches your bow. This action minimizes the surface area that the waves can push on, similar to a surfer paddling out through the breakers. Bear off and regain speed as soon as your boat is on top of the wave. Maintaining steerageway is crucial; a smaller sail plan will help, as will keeping your speed up.

AVOIDING A LEE SHORE

REMEMBER

A *lee shore* is a shoreline to leeward (downwind) of your boat, toward which the wind is blowing. If the shoreline is an island, the island's windward shore is a lee shore. A very important rule of heavy-weather sailing is to avoid getting close to a lee shore. As the wind builds, it's essential to have an escape route of open water downwind of you. Then, in a worst-case scenario, you can simply drop your sails and drift until the storm abates. A lee shore forces you to sail close-hauled — the most demanding point of sail — to get away from its dangerous shallow waters and boat-busting solid objects.

WATCHING OUT FOR ACCIDENTAL JIBES

Accidental jibes are bad, and any jibe in strong winds can be dangerous. When the boom comes crashing to the other side, woe to the person whose head is in the way. An unintended jibe not only endangers any crew in the path of the boom or the mainsheet, but can also put tremendous (maybe even excessive) forces on the mast and boom. You can avoid accidental jibes by being vigilant in your steering and by never letting the boat get near a *dead run* (with the wind straight behind you). Waves can easily throw the boat off course by 10 or even 20 degrees, so in heavy air, keep the boat on a broad reach.

Using an engine

Normally, sailing is faster than motoring in heavy air. But in extreme conditions, you may find that using the engine is safer and more comfortable. Often, you'll keep the smallest sail up for some added propulsion, but you might even drop all sails and just use the engine alone. If you have a reliable engine that's easy to use, consider these pointers before you use it in heavy weather:

- **Consider motorsailing.** Especially when your destination is to windward, the best tactic may be *motorsailing,* in which you keep up a reefed mainsail or small jib and use the motor at the same time. Motorsailing still provides some power from the sail. Also, if your engine fails, doesn't have enough horsepower, or runs out of gas, the last thing you want to do is try to hoist the sails while wallowing about.

- **Don't let the boat heel too far.** If you motorsail, the force of the wind may cause the boat to heel so much that the cooling-water intake comes out of the water, which causes the engine to overheat. Other systems on the engine may not like excessive heel either; keep an eye on the engine's vital signs, including the temperature, and ensure that water is coming out of the exhaust.
- **Make sure that all lines are out of the water before you start your engine.** And keep those lines out of the water; nothing ruins your day faster than having a jib sheet or halyard tail get wrapped up in a propeller. For tips on solving that mishap, see Chapter 15.

Reducing your sail power

The force of the wind increases by the square of the velocity, which means that at 14 knots, the wind force on your rigging and sails is double the load on the boat at 10 knots — and that's before you add in the effect of the waves. Sailboats and their parts can stand only so much load before they begin to break. Stronger winds make your boat and sails more difficult to handle. As the wind speed increases, anything you do to reduce those forces on the boat and sails can make a big difference.

The first step is to depower your sails, an important subject that we cover in depth in Chapter 12. The next step is to reduce the boat's sail area, or *shorten sail.* You can shorten sail in three ways: by dropping a sail, reefing a sail, or changing to a smaller sail. All three methods have their pros and cons, depending on the boat and the conditions.

Dropping a sail

Dropping a sail is a pretty extreme tactic on a catboat (which has only one sail), but sailors commonly use this tactic on sloops of all sizes. Should you drop the mainsail or the jib? The answer depends on the boat and the conditions. Dropping the jib and sailing with the mainsail alone is appropriate under the following conditions:

- **When the jib is very large:** Dropping a *genoa* (large, overlapping jib) significantly decreases your sail power, especially if the mainsail can be reefed.
- **When the boat handles well with the mainsail alone.**
- **When the jib is set on a roller furler (see Chapter 4):** Rolling the jib partway is really easy; see whether that setting works and then roll the jib up all the way if necessary. Do this as an interim step as the wind builds; then plan your next move.

Sometimes, dropping the mainsail and sailing with the jib alone is appropriate, as in the following situations:

- On boats where the mainsail isn't reefable and on dinghies rigged in such a manner that dropping the jib causes the standing rigging to loosen dramatically.
- When the jib is smaller than the main. In extreme conditions, such as squalls, the reduction in sail area (and, thus, the load on the boat) is more dramatic.

As you lower either sail, keep it under control, bunched up so that it doesn't blow around, until it can either be sent down below deck or lashed down on deck securely so that it can't flog about.

TIP

If you must send the crew to the foredeck for a sail change in rough seas, turn the boat onto a very broad reach (no accidental jibes, please) to reduce heel and wave motion. Then everyone on deck can move around on a relatively steady, flat surface.

Turning downwind can also steady the boat's motion to enable a crew member to work up the mast. Once when Peter was skippering *Courageous* — Ted Turner's famous 12-Meter —in Perth, Australia, the mainsail got stuck at the top of the mast, and the crew couldn't lower it. They had to send a crew member 90 feet up in the air to fix the problem. The wind was blowing 28 knots, and the waves were steep and choppy. The crew knew that he couldn't fix the problem and brace himself from the pounding on an upwind course; the length of the mast accentuated the boat's motion too much, so Peter had to turn downwind to level the boat and smooth out the ride. Still, it took nearly 25 minutes to solve the problem. By then, the boat was almost 4 miles farther from home, but at least the crew member that went aloft was safe!

Reefing

Reefing is a system of reducing a sail's exposed area and/or mast. If your jib or mainsail has a roller furler, rolling it up partway reduces the sail's exposed area. Without roller furlers, reefing of mainsails (and some jibs) requires special equipment on the sails, spars, and boat. Most dinghies and many small keelboats don't have this type of reefing equipment, but a larger keelboat will likely have reefing systems. Reefing is an intermediate step (as the wind becomes stronger) before dropping a sail (or changing to a smaller/stronger one). An old saying is still as valuable today as it was in the days of the square riggers: "When in doubt . . . reef 'er."

REMEMBER

Make sure to rig the lines and equipment used to reef the sails as soon as the breeze starts to pick up — or, even better, before you leave the dock if any chance exists that you'll need to reef.

SLAB-REEFING THE MAINSAIL

Slab-reefing (or *jiffy-reefing*) the mainsail entails lowering it partway and attaching it by a "new" tack and clew built in the sail for this purpose. Here are the key components, some of which appear in Figure 7-1:

- **Boom lift:** Also called a *topping lift,* this line or wire holds the boom up when the mainsail is partially lowered. Some boats employ a solid boom vang to keep the boom up instead.
- **Reefing line:** This strong line is led to a pulley near the back of the boom and up the mainsail leech to or through the heavily reinforced *clew cringle* (the aftmost reef point).
- **Reef cringles and reef points:** These reinforced holes in the sail are employed as the "new" clew and tack when reefed. *Reef points* are holes aligned between those reef cringles to help tidy the foot of the sail when it's reefed.

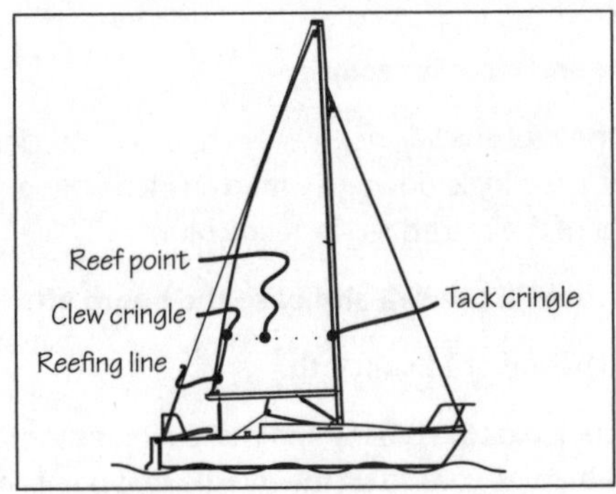

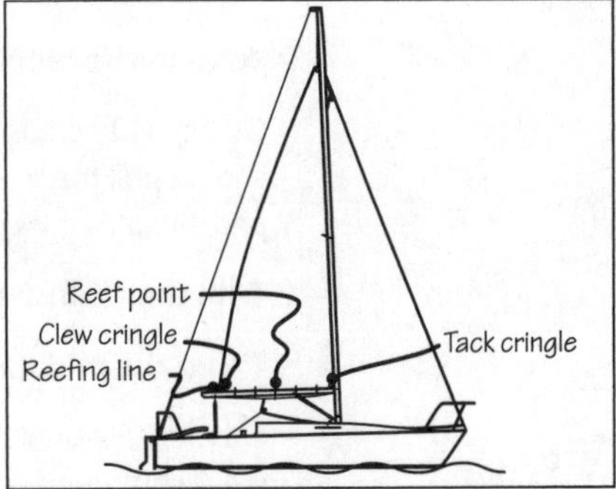

FIGURE 7-1: Left: The parts of a reefing system. Right: A reefed mainsail.

The *tack cringle* (forwardmost reef point) must have some sort of arrangement (strong metal hook, rope system, and so on) near the gooseneck to which it's secured when reefed.

To slab reef a mainsail under way, follow these steps:

1. **Ensure that the reef line is rigged properly.**

   REMEMBER

   Perform this step before you set sail. Feeding the reef line through the clew cringle after the mainsail is hoisted can be difficult.

2. **Have the helmsperson steer a steady course.**

   Close-hauled or close-reaching is preferable because the mainsail drops more easily.

3. **Take the slack out of the boom lift, and *cleat* it (tie it off securely).**

   This step keeps the boom from falling onto heads and into the cockpit when you lower the mainsail. If your boat has a solid vang that supports the boom, you can skip this step.

4. **Ease the boom vang and mainsheet until the main is fully luffing.**

   The main should be luffing throughout the reefing procedure so that it will lower and reef easily. Conduct all reefing activities from the windward side to minimize the danger of getting hit by the swinging boom.

5. **Ease the main halyard — slowly.**

   Gather the dropping luff until the person standing at the mast can secure the tack cringle near the gooseneck with the system provided.

6. **Slowly rehoist the main halyard.**

   Ensure that the luff feeds smoothly during hoisting, and tension the halyard very tightly.

7. **Tension the reef line, and cleat it securely.**

   On bigger keelboats, the reef line will need a winch to get sufficient tension. It should pull the "new" clew cringle down to within an inch or two of the boom and aft so that the foot of the reefed sail is nearly taut.

8. **Trim the mainsheet to refill the sail and ease the boom lift.**
9. **Tie up the middle of the lowered sailcloth.**

   This step is optional, but it aids in visibility and makes things more shipshape. We recommend using bungee cord to tie the middle reef points around the lowered sailcloth and boom. Then if the reef line breaks or slips, the sail won't shred.

You can see a properly slab-reefed main in Figure 7-2.

FIGURE 7-2: Shortened sail for heavy air: A reefed mainsail and smaller, heavy air jib.

REMEMBER

Some mainsails are rigged to "roller reef" inside the mast; others may have more than one set of reef points. Which set you use is determined by how small you want your mainsail to be. The first step down in size is the *first reef*, the next step down is the *second reef*, and so on.

REEFING THE JIB

Occasionally, you may find a jib with reef points, just like a mainsail. The most common (and easiest) way of reefing the jib is with a roller furler, but as the sail rolls up, it loses its designed shape. (In Chapter 12, we discuss the importance of sail shape.) So the only racing boats that rely on a roller furler for reefing are the shorthanded round-the-world boats. No one in their right mind wants to go up to the bow and change jibs or wrestle a sail back on board when they're alone in a 60-knot storm in the Southern Ocean.

Changing down headsails

Another way to reduce sail area is to switch to a smaller jib, if your boat has one. Most dinghies and small keelboats come equipped with only one jib. But as keelboats increase in size, it's more common to find an extra sail or two on board. A sail's bag (and the corners of the sails in them) should be clearly marked. Generally, on a large race boat, jibs are numbered 1 through 4, with 1 for light air and the smaller number 4 for heavy air. Here's an easy way to drop and change headsails:

1. **Turn the boat downwind onto a very broad reach to reduce heel and make moving around on the foredeck easier for the crew.**
2. **Lower the old, bigger jib, and fold it (check out Chapter 16).**

   Bag the jib, and put it down below.
3. **Rig the new, smaller jib and its sheets (refer to Chapter 4).**
4. **Hoist the new jib.**

   Crank the halyard good and tight.
5. **Bring the crew back into the safety of the cockpit and then turn up onto your desired course, trimming the sheet accordingly.**

For most sailors, sail changes are few and far between. A corollary of the "When in doubt, reef 'er" policy is to err on the side of putting up too small a jib initially — especially in a building breeze.

When conditions are deteriorating, over-reducing sail area is considered to be prudent seamanship. Even if you *can* sail the boat under the current conditions with a double-reefed main and a small jib, deciding to lower the mainsail and sail to shore at half-speed under jib alone is perfectly all right.

Recovering from a Capsize on a Dinghy

In strong winds, a major safety concern on a dinghy or small catamaran is *capsizing*, or having the boat flip over. If you're sailing a keelboat, you can skip right to the section "Staying on Board," because that lead keel prevents the boat from capsizing (unless you're in a hurricane!). Capsizing can be a nuisance, but don't fear it; it can also be fun and should be part of every sailor's introductory dinghy-sailing lesson. Given proper preparation and practice, you can handle a capsize easily.

TIP

When the boat flips upside down, all the loose gear in the boat floats away (or sinks), so always make sure that everything is well stowed or tied to the boat.

Centerboard boats fall into two categories with respect to capsizing:

- **Self-righting:** Those in which the crew can right the boat and then sail away
- **Swamping:** Those that *swamp* (fill with water) when they flip, which usually requires outside assistance

REMEMBER

The difference is in the design of the boat and whether it has sealed flotation tanks. All modern dinghies are designed to be self-righting. Assuming that you drained the flotation tanks before sailing and ensured that all drain holes were plugged before sailing, you should be able to right the boat. Avoid sailing in a boat that swamps when no rescue powerboat is available. Catamarans don't swamp, but they can be tricky to get upright. For tips on getting a catamaran up after a capsize, see Chapter 11.

The anatomy of a capsize

A boat can capsize in two ways: by tipping over to leeward or by tipping over to windward. A leeward capsize is common in strong or puffy winds; the boat simply heels too much and blows over, as Figure 7-3 shows. A windward capsize, also called a *death roll*, usually occurs when you're sailing downwind. The boat starts rolling back and forth until finally — *crash!* it sounds ominous, but you're only going to get wet.

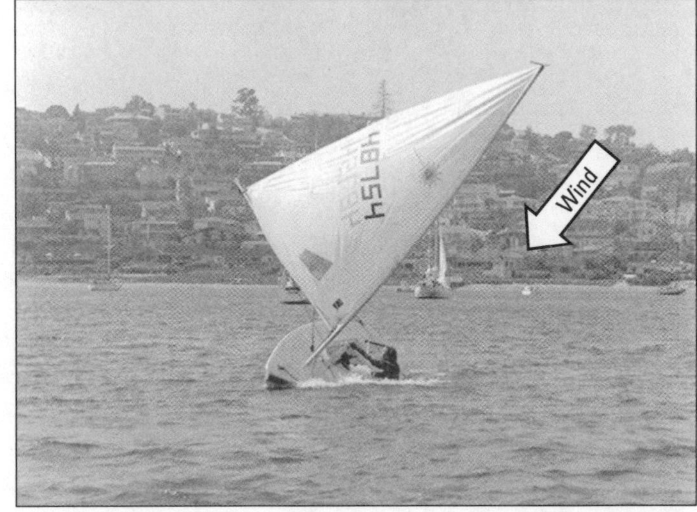

FIGURE 7-3: Capsizing to leeward (top) and to windward (bottom) — the death roll.

Photos courtesy of Sally Samins

Righting the boat

When you're sailing a dinghy or small cat, the question isn't *whether* you're going to capsize but *when.* After you capsize, the sooner you start righting the boat, the quicker and easier the recovery will be. If you dally, the boat may keep rolling until the mast is straight down — a situation called *turning turtle,* because the hull of the boat looks like a turtle shell. Righting a boat that has turtled is *much* harder than righting one that's on its side. So the minute you capsize, quickly hustle through the following steps (see Figure 7-4):

A

Get weight on centerboard as soon as possible to keep mast from sinking down. Best orientation is wind blowing onto the hull towards the mast tip.

B

As boat comes upright, both crew climb into boat while it's easy.

C

With sheets uncleated, the sails will flap while you get things sorted to sail again.

FIGURE 7-4: Getting your boat upright.

Photos courtesy of Sally Samins

1. **Ensure that your crew is safe and happy (well, relatively).**
2. **Get weight on the centerboard as quickly as possible, either by climbing over the high side or swimming around.**

   Don't delay; if you do, you may risk having the boat turn turtle.
3. **Make sure that all sheets are uncleated and loose.**

   Otherwise, the sails will fill as you right the boat, and you'll probably capsize again. You can lean over the hull to watch and talk to the crew, who should be swimming in the water while performing this step and then waiting in the water to climb aboard (see step 4).
4. **While standing on the centerboard, pull on the *rail* (edge) of the boat, and pump your weight to get the mast to come out of the water.**

   You're providing the leverage to bring the boat up. By holding on to the hiking straps, your swimming crew can get scooped into the boat as it comes upright. Having their weight in the boat as it comes up also helps prevent capsizing again immediately (a very common occurrence, especially if the mast is to windward).
5. **When the boat is upright, help everyone back on board while the sails luff.**

REMEMBER

Always get all your crew on board the boat as soon as it's upright. Just let the sails luff; you can worry about getting going again after everyone is safe and you've checked the boat.

Sometimes, especially in wavy conditions, righting the boat is difficult because the waves keep trying to turtle the boat. One effective technique of righting the boat under these conditions is to have the swimming crew hold on to the bow. The boat will naturally drift with the wind until the bow points directly upwind. With this technique, the crew keeps holding on to the bow until the boat is upright.

TIP

If you can't pull the boat upright by yourself, get the crew to provide more righting force by climbing up on the centerboard and leaning out together, as Figure 7-5 shows.

Rescuing a swamped dinghy

Dinghies that swamp are much more time-consuming to get sailing again, and doing so probably requires outside assistance. So never sail a boat that swamps without other boats around, and always make sure that you have a good bucket, or *bailer*, or two aboard in case you flip. Tie in these bailers so that you don't lose them when the boat rolls.

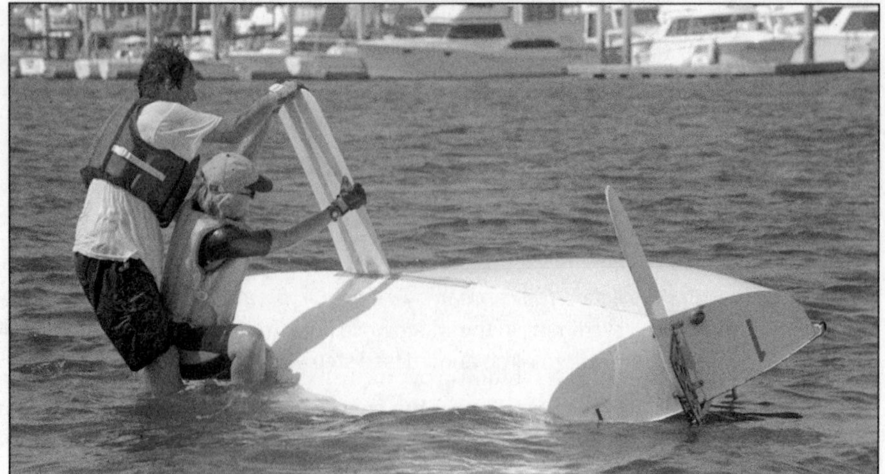

FIGURE 7-5: Righting a turtled boat takes more effort and both crews' weight to lever the mast and sails up and parallel to the water.

Photo courtesy of Sally Samins

If you capsize in a "swamper," you must first uncleat the sheets and bring the boat upright (albeit full of water) by pulling on the centerboard in a similar manner to a self-righting boat. Then climb in over the *transom* (back end) so that the boat doesn't capsize again, and start bailing like mad. If you're fast and can keep the boat upright, you can usually gain on the floodwaters slowly and get the boat dry. But be forewarned: A boat half filled with water is very unstable and can flip again easily. You may find that lowering all the sails will help the boat balance while you bail.

A much easier way to bail out the water is to get a tow from a motorboat. A motorboat with a well-secured tow rope can slowly pull your boat so that the bow raises and the water flows out over the transom. The sail(s) should be lowered to prevent reflipping. If you're in the boat, stay low and far aft; if you're in the water, hang on to the transom to help raise the bow. Soon, the water will be down to a level that you can bail with a bucket. Some dinghies have cockpit self-bailers that you can open to help drain the water, but they work only if the boat is moving.

REMEMBER

If you capsize and can't right the boat, or if you find yourself in the water with your boat swamped, *stay with the boat.* The boat is like a huge life ring, and you're much safer with the boat than without it. If the boat has turtled, try to get out of the water by sitting on the overturned hull, and wait for help. If you're in the water and tangled in lines, stay calm, and untangle yourself.

Rescuing a Man Overboard

Obviously, men, women, and children fall overboard, but *man overboard* is the hail that most people remember from old movies, and it's still the hail most commonly used when someone goes into the drink. In recent years various safety organizations have tried to make this term more politically correct with "crew overboard" or "person in the water" – but none of these have ever stuck... probably since "man overboard" is so ingrained in our heads. So, since safety is no accident, we are going to keep things simple and retain the age old saying here.

This talk about falling overboard may sound melodramatic, but going for an unexpected swim in bigger boats and rough conditions is probably the biggest danger facing the sailor. You and your crew need to prepare to deal with such a situation *before* it happens. Waiting until someone is actually in the water is too late.

Avoiding this situation by staying on board is the best advice; using a life harness can help. Wearing a life jacket can help you if you fall overboard, but the key to your rescue is how the rest of the crew on the boat responds.

Successfully retrieving someone from the water involves four key steps. The following sections discuss each step of a man-overboard drill in detail. The steps assume that you're sailing a larger keelboat, but most of the principles apply equally well to smaller boats.

Each of these steps requires practice so that the crew works together to complete them automatically in an emergency. You can practice by retrieving a hat or fender. If you get sunburned in the time it takes to get the hat or fender back, you probably need more practice (and more sunscreen).

If you're thinking about heading offshore, we recommend taking a Safety at Sea course with hands-on training (not an online course). In the United States, you can find internationally recognized (by World Sailing) courses through US Sailing (`https://www.ussailing.org/education/adult/safety-at-sea-courses`). Peter has to update his international certification every five years for many offshore races.

Step 1: Alert everyone, and keep the swimmer in sight

If you see someone fall overboard, yell to alert the rest of the crew to the emergency, but don't take your eyes off that person. You're now the designated spotter. If for some reason, you can't perform that job (you're driving, for example), make sure that someone else is spotting before you take your eyes off the swimmer. If you lose sight of the person, finding them again in the waves can be very difficult. While you're watching, try to reassure the swimmer by shouting encouragement like "I see you! We're stopping the boat. Don't try to swim to us. We'll be right there." Pointing at the person helps too. Tell the helmsman how far away and in what direction the swimmer is located every few seconds, using clear terms such as "three boat lengths, off the starboard quarter."

REMEMBER

Many bigger keelboats have a designated man-overboard button near the helm on a device such as a chart plotter. That button (whether it's on deck or down below) and its operation should be well known to the crew and be pressed as soon as possible to save the location of the swimmer. Then the GPS device immediately starts navigating (range and bearing) back to that saved location. For more information on using a device with GPS, see Chapter 9.

Step 2: Throw stuff that floats to the swimmer

A bigger keelboat should have man-overboard equipment ready to deploy near the transom. Quickly getting a life ring and/or other Type IV personal flotation aids to the swimmer is crucial. (Check out Chapter 3 for more on specific types of flotation devices.) If you've ever gone swimming fully clothed, you know how hard treading water can be, and doing so is even harder in big waves. Often, these safety devices have a flag that makes keeping the swimmer in sight easier. The more you can throw in the water, the better, both to help the swimmer stay afloat and (like Hansel's breadcrumbs) to help you find your way back. Some manufacturers make cool man-overboard modules (search for them online) that have a host of floating devices and signals designed to live at the back of the cockpit for just such an emergency.

TIP

Aim your throw slightly upwind of the swimmer so that it drifts to them. Also, you can probably throw the life ring farther by throwing underhand.

REMEMBER

Even at relatively slow boat speeds, every second moves the boat farther away from the swimmer. That's why the safety gear (or whatever you can throw) has to be readily at hand.

Step 3: Slow the boat

Slow the boat as soon as practical to minimize the distance to the swimmer. No matter what course/method you take to get the boat turned around and return to the swimmer, the closer you are, the sooner you return, and the easier it will be to find them.

How you go about returning to the swimmer depends on myriad variables, including the boat, the crew and its competence, the conditions, what sails are set, and what swimmer-recovery equipment is on board. If it's a sunny day and 5 knots of wind (Peter's fallen off in those conditions before), it should be fairly easy to slow down and make a quick turn back any which way. If it's blowing 30 knots and big seas, even tacking the boat is difficult, requiring more time and care to avoid causing additional problems.

We show two return/recover methods in this section, but realize that each situation is unique, and no single method will be right all the time. The decision on which method to use should be made by the person in charge.

REMEMBER

These two methods provide important elements to consider when you decide how you're going to deal with a man-overboard situation. Regardless of the technique you use, practicing is important. These routines are designed for larger keelboats, but if you're sailing on a dinghy or small keelboat and drop someone overboard, the general principles still apply. You may not have a life ring to throw to the swimmer, so getting back to them quickly is crucial.

Figure-eight

The first method is a variation on the classic *figure-eight method* (shown in Figure 7-6), in which the boat slows and sails away from the swimmer until the crew is ready to tack the boat safely. (The sail[s] may have to be dropped and the engine turned on, depending on the conditions.) While sailing away, the helmsman steers a course to facilitate preparation for the tack so that the final approach to the swimmer is a close-reach (the easiest course to control speed under sail) recovery.

The first half of the path you sail with this method will depend on the point of sail you were on when the swimmer went splash. If you're sailing upwind, turn farther downwind before tacking; if you're sailing downwind, turn up to a close reach before the tack. The goal is to make it easy to be on a close-reaching angle after you tack on your approach to the swimmer.

Another key to this method is that no jibe is required. In heavy winds, jibes can be downright difficult and even dangerous; tacking is much safer and easier. If conditions are mild, however, the quickest way to get back to the swimmer may very well be to jibe rather than tack. The decision of what method to use should be made by the person in charge.

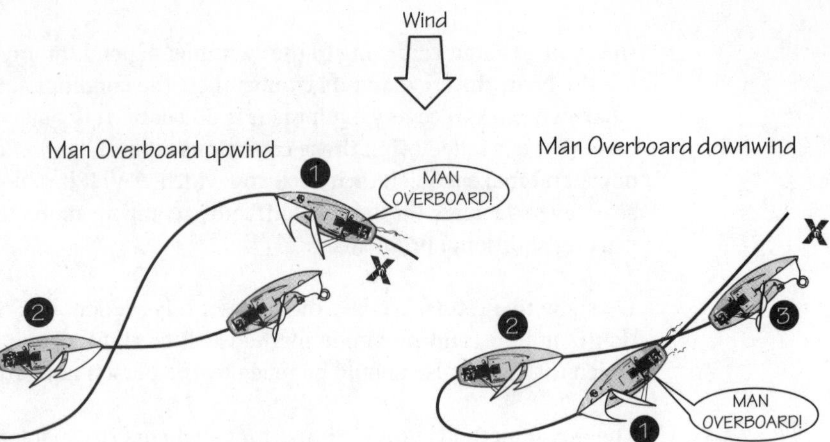
Wind
Man Overboard upwind
Man Overboard downwind
MAN OVERBOARD!
MAN OVERBOARD!
1 Turn to a course where, when ready, you can tack and approach swimmer slowly on a close reach. Don't get too far downwind!
2 Approach slowly with swimmer to leeward.

FIGURE 7-6: Figure-eight method: Your point of sail when the swimmer splashed determines the initial course, which prevents jibes and minimizes turns.

Quick-Stop variation

Another recovery method is a variation on the *Quick-Stop method* and could be called *Man Overboard For Dummies*, as shown in Figure 7-7. It involves the use of an innovative horseshoe-shape recovery device (the original was called a Lifesling) that's attached by a long floating rope to the stern of a boat. This technique can be effective even for shorthanded or inexperienced crews because you just leave the jib cleated and the main luffing. An advantage of the Quick-Stop method is that it keeps the boat closer to the swimmer so that you can keep them in sight more easily and (we hope) rescue them more quickly.

If you have only a main and jib set, here's the procedure:

1. **Yell "Man overboard!", throw the life ring and other floatable things, and keep the swimmer in sight.**
2. **Immediately tack the boat, leaving the jib sheet cleated so that it backs (fills on the back side).**

   The backed jib helps pull the boat around onto the new tack.
3. **If you have sufficient crew, drop the jib while bearing away so that you have one less sail to deal with during the recovery.**
4. **Deploy the Lifesling device from the transom.**
5. **Jibe and turn up to a close-hauled course, aiming close to leeward of the swimmer.**

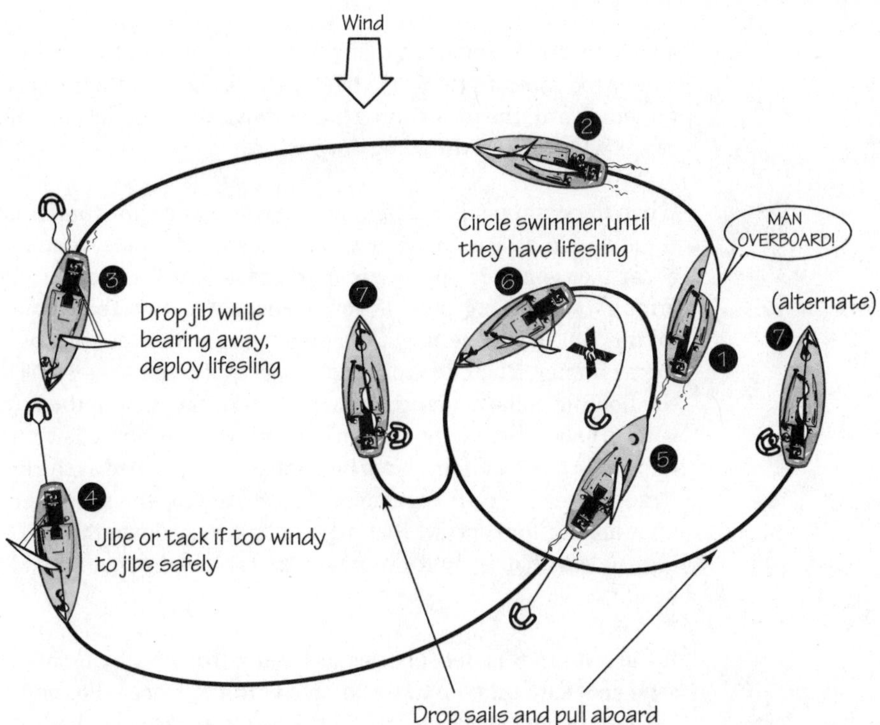

FIGURE 7-7: The Quick-Stop method combined with a Lifesling-type recovery device.

6. **Just past the swimmer, tack and turn in a small circle until the Lifesling or its floating rope reaches the swimmer.**
7. **When the swimmer has hold of the Lifesling, turn toward the wind, and drop all sails.**
8. **Commence the process of pulling the swimmer to the boat and back on board.**

REMEMBER

If you decide to use the engine to get back to the swimmer faster, make sure that you pull all lines out of the water before starting the motor, because getting a line wrapped around your propeller stops the engine. When you get close to the swimmer, put the engine in neutral so as not to endanger them with the propeller.

Step 4: Get the swimmer back on board

Getting back in contact is key. In some cases, the swimmer is able to climb aboard and is more embarrassed than anything else. Many times, though, getting the swimmer back on board can be the most difficult part of a rescue, especially if they're injured. You don't want the swimmer to get overly tired trying to swim back to the boat, so always plan on coming to them. You want to get close enough that you can at least throw them a line. When employing the figure-eight method, approach the swimmer so that they're to leeward of the boat. This way, if you're a little too cautious (which is better than being a little too daring) and end up too far windward, the boat simply blows down to the swimmer. Also, tossing a line is easier when you're throwing downwind.

When the swimmer is within range, throw them a line (preferably with yet another flotation aid attached). After you get them alongside, they may be able to climb aboard, or you may need a group effort to heft them aboard, grabbing under the armpits for the big pull. If you suspect that this technique may aggravate an injury, you may have to get creative to make the retrieval as easy as possible on the swimmer. The LifeSling device can facilitate recovery. The swimmer can put the floating collar under their arms to facilitate lifting them (or hauling them up with a halyard or pully system) aboard. If you don't have a Lifesling, you can improvise one by tying a large bowline in a loop to use as the lifting collar. Another *MacGyver*-like trick is to arrange a rope step for the swimmer. This step can be a line running fore and aft that's draped partway down the hull or a loop (a bowline is best; see Chapter 19 for more on knots) hanging over the side at a comfortable height.

If the swimmer is unconscious or having trouble staying afloat, you may have to send someone into the water to help with the rescue. But don't double your trouble. Before anyone else jumps in the water, make sure that the second person has adequate flotation and a line securing them to the boat.

One good reason to practice man-overboard drills and discuss them with your crew is to decide in advance the best place to get back on board your boat. Don't use the transom of the boat in any kind of rough seas; as the boat bobs in the waves, the transom slams into the water and can seriously injure a swimmer.

Staying Calm If You Fall Overboard

If you fall off a boat, your first reaction may be anger and embarrassment. But you need to stay calm and focused to maximize your rescue chances. We have a friend whose boat sank off the Carolina coast nearly 100 miles offshore. He survived nearly 24 hours afloat, but other crew members didn't. He credits his good fortune to his attitude and mental state. In case you go overboard, even for a few minutes, this section contains some important survival tips.

Conserve energy

The biggest mistake that people make when they fall overboard is exhausting themselves by trying to swim back to the boat. Unless you can *easily* reach a nearby boat, person, or floating object (such as a Type IV life ring), try to conserve energy rather than expend it. Swimming toward the wind and waves is very difficult.

Maximize buoyancy

If the conditions are rough, we hope that you were already wearing a personal flotation device. If it's an inflatable kind, now is the time to pull the trigger! If a floating object is nearby, swim to it, and hold on. Some boating reference books say that your clothing won't affect your buoyancy in the water, and clothing certainly helps keep you warm. In general, we recommend keeping your clothing and footwear on for that reason. A swimming lifesaving course (check with your local YMCA or Red Cross chapter) can provide excellent information on staying afloat.

TIP

You can trap air in your jacket or foul-weather pants to help you float. By sealing all but one opening of a waterproof piece of clothing and then holding the one opening wide to catch air, you can turn this gear into a (leaky) balloon that can help provide support. The same applies to your boots.

Conserve body heat

Because hypothermia is a very real threat, even in moderately cool water, conserving body heat is important. Here are some tips for staying warm:

- **Get as much of your body out of the water as possible.** At the very least, keep your head out of the water. Pockets of air caught in foul weather gear can help.
- **Keep your body in a compact shape.** A very compacted shape is the fetal position, also called the Heat Escape Lessening Position (HELP). With a life jacket on, you can usually stay in the HELP position with your head out of the water, as shown in Figure 7-8. If this position brings your head under water, try keeping your arms and legs together to conserve as much warmth as you can.
- **Huddling with others**. Grouped together, you conserve body heat, provide moral support, and are easier for rescuers to spot (also shown in Figure 7-8).
- **Tighten your life jacket.** A snug fit helps keep you floating higher and burning less energy from treading water. If your life jacket has crotch straps – tightening them will do the same.

In Appendix B, we cover basic first aid afloat, including ways to warm hypothermia victims.

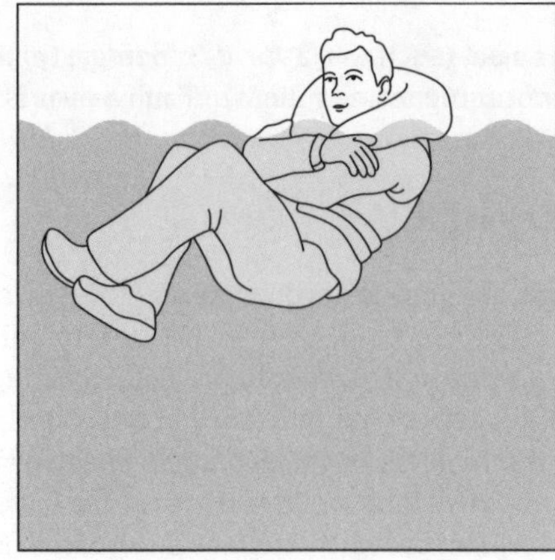

FIGURE 7-8: The HELP position (left) and huddling up (right).

© John Wiley & Sons, Inc.

Make yourself visible

The first time Peter ever sailed at night on the ocean was a thrilling but also somewhat scary experience. Because he was worried about falling overboard, he put a waterproof pocket-size strobe light in his pocket. That way, if he does go overboard he can signal with it to help his team's search. Today, he never sails at night without a waterproof flashlight or headlamp in hand. Peter's friend Cam Lewis, who has raced twice around the world non-stop on huge high-speed catamarans, carries a PLB, which is an emergency radio beacon that sends an SOS signal out to satellites and airplanes. See the upcoming section "Using satellite communications" for more information. A similar signaling device is a personal AIS beacon that transmits a signal that can be received by Automatic Identification System (AIS) devices on other boats. See the section "Automatic Identification System (AIS)" below.

Catching a Tow

At some point in your sailing career, you'll probably be forced to accept a tow from a powerboat. But any time you put your boat's fate in the hands of another boater (which is the case in a tow), you take a risk. To make your towing experiences as carefree as possible, read the following tips:

- **Don't take a tow unless you really need one.** Sailing is fun and the towing boat probably has something better to do.
- **Use a good rope.** An anchor line is an ideal tow line because it's long, strong, and stretchy — all good things for towing. (For more about lines, see Chapter 15.)

- **Attach your tow line securely.** If the loads are moderate (you aren't in heavy weather, and you're not aground), tie your tow line to a secure object. The mast is usually best. Tie it as low as possible around the mast, just above the cabin top or deck. Make sure that the rope isn't chafing anywhere.
- **Use good knots.** Two (or three) round turns around the mast secured with two half hitches are best so you can release the knot safely in a hurry if necessary. See Chapter 19 for details on how to tie that knot.
- **Make sure that the boat and crew are ready before you speed up.** Ask the tow boat's captain not to accelerate until they see a "thumbs up" from you, and then they should increase speed slowly until you give an "okay" sign.
- **Make sure that you can get free in a hurry.** If the powerboat captain is a yahoo, you want to be able to free your boat quickly. A sharp knife works (on the line, that is, not on the yahoo). You may be able to untie the round turns and half hitches in a hurry, even when they're under load. Avoid using a bowline knot; you won't be able to free it easily.
- **Stay away from the tow line.** The line can break and whip directly back behind the mast.
- **Don't tow too fast.** Discuss a comfortable speed with the tow boat ahead of time, and fine-tune that speed with hand signals if necessary.
- **Slow down in waves.** Big waves can add tremendous load, so watch for ones that can surprise you, such as the wake of a ship. If practical, the tow boat should slow down and turn toward the wake to minimize its effect on your boat.
- **Adjust the length of the rope to go downhill.** When you get to a comfortable towing speed, you may want to extend the tow rope to its maximum length to make it easier to steer your boat and to let the stretchy tow rope cushion your ride. Fine-tune the rope's length so that your bow is pointed downhill, riding on the towing boat's wake, which remains a constant distance from you. This little trick really eases the load on the tow line. In most cases, the longer the tow rope, the better (at least two to three of your boat lengths). The only exception is in confined places where tight maneuvering requires a shorter tow line or even a side tow (and slower tow speed).

Communicating and Calling for Help

Our safety chapter wouldn't be complete without a discussion of how to call for help. You probably want to go sailing to get away from phone calls, faxes, and emails, but in an emergency, a communication link can be vital. For coastal sailing, a cellular phone may be convenient, but for safety, we strongly recommend that you use a Very High Frequency (VHF) radio, because VHF Channel 16 is internationally used for emergency communication. Channel 16 is constantly monitored by coast guards and rescue organizations around the world, as well as by many boats and ships.

VHF radios are simply two-way radios with more than two dozen channels. With a VHF radio, you can get in touch with the rescue entity, such as the U.S. Coast Guard (USCG); talk to other boats (not on Channel 16!); listen to marine weather reports; and even talk to marinas and yacht clubs to inquire about slip space for your boat. The radio's range depends on the power of the unit and the height of the antennas of both stations. Talking to another recreational boat, a 5-watt handheld model has a range of a few miles; a 25-watt VHF radio attached to a masthead antenna on a 40-foot mast has a range of roughly 20 miles. The USCG has tall, powerful antennas all along the coastline that extend the working range to 35 miles and sometimes much more. Put a handheld radio in a waterproof bag to keep it dry, and for extended sails, make sure that you have a supply of charged batteries.

You don't need to register a marine VHF radio used on a recreational boat in U.S. waters. But a U.S. recreational sailboat traveling internationally must register the radio and obtain a user license, called an FRN (for FCC Registration Number) from the Federal Communications Commission (`https://apps.fcc.gov/coresWeb/publicHome.do`). For recreational boats from outside the United States, check the requirements, which vary, but many countries require some sort of license.

Using your VHF radio

TIP

Two people can't talk on a VHF radio at the same time. Press the talk button and wait one second before you begin talking. Finish your transmission by saying "Over," release the talk button, and listen for a response. Normal transmissions shouldn't last for more than about 30 seconds.

Here are the common types of VHF radio communications:

- **Radio check:** Once or twice a year and before a major trip, check your radio by tuning to Channel 16 and calling "Any vessel, any vessel. This is the yacht *Babbalubba*, calling for a radio check. Over." Don't waste the USCG's time with a radio-check request.
- **Ship to ship:** For safety and by law in the United States, every vessel operating a VHF radio must monitor Channel 16, so when you're afloat, have your VHF tuned to Channel 16. Doing so makes good sense because when everyone is listening to Channel 16, everyone can help one another as

needed. For general communications, the normal protocol is to first call the other boat on Channel 16 and then switch to another channel as soon as you make contact.

REMEMBER

Channel 16 isn't for chatter. Make contact with the other boat and then switch to another channel.

Channels 9, 68, 69, 71, 72, and 78 are approved for noncommercial intership communication. You can surf to `www.fcc.gov/wireless/bureau-divisions/mobility-division/ship-radio-stations` for a full list of VHF frequencies and their designated uses.

- **Ship to marine telephone operator:** Yes, you can connect to a real telephone by calling the marine operators on channels 24 through 28 and 84 through 86. They typically charge for this service, so we recommend using your cellphone to call another phone.
- **Ship to USCG — EMERGENCY:** Channel 16 is the international emergency channel. See the next section for the proper procedure during an emergency. If you're in trouble, make your primary contact with the USCG (or other rescue organization) on Channel 16, and you'll be instructed if they want you to switch channels.
- **Weather information:** In the United States, marine weather forecasts and warnings are transmitted on special VHF weather channels (Wx-1 thru Wx-8).
- **Digital Selective Calling (DSC):** DSC was developed to increase the performance of a VHF radio, especially in emergency situations, by using a more efficient digital signal. Most modern marine VHF radios are equipped with DSC technology and an easy-to-use DSC button. In the United States, the radio should be programmed with the boat's Maritime Mobile Service Identity (MMSI) number. To find out more about MMSIs, go to `https://www.navcen.uscg.gov/?pageName=mtmmsi`. Although DSC can be used to make a direct private call to any boat or station equipped with a DSC VHF, its greatest utility is in calling for help.

Using the VHF radio in emergencies

If you have a life-threatening situation, make an emergency call on Channel 16 by following these steps (starting with step 2 if your VHF doesn't have DSC):

1. **If your radio is equipped with DSC, lift the red "distress" cover, press the distress button for 5 seconds, and select the nature of your distress from the onscreen menu.**

   Your distress signal will be transmitted, and the radio will switch automatically to Channel 16.

2. **Start your verbal transmission by pressing the talk button and saying "Mayday" three times. Then give the name of your boat three times and your VHF call sign (if you have one) one time.**

WARNING

If your situation is not immediately life threatening – for example you need help such as medical assistance but not emergency evacuation – do not use "Mayday" - start your message by saying "Pan-Pan" (pronounced *pahn-pahn*) three times and then continue with the information described in this list.

3. **Repeat "Mayday" and your boat's name one more time.**
4. **Give your location, either by the distance from an object on the chart (such as "2 miles east of buoy three") or by latitude and longitude.**
5. **Explain your situation *as briefly as possible.***

   You might say something like "Swamped and taking on water, in need of tow or rescue."

6. **State how many people are on board.**
7. **Describe the boat's type, color, and any distinguishing features (such as "30-foot dark red ketch with main and jib hoisted").**
8. **Finish your verbal transmission by saying "Over" (and don't forget to release the talk button so you can listen for a response).**
9. **If no response after listening for a short period, repeat these steps until someone responds.**
10. **When a team from an official rescue service (such as the USCG) responds, follow their instructions.**

If you hear a mayday distress call, figure out whether you're close enough to help by writing down the information and computing your distance. If you can help, speak on the radio directly to the boat in distress, and give your estimated arrival time. If the USCG or other official rescue organization is already on the call, wait for a clear pause in the conversation to share this information. If you can't help, stay off the radio.

TIP

If your boat has a VHF radio, turn it on and keep it tuned to Channel 16, because you never know when you may be able to help somebody who's in trouble.

Using satellite communications

If you're sailing farther offshore (out of VHF range to the shore), the best way to stay in communication or call for help is with satellite radio technology. This hot market has a growing number of options; your choice will depend on your budget and appetite for data.

AUTOMATIC IDENTIFICATION SYSTEM (AIS)

You know those transponders that airplanes and ground controllers use to track airplanes and keep everyone clear of one another? Well, there's a marine equivalent: AIS. All commercial ships carry an AIS transponder (and receiver) that sends basic information (name, position, course, speed, and so on) in digital format on a VHF radio frequency that can be read by any AIS receiver. Though it's not required equipment for recreational sailboats, Peter considers a marine AIS device (one that transmits and receives) to be essential equipment for any sailboat large enough to have a battery and instrument system.

A chart plotter, interfaced navigation software, or even an app on your smartphone allows you to "see" all AIS-transmitting boats within range and their course and speed, displaying their AIS signal on the chartplotter. You can see other boats (and determine whether there's any danger of collision well ahead of time), as well as emergency signals from the pocket-size emergency personal AIS beacons. If someone falls overboard and activates their personal AIS beacon. anyone within range (2 to 3 miles or more) will see their emergency signal and exact location.

Any time Peter goes offshore or sails at night, he has a personal beacon in his pocket! There are two options: a personal AIS beacon that's receivable by any nearby boat with an AIS or a personal locator beacon (PLB) (covered in the "Using satellite communications" section) that sends its signal to the global search-and-rescue network via satellite.

The technology employs radio waves that are sent to a communications satellite (a lot closer than the shoreline VHF antenna) and then routed into the appropriate network: voice, data, and so on. The most familiar device (but not the cheapest) is a handheld satellite phone that can provide basic text and voice communications but typically no Internet access or apps.

The giant satellite domes you see on navy ships and megayachts that provide high-speed web access are out of our league (and where would we mount the antennas?). But communications is big business and changing fast as new satellite networks get launched, bringing high-speed data to remote areas worldwide.

Following are some options for a recreational sailboat to use offshore. Pretty much every type of device has a button for emergencies, but unlike the case with DSC-equipped VHF emergency buttons, the initial recipient isn't necessarily an official rescue entity.

- **Handheld satellite radio:** This type of device will set you back somewhere between a few hundred to a couple thousand dollars — and that's before you buy airtime, which isn't inexpensive. The cost depends on the phone's features (waterproofing, satellite network, and so on). These popular devices are also available to rent. It's prudent to program your sat phone with phone numbers you may need, such as (in the United States) USCG Rescue Coordination for your region.

- **Satellite trackers and messengers:** At the inexpensive end of the spectrum are these often-pocket-size devices, which communicate simply. Some devices only send out your position at intervals; others have limited text-messaging capability. Lightweight and inexpensive, these devices are a great backup option for staying in touch and for use in an emergency.
- **Satellite terminals:** Stepping up in performance (more bandwidth) and cost are satellite terminals, which include a large mounted antenna (ranging from the size of a grapefruit to the size of a beach ball and a base station that can be connected to your boat's network (wired or wireless). Prices are in the thousands of dollars, but again, these devices are available to rent. With the extra bandwidth comes the capability to access more weather information, which is invaluable when planning your route. The Internet data that these devices typically provide isn't yet as fast or inexpensive as at home.
- **EPIRBs and PLBs:** Transmitting on frequencies that are tracked by the worldwide search-and-rescue (SAR) network through satellites and airplanes, these beacons are for use in extreme emergencies. We hope that you'll never have to use one of these devices. Activate them, and they immediately start sending out an SOS signal that's routed to the closest SAR entity. An EPIRB (Emergency Position Indicating Radio Beacon) is a portable and often floating unit that should be stored in an accessible location on the boat. A PLB (personal locator beacon) is a pocket size emergency unit designed to be carried. It works the same way, sending its emergency signal at the push of a button.

IN THIS CHAPTER

» Gauging the wind

» Gathering weather information

» Dealing with fog

» Following the tides and currents

» Sailing with the sea breeze

» Watching the wind shift

» Making the most of your weather knowledge

Chapter 8

All about Weather: Red Sky at Night

When it is evening, ye say, It will be fair weather: for the sky is red.

— MATTHEW 16:2

Weather is important in many sports; you can't play baseball in the rain, and players abandon tennis courts when snow is on the ground. But sailing, more than any other sport, depends on weather, particularly the wind, for its very existence. Without the wind, you may as well be sitting on a raft. Fortunately, in most parts of the world, enough wind is available for sailing much of the time.

In this chapter, we talk about sailing's "playing field": the wind and the water. We discuss how to estimate the present wind and water conditions and how to predict what's going to happen. Having an idea what the weather will do next makes your sail *safer* (so you don't go out when conditions are too windy), *faster* (so you pick the most efficient course), and *more fun* (so you get the best wind for your needs).

Figuring Out How Windy It Is

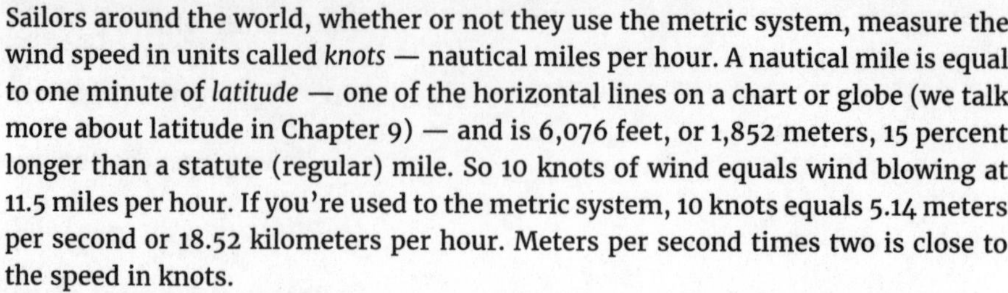

Sailors around the world, whether or not they use the metric system, measure the wind speed in units called *knots* — nautical miles per hour. A nautical mile is equal to one minute of *latitude* — one of the horizontal lines on a chart or globe (we talk more about latitude in Chapter 9) — and is 6,076 feet, or 1,852 meters, 15 percent longer than a statute (regular) mile. So 10 knots of wind equals wind blowing at 11.5 miles per hour. If you're used to the metric system, 10 knots equals 5.14 meters per second or 18.52 kilometers per hour. Meters per second times two is close to the speed in knots.

REMEMBER

Sailors (and weather forecasters) speak of the wind in terms of the *true wind* (the wind that you feel if your boat isn't moving) speed and direction. Be aware that when you're moving, you and your sails "feel" the *apparent wind* — the sum of the true wind and the wind created by the motion of your boat. So even if the wind remains steady, conditions feel windier when you're sailing upwind than when you're sailing downwind. (For more about the difference between true and apparent winds, check out Chapter 11.)

Fortunately, you have another way to judge wind speed: Look at the water. Admiral Sir Francis Beaufort of the British Royal Navy developed a visual scale of wind speed (see Table 8-1) in 1805. He must have been an observant guy (or bored stiff on long sea voyages), and sailors still benefit from his perceptions today. He defined wind speed in terms of a single number: the *Beaufort Force*, which is the first column in Table 8-1. In some parts of the world, weather forecasters still report marine forecasts in these units, although using knots is more common. An especially cool feature of the Beaufort Scale is the remarks about the water's surface shown in the Water-Surface Conditions column.

TIP

This relationship between what the surface of the water looks like and the wind speed really works. Guessing the wind speed every time you go out on the water is fun — and good practice. One of the tips that always seems to come in handy is the one for Force 4. At around 12 knots, a few whitecaps are definitely apparent on the surface.

These descriptions of the water's surface apply only in areas where the wavelets and waves have a long-enough distance to build up, of course, so you need at least a half mile of open water in the direction the wind is coming from. With an *offshore* wind (blowing from the land toward the water), the water can be glassy-smooth right next to a beach, yet the wind can be blowing over 20 knots.

TABLE 8-1 **Beaufort Scale**

Force	Wind Speed (Knots)	Description	Water-Surface Conditions	Dummies *Fun Meter*
0	0	Calm	Smooth, like a mirror.	Good time for a nap.
1	1–3	Light air	Small ripples.	Time for lunch.
2	4–6	Light breeze	Short, small wavelets with no crests.	All right! Now the boat's moving!
3	7–10	Gentle breeze	Larger wavelets with crests.	Hey, this is really fun! Great for beginners.
4	11–16	Moderate breeze	Longer, small waves, some with whitecaps (foamy crests).	Faster is better; time to think about putting on a jacket.
5	17–21	Fresh breeze	Moderate waves with many whitecaps.	Beginners should head for shelter; experienced sailors dream of wind like this.
6	22–27	Strong breeze	Large waves, extensive whitecaps, some spray.	Great fun, but hard work.
7	28–33	Near gale	Heaps of waves, with some breakers, whose foam is blown downwind in streaks.	Only for skilled sailors on well-prepared boats. Staying dry is impossible; lunch is all wet.
8	34–40	Gale	Moderately high waves with edges of crests breaking into *spindrift* (heavy spray); foam is blown downwind in well-defined streaks.	Time to head home, no matter who you are.
9	41–47	Strong gale	High waves with dense foam streaks and some crests rolling over; spray reduces visibility.	Time to rent the movie *The Perfect Storm* and make some popcorn . . . at home.
10	48–55	Storm	Very high waves with long, overhanging crests. The sea looks white; waves tumble with force; visibility is greatly reduced.	Time to put the movie on pause and make sure that all your pets are safely inside the house.
11	56–63	Violent storm	Exceptionally high waves that may obscure medium-size ships. All wave edges are blown into froth, and the sea is covered with patches of foam.	Better hope you used some good knots on the dock lines of your boat.
12	64–71	Hurricane	The air is filled with foam and spray, and the sea is completely white.	I want my blankie!

REMEMBER

Wind direction is defined in the direction *from which* it's blowing, using cardinal points (north, south, east, and west) and their subdivisions (northwest, southeast, and so on) or in degrees on the 360-degree compass. If wind direction is defined in degrees, make sure you know whether it's referenced off true (the default convention for the U.S.'s National Weather Service) or magnetic north. Many weather apps let the user decide whether direction is in true or magnetic degrees. (You can find more about using a compass and about true and magnetic north in Chapter 9.) If the wind is forecast to be *westerly*, it's expected to come *from* the west. If you turn toward the western horizon, a westerly wind blows straight on your face. By paying attention to the wind speed and direction, you become more aware of the overall weather picture — especially when you combine that information with the weather forecast.

The small picture (using your eyes)

Most sailing takes place over the course of a few hours in a relatively small area, whereas most weather forecasts aren't so focused or accurate. A sailor going for an afternoon cruise is concerned with a much smaller slice of the weather pie than a crew heading off to set a record sailing around the globe, but both must look for signs of changing weather. And in both cases, the short-term weather is frequently best assessed by observation rather than blind reliance on a forecast for a larger area. The western sky (in the mid-latitudes) is often the sailor's most valuable weathercaster. This section contains some important tips that help you assess current conditions visually and predict short-term (say, one hour or less) changes in weather.

Here are some visual wind and weather tell-tales for the sailor:

- **The sky:** Clouds (or lack thereof) are an important weather sign. Later, in the section "More than cloud gazing", we review the different types. When clouds change (more, fewer, or different kinds), they often foretell a weather or wind shift.
- **Sailboats on the horizon:** The angle of their sails and their heeling show their current wind. If the boats are upwind of you, those conditions may be filtering down to you.
- **Flags or smokestacks on shore:** They provide definitive evidence of the wind at that location and height.
- **Temperature:** When there's a noticeable change in humidity or temperature, that's an important sign of a wind or weather change.
- **A change in visibility:** If a hazy, murky horizon starts to clear in one direction, more wind will likely come from that direction.
- **The water's surface:** As Beaufort taught us (refer to "Figuring Out How Windy It Is" earlier in this chapter), the surface of the water can effectively portray the wind

speed. Sailors learn to read the water even at a distance. Darker water often means that waves or ripples are causing more wind; a lighter color means less wind.

WARNING

Following are signs of stormy weather approaching:

- Dark cumulonimbus clouds approaching on the horizon (see the next section, "More than cloud gazing")
- Thunder and/or lightning
- Changes in the weather radar on your weather app
- Change in the wind (dies off or blows gently toward the big dark clouds)

More than cloud gazing

Clouds are important to sailors because they help us understand the current conditions and can presage a weather change. Clouds come in all sizes and shapes but fall into three basic types:

- **Cirrus:** The highest clouds, wispy and thin. They signify fair weather — for the next day, at least.
- **Cumulus:** Puffy clouds like cotton balls. The associated weather depends on the clouds' color and size. Cumulus clouds mean fair weather when their bases are high in the sky or when they're relatively thin and bright-white at lower altitudes. The taller (thicker) and darker ones with low-altitude bases are the *cumulonimbus* variety, which foretell ominous weather, including sudden thunderstorms.
- **Stratus:** Layered clouds, very even-looking from underneath. *Stratus* comes from the Latin word for "spread, stretch out, or cover," which is what these clouds do. The associated weather depends on their color, thickness, and altitude. The lower, thicker, and darker stratus clouds are, the more they're associated with rain, wind, and (sometimes) low visibility. Fog is a stratus cloud that touches the ground.

Getting the Scoop on the Weather

Sailors get their weather information from a variety of sources, and none is more accurate than their own observation of present conditions. Because the weather is bound to change while you're sailing, being concerned with what's coming next pays off. We're big fans of all the weather information and forecasts available online and elsewhere, but weather forecasts are never perfect and sometimes completely wrong. The marine weather forecast is the butt of as many jokes among sailors as the TV weather forecast is around the water cooler at the office. But every little bit of information helps, and as you gain more experience in a given area, you develop what sailors call *local knowledge* — the ability to look at the sky and current conditions to forecast the weather.

Experienced sailors know that they should treat the ubiquitous weather information as a resource and never rely on it blindly. Developing your observational skills and increasing your own knowledge of the science of weather will allow you to add value to the forecast (and interpret why things aren't exactly like the forecast).

TIP

Peter and famed sailing meteorologist Chris Bedford created Marine Weather University (`www.marineweatheru.com`) to raise the weather IQ of sailors and offer courses that allow sailors to go beyond their favorite weather app.

It's absolutely important to do some study of the current weather and the forecast before setting sail – no matter whether you're heading out for an hour or a year. A vast amount of weather information is available on the Internet at the click of a button, making it easy and fast to get the forecast. All too many sailors rush to their favorite app to get a forecast, leaving a big hole in their weather prep. They miss out on important information that they need to get the most out of a weather app (especially when it's wrong!). Here's our recommended process for your pre-sail weather preparation (at Marine Weather University, it's called the *forecast funnel*), starting way out at the continental scale and zooming in to the close-up local info available in weather apps.

The big picture

Looking out a few hundred miles or more from your current location is the first step. Initially, you study a surface-weather map. Later in this chapter, in the "Whither the Weather" section, we discuss how to read a weather map and how to recognize the high- and low-pressure systems and fronts that drive the weather on the regional and continental scales. Satellite and radar images at that same larger scale are also part of this first stage of the funnel process.

There are numerous sources of this information, including many weather apps. Most big countries have a national weather service that may provide the best route to this info and many of the steps of the funnel. In the United States, the National Weather Service (NWS) home page (`www.weather.gov`) opens the door to an overwhelming amount of information, including surface charts. The NWS's Ocean Prediction Center (`https://ocean.weather.gov`) provides similar information for the Atlantic and Pacific offshore and coastal waters, and sailors may find it a bit more suited to their needs. The graphics cover a lot of the country, and the page provides links that enable you to drill down to the NWS's marine forecasts (see "Official marine forecasts" later in this chapter).

The human touch

A lot of weather information is available in depersonalized digital format, but the next step in our process is to try to find some guiding analysis from a professional meteorologist. For day-sailing in the United States, a good place to start is the NWS website (again). Forecast Discussion is a great text-based product that's updated a few times a day at regional NWS offices; it provides a good combination of big-picture interpretation of the weather map, observations, reviews of the various forecast tools (weather models), and how the forecaster thinks the regional and local forecasts will pan out. You can get to your regional office's discussion by entering your location on the NWS home page. Outside the United States, the best starting point for forecaster input is the national weather agency of that locale.

Official marine forecasts

Notice that we haven't gotten to weather apps yet? There's a method to our process. Next, you find your local marine forecast, ideally in text or voice format. In the United States, the NWS provides regional marine forecasts that are updated several times a day, available online, and sometimes via VHF radio on the special WX channels. (See Chapter 7 for details on using VHF radio.) One good reason not to bypass this step is that any official warnings or watches (thunderstorms, big waves, fog, and so on) are shared in some weather apps.

Observations

Knowing what's happening around you is how we started this chapter — by reminding you that it's essential for sailors to open their eyes to the weather. Many parts of the world have great sources of live (or recent) weather observations (weather buoys, shore stations, and ships) compiled and presented by national weather organizations. Many weather apps tap into these observations, and some add proprietary weather observations — usually only wind speed and direction, but that information is important to us sailors.

WARNING

You should be wary of observation data, because not all of it is created equal. Make sure that you know the time of the observation (some sites report irregularly) and any limitations that would make it less than helpful. A weather buoy's recent info from 10 miles offshore might have pretty accurate wind data compared with a private weather station bolted to a big building that shields it from the wind.

At this point, you might zoom in and focus a bit more on the local region. If a frontal passage or thunderstorm is in the forecast, you should be closely monitoring the weather radar on an app or on a national weather-service site to stay safe. We discuss these weather features later in the "Squalls" section.

The digital domain

Okay, it's time to talk about the specialty of weather apps: displaying forecasts from weather models. Weather models are complex programs based on the science of fluid dynamics and meteorology that start with an initial set of conditions and run forward in time to produce a forecast. When we wrote the first edition of this book, relatively few weather models didn't have the resolution to provide a local wind forecast; they were run on computers that have long ago been put out to pasture, replaced by today's speedier brethren.

Today, weather models are ubiquitous. Although the global models run by the United States, European Union, and a few other international sources are still incredibly valuable to forecasters, a new generation of higher-resolution weather models that cover smaller areas give sailors a lot of good (and sometimes not-so-good) information to digest about local sailing forecast. These models are much more effective at discerning local nuances that sailors care about, such as sea breezes and local geographic effects. For more on these local features, read on.

It's all too easy to look at the beautiful graphics and tables of wind speed and direction in a weather app and think you have the answer. And armed with the knowledge you've garnered in the previous steps of the forecast funnel, this data can be darned useful. But because most weather apps simply repackage data provided by government weather services, it's important to be a bit of an informed consumer when it comes to looking at the forecast in your app. If possible, try to look at the output of several weather models. It's also important to know which models are global (excelling at big-picture forecasts) and which are regional or local (better at capturing the forces that drive your local sailing weather).

But even though we recognize the limitations of global models in forecasting local sailing weather, we also must appreciate that weather models are like baseball players; they all have their good and bad days. Picking the best model(s) for the day is what those professional meteorologists do, based on their knowledge of the field. They often use the "ensemble method" where they look at the forecasts in a bunch of models to see a trend and use the average (or some variation) as their forecast. Sailors can use the same technique as sailing-oriented weather apps often allow us to see several weather model forecasts (such as for wind speed and direction at 11 a.m. at a particular point) in a table or graph. Then, we too can see the ranges in weather model world, which can be extremely helpful info. If one model is predicting 30 knots of wind from the north and another calls for 10 knots from the south – we might have less confidence in the forecast than if all the models show very similar speed and direction.

The forecast-funnel process doesn't stampede to a single weather model output in an app; it takes a more logical route in painting a picture that helps you decide whether to go sailing on any given day, knowing what range of conditions to expect and why those conditions may transpire. It's essential to become familiar with the weather information available in your area and work through the forecast-funnel process by researching, saving links, and finding the weather apps that work best for you. If you're sailing in a new area, talk to some locals to find out where they get their information.

WEATHER ON OCEAN PASSAGES

Ever wonder how sailors on extended offshore voyages, outside the range of VHF radios and cellphones, get their weather information? They use satellite radio communications (see Chapter 7), of course, but the bandwidth may be extremely limited, depending on their hardware and the satellite network they're using. Commercial forecasting services can send email forecasts for a cost, but most sailors roll their own weather forecasts by accessing weather info and forecasts online.

Again, cost and bandwidth are super-limited, so sailors often rely on downloading the raw output of weather models in a universally accepted compressed format called Gridded Binary (GRIB). GRIB files contain weather model data selected by the user, such as wind, precipitation, and wave height, which can be loaded into various viewers or computer programs that do navigation and weather routing for analysis and planning purposes.

When Peter is navigating in an ocean race (such as Los Angeles to Hawaii), he uses weather-routing software (`www.expeditionmarine.com`) to analyze various weather models and calculate the optimum route to take. This software starts with a forecasted wind and current, the boat's *polars* (predicted boat speed at various wind speeds and angles), and the desired destination; then it tries hundreds or even thousands of possible routes to figure out which one is fastest. New weather model GRIBs are available every few hours, so throughout a race, Peter repeatedly runs route-optimizing software and studies the forecasts to determine the best way to go.

Weather routing is part art, part science, and part luck. Another, less hands-on option is to have an online service such as `www.predictwind.com` do your weather routing in the cloud.

When you're planning a long ocean trip, a *pilot chart* (available at `https://msi.nga.mil/Publications/APC`) can be invaluable. These neat ocean charts show historical wind information averaged by month at locations around the globe. Another cool source of historical ocean wind data is `http://numbat.ceoas.oregonstate.edu/cogow`.

VISUAL WARNINGS

Some marinas and yacht clubs around the United States display small-craft-warning flags. (During the nighttime hours, they may use lights.) These flags, shown in the following figure, are based on the marine weather forecast and indicate expected wind strength or wave conditions. The gray-shaded areas are red in real life.

Small-craft warning Gale warning Storm warning Hurricane warning

Whither the Weather

Although you can use all this weather information at face value, you get more out of it if you understand some of the principles behind it, such as why the wind blows. Many variables affect the weather on both a global and local basis, making the science of meteorology quite complex. But the primary forces that shape weather are temperature and air-pressure differences. In this section, we look at the science behind the big picture of the weather around the planet and then zoom in.

The big picture: Temperature and pressure differences

If every part of the Earth's surface were the same temperature, you'd see very few changes in the weather. But because the sun's rays strike the equator at a more perpendicular angle than at the poles, a temperature differential results. On a global scale, this surface-temperature differential (hotter near the equator, colder near the poles) combined with the *Coriolis effect* (a global centrifugal force that we discuss in the nearby sidebar "The Coriolis effect") creates belts of weather that ring the globe. Near the equator are the *doldrums* — a belt of light, shifty, and unpredictable weather. The *tropics* enjoy relatively steady easterly winds (northeast winds in the Northern Hemisphere, southeast in the Southern Hemisphere),

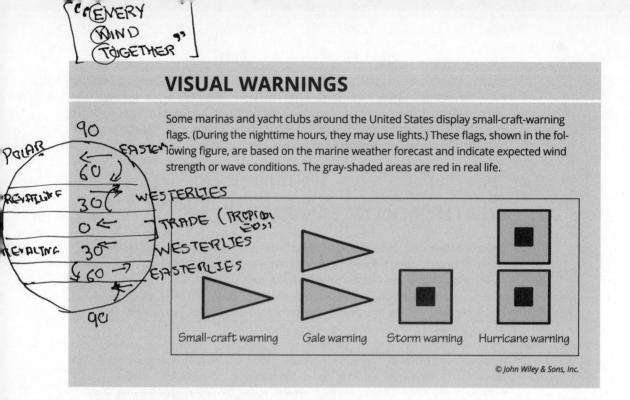

dubbed the *trade winds.* The mid-latitudes on both sides of the equator are home to the *westerlies* (winds from the west), interspersed by waves of low-pressure areas circling the globe.

Our atmosphere is a gas that expands and contracts with temperature changes, and on a global scale, the resulting pressure differences drive the wind. Wind is simply air in motion trying to get to a position of equilibrium by moving from an area of high pressure to one of low pressure. On a weather map, pressure is depicted by lines called *isobars,* which connect points of equal air pressure. Think of a weather map as if it were a topographic map, with the areas of high pressure being mountains and the places with low pressure being the valleys. Wind flows around high- and low-pressure areas, spiraling downhill at a small angle to the isobars. Thanks to the Coriolis effect, wind spirals clockwise (in the Northern Hemisphere) out of a high-pressure area and counterclockwise into a low-pressure area, as Figure 8-1 shows. In the Southern Hemisphere, the direction of rotation is opposite.

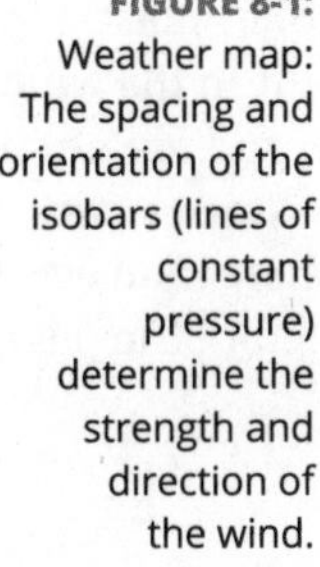

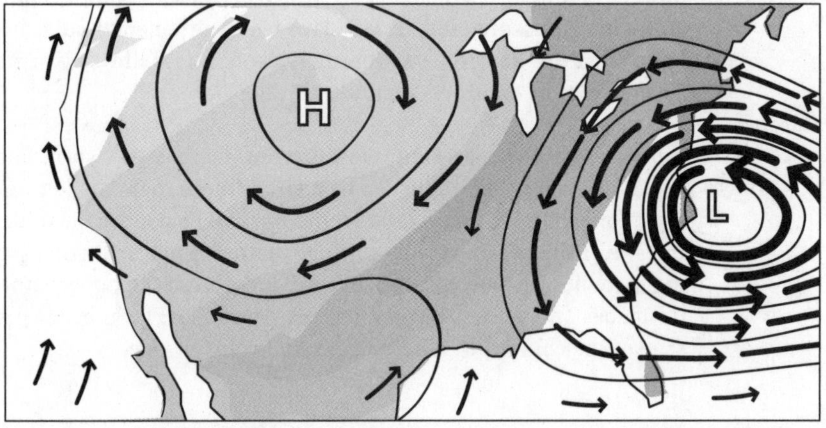

FIGURE 8-1: Weather map: The spacing and orientation of the isobars (lines of constant pressure) determine the strength and direction of the wind.

© John Wiley & Sons, Inc.

The closer together the isobar lines are, the steeper the mountain or valley is, and the faster the wind blows. The weather map of a hurricane shows incredibly tight isobars ringing an immensely deep low-pressure area.

REMEMBER

A *barometer* — a good piece of equipment for a large cruising boat — measures air pressure. A surface weather map also depicts air pressure. By paying attention to the changes in pressure, you can get a better idea of what will happen with the wind, especially if you're armed with weather maps and forecasts. Here are a few general rules regarding air pressure and weather:

» **If pressure is very high or is going up, the weather is or soon will be nice.** High pressure is associated with clear, dry weather.

» **If pressure is very low or is going down, batten down the hatches; you're in for a storm.** Low pressure is associated with cloudy, rainy weather.

In the temperate mid-latitudes on both sides of the equator, the big weather systems that carry our local weather usually move from west to east. Even when the local wind is blowing out of the east, the weather system (high- or low-pressure area) contributing to local weather is traveling from west to east, usually at around 10 to 15 knots. The *jet stream* (a band of very-fast-moving air high in the atmosphere) is related to this dynamic, causing mid-latitude surface weather motion. In this part of the world, pay special attention to the weather on your west side for an indication of what to expect.

Low-pressure areas and fronts

Nasty, windy, rainy weather is associated with low-pressure areas. A complex process that involves the meeting of two air masses of different temperatures creates a low-pressure area, or *low.* Two fronts often emanate from the center of the typical mature low on a weather map (and in real life): a warm front followed by a cold front, as Figure 8-2 shows.

A *front* is a line separating two different air masses (warm and cold, moist and dry) and often is distinguished by a large (more than 20-degree) shift in the wind direction when it passes. Cold fronts typically pack the most punch and are often the site of the most extreme sailing weather. *Squalls* (smaller-scale storms packing incredibly strong winds delivered down from the upper atmosphere) and even tornadoes and *waterspouts* (waterborne tornadoes) can occur just before the passage of the cold front, where warm and cold air meet.

THE CORIOLIS EFFECT

The fact that wind doesn't simply roll straight down a high-pressure "mountain" can be disconcerting. The reason is the Coriolis effect. Because the Earth is a huge spinning ball (a very, very huge spinning ball), air molecules heading "downhill" from a high-pressure area get pulled off-course into a curve.

No, the Coriolis effect isn't why a baseball pitcher's curveball frustrates batters, and it isn't even the reason why water spins down a toilet or sink drain (although your science teacher may have used that as an example). The Coriolis effect comes into play only on larger, regional or planetary scales.

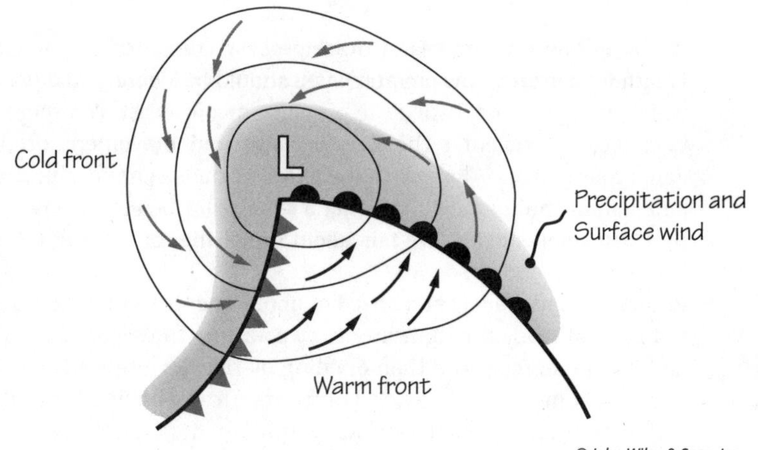

FIGURE 8-2: A Northern Hemisphere low-pressure system and fronts. It typically travels east as it matures and decays.

The weather around a typical mature Northern Hemisphere low has three distinct sectors:

- The weather in the area to the north of the warm front is often described as dismal, with a thick layer of stratus clouds blanketing the entire sky (refer to "More than cloud gazing" earlier in this chapter). If the air cools enough, you get steady drizzle or rain.
- The weather in the sector between the warm and cold fronts is warmer and more humid. A warm, moist wind comes from the south. When the sun begins to heat the ground, the air near the ground decreases in pressure and begins to rise, forming cumulus clouds and, if conditions are right, thunderstorms.
- The western sector behind the cold front is usually cooler and drier. The wind is from the west to northwest and can be quite blustery.

REMEMBER

In the Northern Hemisphere, if you stand facing the wind, the center of the low-pressure system is to your right. In the Southern Hemisphere, this orientation is the opposite due to the Coriolis effect.

Squalls

Thunderstorms, or *squalls*, are sudden, sometimes-severe storms that are usually localized. Although they may precede the passage of a cold front, they can also occur when a landmass heats up (with hot air rising into cooler air aloft) during a sultry, summer day. Puffy white cumulus clouds building vertically into darker, anvil-shape cumulonimbus clouds are visual indicators of developing squalls. Winds (probably not shown in your weather app) can build to over 60 knots quickly, because they tap into fast-moving air in the upper atmosphere, and come from any direction. Lightning is common.

If you follow our forecast-funnel process (refer to "Getting the Scoop on the Weather" earlier in the chapter), you should be aware of the possibility of squalls, which are small and difficult to pinpoint in a forecast. Weather radar is often your best tool for tracking the development and movement of these sometimes-dangerous storms. Along with the telltale clouds, a noticeable drop in temperature and distant thunder are signs that a squall may be near. Some old salts claim that they can smell squalls. We talk about preparing for squalls in Chapter 15.

REMEMBER

Because sound travels at a speed of about one-fifth of a mile per second, you can tell how far away the lightning is by counting the seconds between the lightning and its thunderclap and then dividing by five. Five seconds means that the lightning is about 1 mile away. If you're metrically inclined, count the seconds and divide by three to get the distance in kilometers. Three seconds means that the lightning is 1 kilometer away.

TEN GOLDEN RULES OF SKY WATCHING AT SEA

Sailors have been watching the sky for centuries. Before the days of weather forecasts, sailors who could foretell the weather by paying attention to Mother Nature's signs had a big advantage. Here are some of the golden rules that have been passed down over the ages:

- Red sky at night, sailors' delight; red sky at morning, sailors take warning.
- When the sky changes, so will the weather.
- Mackerel sky, 24 hours dry. (This type of sky has high clouds that look sort of like fish scales.)
- Dew on decks, wind from the sea; no dew on decks, wind from the land.
- When the wind speed exceeds the temperature, sailors should head for home.
- A halo around the moon means rain or snow. The larger the halo, the nearer the precipitation.
- Rainbow to windward means rain is coming. Rainbow to leeward means rain has ended.
- The higher the clouds, the finer the weather. (A lowering ceiling foretells rain.)
- When smoke descends, good weather ends.
- Seagull, seagull, sit on the sand; it's a sign of rain when you're at hand.

Facing Up to Fog

Nothing can strike fear (or at least a sober thought or two) in the heart of an experienced sailor like being caught in a strange area in dense fog. When a bank of fog as thick as pea soup surrounds you, visibility can drop to less than a boat length, making safe navigation and avoiding other boats extremely difficult, regardless of your skill and the available navigation aids.

Fog occurs when air contains more moisture than it can hold in gas form. When the temperature drops below the *dew point* (the temperature at which the air becomes saturated with water vapor), the excess water vapor condenses and becomes visible. Fog comes in several types, but the same conditions occur in every kind: Moist air gets cooled (usually by water, which is why fog is more likely to appear over cold water) until the air temperature drops below the dew point.

Because fog usually rolls in from the sea slowly, you generally have enough time after first spotting it to turn around and hightail it back to the shore before the fog socks in completely. For more information about navigating in fog, see Chapter 9.

Going with the Tide and the Current

The *tide* is actually a giant wave that circles the globe roughly twice a day. The gravitational effect of the moon (and, to a lesser extent, the sun) pulls on the Earth's oceans (lakes are too small to react to this pull), causing two humps, or wave crests — one directly under the moon and the other on the opposite side of the globe — that follow the moon in its 24.8-hour path around the Earth, as Figure 8-3 shows.

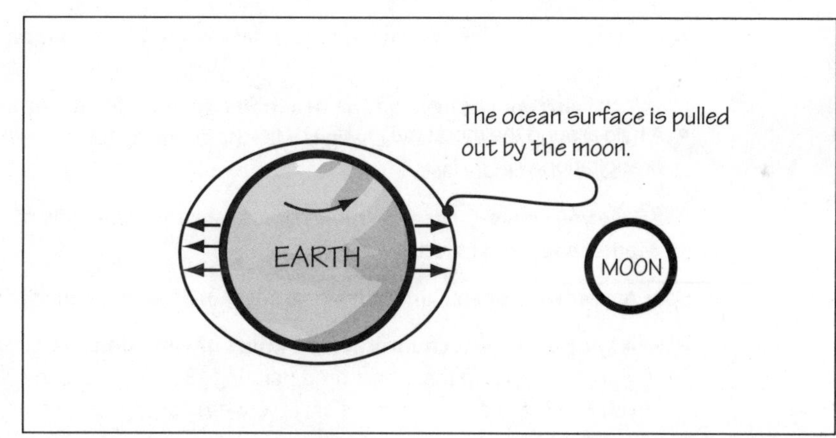

FIGURE 8-3: The moon and the sun pull on the oceans, creating global waves called tides.

THE MOTION OF THE OCEAN

If the moon's pull is constant as it orbits the Earth, why is the tidal range 15 feet (5 meters) or more in some parts of the world and only a few inches in others? The mathematical answer can make a university student's head hurt, but in practical terms, these differences are due to the shape and proximity of landmasses, the underwater topography, and the wind.

Fortunately, most coastal regions of the world have tidal predictions readily available online and in many weather apps, so you don't have to do the math to know whether the harbor is deep enough for your boat.

When the moon lines up with the sun, as it does twice every 29½ days (at the full moon and the new moon), those global wave crests get even bigger, and the corresponding *trough* (low part of a wave) gets even lower. In between, at the moon's first and last quarter, the tides are smallest.

As this global wave girdles the planet, it creates water motion called *tidal current. Current* is moving water, and tidal currents that reach 3 knots or more (rivaling the speed of a small sailboat) aren't uncommon. That much current definitely gets your attention! In some narrow bodies of water, such as the Bay of Fundy in Canada, the current comes in and out like a big tidal wave at speeds in the teens.

Flood tide is tidal current coming inbound as the tide is on the rise; *ebb tide* is the outbound tidal current when the tide is going down. You can discover tons of information about tidal currents by looking at a nautical chart of an area. Focus on the underwater topography, because the current runs strongest where the water is deepest.

These tips about tides and currents can help while you're out on the water:

- **Tidal current changes on the beach first.** In a confined area like a bay, the direction of the tidal flow changes with the changing tide near the shores first and in the middle last.
- **Use your eyes:** Current is visible by watching the water flow past buoys and other anchored objects.
- **A river runs deep**: Current flows stronger in deep water than in shallow water.
- **A knot of current counteracts 10 knots of wind on an anchored ship.** If you see a big ship that's anchored pointing 180 degrees to the 20-knot wind, you know that at least 2 knots of current are flowing against the wind out there.

» **Winds or heavy runoff upstream can overpower weak tidal flows, causing them to run contrary to their predicted direction.** Strong winds can create windblown current on lakes (usually less than 0.5 knot) that have no discernible tide.

» **When the wind opposes the current flow, waves get steep and choppy.** This situation makes for a fast but bouncy ride when heading upwind.

» **When the wind is with the current flow, the waves get smoother and more elongated.** Sailors should be attuned to this sort of difference in sea state to "read" the current.

One more type of current is of interest to sailors: the huge continental-boundary currents flowing along coastlines. Two great examples surround North America. On the west side is the cold, southbound *Alaska current*, and along the east coast is the warm, northbound *Gulf Stream current*. These two currents act like strong rivers within the ocean, with average speeds up to 3 knots. In small areas, the speeds can be much higher. A combination of the Coriolis effect, the global prevailing winds, and the orientation of the coastlines cause these boundary currents.

Understanding Sea Breezes

Temperature differences can also cause changes in the weather on a local scale. *Sea breeze* is the name associated with a family of winds generated on sunny and partly sunny days, when the extra heat of the land causes a cool breeze to blow inland. In certain parts of the world, the sea breeze is so predictable during the summer months that you can almost set your watch by it. Summer sea breezes are common in the mid-latitudes.

Here's how sea breezes work: As the land heats, the air rises (sometimes creating puffy cumulus clouds), and an area of low pressure is created over the land around midday. Meanwhile, the water remains cooler, and so does the air above the water. Cool air from the water blows (or, really, is sucked) into the low pressure over the land. If the conditions are favorable (a light offshore wind up at cloud level and a large temperature difference between land and water), the sea breeze can build fairly quickly to 15 knots or more. Figure 8-4 depicts a classic sea breeze.

As the sun drops, the heating of the land diminishes, and so does the sea breeze. In the Northern Hemisphere, watch for the sea breeze to build until midafternoon and then slowly die away. At night, a similar but opposite dynamic (cooling land) can create a thermal-driven *land breeze* blowing from land out to water. Normally, the land breeze is not as strong as a sea breeze.

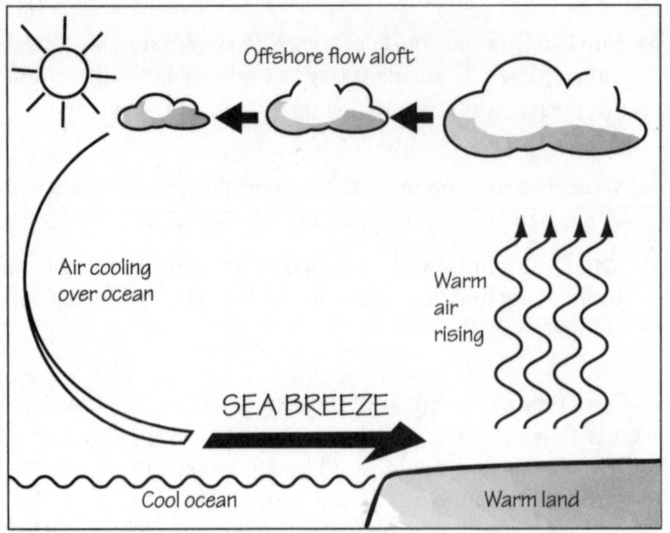

FIGURE 8-4: The dynamics of a sea breeze.

© John Wiley & Sons, Inc.

Recognizing Wind Shifts

Airflow over water is always a bit turbulent, so even the steadiest conditions have little changes in wind speed and direction. When you're sailing near shore in an offshore wind, these wind shifts can be downright maddening (although racers in Chicago's downtown Belmont Harbor claim that they can predict wind shifts by watching doors open at waterside hotels!). Following are some common types of wind shifts:

- **Persistent shift:** A *persistent shift* is one in which the wind moves in one direction very quickly, as in the passage of a front, or progressively, as in the case of a sea breeze gradually trending to the right over the course of the afternoon due to the Coriolis effect. These shifts are sometimes picked up in weather forecasts.
- **Oscillating shift:** When the wind slowly shifts back and forth around an average wind direction, it's an *oscillating wind.* These sorts of shifts usually have a period ranging from less than a minute to ten minutes or so and are usually beyond the scope of a weather forecast.
- **Geographic shift:** A *geographic shift* is a shift in direction or speed caused by land, such as when the wind channels and accelerates through a valley or bends around a headland.

TIP

Every time the wind changes, the opportunity arises to sail faster or take a shorter course to your destination. A clever sailor can take advantage of wind shifts, as you see in the next section, "Using Your Weather Knowledge."

Using Your Weather Knowledge

For safety, know the weather forecast before you sail to avoid going out when conditions are (or will be) too windy or stormy. You can also use your knowledge of the weather, current, wave conditions, and performance of your boat to pick the fastest route. Because the wind is always changing to some degree, here are some good general rules for anyone who's trying to get to their destination faster:

- **When sailing upwind, sail on the longer tack first (if you have one).** The more skewed the course to the destination is relative to the wind direction, the more important this rule becomes. If the course to the destination is 10 miles (16 kilometers) on starboard tack and 0.5 mile (0.8 kilometer) on port tack, definitely go on starboard first, because any wind shift will help you, as Figure 8-5 shows. This same rule applies to a downwind destination.
- **If you expect a wind shift when sailing upwind, sail toward the new wind first.** If your destination is more directly upwind, and you expect a right (clockwise) wind shift, either persistent or geographic, sail on port tack first. See Figure 8-6.
- **Avoid light air.** No matter whether you're sailing to an upwind, downwind, or reaching destination, you won't get there very fast if there's little or no wind. On light-air days, it pays to read the surface of the water to try to keep the boat in the darker patches, where there is some wind.

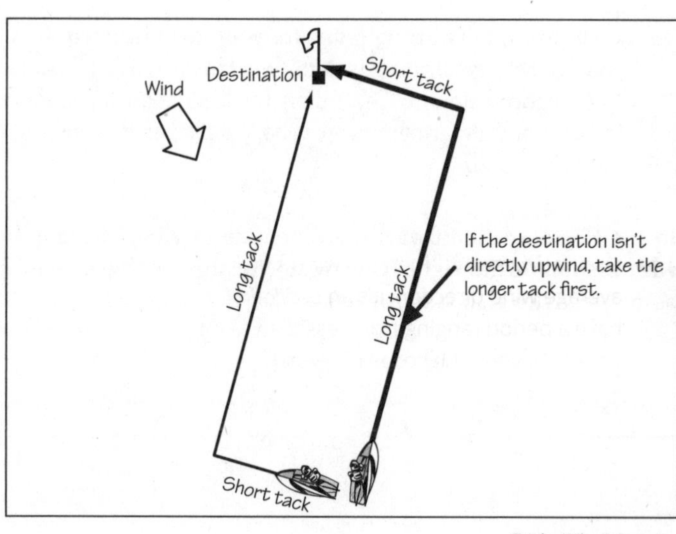

FIGURE 8-5: When your destination is upwind of you but not directly aligned with the wind, sail on the longer tack first to maximize your progress in case the wind changes later.

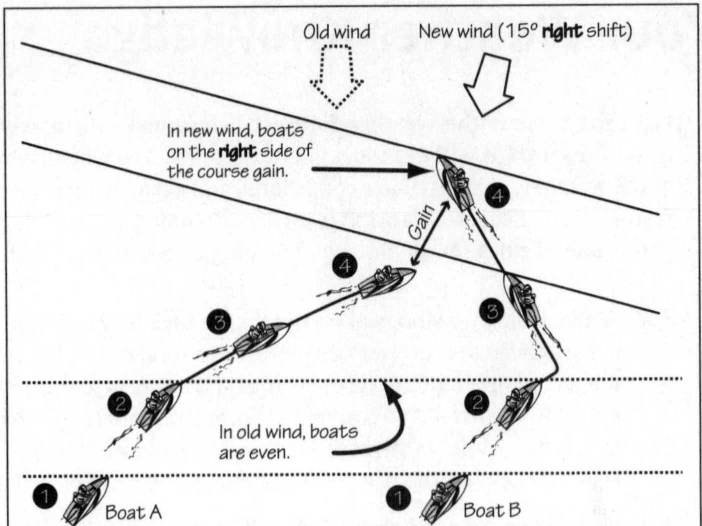
Old wind
New wind (15° **right** shift)
In new wind, boats on the **right** side of the course gain.
Gain
In old wind, boats are even.
Boat A
Boat B
1
2
3
4
1
2
3
4

FIGURE 8-6: Sailing upwind, boats A and B are equal in the "old wind," but at position 3, a new wind arrives, instantly putting boat B ahead, and they tack over and cross ahead.

» **Sail on the lifted tack in an oscillating wind.** If the wind is going back and forth, you want to sail on starboard tack when the wind is in its right/clockwise phase and on port tack when the wind is in its left/counterclockwise phase.

» **Get out of the waves.** In strong winds sailing upwind, take the tack toward the windward shoreline (or an area that's more protected) first to get out of the waves, which slows your progress sailing upwind.

» **On a reach, sail a straight line for your destination unless you expect the wind to change.** If you expect the wind to decrease or shift farther behind, steer slightly below (to leeward of) the destination. If you expect the wind to increase or shift farther ahead, initially steer slightly above (to windward of) the destination.

REMEMBER

In the Northern Hemisphere, an increase in wind speed is normally associated with a shift to the right (clockwise). In the Southern Hemisphere, a "puff" is associated with a shift to the left.

IN THIS CHAPTER

» Navigating by using common sense

» Using navigational aids

» Reading charts and plotting courses

» Determining direction with a compass

» Piloting: Performing basic navigation

» Sailing at night

» Exploring electronic navigation and dabbling in celestial navigation

Chapter 9
Navigation: Holding Your Course

O we can wait no longer,

We too take ship O soul,

Joyous we too launch out on trackless seas,

Fearless for unknown shores.

—WALT WHITMAN

Navigation, as defined in one of Peter's favorite books (*The American Practical Navigator*, by Nathaniel Bowditch, first published in 1802 and revised periodically by the U.S. Navy), is "the process of directing the movement of a craft from one point to another." The history of navigation is replete with fascinating stories of sailors who crossed oceans with limited knowledge of where they were and even less of where they were going. Yet however crudely, they successfully directed their crafts from one point to another and often back again — without any navigation app! The lore of navigation spans the globe. Ancient Polynesian navigators had a rich oral tradition of sailing directions that enabled them to sail to islands well over the horizon by reading nature's road signs like sea birds and waves.

Advances in timekeeping, technology, science, and mathematics enable today's sailors to direct their crafts from one place to another much more easily and accurately. But despite the satellites in the sky that tell you where you are, the link with this rich history of navigation hasn't been completely severed. Many of the skills that you'll find to be the most practical and easiest to use are ones developed centuries ago.

Using Common-Sense Navigation

Whether you're sailing across the pond or across the ocean, you need to use certain basic skills to get there. These basic skills involve being attuned to the elements and using your senses and your judgment to get where you want to go efficiently and safely. Here's how they help:

- **Knowing where you are:** Asking the birds or fish for directions isn't easy.
- **Getting to your destination:** We're not saying that you must have a destination, however; sometimes, it's fun to be spontaneous.
- **Getting there as fast as possible:** We cover some of the getting-there-fast issues in Chapters 11 and 12, but navigation can play a major role in a speedy passage. In Chapter 8, we cover ways to use weather knowledge to plan the fastest route.
- **Getting there as safely as possible:** Safety always comes first, and again, navigation plays a role — by identifying underwater dangers marked on the nautical chart to avoid the ignominy of running aground (see Chapter 15) and by recognizing shipping channels where large commercial vessels have the right-of-way (see Chapter 4).

Although the next section is crucial for sailors on a boat with no compass or chart, these techniques can be equally valuable on bigger boats that have all the navigation goodies.

Judging laylines

When the destination is upwind, so you have to make at least one tack (see Chapter 5) to get there, you have to be able to judge the *layline:* the line beyond which you can *lay* (sail to) the destination on a close-hauled course with no more tacks, as Figure 9-1 shows. Sailing past the layline isn't bad; you simply sail an extra distance. In Chapter 8, we discuss the strategy of which tack to take first in shifting winds. But after you choose your upwind course (a series of long zigzags or many shorter ones), eventually, you must make that final tack, which should be at or beyond the layline. To know where the layline is, you need to pay attention to the wind direction and shifts, and you need to know how many degrees your boat tacks through — the difference between your port and starboard close-hauled headings. In moderate air (10 to 14 knots), most boats tack through 90 degrees or a little less. If there's current, you must allow for its effect too (see Chapter 8).

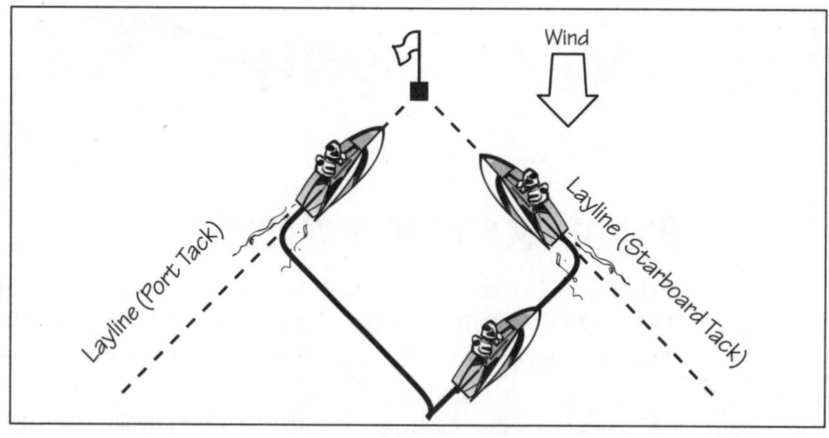

FIGURE 9-1: The layline is the close-hauled track to an upwind destination where no tacks are required.

TIP

When you're sailing upwind, and your destination is *dead abeam* (perpendicular to the boat's heading), tack over to see whether you've reached the layline.

Holding a steady course

If you can see your destination, steering a straight-line course seems like a simple matter. But if current is pushing you sideways, or if your boat is sideslipping excessively due to too much *heel* (too tipped over; see Chapter 11), your course over the bottom, or *course over ground* (COG), is different from your boat's *heading* (the course the boat is steering). If you're sailing on a reach, you can alter your heading so that the boat "makes good" the course you want — the straight line to the destination. If you're sailing close-hauled and slowly drifting downwind of your desired course, you aren't on the layline yet, and you'll need to tack at some point to reach your destination.

TIP

If land lies behind a buoy that's your target, you can use the buoy and land as a *range* (two objects in a line – also called a *transit*) to stay on track, as Figure 9-2 shows. A visual range enables a sailor to determine whether current or wind is pushing the boat sideways and how much to alter course to counteract that effect.

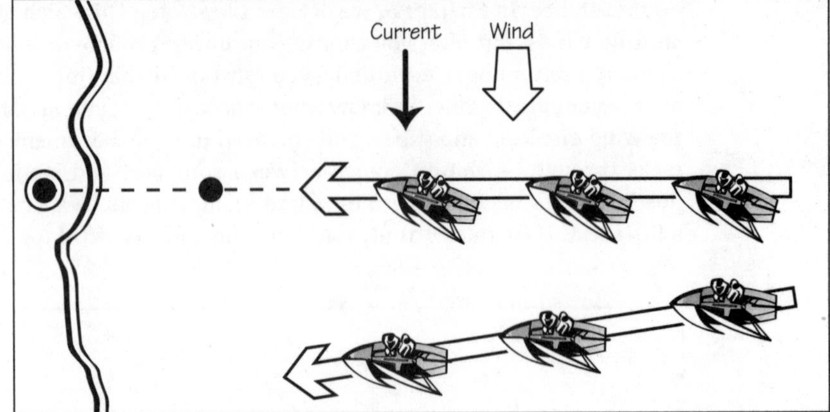

FIGURE 9-2: A range between two objects helps you steer straight in crosscurrents.

Avoiding shallow water

If the water is clear and the wind is calm, the bottom can look amazingly close through the magnifying glass of the water. But this visibility decreases when waves kick up. Use the following tips to avoid potentially dangerous shallow spots:

- **Follow another boat.** By using another boat (ideally, one with a similar or deeper draft) as your guinea pig, you can follow directly behind (at a safe distance, so you can turn if it runs aground) and stay in deep water. This technique is especially helpful when you're entering a strange harbor or following a narrow *channel* (deep-water lane).
- **Look at the bottom.** In the tropics, sandy bottoms get brighter white as the depth decreases, and coral heads become darker.
- **Pay attention to the markers and buoys.** Hang on — we discuss the markers that signal deep and shallow water in the next section, "Relying on Buoys: Aids to Navigation."
- **Slow down.** If you're determined to pass over an area where you think that your keel or centerboard has a chance of touching bottom, take some pace off. You may not avoid grounding, but any contact will be less severe.

- **Stay away from the shoreline.** By definition, the water gets shallower at the shoreline, so stay away from the shore unless you're sure (from a chart or past experience) that the water is deep enough.
- **Watch for waves.** As every surfer knows, waves build up and even break when they "feel" shallow water. Beware of an area with breakers or with waves that seem to mound up bigger than the surrounding waves. And if you see surfers ahead of you, turn around!

Peter used to sail a dinghy with a friend off Key West, Florida. They launched the boat off the beach. Coming home on windy days, when they sailed toward shore, one of them jumped in when the water was chest-deep and held the boat by the bow, while the other lowered the sails and removed the rudder. One day when they were coming in, the coral heads started looking pretty close. They found a nice sandy spot that looked quite shallow, and Peter jumped in, only to find himself swimming in 15 feet of water. The moral of the story is that you want to be cautious about running aground, but judging the depth visually can be deceptive.

Relying on Buoys: Aids to Navigation

Sailors have used visual aids to navigate since time immemorial. A big willow tree may mark a good fishing spot; a promontory may identify the entrance to a harbor. At night, the beam of a lighthouse helps mariners many miles away. An *aid to navigation* (ATON) is any device not on board that helps you determine position or a safe course, or that warns of dangers. Around the world, you find millions of human-made aids to navigation; the most common are buoys. A *buoy* is any floating (albeit anchored) object that can be used for a variety of purposes, including navigation.

Depending on where you are, most (but not all) navigation buoys are laid out in either of two systems or a combination:

- **Cardinal system:** Buoys of specific shapes and colors are laid out to indicate the compass direction to the hazard. The *cardinal points* of the compass are north, south, east, and west — hence, the name. Most European countries, and others including Australia and New Zealand, use the cardinal system in combination with a lateral system.
- **Lateral system:** Buoys of specific shapes and colors are laid out along the edges of the channels or areas of safe navigation. The United States uses primarily the lateral system.

Buoyage systems vary somewhat from country to country, and they vary from region to region in the United States. Fortunately, most of the country is governed by the U.S. Aids to Navigation System (which uses the lateral system), with notable exceptions being the Western rivers, intracoastal waterways, and smaller bodies of water that lie totally within a single state. Conveniently, even those areas use most of the key elements of the U.S. system, which we outline in the following sections. You can ascertain all the important characteristics of a buoy from a nautical chart, as we describe in "Nautical Charts: A Sailor's Road Map" later in this chapter. If you want more details about all the variations in the systems employed around the world, do an Internet search for "International Association of Marine Aids to Navigation and Lighthouse Authorities" where you can learn about the regional systems IALA A & B.

TIP

Around the world, some buoys and other ATONs have no directional (cardinal system) or lateral significance. These ATONs may mark safe water (such as the middle of a channel) or isolated danger, or they may designate a special area or feature for a plethora of reasons.

Knowing your colors

REMEMBER

The most important characteristic of a lateral-system buoy is its color. You may be familiar with the three "Rs" in the expression "red right returning" (from the sea), which describes the basic rule of the U.S. (lateral) buoyage system: When you're coming inbound, entering a harbor, or moving along a channel toward an area that's more protected, you keep the red buoys on your right side. Conversely, you keep the green buoys on your left side. By convention, the red buoys have even numbers painted on them, and the green ones have odd numbers.

Most experienced boaters use the words *port* and *starboard* while they're afloat. In their terminology, in the United States, a red buoy marking a channel should be "left to starboard," which means passing it on your right side when inbound. A green buoy should be "left to port." Interestingly, in most of the rest of the world, including Europe, the convention is exactly opposite. Green buoys have even numbers, and you leave the green buoys on your right side when entering a harbor.

The concept of red buoys being on the right side when you're returning from sea implies that a safe passageway, or *channel,* is bounded by buoys. If the "returning" direction isn't obvious, it's smart to refer to a nautical chart (see "Nautical Charts: A Sailor's Road Map" later in this chapter). Along the Gulf of Mexico and on the Pacific and Atlantic coasts of the United States away from harbors, the red buoys mark shallow spots close to shore.

Identifying the types of buoys

Buoys and other ATONs come in a variety of shapes, which indicate their meaning, as Figure 9-3 shows.

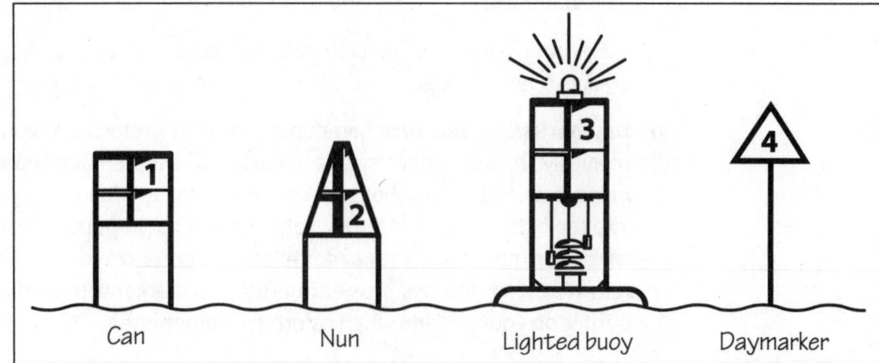

FIGURE 9-3: Aids to Navigation in the U.S. system.

You may encounter the following types of buoys and ATONs when you're out for a sail:

- **Nuns and cans:** The most common buoys (used to mark the edges of the channel) are the red *nuns* (named for their pointed conical top) and the green *cans* (named for their cylindrical shape).
- **Lighted buoys:** Lighted buoys are usually taller than nuns or cans, have a floating base and a superstructure supported by an open framework, display a light signal at night, and often emit a sound (bell, gong, whistle, or horn) as the buoy rolls in the waves. If they're painted solid red (with a red light at night) or solid green (with a green light), they signal the edges of a channel, just like their unlighted brethren. Check out "Navigating at Night" later in this chapter.
- **Junction buoys:** Junction buoys can be shaped like a nun, can, or lighted buoy, but they have horizontal red and green stripes. These stripes indicate the junction of two channels, with the color on top indicating the deeper, or preferred, channel. Red on top means that the bigger channel is to port; in other words, pass the red-topped buoy on your starboard side.
- **Safe Water/Mid-channel/Fairway buoys:** If unlighted, these buoys are balls; otherwise, they're the shape of a lighted buoy (but display a white light) and can indicate safe water at the center (or the beginning) of a channel. All these buoys have vertical red and white stripes.

- **Danger buoys:** By definition, all navigation buoys mark some sort of danger. An isolated danger (such as a rock or other hazard) in relatively open water may be marked by a lighted buoy (white light) with red and black stripes and two black balls at the top. When unlighted, danger buoys can be either nun- or can-shaped and are white with thin orange horizontal stripes at the top and near water level.

  Other informational or regulatory buoys can signal an anchorage, quarantine area, fish nets, dredging operations, or other special purpose.
- **Daymarks/Daybeacons:** Sometimes, in areas protected from waves in relatively shallow waters (such as rivers and human-made channels), *daymarks* are used in lieu of buoys. They're displayed on poles pounded securely into the bottom. As with buoys, color is the most important feature. Pass a triangular red marker with a red reflective border on your *right* side when returning from the sea; pass a square green marker with a reflective green border on your *left* side when returning from the sea.

REMEMBER

With all this talk about "red right returning," don't forget that when you're leaving a harbor, you pass the red buoys (or daymarks) on your left side!

Peter admits it: For all the simplicity of "red right returning," he still gets confused on occasion. His hang-up is the word *returning.* Is he returning *to* the sea (our primordial birthplace) or *from* the sea (to our relatively new home)? Maybe he's the only sailor who has trouble with this concept. Just remember that *returning* refers to returning *from* the sea — coming back to the more protected area.

Nautical Charts: A Sailor's Road Map

Okay, it's time to dive into the fun part of this chapter: navigation skills, including using a nautical chart and a compass. You may wonder why it's necessary to know this stuff, because your navigation app plots your position within a few inches and shows where you're going. It's true that many sailors use a phone app or some other device combining GPS (satellite location) and a nautical chart, just as they use a phone app to navigate in their cars. But relying on a navigation app without knowing how to read and use a chart is a bit like climbing into an airplane and thinking that you can fly the thing because it has a steering wheel.

Though it may seem to be a bit old-school, starting with a paper chart is best. This type of chart is bigger than your phone's screen or a chart-plotter display, making it easier to get oriented and see the big picture. So let's do things the right way: Understand how to read a chart, use a compass, and use your brain before you grab your phone and turn off your mind

Nautical charts are maps for mariners, providing a variety of useful and sometimes invaluable information. Anyone can make a chart, even you. Electronic and paper charts are available from a plethora of sources around the world, including government agencies and public and private companies. In the United States, the National Oceanic and Atmospheric Administration (NOAA) Office of Coast Survey produces the official nautical charts, and its electronic navigational charts (ENCs) are free for direct download. NOAA is in the process of phasing out its paper charts, but it has ENCs that can still be printed; and resellers abound.

Lining up your latitudes and longitudes

Paper charts and ENCs come in a variety of *scales* (coverage areas). To orient yourself to the scale of a particular chart, refer to the scale of *latitude* (horizontal lines on a chart or globe indicating angular distance — 0 to 90 degrees — north or south of the equator), which bounds the vertical (right and left) edges of every paper chart. On an ENC, you may find this same latitude scale on its vertical edge, or a scale/ruler may be displayed somewhere on the chart, usually near the edge. If an ENC has no displayed scale, you'll have to use your app's measuring tool.

No matter where you are on the planet, 1 degree of latitude equals 60 nautical miles. (We have more to say about the difference between nautical miles and statute miles in the section "Measuring the course and distance of a route" later in the chapter.) Each degree is divided into 60 minutes, and each minute is further carved into either 60 seconds or decimal minutes. You can use this catchy phrase to glean distances from latitude (on the edge of your paper chart): "A minute's a mile the world around."

Be careful: The same isn't true of a minute of *longitude,* which varies in distance depending on how close you are to the equator. Vertical lines on a chart or globe indicate longitude, which designates the angular distance (0 to 180 degrees) east or west of the prime meridian. The *prime meridian* is the line of longitude (or *meridian*) that has been arbitrarily given the value of 0 degrees. The prime meridian passes through Greenwich, England, so guess which country established it (and Greenwich Mean Time)!

Latitude and longitude are the navigator's equivalent of streets and avenues in Manhattan (where they run north to south and east to west in a grid). Running at right angles to each other, they provide a universal way of describing your position. While writing this chapter, Peter was at 32 degrees 43.28 minutes north latitude and 117 degrees 13.26 minutes west longitude, or 32°43.28'N, 117°13.26'W. Anyone with the correct chart can determine where he was from those two values.

Deciphering a chart

In addition to latitude and longitude, charts display an enormous amount of information, often coded by a plethora of terms, symbols, and abbreviations. U.S. Chart No. 1 (`https://nauticalcharts.noaa.gov/publications/us-chart-1.html`), published by NOAA, explains every one of these symbols and abbreviations, from the symbol for a pagoda to water depth. U.S. Chart No. 1 is an indispensable aid for finding out how to read a chart and a valuable reference for the saltiest seafarer. Similar publications are produced by chart authorities from other nations (worth reviewing if you're using those charts), and international standards are generally adhered to.

TIP

Private sources of ENCs aren't required to use universal symbols, although they do for the most part. If you're working on an ENC and don't know what a symbol is, you may be able to "query" it with a click to get more information.

Here are some of the most valuable pieces of information displayed on a nautical chart:

- **Buoys and other aids to navigation:** As we mention earlier in this chapter, ATONs come in a huge variety of colors, numbers, letters, shapes, lights, and sound signals. All those details become clear when you understand the code.

  Here's an example: "RW 'SD' Mo (A) WHIS" written next to a little black circle surrounded by a solid magenta circle with a split trapezoid peeking out clearly identifies the location of a red-and-white whistle buoy with the letters "SD" on top, displaying a white light flashing the Morse Code signal for the letter *A* at night and indicating the middle of the entrance to the channel coming into San Diego Harbor. Now you see why you need Chart No. 1!

- **Compass rose/north up:** Most charts are oriented by default as north up (though your app may rotate it for convenience). True north is straight up. On paper charts and some ENCs, a compass rose is displayed for orientation. A *compass rose* consists of two concentric circles, each graduated in degrees (0 to 360) running clockwise from a reference direction (magnetic or true north). The magnetic compass rose is the one that navigators usually use; it's always the smaller inner one. The true compass rose surrounds it. Farther inside the circle is information about the *variation* (the angular difference between true and magnetic north), as well as how the variation changes over time (slowly).

  We have to introduce you to a fact that may shake your belief in Santa Claus: The Earth has two North Poles. *True north* sits properly atop the globe (at 90°N and 0°E). *Magnetic north* (which magnetic compasses think is north because of the Earth's magnetic field) is a few thousand miles away and wanders around a bit because of the molten iron in the Earth's core. Because most sailors use a compass as directional reference, they need to concern themselves only with magnetic north. But just to be safe when discussing compass directions, always indicate which reference system you're using: 270°T indicates true degrees, and 270°M indicates magnetic degrees.

- **Date of update:** Because significant information (such as the position or description of a buoy) can change, having a current chart is important. On a paper chart, you can find the printing date near the corner of the chart, outside the perimeter of the longitude scale. NOAA updates many of its ENCs weekly, but some stay the same for years! Old paper charts make great posters, wallpaper, and gift-wrapping paper!

REMEMBER

- **Depth of the water:** Given a navigator's aversion to running aground, this information is the biggie. On a nautical chart, depth at a particular spot appears as a number that indicates depth below a fixed *datum* (base value), which is normally *mean low water* (the average level of low tide). This number is usually given in units of feet, *fathoms* (1 fathom equals 6 feet), meters, or some combination. The datum and measurement scale (feet, fathoms, and so on) are indicated somewhere on a paper chart, usually on its perimeter. For most ENCs, it's not quite so simple but equally important to understand the depth numbers. Usually, your app (or chartplotting device) allows you to control the scale. Make sure you check those settings and that you know what the numbers mean; 4 meters is a lot deeper than 4 feet! Contour lines that join places of equal depth also help provide a picture of the underwater topography.
- **Hazards:** Shallow water is a major hazard, and charts often use different colors to depict shallow and deep water. (These colors may be user-controllable on an ENC.) Other danger areas, such as rocks that are awash at low tide, have their own special symbols. Even military target ranges are clearly noted.
- **Land:** Because you'll do most of your sailing near land, you can take advantage of the physical characteristics of the shore and any major charted landmarks, such as radio towers and mountaintops.

If you haven't figured it out by now, we think that charts are pretty cool because they possess so much information. Here are some tips on working with and reading charts:

- **Have U.S. Chart No. 1 (or its equivalent) handy.** Hey, you can't tell the players without a program, can you?

» **Fold/zoom the chart to size.** Paper charts usually are much bigger than your chart table or work space, so fold the chart so that you can easily see the area you're interested in. Make sure that you can see a compass rose and a portion of the latitude scale (for measuring distance) when the chart is folded.

On a paper chart, every chart symbol and every rock is always visible. But most ENCs simplify their display as you zoom out to avoid clutter. This ENC zooming problem can be extremely dangerous, however; you need to know where all the rocks are on your route. To mitigate this issue, always zoom in <u>all the way</u> when planning a route, and if you're sailing in unfamiliar waters, make sure to zoom in your navigation app enough to see all the depth and chart symbols, as shown in Figure 9-4.

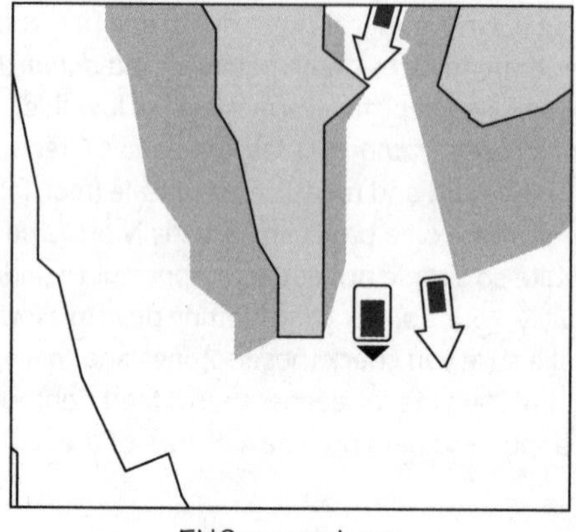

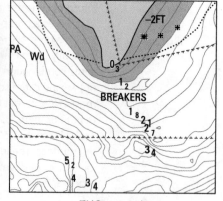

FIGURE 9-4: ENC zoom problem: Important details are omitted when you zoom out.

© John Wiley & Sons, Inc.

» **Get the right charts.** Make sure that you download all the necessary ENCs covering your sailing area on your device before setting out; there may be no Internet connection where you're sailing. If you're using paper charts and traveling to new places, make sure that you have large-scale (close-up) charts of harbors you may want (or be forced) to visit enroute.

» **Orient the chart for ease of use.** Some people like to rotate the chart so that the direction in which they're traveling is straight up. Peter prefers keeping true north up, but that's just his taste.

USING A CHART ON DECK

When you're navigating along an unfamiliar coastline, you may find having the chart on deck to be quite helpful. The down side is that the wind may blow a paper chart overboard (not a good thing), and taking measurements on that chart can be cumbersome at best. Marine stores often sell a collection of local charts on water-resistant paper bound in a spiral binder, which are more convenient to use on deck. Nowadays, Peter generally relies on paper charts for planning purposes, but on deck, he uses ENCs. He prefers portable devices to chart plotters (they're easier to use), and tablet-size devices are much better than a phone for spotting details that are important to your boat's safety (their screens are larger).

Measuring the course and distance of a route

When you're sailing from one place to another, it's helpful to know the course and distance to the destination. This information can be determined with a nautical chart, but the methods vary depending on your chart type and device. On a paper chart, you can measure the distance and compass course between any two points with two of our favorite tools: *parallel rulers* (two straight-edged plastic slats connected by two hinges) and *dividers* (an adjustable metal caliper-like tool with two sharp points). Those devices are rarely employed now (search online to see how to use them if you're interested), replaced by the built-in tools in navigation apps and charts. But we still think that it's important to have at least these paper-chart skills:

- **Create a route between two points on the chart.** Make the route realistic for a sailboat, such as a starting point and an ending point. Use a pencil to draw the points and the line between them.
- **Identify any hazards on your route.** Look at the water depth along the route and in the nearby area. (You may have to sail upwind and not sail the direct route.)
- **Measure the course to sail on your route.** On a paper chart, you have to transfer the direction of the route to a nearby compass rose. Parallel rulers come in handy for this task, but because you have an app that can give you this direction to the nearest tenth of a degree (and probably have no parallel rulers), just eyeball the route's direction on the compass rose.
- **Measure the distance of your route.** Dividers handle this task perfectly, but if you don't have them handy, use your thumb and a finger (or a simple tool) to measure the route's distance. Often, navigators calculate the time it will take to sail the route by using the "speed, time, and distance" formula coming up in the "Dead Reckoning" section.

REMEMBER

1 minute of latitude equals 1 nautical mile. And for marine navigation, we always employ nautical miles rather than statute miles. A nautical mile equals 6,076 feet (roughly 6,000 for easy mental calculations), 2,025 yards (roughly 2,000), 1.852 kilometers, or 1.15 statute miles.

Using a Compass

A *compass* is a device that feels the pull of the Earth's magnetic system and provides a reference direction relative to magnetic north. Sailors use several common types of compasses for navigation and steering:

- **Steering compass:** A steering compass is mounted permanently in a position so that the helmsperson can refer to it when steering. It comes in two basic varieties:
  - *Binnacle or dome compass:* Mounted on a horizontal surface such as a pedestal or deck. This type is easy to read. The binnacle version is common on bigger keelboats with steering wheels.
  - *Bulkhead compass:* Mounted on a vertical surface such as the back wall (bulkhead) of a cabin.
- **Hand-bearing compass:** These small, portable compasses aren't meant to replace a boat's primary steering compass. They make taking a *bearing* (measuring the compass course from your boat to any object, which we discuss later in the "Taking a bearing" section) easier than with a bulkhead compass.
- **Electronic compass:** Electronic compasses use the principles of magnetism and electricity. They're used by autopilots and in sailing instrument systems. Never rely solely on an electronic compass, however; what happens when the battery runs down?

Accounting for deviation

TIP

Unfortunately, compasses don't agree as to the direction of magnetic north. Nearby metal objects (or electrical current) affect a compass's internal magnets and cause it to deviate from magnetic north. To minimize this divergence, mount the compass far from potential sources of interference (such as the engine), and never use iron-based fasteners or fittings within a few feet. You can determine whether a fitting has magnetic properties that would affect the compass by touching the fitting with a magnet.

No matter how careful you are, some deviation (5 degrees plus or minus) is inevitable. So on bigger keelboats whose crews are serious about navigation, it's common to have the compass *swung* (calibrated for deviation error) by a professional. In practice, this process is usually reserved for larger boats (more than 30 feet, or 9 meters) that require compass accuracy to the degree. The manual of an electronic compass will provide instructions on calibration. This usually involves driving the boat around in a couple of slow circles.

Reading a compass

As you may notice, the *compass card* (rotating piece on which the numbers are written) is divided into increments. The four biggies are the cardinal points: north (000°), south (180°), east (090°), and west (270°). Sometimes on larger compasses, the four other points — northeast (045°), southeast (135°), southwest (225°), and northwest (315°) — are also indicated by their initials. On a really large compass, the smallest increments (indicated by hash marks) can be a single degree. Smaller compasses may have a hash mark for every 5-degree increment, which is why the bigger the compass, the better!

If you're sitting directly aft of a dome compass, you can determine your boat's *heading* (direction the boat is pointing toward) by lining up the center *lubber line* (fixed vertical post[s] around the edge of the compass card) with the markings on the compass card. The lubber line indicating your course is the center one in the direction of the bow. You can read your boat's heading on a bulkhead compass in a similar fashion, but notice that the center lubber line is on the back of the compass. Keep in mind that regardless of the compass type, it needs to be mounted "straight" for the lubber line to reflect the boat's heading accurately.

Steering a compass course

When the navigator sets a course to sail and announces it to the helmsperson, they might expect that heading to be followed like a railroad track. Hey, dream on. Holding a compass course is difficult, especially at night and in really wavy conditions. Getting accustomed to the natural movement of the boat in the waves, the effectiveness of the rudder, and the movement of the compass card takes a little while.

Sometimes, such as when you're sailing close-hauled in shifty winds, holding a compass course is just about impossible. (Refer to Chapter 5 for details on sailing close-hauled.) At other times, such as in thick fog, holding a steady course is crucial. The following tips can help:

» **Pick a spot on the horizon.** Steering while looking down at the compass is difficult. Try to pick a spot on the horizon that seems to line up with the desired compass course; then rotate your eyes to the compass only periodically to confirm your heading.

- **Steer an average heading.** In big waves, when the compass card is swinging all around, try to average the desired heading by steering no more than, say, 5 degrees on either side.
- **Concentrate, and get navigation updates.** In difficult conditions, or when you're sailing in an area with hazards you want to avoid (such as a shipping channel or shallow water), the navigator (or the person who's running the navigation app) should be monitoring your position and track, providing you any necessary feedback and updates. As in a car, it's best if the driver isn't the person who's looking at the navigation app. Hey, driving is a hard job!

Basic Navigation: Piloting

Now you're in for the really fun part of navigation: using piloting skills. *Piloting* involves making frequent determinations of position (or a line of position) relative to geographical points. Navigation apps make this task so easy that many people never see the need to use "old-fashioned" piloting skills. But you're here because you know that jumping straight to the app without understanding the fundamentals leaves a big hole in your education that could put you at risk. Also, learning is fun!

Using a speedometer and a depth sounder

Navigators rely so much on a boat's speedometer and depth sounder that these devices deserve a little more explanation.

A *speedometer* serves the same function on a boat as on a car, telling you how fast you're going. A tiny paddlewheel fitted under the belly of the hull drives most boat speedometers. *Note:* A speedometer only tells your speed through the water, not speed over ground, because it doesn't factor in current (see "Figuring in current and leeway" later in this section). Like any sensor, this instrument will benefit from some calibration for accuracy.

A *depth sounder* simply uses sonar waves to measure the distance to the bottom and displays this depth on a dial or digital readout. You can compare this depth with the information on a chart to help determine your location (and avoid sailing into shallow water).

REMEMBER

Your depth sounder isn't measuring from the surface, so you must add the distance of the sensor to the waterline or apply a calibration correction to the instrument when comparing to depth on the nautical chart.

Taking a bearing

Unless you're right on top of a known point, such as a government buoy (which is illegal, by the way), you can determine your position without a navigation app by establishing a series of *lines of position* (LOPs): lines through some point on which you presume your boat is located as a result of an observation or measurement. Being able to take a compass bearing (see Figure 9-5) is an important skill for any sailor. To help you pinpoint your location, you must take a bearing of an object of known position, such as a buoy or a mountain peak, not a moving object or an object that isn't on your chart. Take the time to master these skills; you never know when the battery may run out on your navigation app!

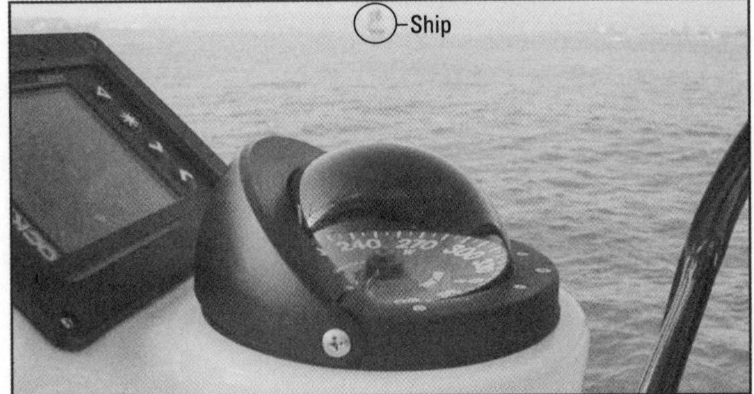

FIGURE 9-5: Taking a bearing: The approaching ship bears about 253°.

Photo courtesy of authors

The procedure for taking a bearing depends on the type of compass you use. (Bulkhead compasses don't lend themselves to taking a bearing, for example, because you can't look through them.) But the basic principles remain the same. Just follow these steps:

1. **Pick out the object on which you intend to get a bearing.**

   If you're close to the shore, you might pick a mountain. Make sure that the object appears on your nautical chart! Buoys are okay, but they can move slightly. Fixed objects (lighthouses and objects on land) are best.

2. **Situate your eyes so that an imaginary line from the object to your eyes passes through the center of the compass (which is close enough to read).**

3. **Read the compass bearing on the far side of the compass that's crossed by that imaginary line.**

TIP

Taking a bearing requires a good imagination — and sometimes several readings. The key is visualizing the imaginary line from the object to the compass.

4. **With the compass course of the bearing now known, go to your chart, find the object or point that you measured and transfer that bearing from the compass rose, and draw a line emanating from your measured point.**

   Note this LOP and the time of day. Theoretically, your actual position is somewhere on this line. Get a second LOP concurrently (best if it's at close to a right angle from the previous one) using the same process and plot it on the chart to obtain a position fix (see Figure 9-6).

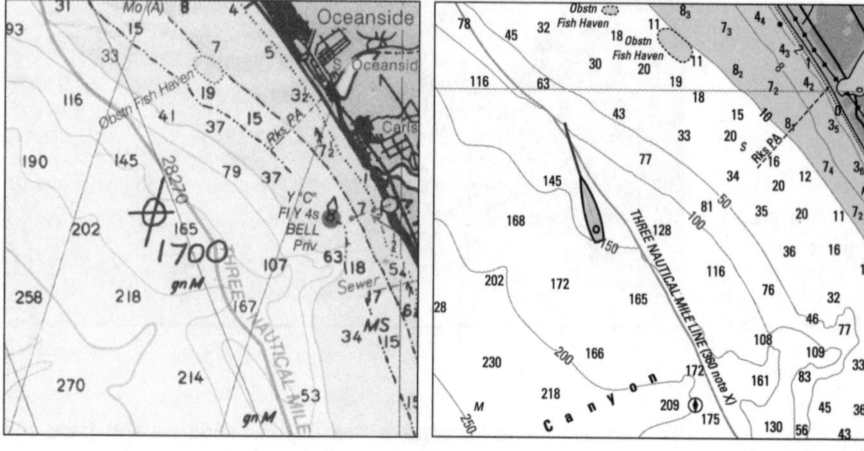

FIGURE 9-6: Your position is where two LOPs intersect (left). An app does all the work (right), but its battery can die.

To get a highly accurate line of position, try this cool (albeit uncommon) method: When you visually line up two points that are on the chart, you can plot them as an LOP. This type of observation is called a *range* or *transit*. Long Island Sound, where Peter grew up, has a great range that occurs when two huge smokestacks line up on the Long Island shore. Because Peter sailed up and down the sound quite a bit, he drew a line on the chart for this range and always watched for it.

Fixing your position without a navigation app

Where two lines of position taken at the same time intersect, you can fix your position on the chart, as Figure 9-6 shows. An accurate fix is every navigator's goal, but error can creep in and degrade accuracy in many ways. To minimize error, remember these tips:

- **Take bearings on objects at right angles to each other.** You can get the most accurate fix from two given LOPs when they're at 90 degrees to each other. When two LOPs cross at a shallow angle, even a small error in one of the bearings can lead to a large error in the fix.
- **Three objects are better than two.** By taking bearings on three objects (ideally, about 60 degrees apart), you further minimize error. Your fix will probably end up looking like a triangle rather than a cross, of course, but you can assume that you're in the middle of that triangle (refer to Figure 9-6 earlier in this chapter).
- **Take bearings on nearby objects.** The nearer the object, the less effect an error in bearing has on your fix.
- **Take two or three readings for each object.** Multiple readings minimize any errors you may make in taking the bearing.
- **Use ranges whenever possible.** Ranges are really accurate.
- **Cross-check your fix with the depth sounder (if you have one that you know to be accurate).** Don't forget to account for the height of the tide above (or below) mean low water. Comparing the measured depth with the depth on the chart is akin to getting yet another fix.
- **Write down the time of the fix next to it to aid in dead reckoning.** We cover this topic in the following section.

WARNING

Don't dally when taking bearings. This method of position fixing with multiple LOPs assumes that all the LOPs are taken concurrently. If it takes five minutes to get your second and third bearings, and your boat is moving the whole time, the accuracy of the fix will be degraded.

Dead reckoning

Dead reckoning (DR) is the process of determining position by advancing a previous position for course and distance. (Also, *Reckoning* is one of Peter's favorite albums by the Grateful Dead.) By definition, using DR isn't as accurate as using a navigation app or fixing your position with accurate LOPs, but it's an invaluable skill for long-distance sailors and navigators.

To be able to perform DR calculations, you must understand the important relationship between speed, time, and distance. Speed (always expressed on a boat in *knots*, or nautical miles per hour) is simply distance (nautical miles) divided by time (hours). If you're good at basic math, you'll have no problem remembering the following equations:

S = Speed (knots) D = Distance (nautical miles) T = Time (hours)

$S = D \div T \quad D = S \times T \quad T = D \div S$

REMEMBER

If you know two of the three quantities, you can determine the third. When performing DR, you use this formula most commonly to calculate distance traveled. If you know your average speed (from your speedometer) and the time you traveled, you can calculate the distance. Furthermore, if you know the average compass course you steered, you can advance your position on the chart from your last known (or estimated) position.

Suppose that you fix your position on the chart with three bearings taken at noon. Then you steer an average heading of 090° at 6.8 knots for 25 minutes. You can calculate the distance traveled as follows:

$D = S \times T$

$D = 6.8 \text{ knots} \times (25/60)$

$D = 2.83 \text{ nautical miles}$

Therefore, you can establish your DR position at 12:25 by measuring on the chart 2.83 miles along a course of 090°M from the noon fix. The updated location is your dead-reckoned position, and you can mark it on a paper chart as such with an encircled dot, the letters *DR*, and the time of day.

TIP

Use the six-minute rule: When determining distance traveled, you must often use a time interval of less than one hour, creating a cumbersome math problem. But because six minutes is one tenth of an hour, you can use this increment of time to ease your calculations. For example, a boat going 6.8 knots travels 0.68 nautical miles (nm) in six minutes, or roughly 1.4 nm in 12 minutes, and so on.

Figuring in current and leeway

When you're advancing your position with DR, you may also need to consider two types of movement that aren't measured on the speedometer and compass:

- **»** *Leeway* is the sideslipping motion that occurs when a heeled boat sails along. It occurs most often when you're sailing upwind or on a close reach. The impact of leeway varies from boat to boat and is almost impossible to measure, but it can be estimated at 3–5 degrees, depending on the boat and how much it heels.
- **»** *Current* has a similar invisible effect on the boat's progress. For more on currents, see Chapter 8.

Keeping a log

Given the importance of staying on top of your speed (or distance traveled) and heading, you can see why all serious navigators kept logs in the paper-chart days. A *log* is a historical record of various pieces of information; your weather app or chart plotter might very well save one for you. Common items of entry in a navigator's log include

- **»** **Average heading (since the last entry):** Whenever the boat changes course (say, after a tack), make a new entry.
- **»** **Average speed since the last entry:** Pay attention, and make your best guess.
- **»** **Given course:** The given course is the one desired by the navigator.
- **»** **Log reading:** Most instrument systems have a log, which is a nautical odometer (as opposed to the log you're writing in).
- **»** **Time:** Time is normally recorded in 24-hour format (so 1:00 p.m is 1300).
- **»** **Weather information:** This includes wind speed and direction, cloud cover, and barometric pressure, etc.
- **»** **Other comments:** Comments might include what sails are up, who is driving, what maneuver was just made, and what was for dinner.

TIP

When should you keep a log? Obviously, you don't need one when you sail a dinghy in familiar waters (and you don't have a place to store it anyway) or when you go on a short harbor cruise. If you're crossing the ocean, even if you have a powerful navigation app, it's definitely prudent to keep a log. Otherwise, use your judgment. Keep a log any time doing so can add to the boat's safety (or for fun and the memories).

Special Piloting Techniques

The key to safe navigation is making it as easy to perform as possible. We began this chapter with a section on common-sense techniques because often (such as in your home waters), you can perform the necessary tasks and keep the boat safe without looking at a chart or your app.

But careful, skilled use of a navigation app and/or rigorous DR, and/or frequent fixing of your position all have their time and place. Navigating at night in a new location with many shoals and hazards is an example. Much of the time, your task requires a level of navigational effort somewhere between the two extremes. This section provides some helpful techniques that are worth learning even if you rely on an app or chartplotter.

Danger bearing

Often, an entrance channel to a busy harbor is marked by two navigational aids (*range markers*) that, when aligned, indicate a safe course — sort of like landing lights on an aircraft carrier. Sometimes, lighthouses display a different-color light (red instead of white) in one sector of their sweep. The edges (where those colors meet) are *danger bearings:* On one side, the boat is safe; on the other side, there could be shallow water.

The navigator can also determine a danger bearing from information gained from the nautical chart. For example, if your present course requires you to sail around an island with rocky shoals on one side, you can plot an LOP as a danger bearing tangent to an obvious landmark or navigational aid of which you want the boat to stay outside, as shown in Figure 9-7. By monitoring the compass bearing to this object and comparing it with your danger bearing (measured on the chart), you can avoid the hazard without having to keep running down to the chart table and plotting your position.

TIP

Add some padding to the danger bearing. For example, if a bearing of 350 degrees to a buoy just skirts a shoal, add (or subtract, depending on which side of the line is safe water) 5 to 10 degrees, especially as you get close to the danger.

Distance off

You can fix your position on a chart with two LOPs you obtain from bearings, but you can also fix your position if you have one LOP and know your distance, or range, from that object. You simply find the point at which the LOP crosses the *circle of position*, marked by a circle whose radius is the distance you are from its center. You can obtain a circle of position in many ways. Two of the most helpful methods are judging distance and doubling the relative angle.

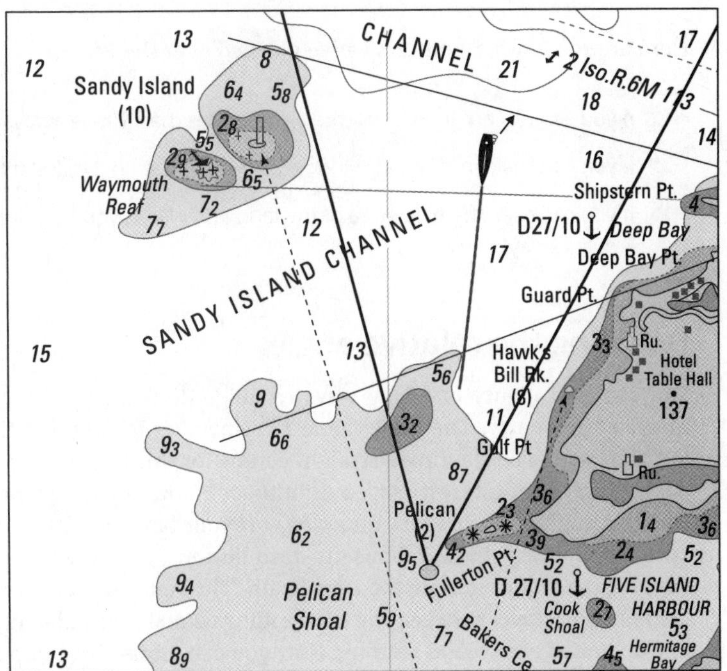

FIGURE 9-7: Two danger bearings provide limits for a safe approach from the north.

Judging distance

Every top navigator likes to think that they have the ability to judge distance as well as a pro golfer or caddie. The skill comes from practice. Any time you're out on the water or on the shore, you can practice by making a game of judging distance. It's fun to involve the whole crew to make their guess and then check the navigation app!

Peter likes guessing distance, and he does it all the time. He's stored away in his mind's eye a catalog of what certain distances look like. He knows, for example, that the distance across Skaneateles Lake (New York) from his dock is 2 miles, and he knows what that distance looks like by heart. So when something is about 2 miles away, he asks himself whether it's closer or farther than the other side of the lake. His brain has also stored away what 6 miles looks like from all the time he's spent staring out of airplane windows. And of course, 100 yards is ingrained from his early years playing on a football field. You see, your brain already has a catalog of what certain distances look like.

Here are some other pointers we've gleaned over the years:

- If you can discern individual trees, you're less than 1 mile away.
- If you can make out house windows, you're less than 2 miles away.
- If you can't see the true edge of the land and water, you're more than 3 miles away.

Doubling the relative angle

You can find plenty of tricky ways to judge distance by using the science and magic of geometry. The easiest one to remember is doubling the relative angle, but you have to be steering a straight course for this technique to work. When you pass an object of interest (say, a lighthouse), note the time when it's 45 degrees (relative angle, not compass direction) off your bow. Pay attention to the average speed, and when the lighthouse is dead abeam (90 degrees to the bow), you've doubled the angle, so note the time again. Through the wonders of geometry, the distance you travel between the two readings equals your distance from the object at the time of the second reading. Now you can plot a circle of position and take a bearing on that object, and you'll have a fix.

Navigating in Fog or Reduced Visibility

By definition, you can't see anything in fog, so make sure that your navigation device is charged if you expect low visibility. The skills of dead reckoning can become crucially important to avoid getting lost or worse. Here are some good rules to keep in mind when fog descends:

- **Be aware of the potential for fog.** In Chapter 8, we discuss how and when fog forms. Don't sail far from home if fog is in the forecast.
- **If fog starts to roll in, react.** Fog won't totally blanket you without some warning, so quickly figure out your compass heading back to the harbor.
- **Assuming that you have a chart, immediately fix your position as accurately as possible.** If you don't have a chart or are simply day-sailing, immediately set your course for the closest safe haven (such as home).
- **Follow the procedures for keeping accurate DR.** And if you have a depth sounder, use it, especially if you're passing areas with steep transitions in depth that can help in getting a fix as described above in the section "Fixing your position without a navigation app."

» **Listen for buoys and foghorns.** The nautical chart (and good ol' U.S. Chart No. 1) indicates what navigational aids make certain sounds.

» **Listen for other boats.** In low visibility, every boat is required to post a lookout. Keep in mind that sound does weird things in fog, so pinpointing the location of a sound can be difficult.

» **Make sound signals.** In low visibility, the International Regulations for Prevention Collisions at Sea (COLREGS) require a sailboat (39 feet, or 12 meters, or longer) to make one long horn blast followed by two short blasts at least every two minutes. For the other rules of the road, see Chapter 4.

Even though we encourage you to master the traditional skills of navigation, sailing in foggy conditions or in low visibility is a good time to pay attention to your navigation app or chart plotter.

Navigating at Night

When night falls, you lose some, but not all, of the visual information that's important to a navigator. Even in familiar waters, the arrival of night is a good time to break out the nautical chart and increase the level of your navigational efforts. One of the most important aspects of coastal navigation at night is identifying lighted buoys, lighthouses, and other boats.

Lighting up the nighttime sky

At night, certain buoys, daymarks, and navigational aids such as lighthouses display lights to help mariners find their way. To prevent confusion, navigational aids are lit in a variety of ways, using color, pattern, and *period* (interval between flashes) to help with identification at night. Typically, solid red and green buoys — so important in defining a channel — are lit with corresponding red and green lights. Lighthouses and midchannel fairway buoys often feature a white light. On a nautical chart, abbreviations such as "F" for "fixed, unblinking" and "FL X sec" for "flashing at X-second intervals" indicate the characteristics of each light.

U.S. Chart No. 1 can help you decipher the abbreviations defining the characteristics of the light. You usually need to view two or three cycles of the light sequence to be sure that you've positively identified it. Realize also that the lights on buoys have a much shorter range (about 2 miles, and even less in big waves) than lighthouses. You may have an easier time identifying a buoy or lighthouse if you first calculate (on the chart) its expected bearing and then look in that direction.

Recognizing other boats at night

All boats are required to have navigation lights (also called *running lights*) at night, including dusk and dawn, and whenever visibility is reduced, such as in fog, heavy rain, or haze. Power boats, larger commercial ships, and other seagoing craft have required lighting configurations that vary considerably depending on the type of boat (or barge or submarine). But most vessels have red and green lights to identify port and starboard, respectively, and have some kind of white stern light while under way. Larger ships display really bright fore-and-aft range lights that help you determine which way they're heading.

Figure 9-8 shows the running lights on a typical sailboat and on a larger ship (more than 164 feet long, or 50 meters). You definitely want to get out of the way if you can see both the red and green bow lights of any vessel coming at you, or if that vessel's bearing remains the same for a long period.

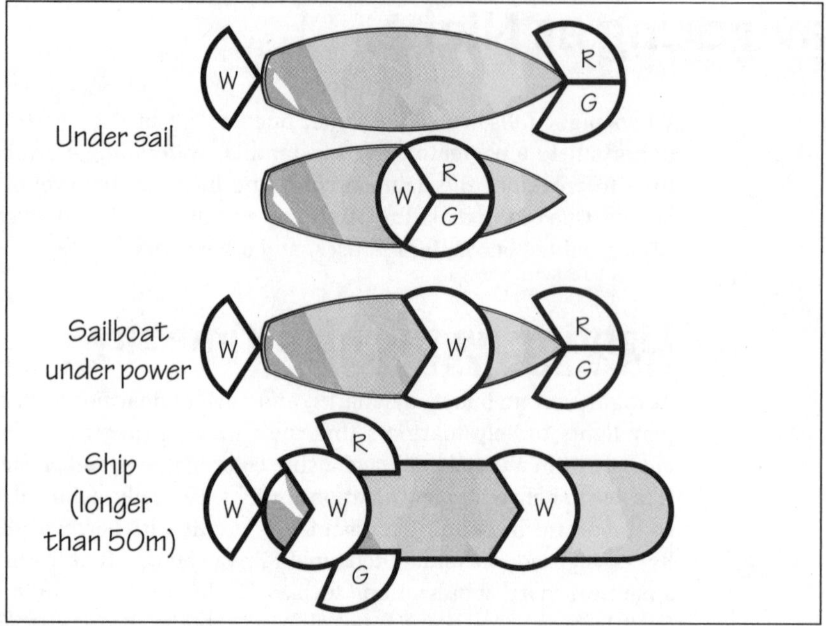

FIGURE 9-8: Navigation lights required on a sailboat and on a large ship.

At night, keeping interior and deck lights to a minimum helps the night vision of those on deck, especially the navigator, who may be going back and forth between the chart table below and the cockpit. Most boats have interior lights that switch to red mode for night operation, because red light doesn't affect night vision the way that white lights do. Personal flashlights (we recommend headlamps) should have a red or blue mode for the same reason.

Keep in mind that red lines and symbols on a chart look faint and gray in red light.

Electronic Navigation: GPS, Navigation Apps, and Chart Plotters

As we stress throughout this chapter, understanding and being conversant in the "traditional" skills of piloting and DR on a paper chart are important even if you rely mainly on navigation apps and devices. Now it's time to take a look behind the curtain of this powerful technology. For simplicity, we'll refer to all electronic navigation devices, apps, computer programs, chart plotters, and the like as apps.

A crucial element of all navigation apps is satellite navigation technology known broadly as the Global Navigation Satellite System (GNSS). The U.S.'s Global Positioning System (GPS) service — currently, 24 globe-circling satellites — was built first and is the common generic name for this technology, though other governments (including Russia, China, and the European Union) have their own systems running or in development. A GPS receiver receives signals from satellites and calculates your current position and movement. You don't need to know how it works to use it.

How accurate is GPS?

According to the U.S. government, a typical GPS-enabled smartphone is accurate to within 16 feet (4.9 meters). High-end marine-grade GPS devices average quite a bit better. Your unit's accuracy depend on its receiver design and features, what satellites it tracks (the more, the better), atmospheric conditions, and any signal blockage.

If you really love all this stuff, head to the Internet to get the latest information on this evolving technology. Check out the websites of GPS manufacturers or surf to `https://www.gps.gov`.

Getting the most out of your navigation app

It's amazing to see how much navigation has changed since we wrote the first edition of *Sailing For Dummies* in 1998. As we stress throughout this chapter, before you begin relying on your app, understand how to read a chart, including the symbols and abbreviations (which look small on a tiny screen), as well as the basic skills of piloting and DR. Also beware of the ENC zooming problem we discuss earlier in the section "Deciphering a chart." With all that in mind, here are some important elements for getting the most out of your navigation app. We call this part *Electronic Navigation For Dummies*, and you should treat it like your presail checklist:

- **Read the manual.** Every app is a little different in its logic and set up – take the time to make sure you understand how your app works and its features. You may find it helpful to do some surfing to find some instructional videos on using your app.
- **Configure your settings.** The power of these apps is incredible, but despite all those features and controllability, you can still make a catastrophic error. A simple example is depth settings. If you're looking at the app's chart screen and see that the depth ahead 3 meters (because there's a big 3 sounding on the chart), you'll be really sorry when you sail over that spot in a 5-foot-draft boat at low tide and discover that unit was showing you depth in feet, not meters. Here are some of the app settings to run through and confirm, along with our recommendations:
  - *Depth:* Set it to whatever units you like. We recommend using the same units in which you think of your boat's draft. Some apps have autocorrection for the current state of the tide; make sure that you know whether that setting is on or off.
  - *Speed:* Set it to knots.
  - *Distance:* Set it to nautical miles (although at times, we like boat lengths and meters).
  - *Compass:* We always set it to magnetic north so that it matches our compass.
  - *Position:* We like degrees, minutes, and decimal minutes, but the setting is up to you.
  - *Shallow water/depth shading:* Most apps allow you to change the color of the water on the chart a particular depth in their settings. We set the shallow water color a few feet deeper than our boat's draft.
  - *Chart display:* You might have a multitude of options, including layers, overlays, orientation (north up, heading up, or course up), boat size, AIS (see Chapter 7), and weather.
  - *COG and SOG damping:* We like to set the damping for GPS-derived course over ground (COG) and speed over ground (SOG) quite low (2-5 secs) so that they update quickly.

TIP

SOG and COG values are super-accurate. Comparing SOG with your instrument boat speed in an area with little or known current can help you calibrate your speedometer. Comparing COG with your compass heading can help you understand compass error (or leeway or current effect).

- **Download your charts ahead of time.** Many apps rely on an Internet connection to display the chart, but they also allow you to download the chart data for a user-selectable region so that you can navigate effectively without an Internet connection.
- **Learn and become proficient in basic chart plotting.**

  Practice skills like the following:

  - Zooming and panning around the chart
  - Finding your boat on the chart
  - Measuring distance and direction between two points on the chart
  - Measuring distance and direction between your boat and any point
  - Creating, saving, and reopening waypoints
  - Creating, saving, and reopening routes (combinations of waypoints)
  - Displaying your track (historical position) on the chart
  - Displaying and controlling the length of a predictor line emanating from the bow of the boat in the direction of your COG
  - Querying chart symbols that you don't understand
  - Configuring and displaying information such as waypoint range and bearing (in nautical miles and magnetic degrees), waypoint ETA, waypoint cross track error (the measurement of how far off course you are), COG and SOG (in magnetic degrees and knots, respectively), and your position (in latitude and longitude)
  - Displaying AIS data and querying individual targets (if available)

  Pretty much every navigation app has a man-overboard (MOB) feature that allows you to save your position at the push of a button and then automatically switch modes to navigate back to that location. Many boats have more than one navigation app. Make sure that everyone on board knows how to operate the MOB feature on every device.

- **Keep a digital log.** A log can help you determine how far you've gone over a certain period, which can be helpful for navigating or for knowing whether you set the world sailing speed record for a 24-hour run. (You need to sail more than 700 miles in a 24-hour period at an average speed of more than 30 knots to be close.)

When Peter is the navigator in a race or just cruising, he likes using a laptop computer interfaced with the GPS and sailing instruments because it helps him make better decisions. Over the past few years, he's enjoyed working on the development of special navigation software (`www.expeditionmarine.com`; see Figure 9-9) that combines the features of basic chart plotting and navigation with weather analysis, routing, and performance optimization. Because technology continues to evolve quickly, being on the cutting edge is fun for him.

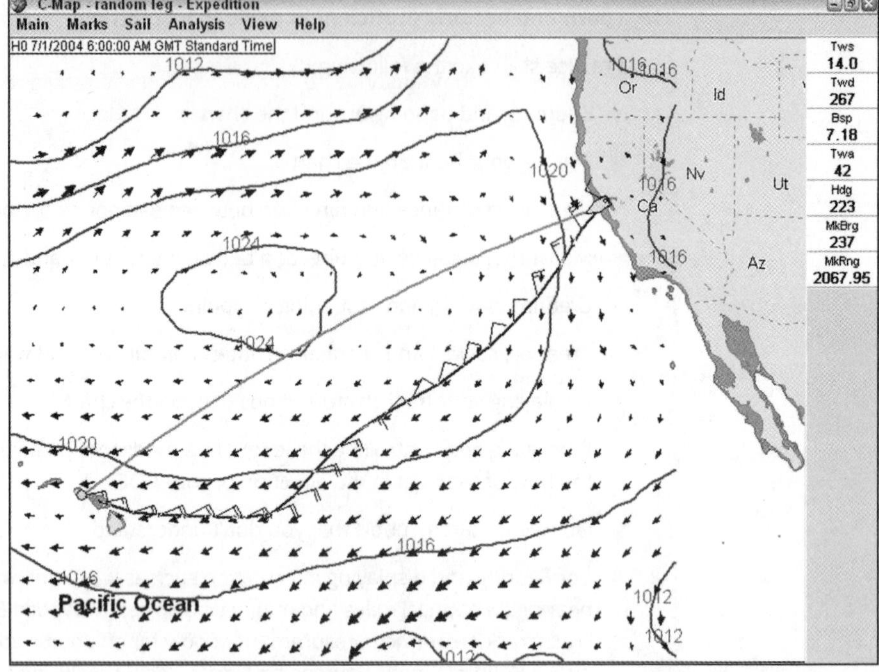

FIGURE 9-9: Weather routing: Navigation software helps you navigate and plan the fastest route for your boat in the forecasted winds.

Wishing on a Star: Celestial Navigation

From high-tech to traditional, *celestial navigation* (navigating by celestial bodies such as stars, the moon, and the sun) is the coolest form of navigation. Using this system puts you in a league with the greats: Galileo, Copernicus, Magellan, Columbus, and Cook. Well, maybe that's a bit of a stretch, but the fact that you can determine where you are in the world, to an accuracy of less than a mile, with a *sextant* (a device that accurately measures the angular height of a celestial body over the horizon), a watch, and some books of tables is pretty amazing. And you need one other thing: a clear or partially clear sky during daylight, dawn, or dusk hours. Nighttime and clouds put a real damper on celestial navigation because you need to see the celestial object and the horizon.

A general book like this one is too small to do justice to celestial navigation. Fortunately, you can find many good books on the subject. Peter's favorite is *Kindergarten of Celestial Navigation,* by Joseph Sellar. It's no longer in print but worth it's weight in gold if you can find a copy.

The basic principal of celestial navigation is easy to grasp. If you can measure the angle between the horizon and a celestial body of known position at a certain time (thank you, Copernicus and friends), you can generate a circle of position. You're somewhere in that circle of position. Get another reading from a different celestial body or the same one at a different time, and if you haven't moved, the two circles of position cross at your location (and also at a point on the other side of the planet, where you obviously aren't). Figure 9-10 shows an example of celestial navigation geometry.

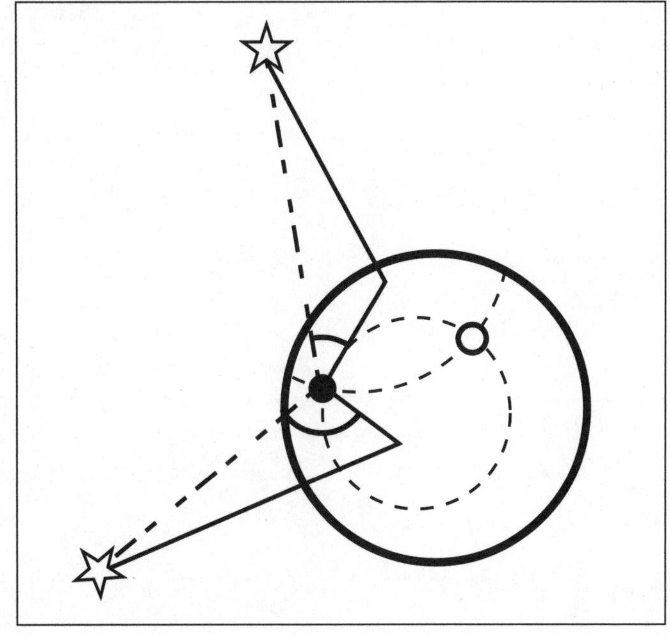

FIGURE 9-10: In celestial navigation, you generate a circle of position on which you're located. Two celestial sights give you two circles and narrow your possible position to two points.

WARNING

No matter how many GPS devices and apps you have on board, never head into unfamiliar waters without a backup plan, which could be a second app or the basic tools required for coastal piloting on a paper chart. Never, ever make a major off-shore passage (such as crossing an ocean) without having a sextant, instruction book, and the requisite books (tables and almanacs), or a calculator or PC with all that information stored inside.

IN THIS CHAPTER

» Dropping anchor — and picking it back up

» Anchoring under sail

» Troubleshooting anchoring problems

» Picking the right anchor and rode

» Taking care of the ground tackle

» Using two anchors and other objects

Chapter 10

Anchors Away: Anchoring Your Boat

Anchors aweigh, my boys,

Anchors aweigh!

Farewell to college joys,

We sail at break of day.

—ALFRED HART MILES

Although nowadays, many quiet little coves that used to be perfect for a peaceful night at anchor are filled with mooring buoys and marinas, you can still find that special special spot that's all your own. So knowing how to anchor is important for those times and when you run out of wind. And when you're ready to travel and charter a sailboat in an exotic place, you'll almost certainly want to anchor.

Anchoring your boat is more involved than tying it to a mooring, because you're responsible for lowering the anchor and making sure that it's secure. This chapter focuses on everything related to anchors, from dropping and retrieving your anchor to choosing the best anchor and gear.

Looking at a Basic Anchor

How do you keep a floating object anchored? One way is to find a heavy rock underwater, dive down, and tie a strong rope to it. But what happens when you want to leave that spot and go someplace else? Hauling that enormous rock on board may be impossible. You can just cut the rope attached to the rock, but what would you do if you want to anchor the next night? (Also, you'd be littering.)

Another problem with the rock method is wind or current. A strong wind pushes very hard on your boat, which in turn pulls very hard on your rock — so hard that it may simply slide or roll across the bottom. Fortunately, you have a better way, thanks to the invention of properly designed anchors.

Most anchors have the following characteristics, as Figure 10-1 shows:

- They sink! (An anchor wouldn't work very well if it floated, would it?)
- They have holding power, thanks to one or more prongs or points called *flukes.* These flukes act like the blade of a shovel to dig into the bottom. Because the flukes help grip the bottom, the anchor can weigh less, making it easier to bring on board.
- They have a long arm, or *shank,* providing mechanical advantage to help the flukes dig in.
- They have features that help keep the fluke(s) dug in when the wind or current shifts and the boat pulls from a different direction.
- Despite their holding power, they can be "unstuck" relatively easily when they're pulled from directly above.

If the wind and/or your engine dies, knowing how to anchor is an important safety skill. The anchor may be stored below deck, but on many bigger cruising keelboats, it may already be rigged and ready to go up on the bow. When stored below deck, the anchor line should be nicely *flaked* (neatly folded), with the anchor and chain on top. *Ground tackle* is the term for the entire package: the anchor plus the *anchor rode* (the line and chain that attach the anchor to the boat).

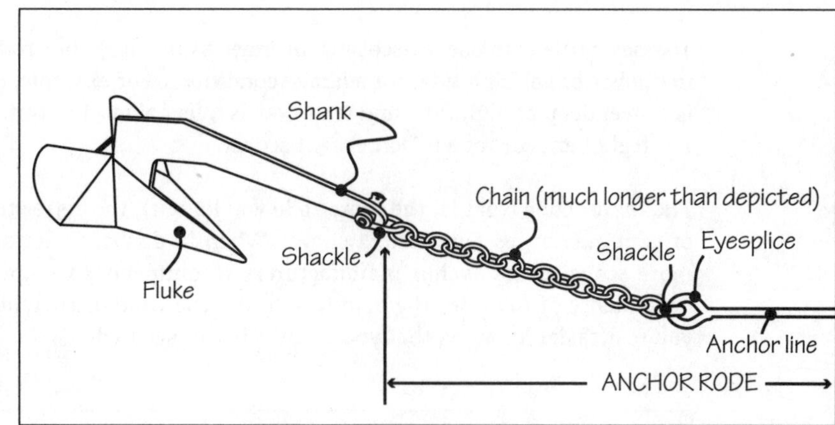

FIGURE 10-1: A Delta/Rocna-style anchor and the components of its anchor rode.

Adding chain: Why it helps

Attaching a length of chain to the anchor ensures that the boat's pulling force on the anchor comes from the all-important horizontal direction, parallel to the bottom, so that the flukes stay dug into the bottom (check out Figure 10-1). In addition, chain doesn't chafe if it's dragged over sharp rocks on the bottom. The anchor rode on most larger charter boats is solely chain, with no rope at all. In extreme anchoring conditions (strong winds or a long stay), more or only chain is the way to go.

On JJ's 48-foot cruising sailboat, the primary anchor rode has more than 30 feet of chain between the anchor and the line. But the rode for the smaller "lunch anchor" (used when taking a short break) has just 10 feet of chain so that it's easier to haul back up on deck.

Getting the scoop on scope

In the cartoons, Popeye simply drops the anchor and rode over the side until it hits bottom and then cleats it off. In the real world, you need to let out much more rode than the depth of the water.

Scope (the ratio between the length of anchor rode you let out and the depth of the water *plus* the distance from your bow at deck height to the water's surface) is an important concept to understand when anchoring. Too little scope, such as Popeye's 1:1 scope, is impractical and dangerous; the pull on the anchor is vertical, and your boat dislodges the anchor at high tide or on the top of any wave. Increasing the ratio of scope allows the anchor to be pulled in a more horizontal direction, which greatly increases its holding power.

The basic rule is to use 5:1 scope (five times as much anchor rode as the distance to the bottom at high tide) for average conditions. For example, if your anchorage is 17 feet deep at high tide, and your bow is 3 feet above the water surface, let out 100 feet of anchor rode to achieve 5:1 scope.

The more scope (that is, the more rode you let out), the better the holding power of your anchor, as Figure 10-2 shows. When in doubt . . . let out more rode for more scope. Some anchor manufacturers recommend 7:1 scope. As long as you have plenty of room for the boat to swing if the wind or current shifts direction, you rest easier knowing that your boat is better secured.

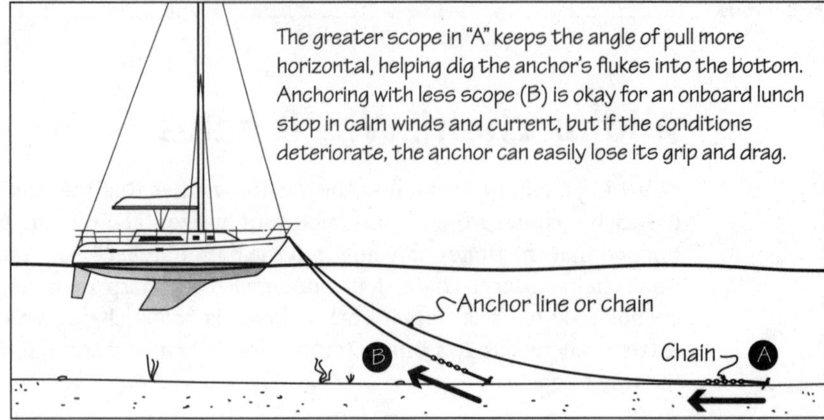

The greater scope in "A" keeps the angle of pull more horizontal, helping dig the anchor's flukes into the bottom. Anchoring with less scope (B) is okay for an onboard lunch stop in calm winds and current, but if the conditions deteriorate, the anchor can easily lose its grip and drag.
Anchor line or chain
Chain
B
A

FIGURE 10-2: More scope gives the anchor better holding power.

© John Wiley & Sons, Inc.

If the conditions are very mild, and you plan on stopping for only a short break and staying on board, you can probably get away with laying out less scope (not less than 3:1) or using a lighter anchor with less chain. Less scope means less work hauling in that anchor rode when you want to get under way. Check out "Choosing the right anchor line" later in this chapter for tips on marking your anchor-line length.

Picking a Good Place to Anchor

To know where to anchor, you need to familiarize yourself with the underwater topography displayed on a nautical chart. From the chart, you can determine the water depth and the type of bottom (mud and sand are better than rock) to find a suitable anchorage. You also need to know how much (if at all) the tide will rise and fall. (See Chapter 9 for more on charts and tides.) On a trip, try to find a local cruising-guide booklet, which will highlight the best anchorages and any special considerations. In some areas, buoys (usually colored yellow) mark a designated anchorage.

For comfort, you want to find an anchorage that's protected from the prevailing wind and wave direction. For safety, you need to find an anchorage that features the following:

- A suitable bottom for securing your anchor.
- Enough depth to prevent the danger of grounding but not so much depth that your anchor rode is too short to achieve a safe scope (5:1 or more).
- Sufficient room for your boat to swing in all directions. (Imagine that the anchor is the center of a circle around which the boat swings.)
- A quiet location out of any channel (less traffic and less current).
- A location protected from waves and strong winds.

TIP

Spending enough time choosing the best place to anchor *before* you drop anchor is much easier than having to pull up your anchor and move.

Finding the lee

Very few anchorages are protected in all wind directions, so your first steps are assessing the current wind direction and reviewing the marine weather forecast. (See Chapter 8 for more information about weather.) A good, protected anchorage is in the *lee* of a nearby landmass, so it blocks the force of the wind and waves. If the forecast is for strong, easterly breezes, for example, you want to anchor just to the west of the protecting landmass.

WARNING

Alongside a *lee shore* (shore facing the oncoming wind and waves) is the most dangerous place for an anchored boat. If the anchor slips at all, you can find yourself getting washed up onto the beach — or worse. Anchoring along a lee shore is like standing in the middle of the road: You may be safe for a while, but your odds aren't so good. The tricky part about picking a good place to anchor is that with a 180-degree wind shift, your nice protected anchorage can become the dreaded lee shore.

Avoiding underwater hazards

You can never go wrong by dropping the hook in some medium-soft mud. Avoid a rocky bottom, because the flukes of the anchor can't dig in, and if they do, they can get stuck. A chart like the one shown in Figure 10-3 indicates the bottom type and shows you underwater hazards to avoid, such as rocks, cables, and shipwrecks. Nothing is worse than getting your anchor so stuck on an object that you have to go swimming or cut your anchor rode away.

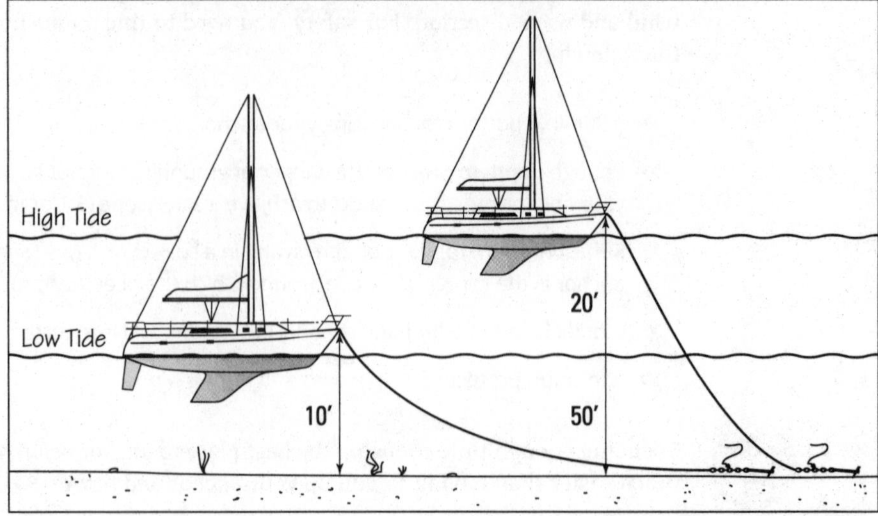

© John Wiley & Sons, Inc.

FIGURE 10-3: With large tidal range, both depth and anchor scope will change. At low tide, the scope is 5:1; at high tide, it's 2.5:1.

Fortunately, the world is becoming more ecologically aware. In the Virgin Islands (where you can enjoy some of the nicest cruising in the world, as we point out in Chapter 17), the local authorities now place mooring buoys at popular anchorages. Because tying up to a mooring is infinitely easier than anchoring, life is much easier for those of us above the water's surface. But the reason for the moorings is to protect the creatures underwater. Dropping an anchor onto a coral reef or a bed of seagrass is a big environmental no-no and causes irreparable damage to these priceless residents of our oceans. Don't do it. If you must anchor near coral reefs or underwater vegetation, take the time to find a sandy patch, or even put on your mask and snorkel to find the best spot before crash-landing your anchor.

Keeping an eye on depth and current

Because charts indicate the water depth at *mean low water* (average low tide), seeing spots that are deep enough for your boat is easy. In big waves or a swell, allow a few more feet of clearance for when the boat is down in the trough. Better yet, avoid anchoring in waves; the idea of anchoring is to relax and get a break from the open-water conditions (refer to Figure 10-3). Your weather app or a local tide book will help you ascertain the tidal range. Avoid anchoring in places with strong current, because it puts more load on the anchor, just like increased wind. For more on currents, see Chapter 9.

Staying away from crowds

Avoid crowded anchorages, where you're restricted in the amount of scope you can let out. In a squall, one of these neighboring boats may drag its anchor — possibly into your boat! A boat at anchor swings with the wind and current, so make sure that your boat is free to swing in a circle around the anchor (see Figure 10-4).

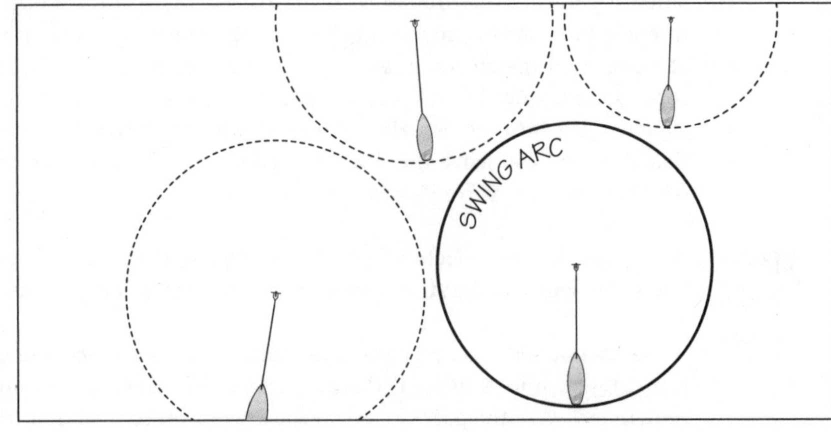

FIGURE 10-4: Allow room to swing around the anchor when the wind/current change.

TIP

Etiquette at anchor says that the most recent boat to anchor must pick up and move if the wind or current shifts (or someone's anchor drags) and the boats are getting too close together.

If you must choose a spot in a crowded anchorage, check out your potential new neighbors. A large powerboat may run a noisy generator all night. Netting on the lifelines and Mickey Mouse swim floats signify the delights of small children on board. Be respectful. Don't be the chief noisemaker. Keep in mind that in strong winds, halyards can beat a very loud tune, so tie them off away from the mast.

Getting Ready to Anchor

After you study the harbor carefully and find the perfect spot, you want to get that anchor to dig in securely on your first try. Anchoring can be stressful, and knowing that the folks on nearby anchored boats are watching your every move doesn't help. It's much easier to do your reconnaissance and make accurate anchoring maneuvers under power with all sails down. (Because you must anchor without using an engine sometimes, we have an "Anchoring under Sail" section later in this chapter.)

Wait to drop the anchor until the boat is stopped dead in the water and just beginning to drift backward, similar to picking up a mooring (refer to Chapter 6). It's a lot easier to go backward on a sailboat under power. Anchoring under power also has the advantage of letting you clear the *foredeck* (area on deck in front of the mast) of sails before you get started so that the crew has space to prepare the anchor rode without stepping on or dirtying the sails.

A common anchoring mishap is caused by not letting the anchor rode run out smoothly during the drop and as you back away from it. Murphy's Law is definitely in force during anchoring. You should pay out the rode at the right time and at a pace that matches the reverse movement of the boat. If your anchor rode has rope, you may need extra preparation. The knots and tangles that a long piece of rope can get into are amazing. We hope you check that the anchor line is neatly flaked before you leave the dock, but checking it again right before you drop — while the skipper is finding the ideal anchorage — is still a good idea.

REMEMBER

When the skipper selects a spot, make sure that the crew dropping the anchor know the depth so that they can prepare and release enough anchor rode.

If the anchor rode has rope, take the time to lay out *(flake)* enough line so that it can run out smoothly until the anchor touches the bottom, and neatly coil the remainder (with the part closest to the anchor on top) so that it's ready to run. If your anchor rode has rope, and your boat has a *chain locker* (compartment in the bow that holds the anchor rode "preflaked"), you need to pull out and arrange only enough rope for the anchor to hit bottom. If the rope in the chain locker was stored correctly, the rest should pay out cleanly as the boat is backed away from the anchor and you add the necessary scope.

Make sure to lead the anchor line over an anchor roller or through a *fairlead* (also called a *bow chock*) and under the *bow pulpit* (the metal frame surrounding the bow to which the forward ends of the lifelines attach), as Figure 10-5 shows. Always tie the end of the anchor line to a secure point on the boat, such as a deck cleat or the mast, before dropping anchor. The ocean floor is littered with anchors from boats whose crew let out "just a little more line" before tying it off.

If your anchor rode is all chain, and the anchor is already poised at the bow in its roller (as is the case in most larger charter sailboats), the preparation and manual labor will be much easier, as the anchor chain will pay out from chain locker with the push of a button to turn the *windlass* (anchor winch drum mounted on the foredeck; described in "Dropping the Anchor" later in this chapter).

Before anchoring, make a final inspection of the anchor line for chafe, check that any shackles are tight, and make sure that the bitter end of the anchor rode is tied securely to the boat (because you're in for an expensive "oops" if it isn't).

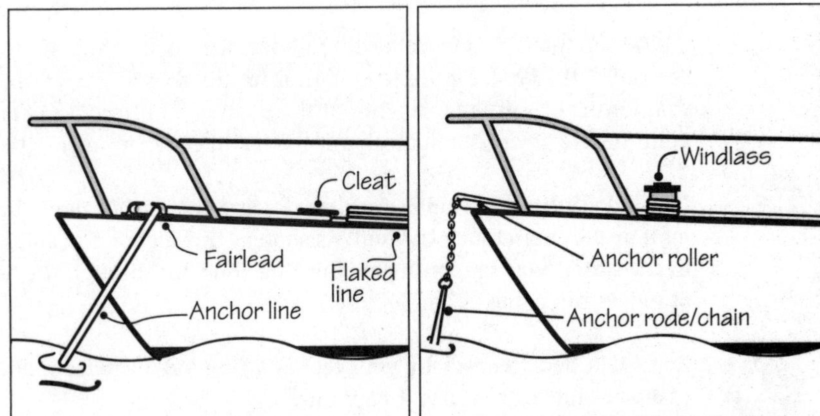

FIGURE 10-5: Two systems for tying off your anchor line.

© John Wiley & Sons, Inc.

Follow these steps when you're preparing to drop the anchor:

1. **Approach the spot from several boat lengths to leeward and then turn the boat head-to-wind.**
2. **Slow the boat, and stop right over the desired spot for your anchor.**

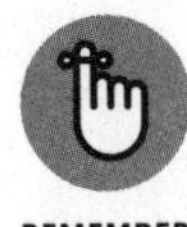

REMEMBER

This spot isn't where the boat sits; it's where the anchor sits. The boat lies downwind (or *down current*) of this spot. As the wind or current shifts, your boat will swing around this spot (ideally, without dislodging the anchor) in a 360-degree circle.

3. **Give the signal.**

TIP

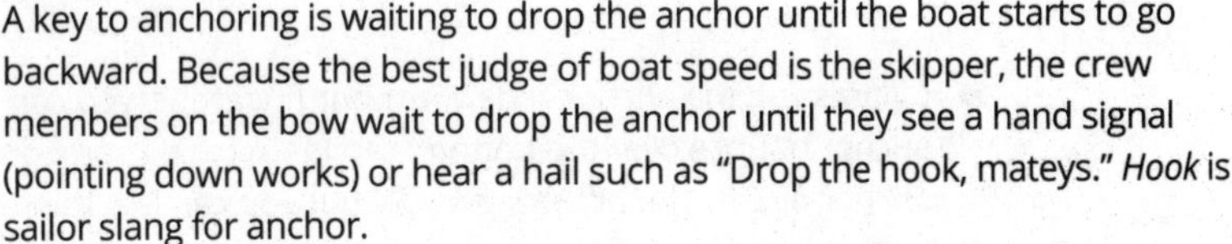

A key to anchoring is waiting to drop the anchor until the boat starts to go backward. Because the best judge of boat speed is the skipper, the crew members on the bow wait to drop the anchor until they see a hand signal (pointing down works) or hear a hail such as "Drop the hook, mateys." *Hook* is sailor slang for anchor.

REMEMBER

Hails can be difficult to hear in a strong wind. Hand signals are better.

4. **Drop the anchor.**

See the next section.

Dropping the Anchor

The safest way to lower the anchor and the chain over the side is to lower it slowly hand over hand or under the control of an anchor windlass (if your boat is equipped with one). A *windlass* looks like a winch drum mounted near the bow in line with a bow-mounted anchor roller that allows the anchor rode to drop smoothly over the rail of the boat. Figure 10-5 earlier in this chapter shows an electric windlass that lowers or raises the anchor at the push of a button. A manual windlass gives your muscle power some mechanical advantage when raising the anchor.

If you don't have a windlass and are letting the anchor down by hand, try not to let it or the chain touch the hull. As soon as the anchor and all the chain are safely in the water, you can let the anchor line slide out through the bow chock. (A pair of gloves can come in handy here.)

WARNING

Keep your body (especially your feet and fingers) away from and out of the loops of anchor line or chain as it pays out.

You can tell when the anchor touches bottom: Either the rope stops paying out so fast, or you feel the weight of the anchor disappear as it settles in. The foredeck crew's job isn't over when the anchor hits pay dirt; you need to let out sufficient *scope*, or extra rope (refer to "Getting the scoop on scope" earlier in this chapter) at a controlled pace so that the rode never gets tight. When enough line to achieve the desired scope is out, the foredeck crew cleats off the anchor line (or stops the windlass) and gives the signal to the helmsman that you're ready to *set* (dig in) the anchor.

Digging In for a While

You can ensure that your anchor is set and holding in a couple of ways:

- By pressing the anchor rode with your fingertips, you can sometimes feel the anchor bounce over the bottom, similar to taking someone's pulse. When the anchor digs in, the bouncing stops, but you can feel the rode stretching as the boat surges in waves.
- With the boat in reverse, you may be able to see the bow dip when the flukes of the anchor grip the bottom.

If you feel jerking motions, the anchor is dragging along the bottom. If your anchor keeps dragging, you can try either of the following techniques to get the anchor to set:

- **Let out more scope.** The anchor is probably skipping along the bottom, and with more scope, the anchor can dig in.
- **Give the anchor line a quick tug.** This technique works best on a smaller boat.

If the anchor keeps dragging, you may have to pick up your anchor and try again.

When your senses tell you that the anchor is holding, try to confirm it by watching landmarks or a range. Figure 10-6 shows a method to track your boat's position at anchor and see whether your anchor is dragging. By sighting through two objects abeam, you can establish a *transit* to track your position.

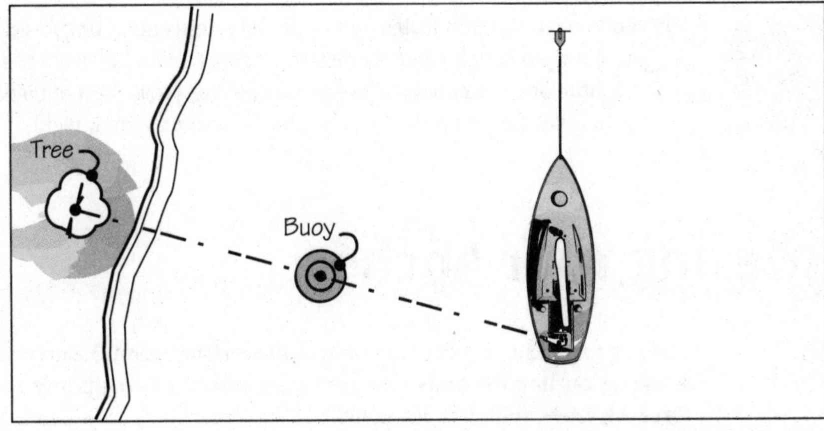

FIGURE 10-6: Is your anchor holding? Use a transit with two objects roughly abeam.

© John Wiley & Sons, Inc.

In addition, a navigation app can also be used to watch the boat's historical position (track) while anchored.

To be doubly sure that your anchor keeps on holding, try the following:

- **Make sure you have enough scope.** Consider the expected conditions, your type of anchor and rode, and the anticipated length of stay.
- **If a convenient transit isn't available, take a few compass bearings on some distinctive landmarks.** Fixed land is best, but you can also use buoys for reference. Use objects that are abeam (perpendicular to the anchor line) for accuracy. For more information about taking bearings, see Chapter 9.
- **Share the transit with your crew members.** Then they can double-check that you're securely anchored.
- **Write down these safety bearings so that when your insomnia kicks in at 2 a.m., you can reassure yourself that your boat is okay.** Remember that your range and bearings change if the boat swings with wind or current shifts.

» **Listen to your navigation system.** Your navigation app or the boat's chart plotter (if you have one) may have an "anchor watch" alarm that rings if the boat moves out of a set area. See "Tackling Anchoring Problems" later in this chapter for tips on using electronics while at anchor.

» **If you're still concerned, dive down with a mask, and inspect the anchor, chain, and rope.** This advice works only in the daytime, of course, and it's easiest to follow if you're anchoring in shallow, clear water in the tropics.

REMEMBER

» **Follow Navigation Rules.** International rules require anchored sailboats longer than 7 meters (22.97 feet) to display a black ball from the mast during daytime and a 360-degree fixed (not flashing) white light at night. Even if your boat is smaller, it's prudent to display an anchor light at night.

Retrieving Your Anchor

The key to picking up the anchor is teamwork between the crew and skipper. After agreeing on hand signals and assigning positions, including the key role of the foredeck crew, follow these steps:

1. **Slowly motor directly toward the anchor.**

   The helmsman probably needs the crew (who are performing step 2) to occasionally point left or right to help keep on track.

2. **As the boat is moving toward the anchor, the crew pulls the slack out of the anchor line.**

   Moving up on the anchor creates slack in the rode. Even if you don't have a pushbutton windlass, this task shouldn't be physically difficult, because you're simply pulling in limp line.

3. **When the boat is directly over the anchor, the crew signals for the helmsman to stop.**

   We use a closed-fist hand signal.

4. **Shift into neutral while the crew securely cleats the anchor line (or stops the windlass) after pulling out *all the slack* so that the anchor line is vertical.**

5. **When the rode is secured, the crew signals that the helmsman can start slowly going forward again until the anchor comes free.**

   Because the anchor rode is now pulling up and forward (the opposite direction from how it was dug in) on the anchor, the flukes usually lift out of a muddy bottom easily.

TIP

Don't blow out your back; let the boat's engine do the tough work of getting the anchor free of the bottom. You can tell when the anchor is free because the bow bounces up slightly and the anchor line has less pressure on it.

6. **When the anchor is free, put the engine back into neutral and begin the hardest part of the exercise: raising the anchor to the deck.**

   If you're lucky enough to have an electric windlass, you may not even break a sweat. A manual windlass provides mechanical advantage but still requires muscle power to crank it; otherwise, get ready to pull and pull and pull some more.

REMEMBER

   If your boat has an anchor windlass, make sure that you understand exactly how it works before using it. Keep your hands clear of the moving parts, and operate it as you would any other powerful tool — slowly and carefully.

   Regardless of the equipment on board, let the engine do all the work until the anchor breaks free from the ground. Take extra care to keep from dragging the chain (and anchor) along the hull.

7. **Before you bring your trusty anchor back on board, take a look at it as it clears the water, and clean it if necessary.**

   Chances are that the anchor has some remnants of its temporary home still attached to it. Mud or sand may come off with repeated dunkings. If not, grab the old standbys — a bucket and a brush — to clean the sticky stuff off the anchor and chain before storing them.

8. **Put the anchor away.**

   If your anchor gets stored on a bow roller, make sure that it's safely secured in place before setting sail. If your anchor, chain, and line get stored in a compartment on the bow, make sure that the anchor line is neatly flaked back and forth in long sections so it stays untangled. If you're storing the anchor down below, see Chapter 4 for details on how to coil a rope.

Anchoring under Sail

Anchoring under power is much easier than anchoring under sail; the sails are out of the way, the boat is easier to control, and the entire crew can concentrate on the task at hand. But if you don't have an engine, anchoring under sail is certainly possible and may be necessary if the wind dies.

REMEMBER

We recommend dropping, folding, and stowing the jib (or furling, if your boat has a roller furler) before approaching the drop spot so that the anchor team has room to do its work.

The key to anchoring under sail is boat control — slowing the boat to a stop at your desired anchor drop spot and then *backing the mainsail* (pushing the boom out so that the main fills backwards) to go in reverse until enough scope is out to get the anchor to set. When you first back the main, put the tiller or wheel in the center. After you start sailing backward, you can swing the stern to the left (to port) by turning the helm to the right (to starboard), and vice versa. Be careful not to oversteer; a little rudder movement goes a long way. Practice going backward out in the open with no anchor involved until you get it right. After you master sailing backward, the steps for dropping the anchor are the same as in the preceding section.

All boats are less maneuverable at low speeds, and sailboats can be tricky to get going again. So the toughest part of anchoring under sail is that for a moment, you intentionally stop the boat, and you lose steerageway until you pick up speed in reverse. This loss of maneuverability is why we recommend practicing first in open water. Leave your mainsail up (and luffing) until you're sure that you're safely anchored so that you can easily escape under sail if you have any problems.

REMEMBER

If you do lose steerageway and are stopped, pointing straight into the wind, you're simply in irons. As in the case of anchoring under power, you want to drop the anchor and begin going backward to add scope. But if you aren't yet at your desired anchoring spot, you need to get out of irons and get moving forward again. Put the tiller or wheel to one side until the boat is pointed on a reaching angle; then you can trim your sail and get going again. (See Chapter 5 for more information.)

Tackling Anchoring Problems

As the preceding sections illustrate, you need to consider many factors before anchoring. Whether you plan to leave your anchored boat for a picnic on the beach, go for a quick snorkeling trip, or just want some peace of mind while you fall asleep down below while at anchor, here's our "what-if" section, offering solutions to the most common anchoring problems:

- **You lose your anchor.** Who gave the anchor a "heave-ho" without first tying the bitter end of the anchor line to the boat? If you don't have a spare, you'd better head for a dock. This possibility is why it's so important to check your ground tackle — and every shackle — carefully before using it.
- **You start swinging too close to another boat.** Some boats "sail" around quite a bit under anchor, powered by the force of the wind on the mast and hull. You can't do much to prevent this movement. But if you're swinging too close to another boat, either due to "sailing" or a shift in the wind, one boat (or

both) has to pick up anchor and move farther away, or put out a stern anchor to keep the boat from swinging. (For more on setting a second anchor, see "Looking at Advanced Techniques" later in this chapter.) Etiquette says the boat that anchored last has to move, but if no one is aboard the other boat, you've pulled the short straw.

- **You think your anchor starts dragging, maybe hours after you anchored.** Keep in mind that your boat swings around the anchor (in a circular arc) depending on changes in the direction of the wind and current. The compass bearings that you took to double-check that you were securely anchored won't be valid if your boat swings 180 degrees, because the current switches direction. If the other boats in the anchorage seem to be in the same positions relative to one another, but all of them are pointing in different directions, you've probably swung. Before going to sleep, make sure that you have a strong mental picture of the anchorage and your boat's position. An anchor alarm on your navigation device will help you rest easier (until it goes off!).

  When anchoring overnight, Peter sleeps lightly and checks things on deck periodically, especially during the first few days of a cruise. He always has his phone in bed with him, running a navigation app that is plotting the boat's historical track. He zooms way in so that he can see movements of even half a boat length. When he awakens, unless he sees a big movement (which might be due to a benign wind or current change), he can roll over and go back to sleep.

- **The weather starts getting nasty.** The added load from increased wind, waves, and current may cause the anchor to start dragging. If you know that more wind is coming, consider seeking better shelter. If you decide to stay, let out plenty of additional scope. (In rough conditions, you may need as much as 10:1 scope.) If you have rope in your rode, pull in or let out several feet every few hours to minimize chafe on the line where it goes through the bow chock or roller. If you have a second anchor, you may want to set it (see "Doubling up: Two anchors" later in this chapter).

- **You can't pull up your anchor.** First, make sure that you start directly over the anchor with all the slack pulled out and the anchor rode securely cleated. If the wind shifts, and your boat swings during your stay, you may not be motoring in the right direction to get the fluke(s) to pull out. Try other directions, slowly increasing the engine power to apply more force.

  If you're having a problem getting the anchor on deck after you get it off the bottom, (and your boat isn't equipped with an anchor windlass on the foredeck), you may need to take the anchor line to a winch and grind the anchor up. Make sure that the anchor line has a good lead through the bow chock and back to the winch, without chafing on anything, and stop grinding before the chain touches the hull. Pulling up an anchor by hand can take heaps of strength, so make sure that you're using the strongest people on the boat for the job.

Choosing the Right Anchor

There's no "perfect" anchor. Different types of anchors have their strengths and weaknesses. Most cruising keelboats carry at least a couple of types for that reason. And for something that sailors have used for centuries, it's telling that new designs are still coming out today. Bottom type (sand, grass, rock, and so on), weight and windage of the boat, and holding power required affect which anchor you'd choose if you could wave a magic wand. Most charter/rental keelboats come equipped with an anchor (or two) and rode, but if it's not hanging off the bow roller, you may have to search down below to find it. Although variations abound, sailboats commonly use two basic types of anchors:

- **Lightweight:** The *Danforth anchor* (see Figure 10-7) takes its name from the company that invented it. It's also called the *lightweight* or *fluke anchor.* Because the large flukes bury so well, the anchor is quite lightweight for its holding power. These anchors need a soft sand or mud bottom (two of the most desirable bottom types for anchoring due to their holding potential) to grip properly.

  This anchor is especially popular on dinghies and small keelboats because of its light weight and low profile on board. This anchor isn't perfect, however; the sharp points on its flukes can be troublesome in storage. Cruising sailboats often carry a smaller Danforth as a "lunch hook" with a mostly rope rode for easy temporary anchoring in calm conditions, as well as a primary anchor of the heavyweight type.

- **Heavyweight:** These heavier (for their holding power) anchors have some sort of spade or claw and are arguably the best all-around anchors for larger sailboats (longer than 36 feet, or 11 meters). Their weight helps their performance in hard-to-dig-in bottoms (such as clay, rock, and grass), and when they're dug in, they have a strong grip.

  These anchors come in a multitude of shapes, but the generic names for anchors in this category include Plow, Claw, and Fluke. Figure 10-7 shows three popular anchors of this type. These heavy anchors are often kept secured up forward on an anchor roller hanging out over the bow. You never see this sight on a racing boat; there's too much weight up forward!

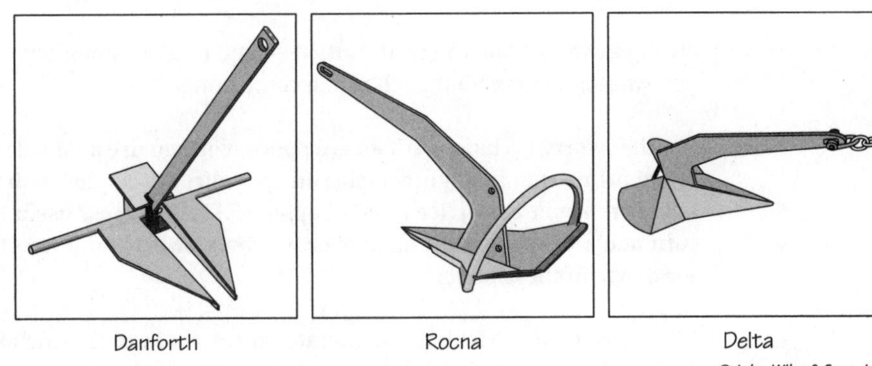

FIGURE 10-7: Three common anchors for sailboats.

© John Wiley & Sons, Inc.

What Size is your anchor?

Size matters when it comes to anchors, and bigger is always better when it comes to staying put but possibly impractical when it comes to storing and handling. A live-aboard cruiser is going to want a bigger anchor than a day sailor/racer. Target anchor size depends on several variables, including the following:

- **Anchor type:** As noted in "Choosing the Right Anchor" earlier in this chapter, lightweight fluke anchors are designed so they don't have to be as beefy as a plow or claw and have the same theoretical holding power. In moderate conditions, a 20-pound Danforth anchor will safely hold a 40-foot (12-meter) sailboat as well as a 35-pound Plow can. You can find anchor-size charts online and at marine stores for guidance.
- **Boat type:** A boat's weight (displacement) gives a good general idea of how hard it will pull at anchor. A loaded-down 40-foot (12-meter) charter sailboat is a lot heavier than a race boat of the same length. But a boat's size and shape also affects the force on the anchor when the wind picks up. Wider (beamier) boats and boats with big masts and lots of standing rigging will pull harder on the anchor when the wind blows on all that stuff.
- **Expected conditions:** Sailors who are cruising for adventure in remote places may have to anchor for longer periods in more extreme wind and wave conditions (and require more grunt in their hook) than those of us who can always head back to our home dock or mooring if a storm is in the offing.

Securing the anchor and rode

The chain is usually connected to the anchor with a *shackle* (a U-shape metal fitting) and to the anchor line (if rigged) with an *eye splice* (a permanent loop woven into the end of the rope) and another shackle instead of a knot. Knots aren't as strong as splices and can come untied — and need we point out that the last thing you want is to have your anchor line come untied?

Another worry is chafe. With an eye splice, you can use a *thimble* (teardrop-shape metal fitting that fits tightly inside an eye splice) to cut down on chafing. (To find out more about eye splices, see Chapter 16.) If you must use a knot, tie a round turn and a couple of half hitches or a fisherman's bend. (See Chapter 19 for the lowdown on these knots.)

TIP

With two strong shackles, you can attach the chain to the anchor line and to the anchor. Use a pair of vise grips or pliers to really tighten the shackles and then *mouse* them: run a few loops of galvanized wire, a small line, or a plastic zip tie" through a hole in the shackle pin to keep it from loosening. Grease the shackle threads first so that they don't freeze up. A galvanized-steel (rustproof) or bronze shackle is best.

Choosing chain

Chain provides an important role in keeping you safe at anchor. (See "Anchoring with all chain" later in this chapter.) If your anchor rode has both rope and chain, the general rule is to have chain that weighs at least as much as your anchor. A 30-foot boat with a 12-pound Danforth anchor, for example, needs at least 16 feet of 1/4-inch chain attached to the anchor. Again, you'll find plenty of sizing guidelines online and at the marine store. As with anchors, shifting up in size and chain length is best if you'll be anchoring in extreme conditions or if your boat is heavier or beamier than average.

Choosing the right anchor line

Don't use just any rope for your anchor line. Here are a few characteristics of a good anchor rope:

- Long enough for anchoring with sufficient scope
- Resistant to chafe
- Stretchy enough to absorb the surging load without yanking the anchor out
- Strong enough to hold your boat in expected conditions

Nylon rope is recommended for anchor lines because it provides the best balance of performance in these key areas.

TIP

So that you can easily tell how many feet or meters of rode you've let out (crucial for figuring out your scope), you can sew or insert small fabric markers into your anchor line at set intervals. Never tie permanent knots in a line for this purpose, because knots weaken the line. Spray paint works well for putting markers on chain.

The basic rule is to use 5:1 scope in average conditions. So assuming that you're anchoring in a maximum water depth of, say, 30 feet, you need more than 150 feet of total rode (chain and rope) for average conditions and more in severe conditions.

WARNING

Resist the temptation to go up in anchor-rope diameter. You get better strength, but you also get less stretch, which is important for keeping the anchor hooked in rough, surging conditions. Also, anchor lines take up enough space on board already; you don't want to increase their diameter unnecessarily.

Maintaining the anchor and rode

A good freshwater hosing after use is important for keeping your anchor gear from smelling like the trash bin behind your local fish restaurant. Because your anchor and rode spend most of the time stored in some dark compartment, inspecting this vital equipment from time to time is important. Check your chain for rusty or weakened links, and examine any anchor line for chafe or wear. If you notice a rusty or weakened link, make sure to replace it immediately.

REMEMBER

The most common place for chafe on an anchor line is where the line has to turn a corner to come on board your boat. A good way to minimize wear is to build a makeshift chafe guard. Slice a short piece of garden hose, and wrap it around the anchor line where it turns the corner over the bow chock. If you're at anchor in rough conditions, periodically pull up (hard) or let out (easy) several feet of anchor line to prevent chafe in one spot.

Anchoring with all chain

Bigger cruising boats (40 feet [12 meters] or longer) often have all-chain anchor rodes (and electric windlasses to pull up all that heavy chain). Obviously, these rodes are much heavier than rope and chain rodes, but chain is also stronger and more durable than rope. A total chain anchor rode enables you to use less scope for given conditions. Although chain doesn't stretch, it can provide critical shock absorption for the anchor because the rode arcs down to the anchor under its own weight. A pulse of wind or wave pushing on the boat simply pulls some of this arc out of the rode, absorbing some of the energy.

Looking at Advanced Techniques

Sometimes, you need to get creative and use two anchors. Or you may need to secure your boat to a seawall (a common method in Europe). We can't complete this anchoring chapter without showing you these two advanced techniques.

Doubling up: Two anchors

Securing your boat with two anchors can help decrease dragging and swinging. One common example is setting two anchors in front of the boat so that when they dig in, the anchor lines create an angle of about 45 degrees (see Figure 10-8). This method is good for really rough weather coming from a fixed direction, because each anchor takes about half the load of the boat's pull. A side benefit is that you can use less scope for the same holding power, but keep in mind that for rough conditions, the more scope, the better. The benefit of two anchors disappears in a big wind shift.

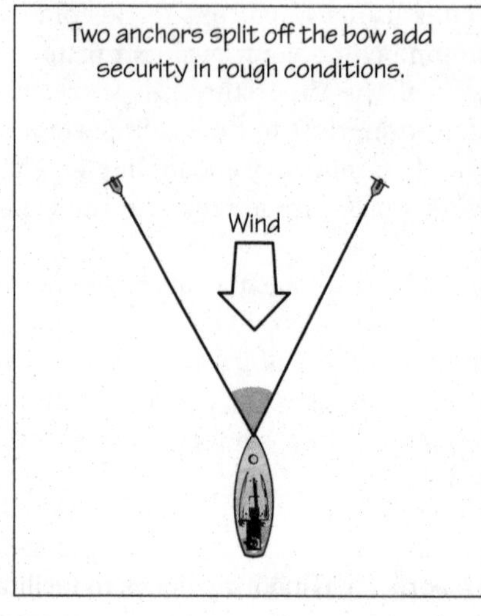

Two anchors split off the bow add
security in rough conditions.
Wind

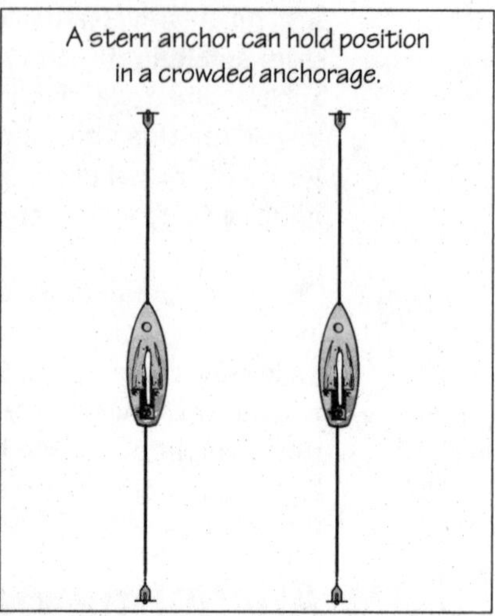

A stern anchor can hold position
in a crowded anchorage.

FIGURE 10-8: Left: Two anchors hold better than one in storms. Right: A stern anchor prevents swinging in mild conditions.

Another common use of two anchors is to set a stern anchor directly opposite the bow anchor to keep your boat from swinging in a crowded anchorage — but only when the weather conditions are quite calm.

Setting double anchors is kind of tricky. You can set them from one boat, but another, arguably easier way is to set the first anchor normally and then send a crew of volunteers out in the dinghy with an anchor and rode to set the second one. Make sure that the bitter end of this second anchor rode is attached to the anchored boat first!

When Peter was with an ESPN documentary team cruising around Cape Horn and the Beagle Channel, the crew used a variation of this anchoring system. The boat was in the middle of nowhere, and often, the water was very deep right up close to shore. To get nestled in as cozily as possible and out of the icy blasts of the *williwaws* (sudden gusts of cold air from the mountains), they dropped an anchor offshore and then took the inflatable dinghy into shore with two lines attached to the back of the boat on big spools. When they got to shore, they found the two strongest nearby trees (or rocks) and tied these stern lines to them (see Figure 10-9). This trick certainly was easier than setting out more anchors!

FIGURE 10-9: Skip Novak's charter boat *Pelagic* nestled into a cozy anchorage near Cape Horn.

Photo courtesy of Skip Novak

Doing it Mediterranean style

Guess where this system is popular? Docking in the Mediterranean style, also referred to as *stern to,* enables you to anchor (or moor) very near the shore and to tie up with your *stern* (back end) close to a bulkhead, or dock — when the water is deep enough. Stern-to is the way the superyachts tie up side by side in Saint-Tropez. Many Mediterranean ports have mooring buoys to facilitate docking. If no moorings are available, and you must use the anchor, simply pick the spot on the shore where you want the stern to end up, and drop the hook the appropriate distance straight out from shore. Then back the boat in slowly (under engine power, please), until you get close to the seawall. Secure two stern lines (one from each corner of the back end) to the seawall, and adjust the tension of the anchor rode so that you don't hit the wall but are close enough to step on shore easily, possibly with the help of a plank to bridge the short gap.

3

Sailing Fast: Taking Your Sailing to the Next Level

IN THIS PART . . .

Satisfy your need for speed (comfortably, of course).

Take part in the fun of kiteboarding and windsurfing.

Get an introduction to sailboat racing.

IN THIS CHAPTER

» Recognizing apparent wind

» Using steering methods to go faster

» Hiking out and trapezing

» Roll tacking and jibing

» Surfing waves, planing, and foiling

» Sailing catamarans

Chapter 11

The Need for Speed: Sailing Fast

I wish to have no connection with any ship that does not sail fast; for I intend to go in harm's way.

— JOHN PAUL JONES

Sailing fast. A powerboater may think that this phrase is an oxymoron, but we've gone sailing with a few professional car drivers, and they've been surprised by how fast sailboats can go. Especially on a boat that's low to the water and gets plenty of spray over the deck, you always feel that you're going faster than you really are.

This chapter looks at ways to sail faster and use your weight to get more performance out of your boat. On all dinghies and small keelboats, how and where you and your crew put your weight can improve your boat's performance. This chapter also shows you how to sail fast boats like catamarans and explores the latest go-fast technique: foiling.

Understanding Apparent Wind

Chapter 5 covers the importance of knowing the wind direction. Many of the go-fast tips in this chapter reiterate the importance of feeling the wind. Before you try to sail faster, however, you need to make a close examination of the wind that hits your moving sailboat. The wind you feel on board your boat, when it's is moving, is the *apparent wind*, which is different from *true wind*, or the wind felt by an anchored boat or a flag on shore.

To illustrate the difference between apparent and true wind, imagine jumping on a bicycle and pedaling down the road. If the day is calm, you feel wind in your face (apparent wind). The faster you pedal, the more wind, right? And if the day is windy, the wind you feel in your face (your apparent wind) is the combination of the *wind of motion* (the wind blowing directly into your face, which you create by pedaling fast) and the *true wind* (the wind blowing over the road).

The same phenomenon happens aboard a sailboat: As you move forward, you create a wind of motion that combines with the true wind blowing over the water, resulting in the wind you and your sails feel: the sailboat's apparent wind (see Figure 11-1).

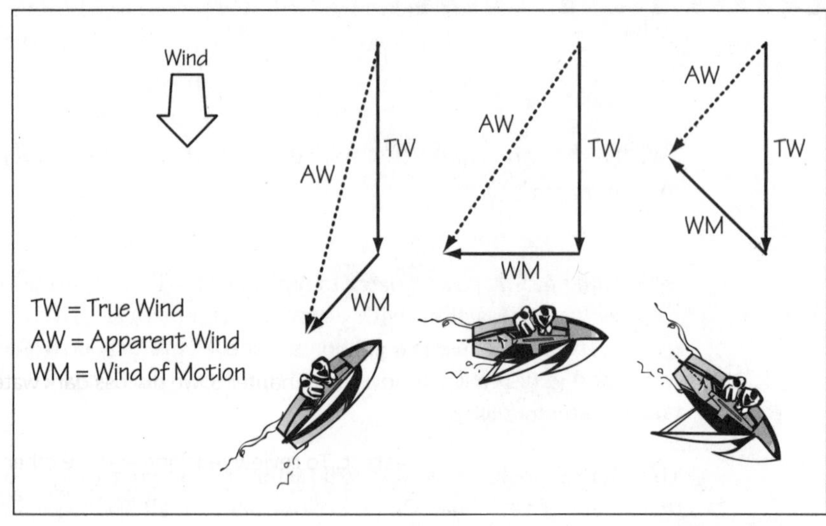

FIGURE 11-1: The apparent wind is a vector sum and is always shifted farther forward (relative to the bow) than the true wind.

On very fast race boats, this capability to make your own wind can have some really amazing results. On most other boats, the difference between the apparent wind and the true wind is more subtle except when you accelerate rapidly, such as when you catch a wave. Here are the key features of apparent wind:

» The faster you go, the more effect your wind of motion has on the apparent wind's direction and velocity.

» Apparent wind is always lighter (less velocity) when you're sailing away from the true wind than when you're sailing toward it. That's why sailing downwind feels warmer than sailing upwind.

» Sailing straight downwind can be slower. Speedy boats such as planing dinghies or catamarans actually sail directly downwind (on a run) to a fixed point more slowly than if they head up and sail on a *broad reach* (deeper than perpendicular to the wind) and then jibe over and broad-reach to that point.

REMEMBER

Don't let apparent wind versus true wind confuse you; the sailor's universe still revolves around the wind that they feel. Just know that as long as your boat is moving, the wind that you and your sails feel is technically called the apparent wind.

Sailing Faster: Go-Fast Tips

A gust of wind hits a beginner's boat, and the boat speeds up, but then the puff goes away and the boat slows again. Keeping your boat fast and getting the most speed out of the conditions requires practice. The following list includes many of the ways to get any boat zooming along and keep it sailing fast:

» **More wind = more speed.** Wind is like boat speed: More is better, but only to a point. Each boat is different, but most boats benefit from increased velocity up to about 15 knots. At that wind speed, beginning sailors should head back to the dock. Going downwind, most boats respond favorably as the wind picks up to 20 knots, but with more wind than that, control becomes a concern. For more on estimating wind strength, check out Chapter 8.

» **In light air, sail for the puffs.** Look for the *dark water,* where the ripples and other signs of more wind are. In Chapter 5, we discuss dark water, which means more wind.

» **Sailing on a reach is fastest.** To review reaching and the other points of sail, refer to Chapter 5. If you had a particular destination in mind and could make the wind blow from any direction, you'd make your course a reach. By sailing on a reach, you can sail on your boat's fastest point of sail and steer a direct course.

» **Sailing to a point straight upwind takes longer than it looks.** Because you have to zigzag your way back and forth to reach a destination directly upwind (as we discuss in Chapter 5), you end up sailing extra distance.

» **Waves matter.** Waves slow you down when you're sailing toward them and can speed you up when you're sailing with them.

» **Wind shifts matter.** Check out Chapter 8 to figure out how to use wind shifts to get to your destination faster.

» **Some boats are faster.** Lots of components determine a boat's speed. As a general rule, a longer boat with more sail area is usually faster, but catamarans and other boats that can *plane* (skim along) or *foil* (lift above the water) are the exceptions to this rule (See the last section of this chapter for more on foiling).

» **Adjust your sail shape for changes in wind speed and direction.** Chapter 12 shows you which ropes to pull to get the perfect sail shape to harness the wind.

Steering Faster: Driving Tips

Just as golfers work on their basic swing, you can improve your driving with practice. To steer faster, try some of the following tips:

» **Steer straight to steer fast.** When most boats are close-hauled or reaching, they exhibit a tendency to turn toward the wind; this tendency is called *weather helm*. Weather helm relates to the balance of all the forces pushing and pulling on the boat, its sails, and its foils. Weather helm is like driving a car that has its front end out of alignment: The tiller or wheel pulls to one side. If you were to release the helm, the boat would turn up until it pointed directly into the wind — dead-center in the no-sail zone.

REMEMBER

But here's something that surprises every new sailor and takes some practice to master: You have to make small steering changes to keep a sailboat going straight. As the wind changes in velocity or the boat changes its angle of heel, the amount of weather helm changes, forcing you to alter the rudder slightly to keep going straight. Although it's disconcerting at first, a little weather helm is natural, and a skilled helmsman develops a good feel for how to make the smallest steering corrections to keep the boat going straight through the changing conditions. Keeping your corrections small also minimizes the speed-robbing drag caused by turning the rudder.

» **Look around.** Find a point (a tree or building) on the horizon where you're headed to make sure that you're steering straight, and look at the sails to make sure they aren't luffing. (Chapter 12 shows you how to use an early warning system called *telltales.*) Then look at the water ahead for approaching wind and waves. Also look around for boats in all directions, back at your point on the horizon, up at the telltales, and so on. Spend 10 to 20 seconds looking at each station.

- **Practice like a pro.** Buddy Melges, the "Wizard of Zenda, Wisconsin," is one of our all-time heroes in sailing. He's won the America's Cup and an Olympic gold medal, but more important, he's a great person who loves to share his knowledge. One time, we asked him how he keeps a keelboat in the groove going upwind in a breeze. He said that he watches the horizon up ahead of the boat and keeps it at a constant heel angle to the bow and luff of the jib. ***Note:*** On a dinghy, flat is fast (sailing with no heel).
- **Find that groove.** *Pinching* the boat (sailing too close to the wind) is obvious because the sails start to luff and lose power. As your boat slows, it slips sideways to leeward more because the rudder and keel (or centerboard) are stalled. If you do stall out and get slow from pinching, ease the sails slightly, bear off 3 to 5 degrees wide of a close-hauled course, and get the water flow going fast again. But you don't want to bear off too far (called *footing*); if you do, you'll be sailing extra distance and away from your upwind destination. Between pinching and footing is the ideal upwind groove, which provides the best compromise of speed versus angle to the wind.

  Trying to reach a point upwind is a balancing act. By pinching, you sail less distance to your destination (because you tack through fewer degrees, as track A in Figure 11-2 shows), but you sail slower. Track B, the intermediate course, provides the best trade-off between boat speed and distance sailed.

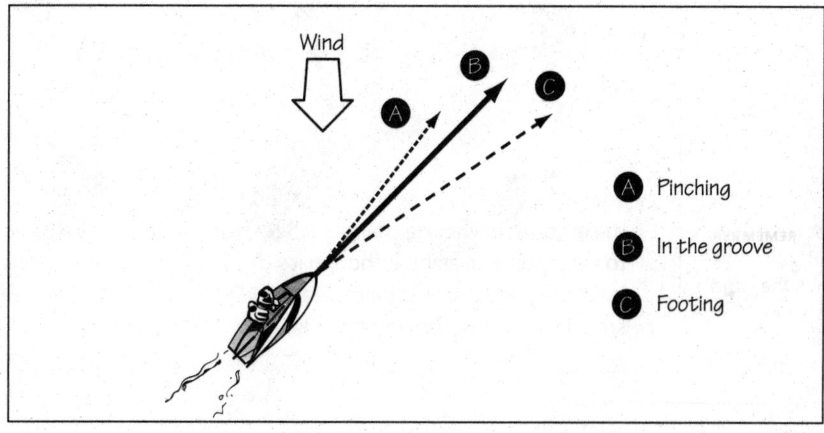

FIGURE 11-2: Three upwind tracks: the pincher (A), in the groove (B), and the footer (C).

TIP

When it's windy, a keelboat's angle of heel can help you find the groove because each keelboat has a maximum heel angle for optimum performance (see Chapter 12). When it's windy, sailing too wide to the wind *(footing)* can cause the boat to heel too far, which can also cause a stall in your rudder (extreme weather helm) unless you let out your sails — but then you're sailing on a reach and not getting closer to that upwind destination (Track C in Figure 11-2). So ease the sails slightly and then head back up to get to that optimum heel angle.

- **React to wind shifts.** All these go-fast tips would be a lot easier if the wind never changed. But the wind is never perfectly steady for long (see Chapter 8). On a sailboat, shifts are named for the effect they have on your sails and the angle your boat can sail (see Figure 11-3). In a *header,* the wind shifts forward. If your sail starts to luff, and you're still pointed in the same direction, the wind has shifted so that it's coming from farther ahead (a *header*). In a *lift,* the wind shifts aft. In either case, you have to alter course or retrim your sails to get back in the groove.

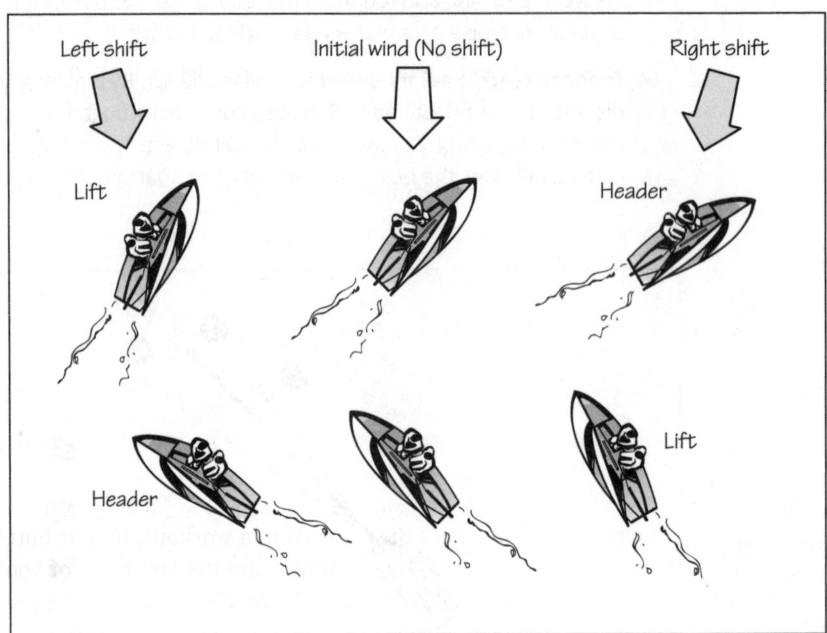

FIGURE 11-3: Wind shifts. In a header, the wind shifts forward; in a lift, the wind shifts aft.

» **Fine-tune your sailing skills on a dinghy.** Because dinghies are much more responsive than keelboats, you develop your feel more quickly when you're sailing a dinghy. In Chapter 5, we cover the basics of sailing a dinghy — an agile, tippy boat. But because dinghies can capsize (some more easily than others), make sure that you review small-boat safety in Chapter 7 and can move your weight quickly. Knowing how to swim is important for dinghy sailing, too, and don't forget your life jacket!

Sailing Flat Is Fast: Ease, Hike, and Trim

The best small-boat sailors can anticipate the changes in wind speed by reading the wind as it comes across the water. They keep their dinghies as flat as possible (not heeled over by the wind) when they're sailing *close-hauled* (toward the wind). Keeping your boat flat is easy in light winds, but to sail like a pro in more breeze when a *puff* (an extra bit of breeze) hits, take one or more of the following three actions to keep the boat from heeling:

» **Hike out.** Lean your weight over the side. Read the next section for tips on hiking your hardest in windy conditions.

» **Ease the mainsail.** Let out the sail slightly to bleed some power from it. When the puff is over, *trim* (pull) the sail back in.

» **Pinch.** Steer the boat a little bit closer to the wind so that the front of the sail begins to *luff* (flutter).

Hiking out

Even on keelboats, moving your weight to the high side helps coax a little more speed out of your boat.

TIP

On a dinghy, *hiking hard* means getting a workout. If your butt is on the rail, you aren't hiking very hard. If your thighs are the last parts of you touching the rail, as shown in Figure 11-4, you're really maximizing the leverage of your body. The following tips can help you hike your hardest in a dinghy:

» **Hook your feet under the hiking straps** (after checking that they're secure and a comfortable length). If you skip this tip, you're going for a swim.

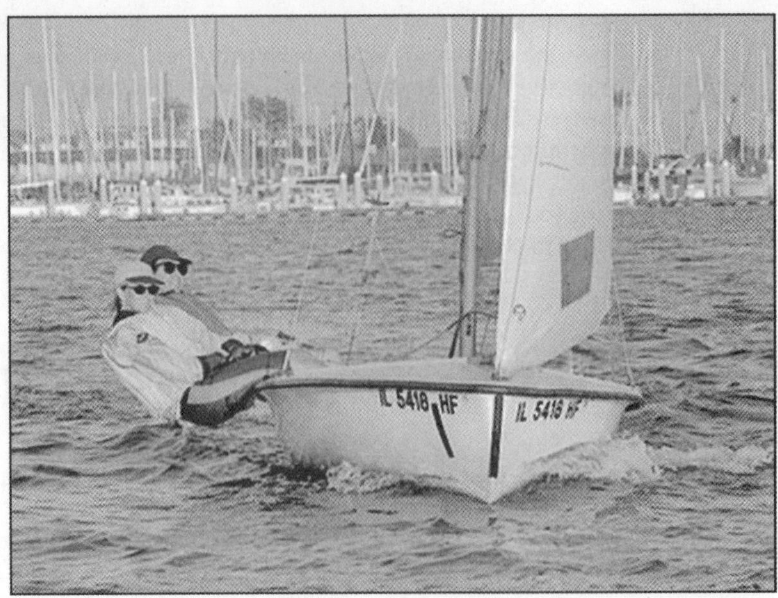

FIGURE 11-4: A dinghy sailor hiking hard.

Photo courtesy of Sally Samins

- **Make sure that the *tiller extension* (hiking stick) is long enough.** The hiking stick connects to the end of the tiller so that you can still steer as you hike out.
- **Make sure that your *mainsheet* (the rope you use to control the trim of the mainsail) is as easy to hold as possible.** Consider adding a ratchet block (see Chapter 5) and/or a cleat (one that's easy to uncleat in a puff!).
- **If you're trimming the jib, hold on to the jib sheet while leaning outboard.** Now you're using arm and leg muscles to hike and getting a great workout.

Trapezing for speed

Imagine that you're sailing on a dinghy in windy conditions and are hiking as hard as you can. Really tall people of equal weight would be able to keep their boats flatter because they have more leverage. Because flatter is faster, off they go. But what if you hike out so far that you're standing on the side of your boat? Then you can pass those boats like you're being shot out of a cannon.

A *trapeze* lets you do just that: stand on the side of your boat to maximize the effect of your body weight. Trapezing is like superhiking. A trapeze system includes a support wire *(trapeze wire)*, which runs from near the top of the mast to a ring just above deck level. It also includes a *trapeze harness*, which you wear with a hook at belly-button level in front, enabling you to hook in to the trapeze wire, as Figure 11-5 shows.

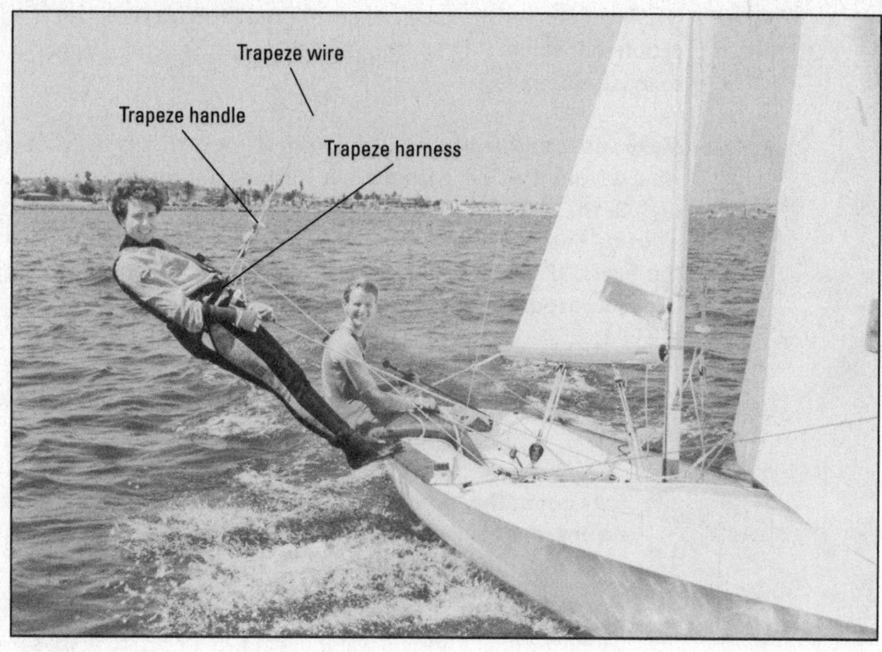

FIGURE 11-5: Pam Healy (JJ's teammate in the 1992 Olympics) on a trapeze.

Photo courtesy of authors

Many dinghies and catamarans are designed to have one or more crew members ride on a trapeze. Trapezing requires athletic ability, balance, and sailing skills (to anticipate wind shifts and to keep from being dragged in the water or flung around the bow by a wave).

The trapeze artist in Figure 11-5 is JJ's 1992 Olympics teammate, Pamela Healy. You're probably wondering how Pam can tack while on a trapeze. As the boat begins the turn, she swings into the boat and unhooks, supporting her weight by holding on to a small handle on the trapeze wire. Then, with her other hand, she uncleats the jib sheet as the boat turns through the no-sail zone. When the boat is on the new tack, she leaps out over the water on the new side, holding on to the handle of the new trap wire. (Yes, the boat has two wires, one on each side.) In her other hand, she trims in the new jib sheet. Finally, she hooks in, and off she goes in one smooth yet fast motion.

Positioning for Proper Fore-and-Aft Trim

Sitting in the wrong position *athwartships* (across the boat) on a dinghy is pretty obvious, because the boat dramatically heels one way or the other. *Fore-and-aft weight position* errors (such as sitting too far back) don't give you an instant indication that something is out of whack, but they're very important if you're looking to maximize speed.

TIP

Make sure that the boat is sitting *on its lines* — that is, level in the water when you view it from the side, with neither the bow nor the stern sitting abnormally low or high in the water. Keeping the boat on its lines usually means sitting somewhere near the boat's *center of buoyancy* (the central point of all the buoyancy forces on the boat). If you could push your boat down with a huge finger, the center of buoyancy would be the point where downward pressure evenly sinks both ends of the boat.

Keep the following basic guidelines in mind to fine-tune your weight position for proper fore-and-aft trim:

- **Stay out of the "ends" of the boat and if you have more than one person on board, sit close together.** Generally, if you sit near the centerboard or keel, you're close to the right spot.
- **In light air, shift your weight forward one or two body widths.** Look at your *wake* (the disturbed water behind your boat) to make sure that you're not dragging your stern.
- **When hiking out or trapezing while sailing upwind, position yourself at the widest point of the boat.** When you trapeze at the boat's *max beam*, you'll generate the maximum leverage.
- **In strong winds, when reaching or running, or if the waves start to come over the bow, move back one or two body widths.** This action keeps the bow out of the water and floats the boat more on the back end, which has a flatter shape, resulting in less drag for high-speed sailing.

Rockin' and Rollin' the Boat

You've heard the expression "Don't rock the boat," right? Well, in most dinghies, if you want to go fast in a straight line, lose the word *don't*. *Kinetics* are techniques for flapping your boat's "wings" (both above and below the water). Kinetics include *rocking* (repeatedly rolling), *pumping* (repeatedly trimming and easing) the sails, roll tacking, roll jibing, and *sculling* (repeatedly turning the rudder back and forth). In windy and wavy conditions, some of these techniques can give you that extra burst of speed that enables the boat to start *planing* (skimming along the surface of the water) and surfing waves.

This section provides several tips to help you master some rocking and rolling in your boat. (Just leave the electric guitar on shore, please.)

Roll tack

Kinetics are so fast that the racing rules restrict them. But intentional rocking is legal during tacking and jibing maneuvers. Experienced dinghy racers have turned this technicality into an art form, rolling the boat during tacks and jibes so effectively that the boat actually accelerates during the turn.

Follow these steps for a successful *roll tack*, as Figure 11-6 shows:

1. **Begin the tack by leaning in slightly, adding about 10 degrees of leeward heel.**
2. **Start turning the rudder just like in any tack.**
3. **When the boat points nearly directly into the wind, hike the boat hard to windward (windward on the original tack) to begin the roll, and trim the mainsheet in tight at the same time.**

   Keep turning!
4. **When your butt is about to get wet, quickly change sides to the new windward side.**

   Normally, you change sides when the turn of the tack is about 75 percent complete (that is, you're almost on the new close-hauled course).
5. **Ease the mainsheet about 1 foot, and trim the jib on the new side.**
6. **As the boat turns onto the new close-hauled course, you and the crew hike (in unison) the boat flat on the new side, trimming the mainsheet back in the amount that you eased it in step 5.**

   The boat squirts forward on the new tack.

WARNING

Be careful — too much roll and over you go in a capsize.

In light air, the skipper's weight alone may be enough to flatten the boat on the new tack. So the crew just moves to the centerline of the boat or whatever position brings the boat level.

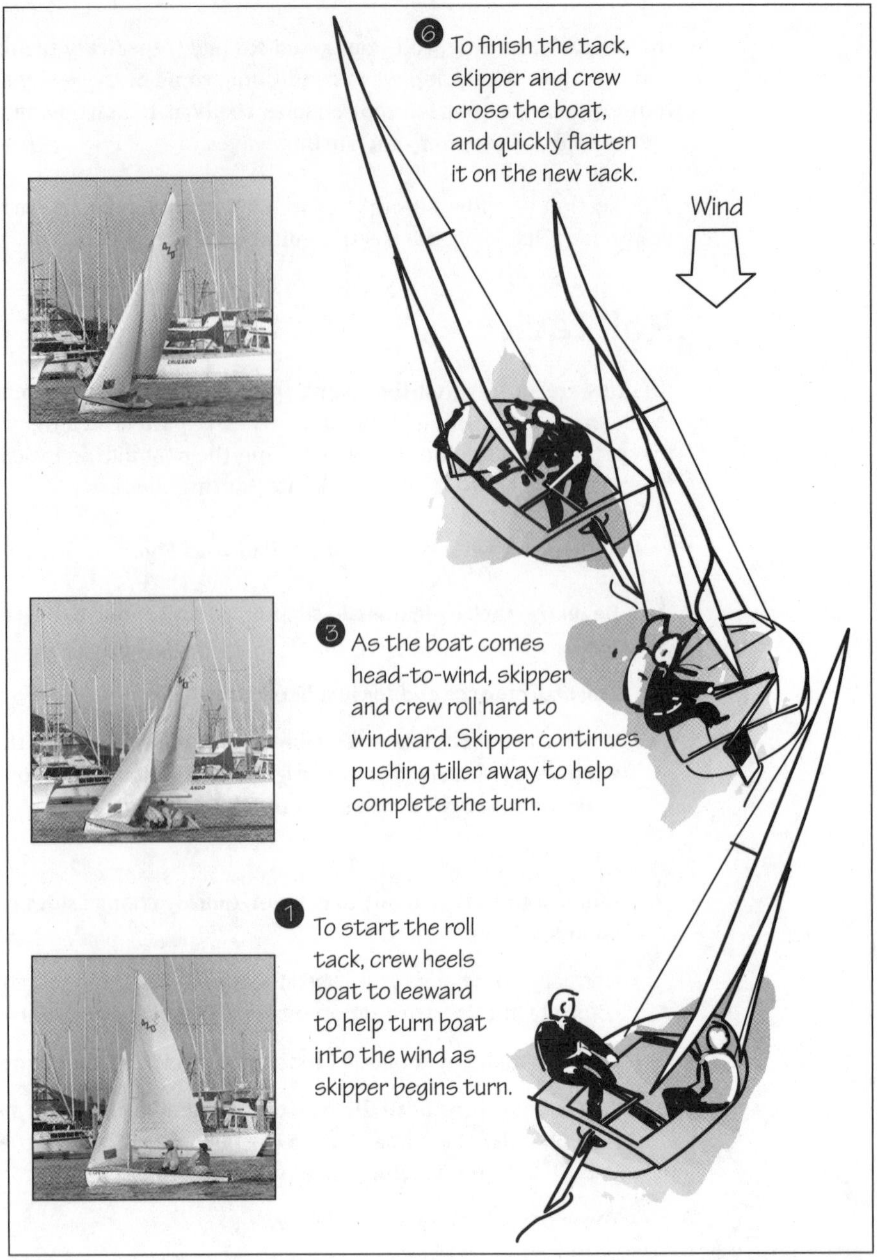

6 To finish the tack, skipper and crew cross the boat, and quickly flatten it on the new tack.

Wind

3 As the boat comes head-to-wind, skipper and crew roll hard to windward. Skipper continues pushing tiller away to help complete the turn.

1 To start the roll tack, crew heels boat to leeward to help turn boat into the wind as skipper begins turn.

FIGURE 11-6: Sequence of a roll tack.

REMEMBER

Roll tacking takes a great deal of practice and coordination between skipper and crew, because you get the biggest roll when the whole crew moves together. Timing is crucial. Starting the roll too early or not hiking hard enough results in a lame excuse for a roll tack that may even slow the boat.

Because of its keel, you and a bunch of your biggest friends won't be able to get much roll out of a keelboat. But by using the preceding rolling tips and keeping your weight on the old windward side until the boat is through the tack, you can still slightly improve the speed of your keelboat tack — especially in light air.

Roll jibe

Roll jibing is very similar to roll tacking and requires just as much practice. Here are the steps to a successful roll jibe:

1. **Heel the boat to windward an additional 10 degrees by hiking out.**
2. **Begin your smooth turn downwind with the rudder.**
3. **Grab the mainsheet, and fling the mainsail quickly across.**

   Alternatively, the crew can grab the *boom vang* (sail control rigged between the boom and the mast) to fling the main onto the new jibe.
4. **Just before your butt drags in the water, quickly switch sides, and gently but forcefully flatten the boat by hiking out with your weight.**
5. **At the same time that you switch sides, give the mainsheet a quick pull in to help acceleration.**
6. **Return the boat to its optimum downwind course, and let the mainsheet back out.**

The initial change in heel for both the tack and the jibe helps start the turn so that you use less rudder motion (which is less drag). The second, more forceful roll gives you that kinetic boost of speed, as though you're flapping the "wings" (sails and underwater foils) of your boat!

WARNING

As the wind comes up, all this rocking and rolling can be a quick ticket to capsize, so be careful. Rocking and rolling techniques work best in light to medium wind. In fact, in heavy air, you may need to hike to windward as the mainsail fills out of a jibe to keep the boat from capsizing. Also, you may need to steer into the turn, as the next section describes.

S-turning in heavy air

An *S-turn jibe* is the opposite of a roll jibe but is the key to staying under control during a jibe when the wind picks up. Follow these steps for a successful S-turn:

1. **Start on a very broad reach.**

   This angle minimizes the turn needed to complete the jibe.

2. **When the crew is ready, bear away (gently) to jibe.**

   Now is the time to pull in the mainsheet fast.

3. **Reverse the helm about 15 degrees at the split second in the turn when the boom catches wind on the new side and begins to blow across the boat, steering the boat back toward the old jibe, as Figure 11-7 shows.**

   This "S-turn" counteracts the momentum of the boom and keeps the boat from heeling too far when the mainsail fills on the new jibe.

4. **A second later, just after the mainsail fills with a bang on the new jibe, reverse the helm again, and steer straight (or wherever you need to steer to be on a very broad reach on the new jibe).**

   Have your crew keep the boat flat throughout this maneuver. Everyone may have to hike out right out of the jibe to keep the boom from touching the water.

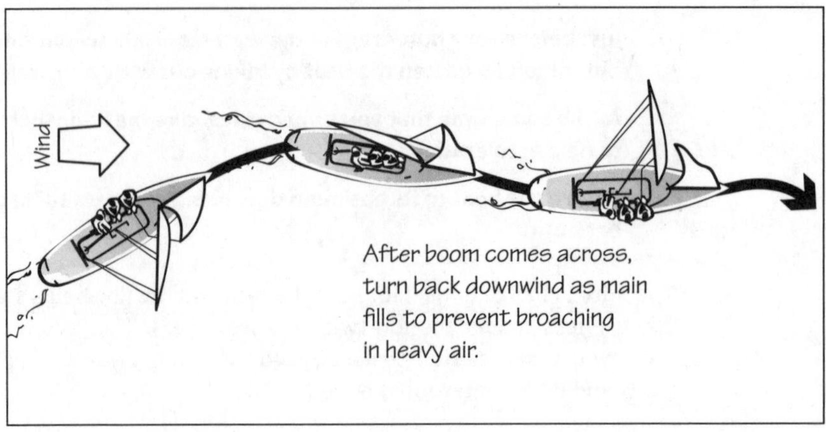

Wind
After boom comes across, turn back downwind as main fills to prevent broaching in heavy air.

FIGURE 11-7: An S-turn jibe.

You've gotta rock it

You can actually rock your sailboat back and forth to generate a good head of steam when absolutely no wind is blowing, as Figure 11-8 shows. On a light dinghy, rocking works better than paddling.

Here's how to rock your boat to generate your own wind:

1. **Put the centerboard/daggerboard all the way down.**
2. **Set the sails to a loose close-hauled trim.**

FIGURE 11-8: No wind? No problem. Rock your boat home.

Photo courtesy of Sally Samins

3. **Have the skipper hold the tiller straight or, if single-handing, let the tiller go where it pleases.**

   Alternatively, the skipper can practice *sculling,* repeatedly turning the tiller hard to one side and then the other, propelling the boat forward.

4. **Violently rock the boat one way.**
5. **Right before the boat begins to capsize (which is always a risk if you aren't careful), violently rock the boat back the other way.**

   Having the primary "rocker" stand up and hold the mast helps.

6. **Continue until you reach your destination or collapse from exhaustion.**

Planing and Surfing the Waves

Nothing compares with the thrill of sailing a small dinghy on a high-speed reach, with water spraying off the bow like a fire hose. You may be going only 10 or even 20 knots, but the sensation of speed is greater than going four times that fast in a car. Really!

Most heavy keelboats are stuck within the bow and stern waves that they create as they cruise through the water. But given enough power from the wind, light dinghies can jump over those waves and skim over the water, similar to a speedboat or a surfer.

If you have enough wind, this skimming action, called *planing*, doesn't require any special action on the part of the crew. As soon as you begin to plane, you know it — because of the huge smile that spreads across your face as you realize that you're going faster than you'd thought possible.

A close cousin to planing is *surfing*. Technically speaking, planing occurs any time the boat breaks free of its own bow and stern wave and then rips along, regardless of the texture of the water's surface. Surfing happens when a wave *crest* (top) grabs the boat and gets it speeding along, sliding "downhill" on the face of the wave.

WARNING

When we talk about surfing the waves, we're not talking about going in close to the shore break. You have a mast overhead, a mast that would get crumpled if you capsize in the surf close to shore — not to mention what would happen to you and your boat.

The great thing about surfing waves is that you can surf ocean swells, powerboat wakes, or anything with a slope to it. Because waves usually run the same direction as the wind, your best chance to catch them is sailing on a broad reach or a run.

Any surfer can tell you that to catch a wave, you need to be going close to the wave's speed. On a sailboat, you may need to use kinetic techniques (such as rocking and pumping) to accelerate your boat when the wave starts to pick up your transom.

To start your surfing career, follow these easy steps:

1. **Get the boat pointed on a broad reach with the sails perfectly trimmed.**

   REMEMBER

   If the boat has a spinnaker, use it for extra horsepower. See Chapter 12 for details on how to use a spinnaker.

2. **If you have a centerboard or daggerboard, pull it up partway.**

   This action reduces the drag underwater and is good practice anytime you're sailing off the wind.

3. **When your boat is pointed downhill on the wave and is starting to accelerate, give a good pump to the mainsheet by pulling it in 3 feet (1 meter) or so very fast and then releasing it immediately.**

   If you're reaching with a spinnaker, you can pump it too. The boat scoots forward and starts to shoot down the face of the wave.

4. **Quickly slide your weight back in the boat to raise the bow out of the water and enable the boat to sit on the flatter (more surfboard-shaped) back half of the hull.**

Now you're surfing, and you can steer the boat straight down the face of the wave. You need to trim your sails, because your apparent wind moves forward the more you accelerate. Refer to "Understanding Apparent Wind" at the beginning of this chapter.

WARNING

Don't get greedy! Don't stay surfing one wave so long that your bow plows into the back of the wave ahead of you, flooding the cockpit with water.

5. **As you get near the bottom of the wave (the *trough*) and the bow starts to point uphill, turn to windward about 10 to 20 degrees to try to stay riding on the downhill portion of the wave or at least build speed so that wave passes under you.**
6. **When you feel the boat slow, slide forward to your normal position.**

Sailing on a Catamaran

If you know how to sail a keelboat or dinghy, you can sail a catamaran, or vice versa. A *catamaran*, also commonly referred to as a *cat*, is simply a sailboat with two hulls instead of one. Figure 11-9 shows a basic cat. Sure, some multihulls are big, heavy cruisers, but we're talking about the kind you launch off a beach, around 20 feet (6 meters) or smaller. Note that a cat has some features you don't find on other sailboats, including a crossbar to hold its unique twin hulls in place, the *trampoline* (rope mesh or fabric surface between the two hulls), full-length battens in the mainsail, and a rotating mast to optimize sail shape.

Because the principles of sailing a catamaran are the same as for any boat, this section focuses on some areas where you run into significant differences.

Making your own wind

The big difference between cats and dinghies is their speed. Cats are faster on almost every point of sail, in every wind condition. The reason for the speed is twofold: The narrow hulls cause very little drag, and the wide wheelbase enables the crew to sit very far away from the sails, providing great mechanical advantage to keep the boat from heeling. The added width is sort of like having a supertrapeze. In fact, many cats have trapezes too!

Although catamarans, like any other boats, can sail directly downwind with the wind dead astern, the faster way to get downwind is to broad-reach one way and then jibe and broad-reach the other way, in a zigzag route. Although you sail a longer distance than when you steer straight downwind, the extra speed generated by reaching up and making some of that magic apparent wind is usually well worth the trouble.

FIGURE 11-9: A catamaran flying a hull.

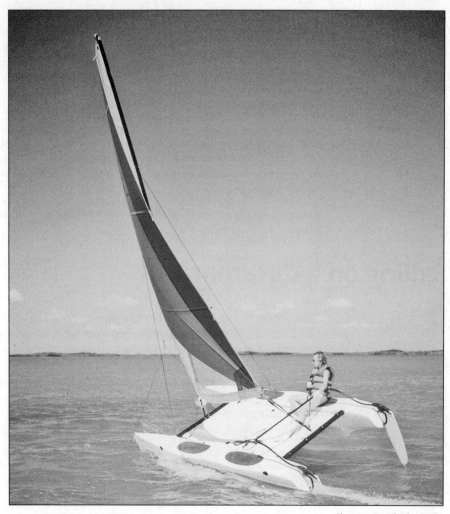

Photo courtesy of Hobie Cat Co.

Flying a hull

A catamaran doesn't heel over; it flies, which is certainly the feeling you get the first time the windward hull (which you're sitting on) lifts up out of the water. *Flying a hull* is the same thing as *heeling* on a monohull; it just looks cooler because the windward hull is so high above the water. If you go too far, though, you invite a capsize (reducing your cool factor to zero).

For maximum speed, you want to have the windward hull just kissing the waves, which minimizes the drag of the craft going through the water but maximizes the efficiency of the sails and foils. You can get the hull back down closer to the water the same way you reduce heel in a dinghy, by

- Hiking out harder (or using your trapeze)
- Easing the mainsheet a few inches to bleed power from your biggest sail
- Turning the boat toward the wind to bleed power from the sails by pinching

Pinching works fine in most conditions. But if conditions are windy, you can fly a hull when sailing very close to a dead-downwind course. In this case, turning the boat toward the wind adds power into the sails, and the boat heels even more. The correct reaction, then, is to bear away more to slow the boat. The only way to know which way (toward or away from the wind) will depower you best is to pay attention to your heading relative to the true wind direction.

Trimming your fully battened sails

Almost all catamarans have a fully battened mainsail — that is, the battens in the sail go all the way from *leech* to *luff* (back edge to front edge). The extra support from the long battens enables the sailmaker to build more area onto a given mast-and-boom combination. Fully battened sails aren't unique to catamarans, but watching the leading edge of the sail for the small bubble that indicates slight undertrim can be difficult because they don't luff as dramatically as "soft" sails. Make sure that your mainsail has *telltales* (see Chapter 12).

Tacking made easy

Not all catamarans are created equal, and some can be difficult to tack. If you find yourself on a cat that wants to get stuck head-to-wind, try these steps:

1. **Make sure that you're going as fast as possible on a close-hauled course.**

   Do this before starting your tack.

2. **Pick a smooth spot in the waves to begin the turn.**

   Hitting a big wave in the middle of the turn can stop your boat.

3. **Turn the boat in a fairly sharp arc.**

   Catamarans lose momentum quickly, so keep that tiller hard over.

If the boat has a jib, keep it cleated on the old tack, and let it *backwind* (fill backward) as the boat turns through the wind. At the same time, release the mainsheet so that it's free to run. The backing jib and eased mainsail combination helps spin the boat down onto the new close-hauled course.

If the boat doesn't have a jib, completing the tack can be difficult. Often, the boat loses too much momentum and ends up stopping as it comes on a course pointed directly at the wind direction. Congratulations — you're in irons. Check out Chapter 5 for directions on getting out of irons. Next time, try jibing instead.

Recovering from a capsize

When catamarans capsize, you can be in for some real excitement. If you aren't careful, you can get catapulted from the high side and land on the sail or the mast. See Chapter 7 for the basics of righting a capsized boat. This section has tips just for cats.

The following steps can help you recover from a catamaran capsize.

1. **Rig your cat with a *righting line.***

   This inventive piece of equipment is a fairly thick (mainsheet-size) piece of rope rigged for easy access in the event of a flip.

2. **Avoid falling off the boat, if at all possible, by holding onto a *shroud* (wire that supports the mast) or some part of the trampoline or hull.**

   If you do fall, try to land feet first (presuming that you have shoes or booties on) with your knees bent.

3. **Prevent the boat from *turning turtle* (flipping over all the way so that the mast is pointed straight down).**

   WARNING

   Recovering from a turtle is much harder than recovering from a regular capsize, when the mast stays horizontal on the water. If you're clever enough to still be high and dry on the upper hull, get off: Your weight on the upper hull isn't helping the situation and may in fact be adding more pressure to sink the mast. Fortunately, most production cats have sealed mast sections or a float attached to the top of the mast that inhibits the boat turning turtle.

4. **Lean your weight (and your crew's) out on the extended righting line (as Figure 11-10 shows) to pull the boat upright.**

   Release the sheets first so the sails don't fill when they do get dry again. Then try to get the boat to rotate around so that the bow points into (or close to) the wind direction. You may be able to rotate the boat simply by standing on the "lower" bow, adding drag so that the stern blows downwind more. If that strategy doesn't work, you can try swimming the bow upwind — a tiring task! Popping the battens in the mainsail so that they're convex (looking down on the boat) can also help you right the boat, because as the sail begins to come out of the water, the wing shape of the mainsail helps lift the mast farther out of the water.

FIGURE 11-10: Using a righting line to add leverage and right a capsized catamaran.

Photo courtesy of Hobie Cat Co.

5. **When the boat begins to come upright, the cat reaches the critical point of balance, and the upper hull falls down fast.**

WARNING

Watch out for falling hulls! Stay clear of the hull and the *dolphin striker* (the support strut mounted to the front crossbeam below the mast), if your cat has one. As the boat comes upright, have the crew hold on to the lower hull to prevent the boat from continuing to roll over and capsize the other way.

If you capsize on a boat that doesn't have a righting line, you may be able to create a makeshift one by tying a rope (the jib sheet may work well) to the mast or "upper" trampoline support bar. The mainsheet is also a possible righting line, but first make sure that it's long enough and rigged in such a way that you aren't pulling up a sail full of water and that the sails will still be fully eased and luffing as the boat is righted. Otherwise, the sails may fill with air as the mast comes up, and the boat may flip over again.

Foiling above the Water

Another way that certain boats gain speed is by lifting up above the water on *hydrofoils*, also simply called *foils* (shaped underwater wings that allow a boat to lift above the surface of the water). Foiling increases speed and efficiency by reducing the drag on the hull caused by the wetted surface and the formation of waves.

Sailing a foiling dinghy, like the Moths shown racing in Chapter 14, requires advanced skills, as the boat can be unstable when it isn't foiling due to its ultralight construction. But newer foiling dinghies like the Skeeta (shown in Figure 11-11) and Fulcrum Speedworks' UFO are more user-friendly, with wider hulls that makes them more stable at low speed. Another option, albeit pricier, is the F101 foiling trimaran.

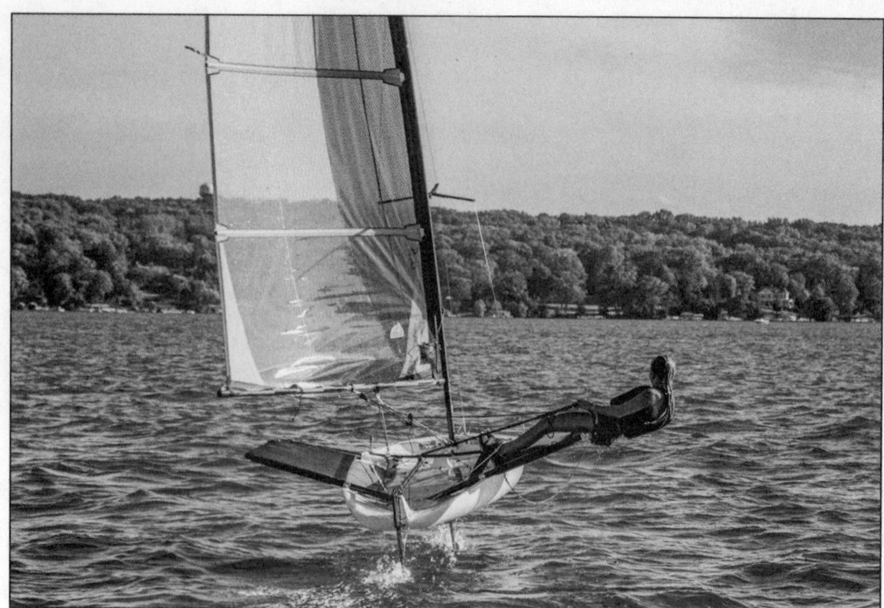

FIGURE 11-11: The foiling Skeeta in action.

Photo courtesy of Harry Melges III

If you do get a chance to try a foiling boat, the best way to get a boat on its foils is to go as fast as possible. In other words, use the go-fast skills listed throughout in this chapter: Start on a reach and hike, and trim and pump the mainsail to get enough forward speed that the flow over the foils will generate enough force to lift the boat up and above the water. Check out Chapter 13 to learn how to foil on a kiteboard and a windsurfer.

IN THIS CHAPTER

» Making sure your sails aren't stalled

» Adjusting the sail shape

» Controlling the power in your sails

» Going fast downwind with spinnakers

Chapter 12
Trimming Your Sails for Speed

A wet sheet and a flowing sea,

A wind that follows fast,

And fills the white and rustling sail,

And bends the gallant mast.

—ALLAN CUNNINGHAM

If your sails are the engines of your boat, the lines you use to adjust your sail shape, also known as the *running rigging*, are your throttle. Because the wind and seas are rarely perfectly steady, the optimum shape of your sail changes according to the weather conditions, just as the wing of a fighter jet is different in shape from the wing of a glider because of their dissimilar speed and lift requirements.

To optimize boat speed, some boats use different sails for different points of sail or wind strengths. For the best downwind speed, for example, you might fly a *spinnaker*, a parachute-like sail.

In this chapter, we discuss how to adjust the shape of your sails, how to control the power in your sails, and how to use spinnakers — all to garner more speed.

When in Doubt, Let It Out

After you get your sails trimmed perfectly at the beginning of the day, you can just *cleat* them (tie them off) and ignore them, right? Wrong. The angle of the sails to the wind can easily change if

- **The wind shifts.** Many factors can cause a change in the wind direction; check out Chapter 8 for more on wind shifts.
- **You turn the boat.** Every course change requires a change in sail trim.

When the angle of the sails to the wind is wrong, the boat slows or may even stop. So how can you tell whether your sails are *trimmed* (pulled in) just right? Looking up at the sails is your best and fastest indication of improper trim. In simple terms, sails can be undertrimmed, overtrimmed, or perfectly trimmed:

- An *undertrimmed* sail — one that isn't pulled in enough — is fairly obvious: The sail *luffs,* which means that it's spilling air and thus losing power.
- An *overtrimmed* sail — one that's pulled in too much — is a more devious animal. It also slows you down, but it's harder to see because it still appears to be full of wind. If you could see the air molecules as they travel over an overtrimmed sail, however, you'd see that the airflow is *stalled* (turbulent, not smooth), as Figure 12-1 shows. As you know from any air-disaster movie, a plane that has stalled can't fly because the wings can't generate *lift* — and lift is what makes a sailboat move.
- A *perfectly trimmed* sail is constantly adjusted to maintain that perfect trim. "When in doubt, let it out" is the first rule. Ease the sheet out until the sail just starts to luff; then trim it back in an inch. Repeat often (unless you're out for a relaxing cruise, in which case just cleat the sheet and grab a refreshing beverage instead).

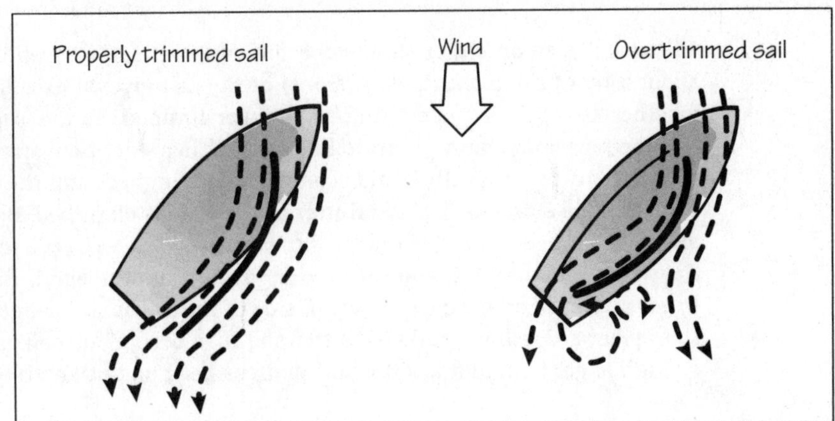

FIGURE 12-1: Wind flow over a properly trimmed sail (left) and stalled flow over an overtrimmed sail (right).

© John Wiley & Sons, Inc.

Relying on Telltales

Another way to tell whether your sail is stalled is to use telltales as an early-warning system. *Telltales* are little strands of yarn or cassette tape that are attached (usually with tape) to the sail. Telltales are more sensitive to changes in the flow than the sail is, so they luff sooner than the sailcloth does. See telltales in action in Figure 12-2.

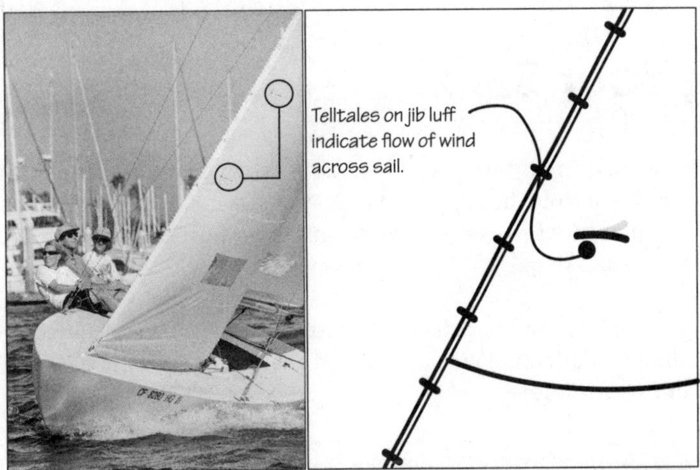

Telltales on jib luff
indicate flow of wind
across sail.

FIGURE 12-2: Telltales on the jib luff help you trim your sail and steer at the correct angle to the wind.

Photo courtesy of Sally Samins; illustration © John Wiley & Sons, Inc.

Telltales placed on either side of the forwardmost sail (the jib, if you have one) about a foot back from the *luff* (front) of the sail give an excellent indication of whether the sail is undertrimmed or overtrimmed. If the sails are perfectly trimmed for your course, both telltales (on either side) flow straight back. If you turn toward the wind, the sail becomes undertrimmed, and the inside, or *windward,* telltale starts to rise and flutter as the flow is disturbed. Because the sail is already trimmed tight, this flutter is the driver's (*skipper's*) cue to turn away from the wind *(bear away).* If you turn too far away from the wind, the air flow starts to get disturbed on the back *(leeward)* side of the sail as the sail gets overtrimmed, so the leeward telltale starts to flutter and then droop. You can ease the sheet out enough to get both telltales flowing again or head up until both telltales flow.

TIP

When you're sailing close-hauled, you don't really have to keep the telltales flowing perfectly all the time. In fact, a little rise by the inside telltale occasionally is okay, especially in stronger winds. That little movement just means that you're sailing a very fine line, and you don't want to sail any closer to the wind.

On a mainsail, telltales on the luff are less accurate because of the turbulence caused by the mast. Therefore, keep looking for an occasional slight "bubble" in the front of the mainsail, indicating that the sail is just on the verge of luffing, rather than relying on telltales. A telltale placed on the leech of the mainsail (by the top batten is best), however, gives you a quick indication when the mainsail is overtrimmed (and therefore is stalled) because the telltale no longer flows straight back.

Shaping Your Sails

REMEMBER

The most important speed control — your boat's throttle — is the sail's sheet, which controls the angle of the sail to the wind. But if you want to eke out another few percent of power from your sails, you must delve a little deeper into the subject of sail shape.

Your sail is really a wing, generating lift as the wind flows past it. Figure 12-3 shows a horizontal cross section of that seagoing wing with the following measurable attributes:

- **Angle of attack:** This term is simply a technical term for the concept you already know as the angle of the sail to the wind. You measure angle of attack as the angle of the wind to the sail's chord; the sheet controls it. Check out "Controlling the power" later in this chapter for more on the angle of attack at various points of sail.

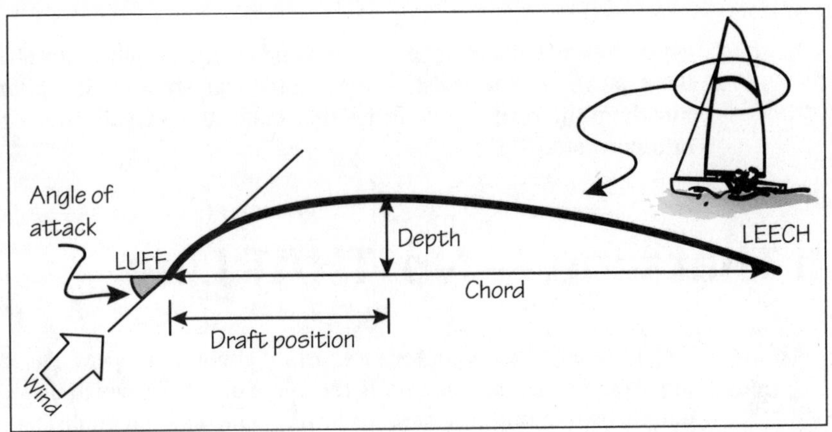

FIGURE 12-3: A cross section of a sail flipped on its side and dissected.

- **Chord:** The straight line between the leading edge (luff) and the trailing edge (leech).
- **Depth:** The fullness of a sail, expressed as a percentage of the depth at the sail's deepest point to the length of the chord.
- **Draft position:** The position of the sail's deepest point, expressed as a percentage of the distance the point is back from the luff to the length of the chord.
- **Twist:** The amount the angle of attack changes vertically in the sail, from bottom to top, as Figure 12-4 shows.

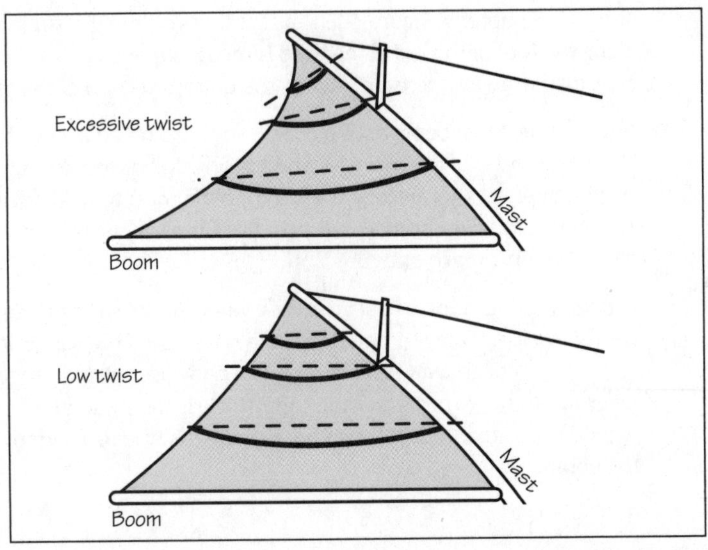

FIGURE 12-4: Mainsail twist viewed from the cockpit.

No one except a sailmaker is concerned with the absolute quantities of depth, draft position, and twist. From a practical standpoint, sailors are interested mostly in the relative quantities that make a given sail deeper or flatter or more or less twisted.

Pull That Line — No, THAT Line

TIP

We've stated it before, but it's important enough to repeat: Far and away the most important aspect of sail trim is the angle of attack, which a sail's sheet controls. Pull the sail in until it just stops luffing, and when in doubt, let it out!

Of secondary importance are a variety of fine-tuning controls. Follow our tuning suggestions in this section to get the sail shape in the correct range for the wind conditions. From there, you can experiment with small adjustments to see whether you can get more performance out of your boat. Here are the basic mainsail controls (shown in Figure 12-5):

- **Mainsheet:** The *mainsheet* is the biggie — the most-adjusted piece of running rigging on the boat — because it controls the sail's angle of attack. When you're sailing upwind, the mainsheet also controls the twist. Read more about twist in "Controlling the power" later in this chapter.
- **Outhaul:** The *outhaul* controls depth in the bottom of the mainsail. Again, getting the outhaul tension in the ballpark is most important, and you can do so by using the same visual cues that you use to determine luff tension (as shown in Chapter 4, Figure 4-13), except that you see the stress or looseness along the foot of the sail. If the wind is moderate or strong, err on the tight side. Increased foot tension flattens the bottom section of the mainsail.
- **Boom vang:** Most boats have a *boom vang* (also called a vang) system to control the twist of the mainsail when sailing downwind. Usually, the vang is a system of pulleys connecting the boom to the mast to hold down the boom. The vang takes over primary twist control from the mainsheet when the sail is eased out on a reach or a run.

TIP

A great starting point is to set the vang when you're sailing close-hauled. With the mainsail perfectly trimmed, pull the slack out of the vang rope and cleat it. Then, as you bear away (turn downwind) and ease the mainsheet, the vang takes up tension. The tighter the vang, the less the twist on reaches and runs. A good rule is to put on enough boom vang that the top batten is parallel to the boom.

» **Traveler:** A secondary control for changing the mainsail's angle of attack is the *traveler,* but not all boats have one. The traveler moves the lower mainsheet attachment point (on the boat) from side to side, thereby changing the angle of attack without changing the sail's twist. When you're sailing to windward in light air after the mainsheet is trimmed for the right amount of twist, pull the traveler to windward so that the boom is on centerline for maximum upwind power. In heavy air, you can reduce power by dropping the traveler to leeward.

» **Backstay:** The *backstay* is the support wire between the top of the mast and the back of the boat. Some smaller boats (and most dinghies) don't have a backstay, and some bigger boats don't have a convenient means to control the backstay tension. But if your boat has a backstay control that's easy to use, you'll love the backstay because it gives you more control of mainsail shape than any control line except the mainsheet. As you tension the backstay, the mast bends, and this bend dramatically decreases the depth of the mainsail.

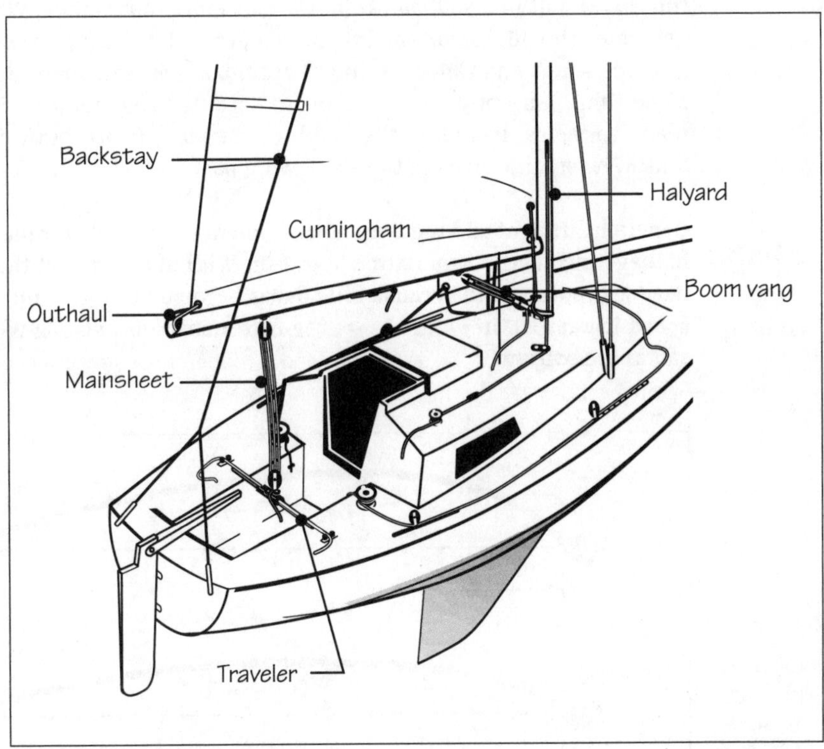

FIGURE 12-5: The sail-shape controls on a basic keelboat.

» **Halyard and cunningham (that clever pig):** The *halyard* is primary and the *cunningham* secondary in controlling the tension in the luff of the sail. Some boats don't even have a cunningham (also called the *downhaul*), a control rope that pulls the luff downward at or near the tack. (In Chapter 4, we discuss the two visibly obvious extremes of luff tension.) Proper luff tension depends on the design and shape of the sail, your point of sail, and the wind velocity. To eke out that last inch of speed, you need to tighten your luff sailing upwind and loosen it downwind. Increased luff tension usually moves the draft position forward and decreases the depth of (flattens) the sail slightly.

Powering Up Your Sails

One great way to picture what variations in sail shape do is to think in terms of power. More power makes you go faster in a race car (until you have to go around the curve), but in a sailboat, things aren't quite that simple. When a wing shape generates the all-important lift, it also generates drag. Therefore, designers of airplane wings and sailors trying to optimize their sail shape are looking for the same thing: an optimized ratio of lift to drag. That ratio varies depending on many variables, including the depth of the wing (sail), draft position, angle of attack, twist, and speed of the air flowing past.

REMEMBER

Generally, in light and medium winds, you need full sails for maximum power; at higher wind speeds, you flatten your sails with more twist at the top because you need less power (and because full shapes become "draggy" and slow as the wind speed increases). In Figure 12-6, the better shape for strong winds is the flatter sail at the bottom.

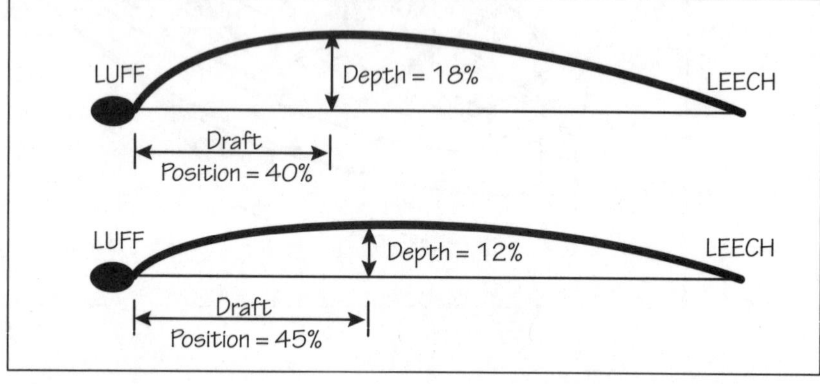

FIGURE 12-6: A fuller, draft-forward sail shape (top) gives you more power for lighter winds.

Controlling the power

We can use this concept of power to describe the effect of variations in sail shape. We start with the most important variations and move to the least important:

- **Angle of attack:** Suppose that your boat is pointed on a *reach* (with the wind coming across the boat), and your sail is luffing — a 0-degree angle of attack. As you trim the sail in with the mainsheet, you increase the angle of attack until the point where the sail gets overtrimmed and stalls, as Figure 12-7 shows. The traveler can also change the angle of attack.

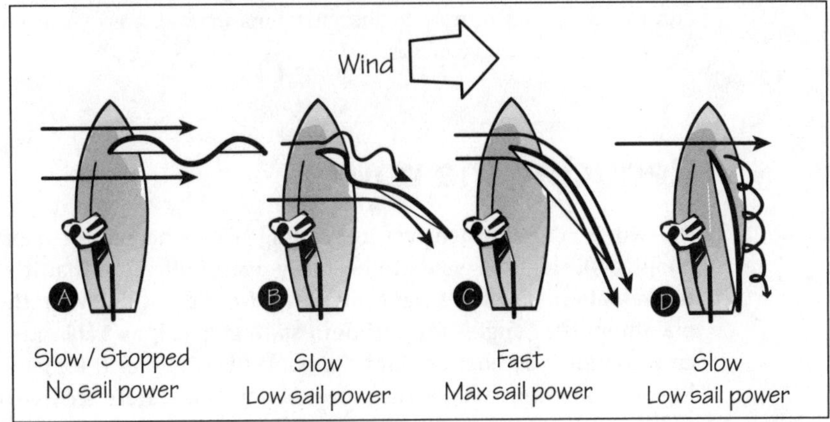

FIGURE 12-7: The angle of attack controls the sail power.

© John Wiley & Sons, Inc.

- **Twist:** If the top of the sail has a 0-degree angle of attack to the wind (it's luffing!), and the bottom of the sail is perfectly trimmed to the wind, the sail has a very *twisty* shape. Power increases with less twist — to a point. (See the nearby sidebar "Why twist at all?") You can power up the sail by decreasing twist to the point that both the top and the bottom of the sail are perfectly trimmed (best angle of attack). The vang and the mainsheet affect twist. For an illustration of twist, refer to Figure 12-4 earlier in this chapter.
- **Depth:** Power increases with depth — at least until the winds get stronger, when a deep shape has quite a bit of drag. You can change the depth by adjusting the outhaul, backstay, and mast bend.
- **Draft position:** Draft position primarily affects the sail's capability to accelerate. Draft farther forward (about 45 percent or so) is a great accelerating shape — good for light or moderate air and waves that constantly slow the boat. Draft farther aft (50 percent or more) is a better shape for straight-line speed in constant conditions. You can move the draft by adjusting luff tension and secondarily by adjusting depth.

WHY TWIST AT ALL?

You may think that zero twist has the most power, but that's rarely the case because of a phenomenon related to friction. At and near the water's surface, friction noticeably slows the true wind as the wind rubs against the water and waves. Moving up toward the top of the mast, the true wind speed increases. This vertical variation in true wind speed causes a situation of great interest to sailors: The apparent wind felt at the bottom of the sails is farther forward (more from the bow) than the apparent wind felt at the top of the sails. (See Chapter 11 for a discussion of apparent wind.) The fact that the wind shifts in direction up and down your sails (as long as you're moving and creating apparent wind) explains why zero twist is usually slow: At some height, the sail is overtrimmed and stalled. In most conditions, to get your sail at the optimum angle of attack at every level from top to bottom (for maximum power), you want to set the sails with a moderate amount of twist.

Reducing the power

On windy days, when you're sailing close-hauled or close-reaching (see Chapter 5), the boat wants to heel way over, indicating that it's overpowered. In this situation, you don't want full power from the sails. When the boat reaches its maximum heel angle (for optimum sailing speed, as Table 12-1 shows) and the crew weight is outboard as far as possible (see Chapter 11 for good stuff about hiking out), you must reduce the power in your sails. Here are five ways to do so:

- **Ease the sheets.** The quickest, fastest, and best way to "depower" your sails is to ease the sheet and decrease the angle of attack. Slowly ease the mainsheet (or the traveler, if it's easier to handle, but keep the jib in unless conditions are really windy), and feel the heel decrease. Stop easing when the heel is at the optimum maximum angle, as Table 12-1 shows. Don't worry if your sail luffs a little bit; you don't want that extra power.
- **Pinch.** Slowly turning the boat toward the wind also decreases the angle of attack. The danger here is that you slow down and stall out your centerboard or keel, so pinching is usually most effective when done subtly and combined with easing the mainsheet.
- **Add twist.** Adding twist is really just decreasing the angle of attack up high, and depowering the top of your sail first is good to do. Add twist by easing the mainsheet and jib sheet slightly. You can also move the jib lead back an inch or three to add twist in the jib, as we describe in "Trimming the jib" later in this chapter.

- **Make the sails as flat as possible.** Bend the mast (tighten the backstay), tighten the luff tension (with the halyard and cunningham), and tighten the outhaul. Some catamarans have systems for rotating the mast to adjust sail shape.
- **If you're still overpowered, reef your sail.** See Chapter 7 for details on how to *reef* (reduce sail area).

TABLE 12-1 **Optimum Heel Angles**

Type of Boat	Maximum Efficient Heel Angle
One- and two-person dinghies	0–5 degrees heel — essentially upright
Larger, heavier dinghies	0–8 degrees
Scows (flat-bottomed dinghies with two rudders)	About 10–15 degrees, to the point where the leeward rudder is straight down
Catamarans	Just enough that the windward hull "kisses" the water
Keelboats	10–25 degrees, depending on the design; you heel more on a keelboat so that the ballast in the keel fin can get some leverage to prevent further heeling

Heel too far, and your rudder and keel will stall and slow you down. When conditions are windy, especially on a dinghy, you have a good reason besides speed and balance to limit your heel angle: If you're heeled over too much, the boom will hit the water when you ease the mainsheet. Check out "Rounding up" later in this chapter to see what happens next in this ugly scenario.

Trimming the jib

The principles of sail shape and trim apply similarly to the jib, but some of the controls we cover in "Reducing the power" earlier in this chapter apply only to the mainsail. Because your jib is the first sail to "see" the wind when you're sailing close-hauled, take a closer look at some of its controls.

REMEMBER

The sheet is the most important control because it affects the angle of attack of the sail. Get the sheet right, and you're doing better than most sailors on the water today! Simply ease out the sheet until the sail begins to luff and then slowly pull it in until the luffing just stops. When in doubt, ease it out! As we discuss in "Relying on Telltales" earlier in this chapter, telltales can be a very effective trim aid on a jib.

The halyard usually controls luff tension on the jib, just like on the mainsail, and the same rules apply. But the jib doesn't have an outhaul to adjust foot tension or a boom vang to control twist. The jib sheet does all that work, with a little help from the jib leads. The *jib leads* (or *jib cars*) are the first fittings (usually, a pulley or fairlead) through which each jib sheet (one on each side) passes as it comes from the sail on its way to the cockpit. (You can check out Chapter 4, where we describe the rigging process of the jib and the jib sheet, if you're feeling a bit confused at this point.)

Jib leads, which typically are adjustable fore and aft, affect the jib's twist. Move a lead too far forward, and as you trim the sheet, it pulls down on the jib leech too much, acting more like a boom vang and less like an outhaul. Move a lead too far aft, and as you trim the sheet, it pulls out on the foot excessively but doesn't pull down on the leech enough. The correct setting is between these extremes, as Figure 12-8 shows.

FIGURE 12-8: (A) Lead too far forward, (B) too far aft, and (C) perfect. The illustration at far right shows the same lead positions.

Photos courtesy of Sally Samins; illustration © John Wiley & Sons, Inc.

As the wind increases, you move your lead back to twist and decrease power in the jib. Some boats, mostly larger keelboats, have several jibs in varying sizes and strengths. In general, you want to use the biggest sail in light winds and the smallest sail in strong winds (for reduced power).

Sailing Fast Downwind

All the principles of trimming sails apply equally well to all points of sail. The only difference is that on the broadest points of sail (when the wind is coming from behind), the boat is heeling less. So to sail faster downwind, you can often increase the power of the sails or put up a bigger, more powerful sail, such as a *spinnaker* (a large, lightweight, balloonlike sail). But if you don't have a spinnaker, or if your crew is on a coffee break and refuses to put it up, you can try some of the following trimming tips for getting more speed from your boat and sails while sailing downwind:

- Make sure that the mainsail and the jib are sheeted properly, right on the verge of luffing. If the wind is coming from too far behind (broad reaching or running), the mainsail can't luff because the boom hits the shrouds, and you may need to *wing out* the jib to get it to fill, as we describe in Chapter 5.
- Ease the luff tension (halyard and/or the cunningham) to make the sails as full and powerful as possible.
- Ease the outhaul to deepen the lower section of the mainsail.
- If the jib is still being trimmed on the leeward side, move the lead forward and outboard (about 1 foot on a 30-foot boat).
- On a dinghy, pull up the centerboard halfway to reduce drag.
- Set the boom vang to limit mainsail twist.

Setting a symmetrical spinnaker

Now for the fun sail: the spinnaker. Setting a spinnaker when you're going on a reach or downwind can be like lighting the afterburners on a jet aircraft. Sailing with a spinnaker is fast, but because it's attached only at the corners, you can easily get into a love–hate relationship with this potentially unruly sail. Fortunately, you have this book, so get ready to love this colorful parachute.

Two types of spinnakers exist: symmetrical and asymmetrical, as Figure 12-9 shows. Flatter asymmetrical spinnakers can also be called *gennakers* because they're designed to be flown like a big jib (*genoa*) but have more sail area, like a spinnaker. They're popular cruising sails because of their ease of use.

We start with the symmetrical spinnaker because as soon as you master that big sail, the asymmetrical is a breeze (bad sailing pun). But, in fact, many of the techniques in this section apply equally to both types of spinnakers.

Gathering your spinnaker equipment

Before you can set a spinnaker, you need the following equipment. Check out Figure 12-10 for a clear illustration:

- **Spinnaker pole:** A lightweight pole that attaches to the mast and supports the tack of the spinnaker when set.

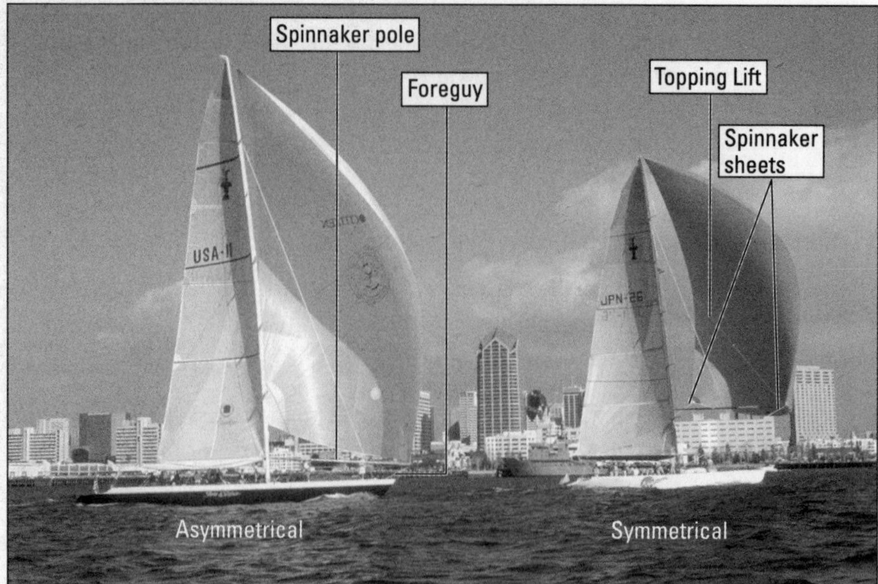

FIGURE 12-9: Two America's Cup boats on San Diego Bay: (left) an asymmetrical spinnaker and (right) a symmetrical spinnaker.

Photo courtesy of Sally Samins

- **Topping lift (also called the *pole lift* or *topper*):** A halyardlike control rope running from the mast, used to lift the outboard tip of the spinnaker pole into position.
- **Foreguy or downhaul:** Rope coming from the foredeck area, used to keep the outboard tip of the spinnaker pole from lifting too high.
- **Spinnaker halyard:** Rope used to hoist the spinnaker.
- **Spinnaker sheets:** Control ropes on either side of the boat used to adjust the sail's angle of attack. When the spinnaker is flying, these sheets change their names: The sheet on the windward side that goes through the fitting at the end of the spinnaker pole is called the *guy* or *afterguy.* The sheet on the leeward side is still the sheet. When you jibe, of course, the sheets swap names because now the wind is blowing on the opposite side of the boat. The number of spinnaker sheets you use depends on the boat's deck layout, size, and jibing method. Some boats employ one sheet per side, and others use two sheets (a dedicated guy and sheet) on each side (lazy guy and sheet method), as shown in Figure 12-10.

Preparing to hoist

Because spinnakers are made of ultra-lightweight cloth, they're most easily stored stuffed into a sail bag, or *spinnaker turtle.* Like its close cousin the parachute, a spinnaker must be meticulously prepared so that it deploys correctly.

Nothing is more frustrating than expecting to see a big, powerful sail fill with air and instead seeing a twisted mass of nylon.

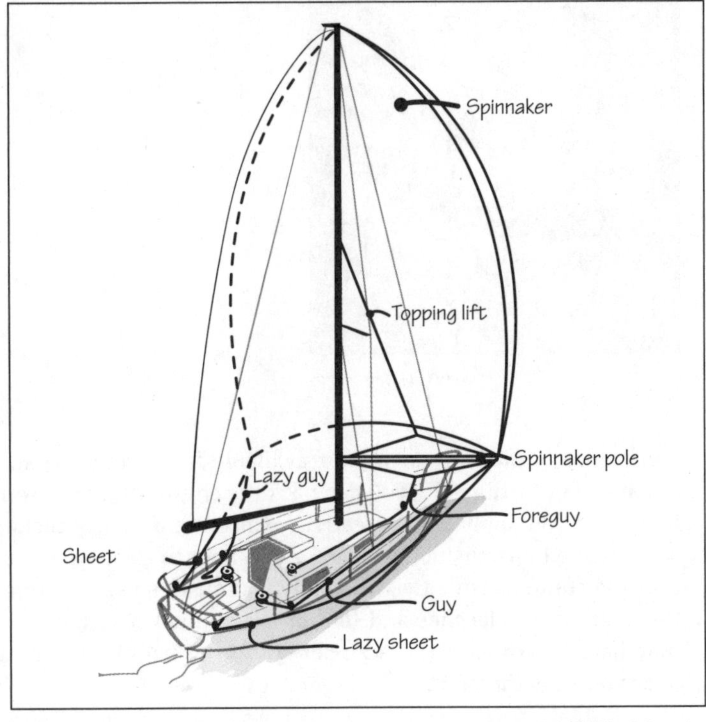

FIGURE 12-10: The equipment for flying a spinnaker. This boat employs a separate guy and sheet on each side.

WARNING

One of the most embarrassing moments in sailing occurs when a crew hoists a sail sideways. Don't laugh, because all of us have done it by mixing up the sail's corners when rigging. To save your pride, make sure that "head" is clearly written on the top corner in permanent marker.

You can choose among several methods of packing the *chute* (sailor's slang for spinnaker), but all of them have one thing in common: When the sail is stuffed back into its bag, all three corners are clearly separated, ready for attaching to their respective sheets and halyard, with no twists in the body of the sail.

As you see in Figure 12-11, packing the chute is easiest on a nice big lawn, where you can stretch the sail out, untangle any twists, and stuff it in the bag carefully, starting on its centerline and working toward the head and the two clews. (Until a symmetrical chute is flying, it's said to have two clews and two leeches.) The three corners of the sail (the head and clews) should be on top.

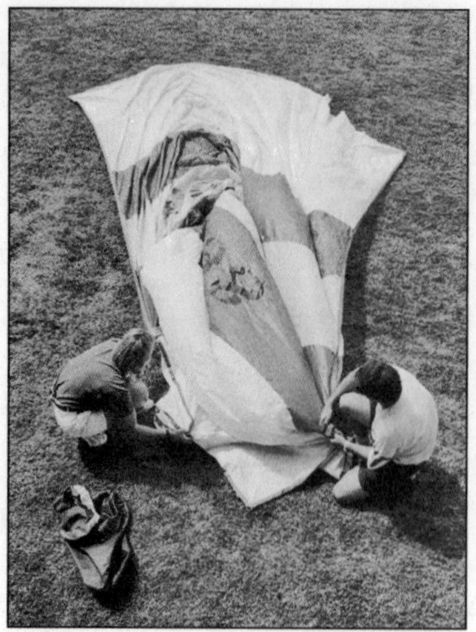

FIGURE 12-11: Packing the chute the easy way, spread out on a lawn.

Photo courtesy of Sally Samins

Sometimes, a nice big lawn isn't available for packing — such as while you're afloat — but fortunately, you can pack the chute within the confines of the boat's interior if you apply some creativity. On a keelboat, try tucking the head of the sail under a bunk cushion or using a slip knot to tie it up forward, and make sure that the chute doesn't twist! Usually, sailmakers use different-colored tapes on the edges of the leeches and foot of the spinnaker to help. Keelboat spinnakers may have Velcro bands or a zipper system to help keep the sail cloth contained once you've gathered it.

On a dinghy, it's best to check that the spinnaker isn't twisted before you launch the boat. Then, on your first take-down, stuff the center of the spinnaker in the bag first and the corners at the end (on top).

TIP

If you're in a rush, your spinnaker still stands a very good chance of setting cleanly if you run one of the leeches (sliding your hands from one edge to the other and making sure there aren't any twists) and don't twist the two corners attached to that edge when stuffing the sail into the bag. Your odds get even better when you run both leeches.

Hooking up the spinnaker

In preparation for the set, the three corners of the spinnaker need to be attached to the three control ropes: the halyard and the two sheets. You may think that hooking up the ropes to the corners is a simple task, but for some reason, this chore is the source of many problems. Here are some tips to make this job easier:

» **All three ropes should follow the same path to the sail.** If the sheets come in under the jib, the halyard should too.

» **Attach the halyard and sheets securely and to the correct corner.** Having written "head" on the head of the sail will really help right now.

» **Make extra-sure that your sheets and halyards are led properly.** Check that you haven't made any loops around stanchions, spreaders, and other paraphernalia in their paths.

Hoisting: The "cruising set"

Being deliberate with each stage of setting the spinnaker pays off. Nothing is worse than a spinnaker filling when it's halfway hoisted, because then the halyard has tons of load as you haul it to the top. Here are the steps for a conservative spinnaker-setting procedure called a *cruising set.* The beauty of this set is that the sail doesn't fill until you're ready for it.

1. **Make sure that the spinnaker is attached to the sheets and halyard properly and that the bag is secured to the boat.**
2. **Connect the inboard end of the spinnaker pole to the mast, attach the topping lift and foreguy to the outboard end, and then raise the pole.**

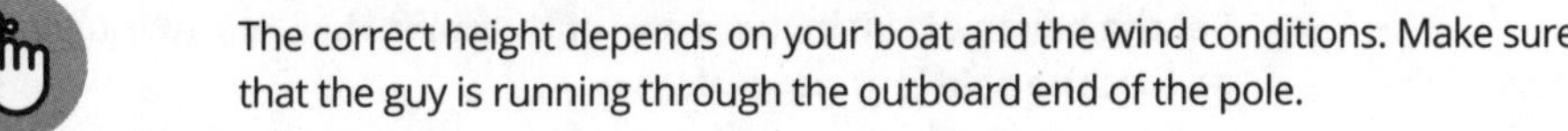

REMEMBER

The correct height depends on your boat and the wind conditions. Make sure that the guy is running through the outboard end of the pole.

3. **Turn the boat onto a very broad reach or run.**

WARNING

Be careful not to jibe accidentally. Turning the boat onto a broad reach or run lets you hoist the spinnaker behind the mainsail — protected from the force of the wind.

4. **Make sure that the crew is ready, and call for the sail to be hoisted.**
5. **As the sail is being hoisted, pull the guy until the clew of the spinnaker touches the pole.**

If you're using winches, make sure that you have enough wraps on the guy's winch drum to take the load when the sail fills. (For more about winch use, see Chapter 5.)

6. **When the halyard is fully hoisted and cleated, set the guy to its proper position, drop the jib, carefully turn the boat onto the desired course, and trim the sheet as required.**

Trimming the spinnaker

Trimming a spinnaker is similar to trimming any other sail. Get the angle of attack correct, and you're off and running. Your spinnaker will inevitably collapse, because it's a relatively finicky sail that requires constant — and we mean *constant* — attention.

TIP

The key to trimming the spinnaker is working through a basic cycle. First, set the guy, then the sheet, and then the pole height. As with every other sail, the control rope that gets the most work is the spinnaker sheet. Here are the steps for spinnaker trim:

1. **Set the guy so that the pole is about 90 degrees to the apparent wind when broad-reaching or -running, and ease it forward so that the pole is almost touching the forestay on tighter reaches.**
2. **Trim the sheet so that the luff of the sail has a small curl in it.**

   If you trim just a little bit more, the curl disappears, and the sail looks completely full. If you ease just a little bit more, the curl gets larger and ultimately causes the sail to collapse.
3. **Set the outboard end of the pole height so that the tack of the spinnaker is level with the clew.**
4. **Set the height of the inboard end of the spinnaker pole (if it's adjustable) so that the pole is horizontal.**

Avoiding a spinnaker collapse

WARNING

If you get a wind shift, or if the driver changes course suddenly or if you just neglect your spinnaker for a moment, it will collapse. Unfortunately, the spinnaker doesn't luff gently when it collapses; it flaps in a loud manner that makes you feel that something is very wrong. The spinnaker can collapse in two ways:

- **Downwind collapse:** In this case, the sail falls into itself, usually caving in on top and ultimately hanging like a limp mass. The cure for a downwind collapse is to turn the boat up toward the wind (about 20 degrees) until the sail fills and/or bring the pole aft (trim the guy) and ease the sheet.
- **Upwind collapse:** When the wind comes too far forward for the trim of the chute (too little angle of attack), the spinnaker luffs completely. The cure is to turn the boat away from the wind until the sail fills and/or trim the sheet.

Jibing the spinnaker

Any maneuver with a spinnaker can be a trial, but thanks to the cruising set (and the *cruising takedown*, which we outline in "Taking the spinnaker down" later in this chapter), the most difficult maneuver is without question the jibe. You know you've jibed successfully when

- The sail fills cleanly on the new jibe with the pole set properly.
- The sail stays full during the entire jibe.
- Nothing (and no one) falls in the water.
- The crew member on the bow comes back into the cockpit with a big smile on their face.

Here are the steps for a successful jibe (and check out Figure 12-12):

1. **Make sure that the crew is ready and in position.**
2. **Turn the boat down to a very broad reach (so that the turn during the jibe isn't very sharp), and retrim the chute accordingly.**

   Work hard to keep the spinnaker full throughout the jibe.
3. **Announce the turn into the jibe by saying "Jibe-ho," "Jibing," "Here we go," or anything else that makes sense.**
4. **As the boat turns, keep trimming the guy back and easing the sheet forward so that the spinnaker stays full (keeps flying).**

   Because the boat's angle to the wind is changing, this step is crucial throughout the maneuver. In a good jibe, you must continue to rotate the spinnaker so that it stays full.
5. **Turn the boat through the jibe while shifting the pole from the old windward side to the new windward side by *tripping* (detaching) the pole ends from the mast and old guy and then reattaching the pole on the new side.**

   REMEMBER

   This step is often the hardest part of the jibe because it requires fancy footwork on the foredeck and coordination on the part of the foredeck team, trimmers, and helmsman to facilitate the switch. During this step, the mainsail must be jibed too. Stop the turn when you're on a very broad reach on the new jibe.
6. **When the pole is attached on the new windward side, the spinnaker is properly trimmed on the new jibe, and the crew is ready, you can turn up to a sharper reach (requiring further trimming of the spinnaker) if you desire.**

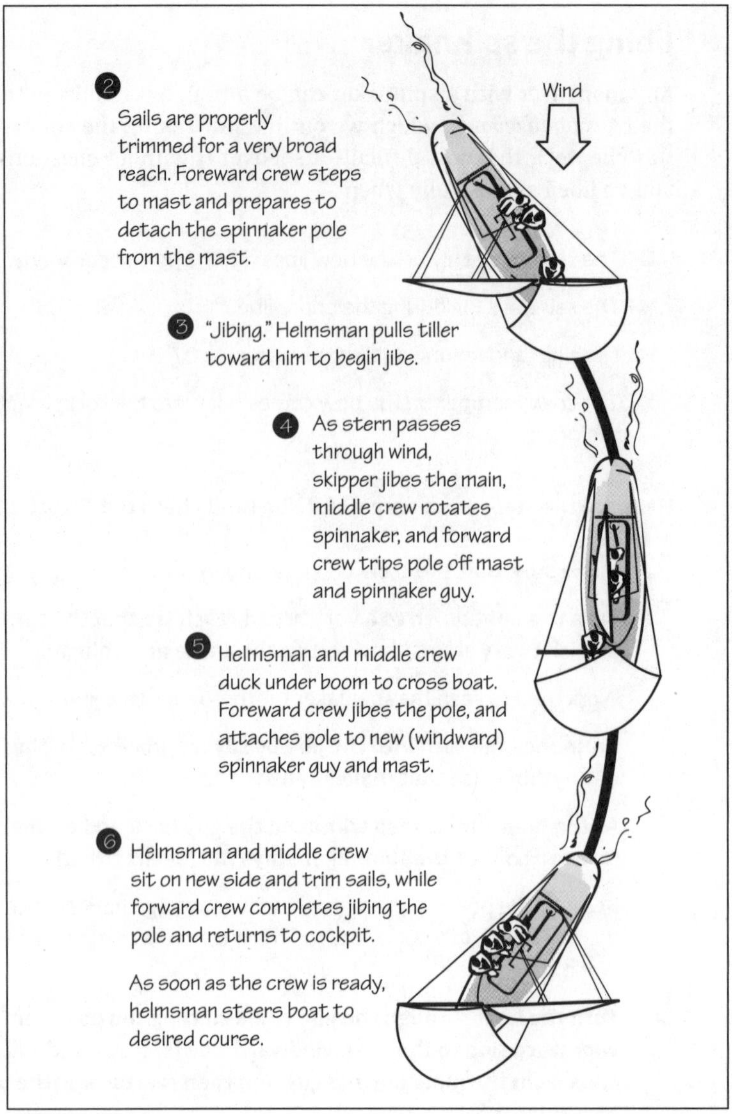

2 Sails are properly trimmed for a very broad reach. Foreward crew steps to mast and prepares to detach the spinnaker pole from the mast.

Wind

3 "Jibing." Helmsman pulls tiller toward him to begin jibe.

4 As stern passes through wind, skipper jibes the main, middle crew rotates spinnaker, and forward crew trips pole off mast and spinnaker guy.

5 Helmsman and middle crew duck under boom to cross boat. Foreward crew jibes the pole, and attaches pole to new (windward) spinnaker guy and mast.

6 Helmsman and middle crew sit on new side and trim sails, while forward crew completes jibing the pole and returns to cockpit.

As soon as the crew is ready, helmsman steers boat to desired course.

FIGURE 12-12: The steps for a successful spinnaker jibe on a three-person boat.

TIP

Think rotation! One of the most common errors in spinnaker jibes is not rotating the spinnaker around as the boat is turned through the jibe. The result is a tangled mess, with the spinnaker often blowing between the forestay and the mast. Practice jibing the spinnaker without the pole to get the feel of rotating the sail with the sheets. In light air, pull the mainsheet in tight (overtrimmed) or even drop the mainsail completely to facilitate this drill.

SWITCHING THE POLE: DIP POLE VERSUS END FOR END

Depending on the type of boat, your *bowman* (forward crew member) can use one of two methods for shifting the pole. The *end-for-end* jibe is common on dinghies and smaller keelboats. During the jibe, the two pole ends are disconnected from the mast and old guy; then they're reattached so that the old inboard end is attached to the new guy, and the pole is pushed out so that the old outboard end can be attached to the mast.

The *dip-pole* jibe is common on keelboats longer than 40 feet (12 meters). During the jibe, the pole's outboard end is disconnected from the old guy, lowered so that it can swing behind the forestay, and then connected to the new guy and raised up into position on the new windward side.

WARNING

Whether or not you have a spinnaker up, a jibe can be a pretty wild maneuver in windy conditions. The force of the mainsail swinging across and filling with a BANG on the new side can generate a major turning force that can lead to a capsize on a dinghy and a *broach* (rapid, out-of-control turn up toward the wind) in a keelboat. In windy weather (more than 12 to 15 knots), the helmsman can perform an *S-jibe* to counteract the momentum caused at the moment the mainsail fills after a jibe, as Chapter 11 shows.

Taking the spinnaker down

The key to a calm and successful takedown is planning it early enough that the helmsman can keep the boat pointing downwind, hiding the lowered spinnaker behind the mainsail until everything is cleaned up. Here are the steps for a *cruising takedown:*

1. **Turn the boat onto a very broad reach, and hoist the jib.**
2. **Collapse the spinnaker by easing the guy forward and pulling in the sheet.**

   The sail collapses and is docile, protected from the wind behind the mainsail.
3. **Grab the sheet, and begin pulling the sail on board.**
4. **Ease the halyard in concert with the sail being pulled in so that it doesn't fall into the water (drops too fast) or require a struggle by the takedown team (drops too slow).**
5. **Stuff the spinnaker into the forward hatch (if you have one) or into the back hatch or spinnaker bag on a smaller boat.**
6. **Lower the pole, and secure it and the spinnaker sheets.**

Dinghies and smaller keelboats often take the spinnaker down on the windward side in races. You can also find several other types of racing spinnaker sets. But all those methods require tons of practice, whereas the cruising set and takedown work on any boat and are the easiest ways to get that colorful sail up and down.

Setting an asymmetrical spinnaker

Asymmetrical spinnakers, or *A-sails,* are a great evolution of the spinnaker. So many small modern keelboats have A-sails that sailors often just call them spinnakers. Configured correctly, they have all the spinnaker's advantages (more speed for downwind sailing) but are easier for the crew to manage.

A-sails have a luff longer than the leech and, unlike the spinnaker, are always set with the same edge (the luff) forward, just like a jib. An asymmetrical spinnaker usually doesn't have a guy; it simply has a tack line that holds the *tack* (front corner) of the sail down to the bow or a built-in bow pole called a *sprit.*

At the clew are two sheets, one for the left side and one for the right, just like a jib. For sets and takedowns, you can still use the cruising method of bearing away to hide the sail behind the mainsail to avoid problems. Jibes are easy because you don't have a pole to shift (except on the few boats that fly these sails from spinnaker poles; more about that in a minute), and the sail is meant to collapse as it jibes, blowing around in front of the boat.

The techniques for preparing the sail for the set are similar to a spinnaker, and when the sail is hoisted, the trimming techniques of an A-sail are also analogous. Some racing keelboats use both A-sails and spinnakers and therefore set the tack of their A-sail on a spinnaker pole. Other racing keelboats use only A-sails but employ a spinnaker pole rather than a sprit. In either case, jibing the A-sail becomes a major production and very labor-intensive. For the combination of A-sail and pole, a plethora of rigging methods are available for setting up the two guys and for shifting the pole from one side of the headstay to the other during the jibe. The bottom line is that these boats are giving up the ease-of-use advantages of an A-sail in the quest for a bit more speed. The trade-off may be worthwhile for crew members on some big racing boats but not for cruisers and recreational sailors.

WARNING

Taking down any type of spinnaker will likely take much longer than you expect. Because it's safest to keep the boat pointing downwind until the sail is safely down and under control, make sure to start with plenty of distance before an obstacle such as shallow water (or, worse, dry land!) forces you to turn upwind.

Losing Control in Strong Winds

Before you read this section, we urge you to read "Reducing the power" earlier in this chapter. If you feel like keeping the power on and finding your boat's limits, you can use all the go-fast tips in this chapter (and Chapter 11) in stronger winds and bigger waves. But we should warn you about two kinds of wipeouts: rounding up and rounding down. The other name for rounding down is the *death roll.* (See why we wanted to warn you?) But don't worry. You'll survive and have a great story to tell.

Rounding up

Broaching, or *rounding up,* can occur on any type of boat on any point of sail, but it's most common when you're sailing off the wind. Rounding up occurs when a massive amount of weather helm (which we describe in Chapter 11) from all the forces acting on the boat causes the boat to "round up" swiftly toward the wind. In a round-up, you feel as though the rudder is gone, because you have no steering control. Actually, the rudder is just stalled. Telltale signs — increasing weather helm and increasing heel — precede a round-up. The following list provides a few ways to avoid this embarrassing (and potentially hazardous) fate when sailing on a windy reach:

- **Ease the boom vang.** This tip is especially important when the boat is heeling so much that the boom is close to the water.
- **Move the crew weight back.** This action keeps more of the rudder in the water. Make sure that the crew is hiking, too.
- **Play the mainsheet aggressively.** In big wind and waves, you must play the mainsail to keep the boat "on its feet." The helmsman should ask the trimmer (sometimes one and the same on a dinghy) for a quick ease if they start feeling weather helm building.
- **"Pump" the rudder.** By rapidly jerking the helm from "straight" to "bearing away sharply" and then back to "straight," you may avoid stalling and help the rudder stay gripped to the water. Make sure to warn your crew so they can brace themselves and hold on.
- **Reduce heel.** See Chapter 11 and this chapter for ideas such as flattening your sails and pulling up your centerboard (if you have one) partway.

TIP

If you do broach, make sure that all the crew members are still aboard and hanging on tight. Then put the helm to center, ease all the sails, and try, with what little forward motion you have left, to coax the boat back away from the wind again by jerking the rudder hard to bear off. If you're flying a spinnaker or an

A-sail, you may need to take it down to get the boat back on its feet. Keep the guy (or tack rope on an A-sail) on tight, and let the sheet out all the way so the sail luffs. You may have to drop the halyard and then pull the sail in from that remaining corner.

Rounding down

WARNING

The *round-down*, or *death roll*, is probably the most spectacular crash. It occurs most commonly on dinghies, resulting in a capsize, although keelboats aren't totally immune. The round-down starts with the boat sailing on a very broad reach, run, or by the lee. (Chapter 5 covers the points of sail.) In strong winds, if you let the spinnaker fly too far to windward of the boat, or if you heel the boat to windward with too much twist in the main, the boat can roll dramatically to windward while it turns "down," away from the wind direction. The forces start to multiply, and soon, you've lost steering control. Rounding down can result in a dangerous accidental jibe.

The following preventive measures can help you avoid the death roll when sailing on a broad reach or run:

- **Don't let the mainsail out too far, and keep the boom vang on tight.** On this point of sail, you want to minimize mainsail twist.
- **Don't sail too low.** Turn the boat toward the wind until you're clearly on a broad reach, the higher, the better — to a point, because as you turn up, you risk a broach and may be steering way off course.
- **Keep your spinnaker pulling the boat forward, not to windward.** If your spinnaker seems to have a mind of its own and is unstable, pull in on both the sheet and the guy to fly the spinnaker closer to the boat.
- **Keep the crew weight in the middle of the boat.** Keep the crew weight balanced, and have your crew members be ready to move quickly to leeward if the boat rolls that way.

If you do capsize in a dinghy, we hope that you read all about getting out of this predicament in Chapter 7. On a keelboat, you end up on your side, as you do in a broach.

TIP

You never have to jibe; you can always turn in the other direction by tacking and then bearing off again. (Take down the spinnaker or A-sail first, please.) In heavy air, try to minimize any jibes — planned or not. And if you do decide to jibe, remember to employ the S-turn technique, which we describe in Chapter 11.

IN THIS CHAPTER

» Picking the right location, conditions, and equipment

» Rigging the sail

» Getting familiar with the board and the sail

» Launching techniques

» Maneuvering with the wind

» Handling common problems

Chapter 13

Kiteboarding and Windsurfing

Let's go fly a kite!

—MARY POPPINS

To describe these watersports geared towards the thrill-seeker, we turned over this chapter's authorship to our daughter, Marly Isler. With her experience as a sailor, kiter, and windsurfer (a triple threat!), she understands why people of all ages are drawn to these fast and flashy facets of sailing and will share with you the building blocks to get you having fun on the water in no time!

In this chapter, I'll introduce you to my favorite kinds of sailing: kiteboarding and windsurfing. Kiteboarding (also called *kitesurfing* or simply *kiting*) and windsurfing (or *sailboarding*) require unique boards and sails (see Figure 13-1), which have been modernized greatly since they were developed in the 1970s. But be forewarned — after you try these high-speed aspects of the sport of sailing, you might just rip out this book's other chapters and never look back!

FIGURE 13-1: (Left) A kiteboarder in Cape Hatteras, NC and (right) the author, Marly, carrying all her equipment to the beach.

Photo courtesy of authors

One great aspect of sailing is that after you master the basics on one boat, you can transfer those skills to other boats with relative ease. Although kiteboards and windsurfers are a little more difficult to sail than other boats because they require more balance and coordination, I'll show you exercises that you can do to get comfortable trimming the sail and staying on the board. Take it from me: The result is definitely worth the effort.

Swimming, Anyone?

Just as with any other type of sailing, I recommend finding a certified instructor to show you the basics. Most kiteboarding and windsurfing schools have special equipment, such as small trainer kites, that let you get the feel of the sport on shore before you head out and get wet — and you're definitely going to get wet. You'll spend most of the first phase of your kiteboarding and windsurfing career swimming!

A kiteboarding or windsurfing vacation may be the best way for you to start. My parents and I took multiple trips to Cape Hatteras, North Carolina, for lessons when we were picking up kiteboarding. The shallow depth, strong winds, and warm water made it an ideal spot to learn. Also, having instructors on jet skis tow us back upwind made the learning curve quicker and the swimming (or "body-dragging") phase much more enjoyable!

REMEMBER

The skills that you develop on other sailboats — being attuned to and feeling the wind direction — are just as important in kiteboarding and windsurfing. The safety rules in Chapters 3 and 7 still apply. Make sure that you check your equipment, that you have sufficiently safe and warm clothing (such as a life jacket and a wetsuit), and that you aren't heading out in conditions that are too windy or rough for your skill level. A qualified instructor can make sure that your experience is as safe (and fun) as possible.

FOILING: THE NEWEST CRAZE

The sport of sailing (and surfing too!) is seeing a huge uptick in interest with the use of hydrofoils. Kiteboarding and windsurfing are no exceptions. Boards with hydrofoils, shown in the accompanying figure, are a speedier way for sailors to move quickly and quietly feet above the water. Wing foiling is an offshoot of foil kiteboarding; the kite is held in your hands rather than soaring above you controlled by lines. Given that a hydrofoil has such sharp wing tips, I recommend receiving proper instruction when you're learning, for safety's sake. So put on that helmet, call your local lesson shop, and get ready to fly. See Chapter 12 for more information on foiling.

Photo courtesy of authors

Parts are parts

The parts of a kite and kiteboard, as well as a windsurfer, are similar to the parts of any sailboat. Your arms become the mainsheet; your body becomes the standing rigging. The biggest difference is that a kiteboard and windsurfer don't have a rudder; you steer each with just sail movements and your body weight. Figure 13-2 shows the parts of a windsurfer.

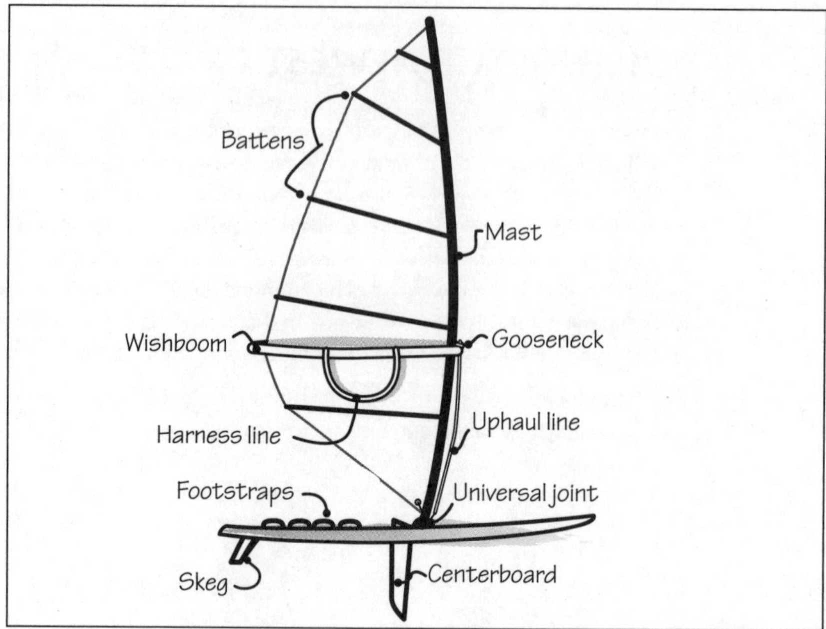

FIGURE 13-2: The parts of a windsurfing sail and board.

Following is a rundown of the distinctive parts and features:

- **Board:** The traditional kiteboard is similar in shape to a snowboard or wakeboard, whereas the windsurfing board is larger and more similar to a stand-up paddleboard or longboard for surfing. The biggest, floatiest board you can find is best for both kiteboarding and windsurfing beginners because it provides the most stable platform.
- **Skegs:** *Skegs* are fixed fins near the stern of the board that provide directional stability Most kiteboards have smaller sets on both sides for dual-directional riding, although some kiteboarders prefer using a small surfboard with only one set of skegs.
- **Footstraps:** Footstraps (which secure your feet) aren't found on all boards.

- **Harness:** A harness is either a seat or waist harness with a hook. In kiteboarding, it's always connected to the chicken loop (described later in this section). In windsurfing, it can be connected temporarily to the harness lines (rope loops off the boom), thereby taking the load off your arms.
- **Sail:** This colorful cloth has hard battens (for windsurfing) or air-filled chambers called *bladders* (for kiteboarding) to help the sail keep its designed shape.

The following parts are kiteboard-specific. You can see some of them in Figure 13-3.

- **Bar:** What your hands hold to direct the kite. The outer points of the bar are where the kite's outer lines begin.
- **Safety line:** A bungee line that connects your harness to the kite lines.
- **Chicken loop and stick:** The lowest parts of the bar system connecting to the harness hook. The other end of the chicken loop is the quick release and the place where the kite's center lines begin. The chicken stick is colloquially called a more inappropriate word for a part of a donkey's anatomy that can't be printed in this book.
- **Kite lines:** Thin, no-stretch lines running all the way to the kite. The number of lines differs from kite to kite, but normally, there are four. The two center kite lines connect to the chicken loop and then run through the center of the bar. The two outer kite lines (also called steering lines) are connected to the ends of the bar.
- **Downhaul:** Strap above the bar connected to the center lines that changes the angle of the sail. The more downhaul, the less power the sail will have.
- **Bridles:** Arrangement of lines beginning on the body of the kite and leading to the center kite lines, one on the port side and one on the starboard side.
- **Pigtails:** A fancy knot system that connects kite lines to the bridles, with the lines looped around a spliced ball at the end.
- **Kite bladders and struts:** Air-filled chambers on the kite. The main air-filled bladder in a kite is at the leading edge of the sail; the smaller air-filled struts go perpendicular toward the trailing edge of the sail. Most foiling or racing kite sails don't have bladders but still have chambers that provide that sail shape structure when the wind blows through them.
- **Inflate/deflate valve:** A valve on the sail for filling the bladders with air.
- **Kite pump:** A modified bike pump used to fill kite bladders with air. Make sure that your pump attachments match up with the kite valve, as each kite brand uses different attachments.

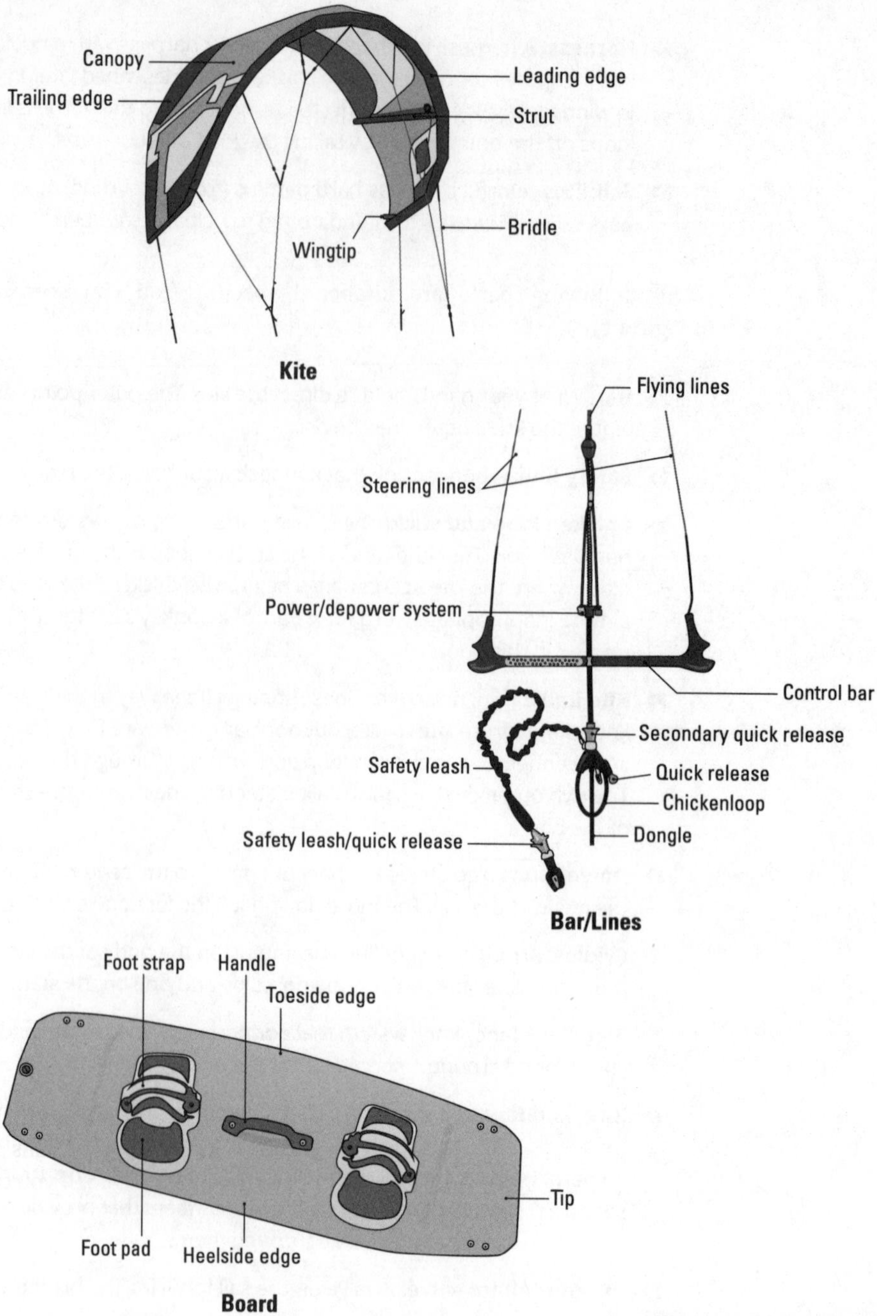

Canopy
Trailing edge
Leading edge
Strut
Bridle
Wingtip
Kite
Flying lines
Steering lines
Power/depower system
Control bar
Secondary quick release
Safety leash
Quick release
Chickenloop
Safety leash/quick release
Dongle
Bar/Lines
Foot strap
Handle
Toeside edge
Tip
Foot pad
Heelside edge
Board

FIGURE 13-3: The parts of a kiteboard.

© John Wiley & Sons, Inc.

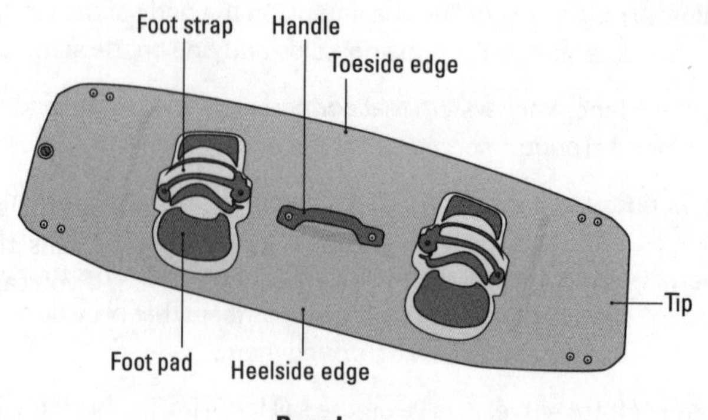

These parts are windsurfer-specific:

- **Mast:** The vertical structure that holds the sail upright.
- **Universal joint and mast base:** Fitting connecting the rig to the board, enabling you to rotate the rig in any direction. The *mast base* is a fitting at the bottom of the mast that connects to the universal joint.
- **Boom (or wishboom):** Wishbone-shaped tubes attached to the mast and sail that allow you to adjust the sail's trim and provide your "handlebars."
- **Gooseneck:** A fitting (often, a clamp) that attaches the boom to the mast.
- **Uphaul line:** A line attached to the gooseneck that helps pull the mast and sail out of the water.
- **Mast sleeve:** The sailcloth tube along the luff of the sail into which you insert the mast when getting ready to sail.
- **Camber inducers:** Fittings in the sail's luff into which the battens sit. Their shape creates a 3D winglike shape for the sail. Camber inducers are used primarily on high-performance (not beginner) sails.

The ideal setup

The ideal conditions for beginning to kiteboard or windsurf include flat water (no waves), warm water, and a steady, moderate breeze parallel to the shore. Because beginners start by sailing on a beam or broad reach (for a review of the points of sail, see Chapter 5), this orientation makes going out and coming in easy. If the breeze is blowing offshore (away from the land), you have to sail close-hauled back to shore — a difficult point of sail for a beginner. When the breeze is blowing onshore, trying to sail away is difficult and frustrating. Kiteboarding and windsurfing in too much wind (more than 16 knots for kiteboarding and more than 10 knots for windsurfing) is nearly impossible for beginners.

REMEMBER

One reason why you may want to take your first few lessons at a school or camp is that the facility will have a wide variety of boards and sails that are ideal for beginners. You may want to delay your first purchase until you can handle slightly more advanced equipment.

Kiteboarding

Kiteboarding is a fast-growing part of the sport of sailing, and it's easy to see why. Even Richard Branson, Barack Obama, and Mark Zuckerberg are part of the kiting community, and they love shredding over the water at top speeds. The ability to fit your kite in a backpack and hold your board also makes it the sport accessible to more people. Good luck trying to carry your sailboat onto a plane!

Rigging up

The first step in kiteboarding is pumping up the kite. Using your kite pump, connect the nozzle to the inflate/deflate valve on the main bladder of the kite (see Figure 13-4). Most kites have a recommended PSI (pounds per square inch) level or firmness written near the valve. It's important to get your kite bladders very firm so that they hold their shape. All that pumping is a great arm workout!

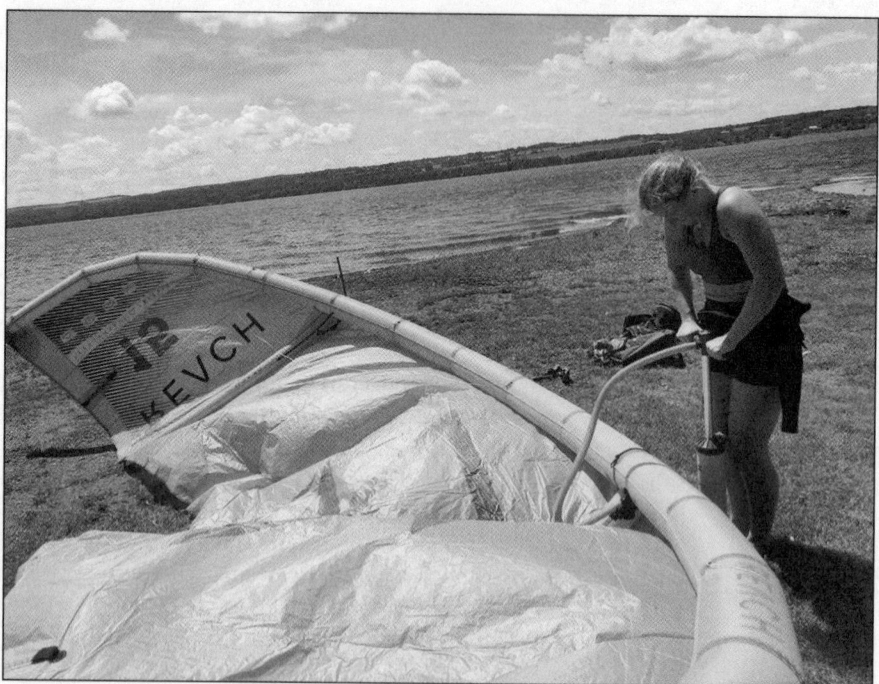

FIGURE 13-4: Marly pumping up her 15-meter kite on Skaneateles Lake, NY.

Photo courtesy of authors

After the kite is filled, the valve is closed, and the pump is disconnected, flip the kite over so that the main bladder is touching the ground and the center of the bladder is pointed toward the wind so that it can't catch air. The cloth in the kite should flap like a flag. You can put your board on top of the bladder to weigh it down, or if you're on a beach, pile some sand between the air-filled struts so your kite stays in place.

The next step — running your lines — requires your undivided attention. Uncoil your lines from your bar, and spool them out downwind of your kite with the bar farthest away from the sail. Then, starting at the bar, walk out the lines to make sure that they're not overlapping or tangled. (I like to walk slowly with the center lines between my legs and the outer lines on the outside of my legs to check that nothing is tangled or knotted.) When you've reached the end of the lines, loop the pigtails to the kite bridle. Even the best kiters take the time to double-check their lines!

Making a not-so-dry run

Have I mentioned that you're going to get wet and look a little foolish when you begin kiteboarding? You can minimize your embarrassment (a little) by getting used to the board and the sail separately before you use them together.

Getting used to kite flying on land with a small trainer kite is a good first step. As you fly the trainer kite on land, you'll see how the kite reacts at different points of the arc (*wind window*), which is shown in Figure 13-5.

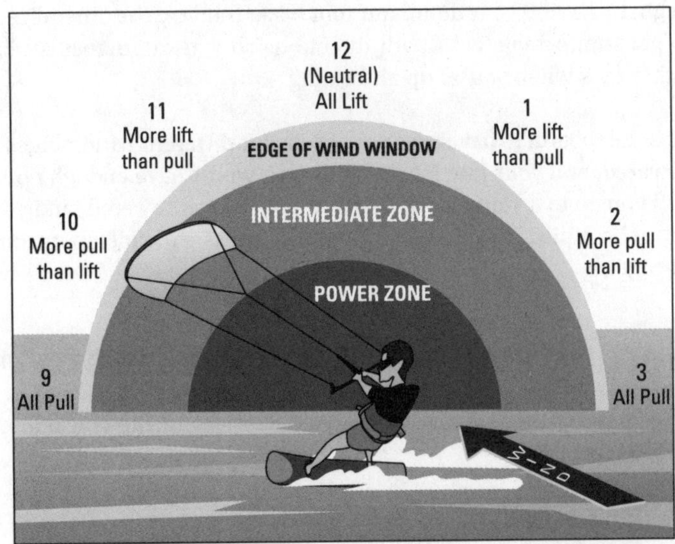

FIGURE 13-5: Your kite has the most power when it's at the sides of the wind window.

You can try some of the following drills to get comfortable with the sail:

- **Keep the kite steady at 12 o'clock.** The kite is calm and sits comfortably at the top of the wind window when your bar is far away from you.
- **Practice power strokes.** The kite has a lot of pulling power when one side of the bar is pulled in and the kite moves near an edge of the wind window. Try some power strokes by trimming in on one side of the bar and bringing the

kite from 12 o'clock to 9 o'clock or 3 o'clock. The force generated from this motion will be what pulls you up and keeps you riding in the water.

» **Kiss the sand with your kite.** Practice slowly dropping your kite to the sand at the very edge of the wind window. You'll need both hands on the bar and little movements to have the kite tenderly touch the ground. This maneuver is how you'll drop the kite to an instructor or kite friend after a kiting session.

» **One-handed kite flying.** Try flying your kite to the right edge of the wind window, take your right hand off the bar, and see whether you can fly the kite with just your left hand on the bar. Then switch sides. This drill will come in handy when you want to go upwind.

After you've perfected the use of the trainer kite, put on your bathing suit or wet-suit, and take a larger kite into the water, sans board. Now you'll practice *body dragging* — using the kite to pull you along the water.

To get comfortable on the board, try wakeboarding behind a powerboat or a jet ski. Begin by having your dominant foot back; then try the other direction. You'll want to get comfortable with both directions so you can maneuver back and forth on either tack when you're up and riding.

REMEMBER

Most kiteboarders have a quiver of sails for different wind ranges. If you're under-powered, and your kite is too small, you won't have enough oomph in the kite to pull you up to a standing position. If you're overpowered, and your kite is too big, you'll be pulled downwind (and your harness will ride up uncomfortably to your ribcage!).

Getting your feet (and the rest of you) wet

After rigging up and connecting your harness to the chicken loop, follow these steps to get going:

1. **Have an instructor or kite friend hold your kite in a C-shape, and walk to the edge of the wind window.**

   If the other person is too close to the wind, the kite will flap like a flag, and if they're too far from the wind, the kite will be pulling you toward it. When the other person is in the correct position, check that your lines are clear (not twisted), and give them a thumbs-up to let them know that they can let go.

2. **Fly the kite to the top of the wind window.**

   At this point, you should grab your board, triple-check your lines, and bid your fellow beachgoers goodbye.

3. **Walk out to knee- or hip-deep water.**

   Sit down with your back to the wind, and put your feet in your footstraps. Keep the toe side of the board out of the water, and turn your board so that it's perpendicular to the wind (which will be coming from directly behind you).

4. **Power-stroke.**

   Power-stroke from 12 o'clock to the direction in which you want to move. Trimming your bar toward you will put more power in the kite. You may need to do a couple of power strokes in a row. Keep your knees bent, and this force will pull you into a standing position.

   You're kiting on a reach!

Here are a few important safety tips to keep in mind when you're getting started:

- If you keep falling forward while trying to get up, try putting your weight on your heels, bending your knees more, and doing shorter power strokes. If you keep falling backward, try doing larger power strokes — even bringing your kite to 10 o'clock or 2 o'clock to start the stroke so that you have more runway.
- When it comes to kiteboard safety, it pays to be extra-vigilant about your lines. When launching, make sure that no beachgoers are directly downwind of your kite and no swimmers are nearby. When you fall into the water, try your best to fall away from your bar and lines; you don't want to get an ankle wrapped!
- If you have a nasty crash, and your board gets away from you, go back to the basics by body dragging. Your board will naturally move downwind with the waves and wind. Try to body-drag upwind, putting an arm out and angling your body on a close reaching course. You may need to do a couple of body-dragging tacks before you've caught up with your board, so stay patient and relaxed!

Changing direction and going upwind

After you're up and reaching along, try to keep your kite stationary at 10 o'clock or 2 o'clock in the wind window. If you get too slow and need more power, do some small power strokes. The higher the kite is and the farther out your bar is, the slower you'll go.

When you get the hang of reaching, you'll want to try going in the other direction. Before you're able to transition (tack or gybe; see the next section), the easiest way to change directions is to bring your kite up to 12 o'clock and sink down into the water as you slow down. Once back in the water, you'll do the same starting technique in the other direction, bringing your kite down along the wind window on the side you want to go toward.

REMEMBER

After some time reaching (and body dragging back to your board after wipeouts!), you'll naturally travel downwind. To go upwind, dig in your back heel to push the aft corner of your board farther into the water, and twist your body to face upwind. If you're comfortable dropping your front-facing hand from the bar and flying the kite one-handed, your body will rotate more and naturally turn upwind.

When you're learning to kiteboard, a nice long beach running parallel to the wind is your best friend. You can go back and forth on a reach (the easiest point of sail), slowly losing windward distance, and then walk back upwind on the beach with your board under your arm and your kite in the air and angled toward the water. There's no embarrassment in the kiteboarding "walk of shame" while you're learning!

Transitioning or tacking/gybing

In kiteboarding, a change in directions is called a *transition*. Here are the steps for transitioning on a kiteboard:

1. **Slow down by bringing your kite to 12 o'clock.**
2. **Edge into an upwind board position by putting more weight on your back foot and bringing the front of your board upwind.**
3. **Switch your stance so that your new front leg is straight and your new back leg is bent; then bring your weight over your new back leg.**
4. **Bring your kite down in a power stroke in your new direction.**

   You're off!

TIP

It's easiest to get going after a transition on a broad reach angle. A long *downwinder* — a long broad reaching kite session in which you plan to end in a different place from the one where you launched — is a good way to practice your transitions. A downwinder with a group of friends is my favorite kiting activity.

Windsurfing

My first windsurfing foray was as a little kid, hanging onto the foot straps of my parents' windsurfing board, my legs kicking up spray. Once I got too big to windsurf from the backseat, I spent countless hours trying to get the hang of going solo. I hope the lessons that follow help make your learning curve a little less steep, as they ultimately did for me so that I could follow in my parents' windsurfing "foot straps."

Rigging up

The great part about windsurfers is that they're easy to rig. High-performance sails, with their long battens and camber inducers, can be a bit tricky to rig, but a beginner's sail should have few (if any) battens. Rigging your windsurfer (especially the sail) is similar in many ways to rigging any sailboat (see Chapter 4). As with some dinghies, you don't have a halyard to hoist; the sail's luff sleeve simply slides down onto the mast. The trickiest part can be securing the boom to the mast so that the boom is at a comfortable height (roughly chest height), so have your instructor help.

Getting used to the board

After you assemble the right equipment, leave the sail on shore for a while, and familiarize yourself with the board in the water. Try these techniques:

- **Practice lying on your stomach and paddling the board.** Try paddling in a circle.
- **Stand up, and work on your balance.** Keep your knees bent and your hands out to the sides, just like a tightrope walker.
- **Move your feet out to each side of the board, and practice rocking the board from side to side.** Try to keep your balance!
- **Walk toward the front of the board, practice turning around, walk toward the stern, and turn again.** You can't do this drill on a small, high-wind board; the board is too small and unstable.

When you feel comfortable on the board, put it back on the beach near your starting point, and get the sail.

Getting used to the sail

REMEMBER

Balance is the first tricky part about windsurfing. The second tricky part is the fact that a windsurfer doesn't have a rudder; you steer the boat with the sail and your weight.

You can get a feel for the dynamics of handling the sail as follows:

1. **Stand with your back to the wind, pull the mast, and sail up on shore, bracing the mast base with your foot.**

2. **Stand to windward of the sail, and hold on to the mast at or near the gooseneck.**

   The sail luffs like a flag with the wind.

   Note: A fully-battened sail doesn't flap like a normal sail.

3. **Face directly downwind, with your back to the wind and the sail pointing downwind away from you.**

   Get comfortable in this luffing, or safety, position, as Figure 13-6 shows, because you'll be in this position quite a bit at first.

FIGURE 13-6: My mom standing on the shore with the sail in a luffing position.

Photo courtesy of Sally Samins

4. **Try tilting the sail to your left and then to your right.**

   When you're on the water, you turn the board by tilting the sail in this manner.

Getting your feet (and the rest of you) wet

After you attach your rig to the board and get in the water, follow these steps to get going:

1. **Put the board in deep-enough water so that the centerboard can be down all the way.**

   Position the board so that the wind blows across one side.

2. **Put the sail downwind of the board so that the mast and board form a T.**
3. **Kneel on the board at the mast base, and grab the uphaul line.**
4. **Stand up, and start pulling the sail out of the water with the uphaul.**

   Use your full body weight. Bend your knees; don't strain your back.

5. **When the sail is all the way out of the water, hold the mast in the luffing position, the way you practiced on land.**

   Your feet straddle the mast.

6. **Holding the mast with your back hand (the hand that's farthest back when you get under way), cross your forward hand over, and grab the boom about a foot behind the mast.**
7. **After grabbing the boom, bend this arm and bring the rig across your body, as Figure 13-7 shows.**

   The sail is still luffing.

FIGURE 13-7: (Left) Grab the boom with your forward hand, and (right) bring the rig across your body.

Photos courtesy of Sally Samins

8. **Take slow baby steps around to the side of the board as you grab the boom with your back hand, about 3 feet behind where your forward hand is.**

TIP

Keep both hands on the boom. Your back arm is the mainsheet. Your front arm is like the *shrouds* (wires supporting the mast). If you pull in your back arm and keep your front arm steady, you trim in the sail and start to move forward.

9. **Pull in your back arm so that you're facing the middle of the sail — perfectly positioned to balance the force of the wind.**

   You're sailing on a reach!

Lean your body back away from the rig as much as you need to keep your balance. You can control the trim of the sail with the position of your arms. To trim in, pull in your back hand. To ease out, either push out your back hand or pull in your front hand. To stop, return to the luffing or safety position by releasing your back hand from the boom and then bringing it forward to hold on to the mast or uphaul line. By now, of course, you're great at the other method for stopping: falling in.

REMEMBER

If you fall, make sure that you always swim back to the board right away; otherwise, it may drift off. Use the board as your swim platform to take a break.

Whether you're taking a learn-to-windsurf vacation in the Caribbean, getting lessons at a local lake, or visiting a friend's beach house, keep these points in mind as you practice your windsurfing skills:

- When you fall in, try to fall backward on your butt instead of jumping feet first. Otherwise, if the water is shallow, you can twist your ankle.
- As you come back to the surface after a fall, put your hands above your head so that you don't hit your head on the sail or board.
- If you find that you keep sliding off the board, ask the school or rental shop for a different board. The board's original nonskid surface may be worn off. We've also seen boards that have suntan lotion all over them and are as slippery as a seal. For traction, and for protection from any coral or rocks when walking out, some people swear by rubber booties.

Steering the board

After you master getting moving, you'll want to know how to turn. Many beginners get the first part right, but then they keep going and going because they don't know how to turn around and get back, or they're so fearful of attempting a tack that they get too far from shore. (If this scenario happens to you, hope that your instructor has a motorboat!)

REMEMBER

Here's a great drill to practice. With the rig in the safety position, lean it to the right so that the board swivels left; then lean to the left so that the board swivels right. Keep practicing until you can turn the board 360 degrees. As the board turns, take baby steps around the mast base to keep your back facing the wind direction.

When you pull in the sail and are moving forward, you can steer by leaning the rig forward or backward while keeping the sail sheeted in with your back hand, as Figure 13-8 shows. On a short high-performance board, you use your body weight to help turn.

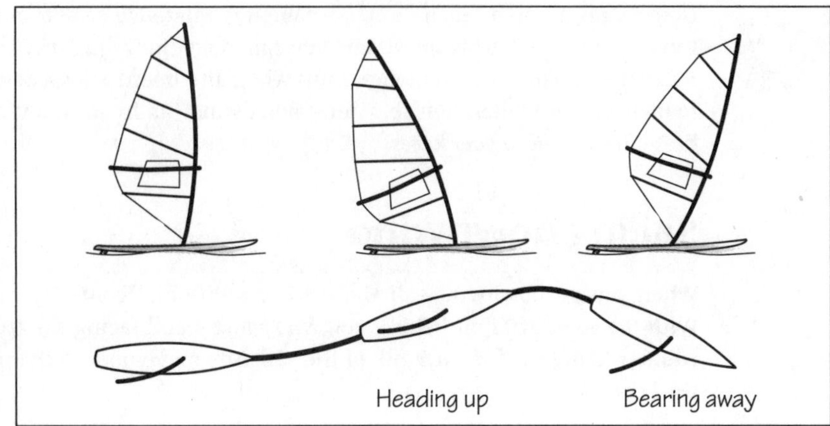

FIGURE 13-8: To turn toward the wind, tip the sail back (center); to turn away from the wind, tip the sail forward (right).

As you experiment with turning, you quickly discover that sailing upwind and reaching are very similar, but sailing on a run is a real challenge. Therefore, the first maneuver a windsurfer tries is a tack rather than a jibe.

Tacking

In Chapter 5, we define *tacking* as maneuvering through the no-sail zone so that the wind is blowing on the opposite side of the boat. Here are the steps for tacking on a windsurfer:

1. **Tilt the rig aft (toward the back), and trim the sail to turn the board toward the wind.**
2. **When the board is pointed directly almost toward the wind in the no-sail zone, step your forward foot around the front of the mast so that you end up straddling the mast with your back to the wind.**

3. **With the sail luffing, continue taking baby steps to the other side of the board as you lean the rig sideways to get the board pointed on a reaching course on the new tack.**

   The wind is coming over the new side of the board.

4. **As the board bears away, cross your new forward hand over to grab the boom (refer to "Getting your feet [and the rest of you] wet" earlier in this chapter), and pull the sheet in with your back hand.**

   Take your final baby steps so that you're standing on the new windward side and facing the sail. Off you go!

TIP

Going straight on a reach or close-hauled is relatively easy to master because all the forces are pretty balanced, and you can make fine adjustments with your arms. Balancing becomes a challenge only when the board slows down (such as in a maneuver) and when you're sailing downwind. As in so many other sports, the best advice is *bend your knees!*

Sailing downwind

When you go downwind, all that nice stability and control go out the window. With the wind straight behind you, you must stand facing the front of the board, counteracting the forward pull of the sail. Any movement to the right or left rocks the board.

To begin downwind sailing, follow these steps:

1. **Start by sailing on a reach.**

   The wind is blowing across the board.

2. **To bear off on a broader reach, tilt the mast forward to turn the board down (away from the wind), constantly moving your feet and rotating your body to counteract the sail's force.**

   As the wind comes more from dead behind, the force on the sail may feel more powerful.

3. **To counteract the force on the sail, bring both hands closer to you or take a step or two back — thereby tipping the top of the sail backward — until you feel that you can control the sail.**

   If you get hit by a huge puff, you can always release your back hand (the hand closest to the *clew,* or back corner, of the sail) and luff the sail to keep from being pulled forward into the water.

REMEMBER

Bend your knees to maintain your balance.

Jibing

When sailing downwind, you may want to try a *jibe* — a maneuver in which you change tacks by turning away from the wind. Jibing on a short high-performance windsurfer can be downright thrilling, like carving a turn on a slalom water ski or on a snowboard. But on a big *longboard* (trainer windsurfer), tacking around and then bearing off is much easier than jibing because the big board is tough to turn.

The easiest way to jibe is simply to unload the sail and revert to the safety position, holding on to the mast near the gooseneck. Tilt the rig, and walk around to the "new" windward side to turn the boat until it's pointed on a comfortable reaching course. Then get going again in the standard fashion.

TIP

Sailing straight downwind in anything but light air is a pain on a longboard. So if I need to get to a downwind destination, I sail on a broad reach across the wind, jibing (or tacking) each time I want to zig or zag back the other way. If conditions are windy, this approach is a really fun way to get downwind, because your board creates its own wind and flies across the water.

Keeping in balance

Anticipating wind shifts helps you keep the sails trimmed properly — which means that you stay drier, too. Here are some tips for staying balanced when the wind changes:

- As a puff of wind hits, lean your weight out more. Be ready to let out your back hand and pull in your front hand to ease the sail slightly so that you stay balanced and don't get pulled over.
- If you anticipate the end of the puff, bring your weight to the center as the wind dies away.
- If the wind dies suddenly, bend your knees and get your torso over the top of the board quickly to avoid falling backward into the water.

TIP

If you've ever been skiing, you know how easily you can pick out the beginning skiers coming down the hill. The same principle applies with windsurfing; just look for the guy with his butt sticking way out. If you want to look cool, tilt your hips forward and bend your knees!

Kiteboarding and Windsurfing Safely

The ability to rescue yourself is crucial to kiteboarding and windsurfing safety. While you're kiteboarding, remember the three safety options available to you:

- When in doubt, let it out. Your first step when you're feeling unsteady is parking your kite at 12 o'clock and letting out your bar.
- If you're still feeling unsafe, use the quick release above the chicken loop to have your safety bungee engage, causing your kite to lose its shape and any power. Using the quick release normally results in a "spaghetti dinner" — a big, tangled ball of lines.
- The last safety measure is deploying the safety bungee, which disconnects you from your kite. (It sounds like a kitemare!)

If you have a problem such as a dying breeze or broken equipment on a windsurfer, you can always paddle the board and the rig back to shore, as follows:

- Try laying the rig over the stern of the board so that it's partially out of the water, lie or kneel on the board, and start using those arms. The problem with this technique is that the sail is like a big brake dragging in the water. If conditions are windy, or if you have a long distance to go, derigging the sail may help. Release the outhaul, roll up the sail along the mast (or, if the sail is fully battened, slide it off the mast and then roll it up), fold the boom up against the mast, and start paddling.
- In a windsurfer emergency, always stay with your board; it's your primary source of flotation. Staying out of the water on the board keeps you much warmer. If you try to paddle back to shore, but the extra *windage* (drag) of your rig components make forward motion difficult, you can always sacrifice the rig to Poseidon to save the board — and yourself.

TIP

While you're sailing, make sure to keep an eye on your distance from shore. Try a tack or a jibe after a few minutes so that you don't sail too far from shore.

If you need to signal for help, wave your arms high above your head.

IN THIS CHAPTER

» Identifying the top trophies in racing

» Racing in different parts of the world

» Discovering how sailboat racing works

Chapter 14

Racing Sailboats: Going for the Gold

O Captain! my Captain! our fearful trip is done,

The ship has weathered every rack, the prize we sought is won,

The port is near, the bells I hear, the people all exulting.

— WALT WHITMAN

As you read this chapter, one fact becomes obvious, so we may as well state it up front: We love sailboat racing. It's our passion, so this chapter is very biased. But hey, at least we're warning you.

We've competed at all levels, and sailboat racing has enriched our lives in many ways. JJ has been racing sailboats since she was 8, and Peter started racing at age 13. JJ represented the United States in two Olympics, winning a bronze medal in 1992 with teammate Pamela Healy and a silver medal in 2000 with Pease Glaser. Peter was navigator for the Dennis Conner–skippered *Stars & Stripes* boat that won the America's Cup in 1987 in Perth, Australia. The victory tour included a trip to the White House and a New York City ticker-tape parade.

Whether you plan on embarking on a racing career or just want to know what the boats that you see racing on the water (or on television) are doing, this chapter introduces you to the incredibly diverse sport of sailboat racing — everything from the biggest prizes in racing to the types of sailboats that race to what you can do if you're interested in competing.

Winning the Top Trophies in Sailing

Sailboat racing comes in many forms, from casual weekend racing to grand-prix professional racing with television coverage and even prize money. This section looks at the world's best-known races.

The America's Cup

The America's Cup is the oldest international sporting event in the world. The event started in 1851, when a group of Yankees sailed their quick schooner, *America,* over to England looking to race (and wager) against some suckers. They were unsuccessful in drumming up a challenge for money, so they entered a race around the Isle of Wight in southern England, and the rest is history. *America* beat 14 British boats around the course (although some controversy ensued over whether the Yankees skipped a mark of the course) and took home a sterling-silver ewer, renamed the America's Cup after the boat that won it.

For 132 years, the America's Cup trophy (shown in Figure 14-1) was in the possession of the New York Yacht Club — the longest winning streak in the history of sports. But in 1983, a team of Aussies with a very fast boat with a winged keel carried the Cup down under. A U.S. crew led by skipper Dennis Conner (with Peter as navigator) representing the San Diego Yacht Club went to Perth, Australia, and won the Cup back in 1987. The winner gets to choose the location of the next event, so Cup races have subsequently taken place in San Diego (California, USA), Valencia (Spain, when a winning Swiss team was the defender), and Auckland (New Zealand).

The America's Cup is a match-racing competition that typically features an elimination series among the challenging teams to decide who races the defending team in the America's Cup match — a multirace series.

In recent years, the Cup races have taken place every three or four years, in increasingly innovative and technologically advanced boats including foiling catamarans (shown in Figure 14-2) and foiling monohulls in 2021. For most of the Cup's history, the fastest boat usually wins, so teams pour millions into the design and construction of these specialty yachts. For the latest America's Cup news, check out `www.americascup.com`.

FIGURE 14-1: New Zealand's Peter Burling holding the coveted America's Cup.

© Chris Cameron/Photosport via Associated Press

FIGURE 14-2: New Zealand's foiling catamaran racing to victory in the 2017 America's Cup in Bermuda.

© Gregory Bull/Associated Press

The Olympics

Most sailors consider the Olympics to be the premier sailing competition and the purest test of sailing skill, because the boats are strictly *one design* (built to very strict measurements to ensure equality). Sailing has been part of the Olympics since the Paris Games in 1900.

Olympic sailing awards gold medals to the winners in 10 classes of one-design boats, from several types of one- and two-person dinghies to a catamaran and foiling kiteboards and windsurfers. Men and women compete equally in several of the classes. JJ competed in the 470, a fast, two-person trapeze dinghy with a spinnaker (shown in Figure 14-3).

FIGURE 14-3: JJ and Pam Healy planing at high speed in big waves in their Olympic 470 — on their way to the bronze in the '92 Olympics.

Photo courtesy of Geri Conser

The Olympics allow only a limited number of countries per event and then only one team per country per class of boat. The world's best sailors often try for many years to earn a spot in the Olympics. Racing at the Olympics takes place over many days, with multiple races per day, so individual sailors can compete for only one medal per Games.

Racing Sailboats All Over the World

Boats come in thousands and thousands of types, and you can race any type. Additionally, races take place all over the globe, from Cape Horn to the fjords of Norway. You can race model boats on ponds and ice boats on frozen lakes. Some races are around *buoys* (anchored, floating turning marks), and other races go offshore from point to point. Here's a look at the many types of racing.

Fleet racing: All together now

Races can be as short as ten minutes, or they may last for months. You can race *one-design* (in which all the boats are identical) or under a *handicap* system (in which boats of different types race together, with the faster boats owing time to the slower boats). The majority of sailboat racing is done in fleets (hence the term *fleet racing,* in which many boats compete).

One-design racing

Maybe the most competitive sailing in the world is in the incredibly diverse world of one-design dinghy, keelboat, catamaran, and sailboard racing. Races are hosted literally around the globe, and many of the most popular classes (both Olympic and non-Olympic) have exceptionally well-organized regional, national, and international circuits. Because the competing boats are almost identical, one-design racing provides the purest test of a sailor's skill. One-design racing is the backbone of the sport of sailboat racing, and virtually all the world's top sailors have spent most of their sailing lives in one-design competitions.

There are also professional one-design events with sponsorship, TV coverage, and prize money. Probably the most exciting one to watch is SailGP (`https://www.sailgp.com`) in the foiling catamarans, similar to those used in the 2017 America's Cup (refer to Figure 14-2 earlier in this chapter).

Handicap racing

Handicap (rating rules) racing allows boats of different types to race against one another by calculating how much time the faster (usually, bigger) boats owe to the slower boats. Fully crewed yachts more than 36 feet (11 meters) long race in a variety of grand prix–level events around the world. Some crews are professional, and many top international sailors travel from race to race, living out of duffel bags. Popular major events are in Sardinia, Trieste, Kiel, Palma, San Francisco, Newport, Bermuda, Sydney, Key West, Chicago, and the Caribbean.

Box rules and development classes

Box rules allow boat designers to exercise some creativity as long as the boat fits into a "box" of parameters (usually, length, width, and sail area). Then the boats compete evenly with no handicap. Some classes, often called *development classes,* encourage design and construction creativity.

Team racing

Team racing, usually sailed in two-person dinghies, is extremely exciting. The most common format has six boats racing, three boats per team, although there are also 2v2 and 4v4 competitions. Tactics and boat handling are crucial to this exciting aspect of the sport, as competitors try to hold back their opponents to enable their teammates to catch up and pass to get their whole team in a winning combination of finish positions.

Distance racing: Point to point

Distance racing harks back to the clipper ships of the mid-19th century. The desire in Europe and the eastern United States for goods such as tea from China forced shipping companies to build faster ships. The clipper ships, probably so named because they moved at such a fast clip, were sleek, narrow ships with enormous sail area and lengths up to 300 feet (91 meters). The discovery of gold in California and Australia heightened the need for cargo space and delivery speed, yet the trip from New York to San Francisco was an arduous 15,000-mile route around stormy Cape Horn. *Flying Cloud*'s record-breaking trip of 89 days in 1851 was front-page news, and the captains of the fastest clipper ships were heroes.

Many famous distance races today follow the same trade routes as the clipper ships of the 19th century. Transatlantic races run from Cape Town to Rio de Janeiro, Los Angeles to Hawaii (the famous Transpacific Yacht Race nicknamed the "Transpac"), Chicago to Mackinac Island, and Newport to Bermuda, to name a few. Yet today, the fastest boats carry as little cargo as possible, and the crews eat freeze-dried food and make their own drinking water with a desalination system. Following distance races on the Internet is fun, because tracking software shows you the boats' courses, and crew reports make you feel like you're on board (except that you get clean clothes, fresh food, a dry bed, and warm showers).

Another major offshore race is simply called The Ocean Race. Similar 60-foot-plus boats with mixed crews race around the world with stopovers in various ports. The longest and most grueling legs are in the Southern (Antarctic) Ocean, with the competitors blasting downwind at full speed and dodging icebergs. That part of the race makes for some great television coverage. Check it out at `www.theoceanrace.com`.

The exceptionally rugged (and possibly antisocial) sailor can compete in a non-stop around-the-world race — alone! It takes a really special person to want to be in a high-tech sloop, racing as fast as possible around the globe solo for more than a month or two. Needless to say, doing so is very dangerous, but check out the Vendee Globe race (`www.vendeeglobe.org`). The Mini Transat class, 21 feet long, provides popular (and lower-budget) single-handed offshore racing to a mostly European fleet of sailors (`www.minitransat.fr/en`).

Understanding a Sailboat Race

This section has the big picture of what you need to know to race in the most common type of sailboat race: a *fleet race* (many boats competing) around a course defined by *buoys*. Don't worry — you'll be back at the dock in time for dinner and a nice hot shower!

Preparing the boat

REMEMBER

Anyone with a boat can find a race to enter. But to maximize your chances of performing well, you need to prepare your boat and crew. One of the most important aspects of racing is boat speed. If your boat is slow, you can still win a race by using clever tactics and maneuvering better than the competition, but winning is much easier with a fast boat. Boat speed comes through preparation — refining your equipment so that it's fast and easy to sail. Making sure that your boat can handle the stress of heavy winds and big waves can help you avoid the agony of a breakdown. Even the little things, such as polishing your boat's bottom, can make the difference between winning and losing.

Preparing the crew

Some boats are sailed single-handed; others, you race with a large crew. No matter how many people are on board, the abilities, motivation, and teamwork of the crew members are critical to success. A blown maneuver, such as a spinnaker takedown at a mark rounding, can cost dearly, but a good crew can make an average driver look like a superstar. The crew constantly feeds the driver information about wind shifts, wave conditions, and boat-on-boat positioning so that the driver can steer as quickly as possible without looking around too much. The more competitive the racing is, the more important it is for the entire crew to work smoothly as a team.

Entering the race

Local sailing and yacht clubs run most races. A document called the *Notice of Race* explains the basic details of the *regatta* (a series of races scored together as a whole): when the racing starts, what type of boats can enter, if you need to pay an entry fee, when you can register, who is organizing the event, and so on. You can usually find a club's upcoming race schedule on its website, with links to registration and the Notice of Race.

The *Sailing Instructions* (SIs) cover important details, such as a schedule of races, a chart of the race area, and the type of race courses. Figure 14-4 shows you a windward–leeward course, typical of an around-the-buoys race. The starting and finishing lines are imaginary lines between an anchored race-committee boat and a buoy.

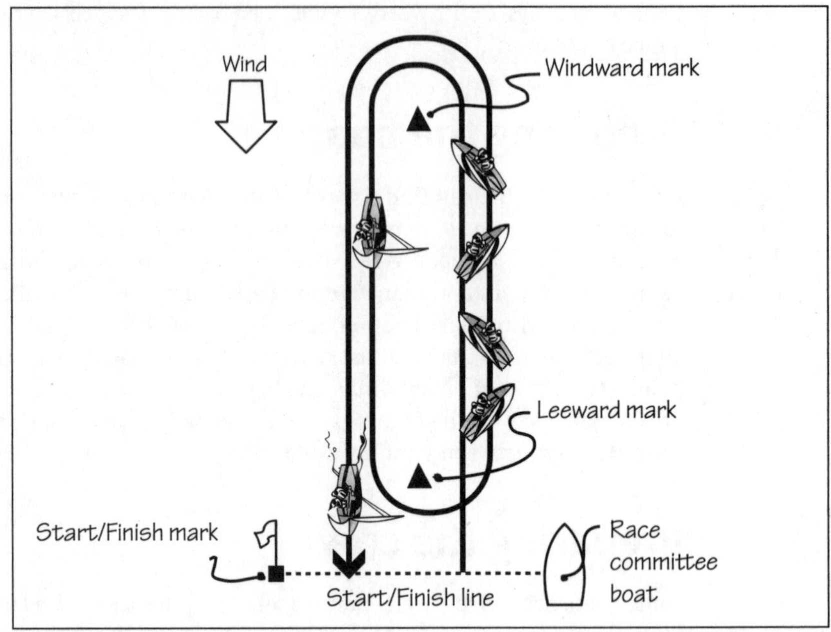

FIGURE 14-4: A common windward–leeward course, including the start/finish line.

© John Wiley & Sons, Inc.

A skippers' or competitors' meeting may precede the first race. The meeting is a good chance to ask questions and find out more about the upcoming event.

As soon as you know what time the first race starts, figure out when you want to leave the dock, and make sure that your team arrives early. You need time to check the notice board (the SIs describe its location), pack your gear bag or change into your sailing clothes, and rig your boat. On race day, it may take longer to launch your boat than normal, with everyone leaving at the same time. In deciding when to meet, factor in how long it will take you to get to the race-course area, and give yourself close to an hour at the racing area before the start of the first race of the day.

Before the start, crews develop their racing strategy by carefully monitoring changes in the wind direction and velocity and by watching for variations in current. Based on their observations, crews may develop a game plan to favor one side of the course because it has more wind or some other advantage. Crews also may use the time to practice maneuvers.

Finally, you can remind your child to apply sunscreen and go the bathroom before heading out on the water; they'll thank you later.

Getting a good start

The start is often the most important part of the race. A good start can propel you into an untouchable position — or at least give you a better shot at a top finish. A series of sound and visual signals from the race-committee boat counts down the time to the start.

The goal is to be just behind the starting line at full speed, just as the countdown clicks to zero and the starting gun fires. That sounds easy, but all the other boats are trying to do the very same thing. Another prestart consideration is which end of the line is "favored" with respect to the wind conditions and your competitors (see Figure 14-5). Sail to the middle of the starting line and point your bow into the wind. If your bow is pointing toward one end of the line, that end is favored (assuming that the first mark is upwind).

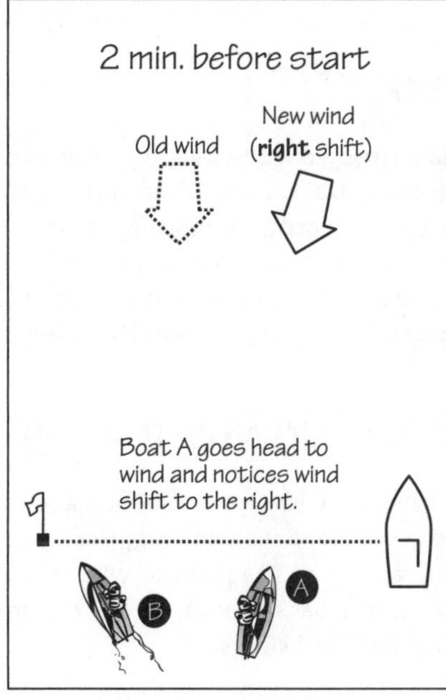

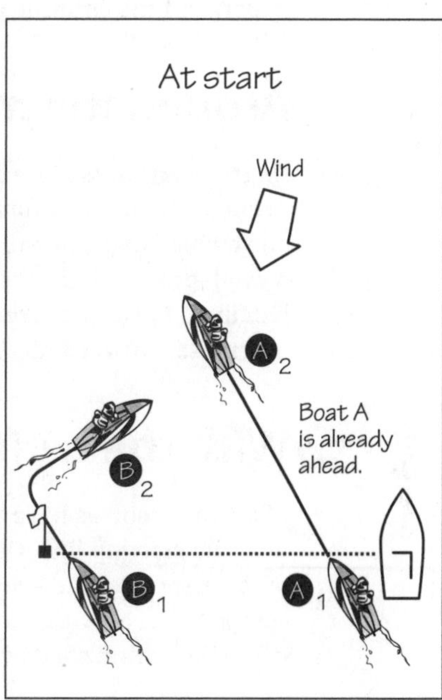

FIGURE 14-5: A wind shift to the right makes the right end of the starting line favored.

If boats start prematurely, the race committee can recall specific boats (using flags and hails) or call the whole fleet back for another try.

Against the wind: The first leg

The first turning mark is commonly positioned directly upwind of the starting line. As you discover in Chapter 5, no sailboat can sail straight into the wind, so on the first leg, the fleet works its way to the top mark tack by tack. A boat can reach the mark by tacking only once, of course, but often, because of wind shifts and other competitors, boats must make more tacks. Strategic considerations include wind shifts; even a 5-degree wind shift affects the positions in the race. Boats that head to the right side of the race course (by first sailing on port tack) benefit greatly from a clockwise shift, as Figure 14-5 shows. But if the wind goes counterclockwise, those same boats lose out — which is why, before the start, you try to figure out what the wind will do and why, during the race, you keep looking for clues to what the wind will do next.

While racing upwind, you must also focus on keeping clear wind in your sails and avoiding the exhaust (disturbed air) coming off a competitor's sails. The boats ahead often try to "cover" their competition and force them farther back. While employing these various tactics, crew members try to keep the boat sailing at maximum speed, adjusting the sails and their own positions on the boat to stay in perfect tune with the changing wind conditions.

Around the mark

On the open course, the boats spread out across a mile or more; then they all converge at the mark before turning the corner. When turning the first mark to go downwind, many boats set the colorful spinnaker, as shown in Figure 14-6. A well-practiced crew can gain valuable boat lengths with deft boat and sail handling. Luckily, universal sailing rules cover which boat has the right-of-way; otherwise, crowded mark roundings would be complete chaos.

With the wind: The downwind leg

Many race courses have two buoys: a *windward* (top) and a *leeward* (bottom) mark near the starting line. On the second, downwind leg, the crews continue to focus on boat speed while keeping an eye on the puffs of wind and the position of the competition. Now the crews in the back boats have the opportunity to attack by using their wind shadows to slow the leaders.

FIGURE 14-6: On the downwind leg, the crews try to get every ounce of speed out of their spinnakers.

Photo courtesy of Sally Samins

The finish gun

Like the starting line, the finish is an imaginary line between two objects, usually a buoy on one end and a flag on the committee boat on the other. No sound is sweeter than the blast of the gun as you cross the line in first place, but you don't need to win every race to win a regatta. You just need to be in the top group consistently.

Knowing the Rules of the Game

To play a game with other people, you have to agree on the rules. The governing body of the sport, World Sailing, updates the *Racing Rules of Sailing* every four years.

If you want to learn the rules, get the latest edition of Dave Perry's book, *Understanding the Racing Rules of Sailing* (US Sailing Association). This well-written book covers the most common racing situations and helps you understand the tactics of racing while teaching you the rules. You can download a copy of the racing rules at `https://www.sailing.org` or download a racing-rules app. To give you an idea of how the rules work, we outline the seven most basic rules in sailboat racing in the following list:

- **Avoid collisions with other boats and any buoys or turning marks.** Sailboat racing isn't bumper boats.
- **You must start properly.** The starting line is meant to be crossed after the starting gun. If you cross before the gun fires, you have to go back and restart.
- **Starboard tack has the right-of-way over port tack.** This rule and the following two rules are in force under the rules of the road (for nonracing sailboats) and the *Racing Rules* (for racing sailboats only). See Figure 14-7.
- **The leeward boat has the right-of-way over the windward boat.** This rule applies when two boats are on the same tack; if they're on opposite tacks, the preceding rule applies, and starboard tack has the right-of-way over port tack. Refer to Figure 14-7.
- **The overtaking boat must keep clear.** Makes sense, doesn't it? The boat that's passing must stay out of the way of the boat that's being passed.
- **When rounding marks, the inside boat is king.** If two or more boats approach a turning mark or some sort of obstruction while overlapped, the boat on the inside of the turn has the right-of-way.
- **You can make amends — sometimes.** The penalties in sailing vary depending on the SIs. Some regattas allow you to exonerate a foul (when you break a rule) by immediately sailing two complete circles (two tacks and two jibes) or by accepting a percentage penalty to your finish score. In many races, however, if you foul another boat, don't take a penalty, and are found guilty in a postrace hearing, you're disqualified from the race. Ouch.

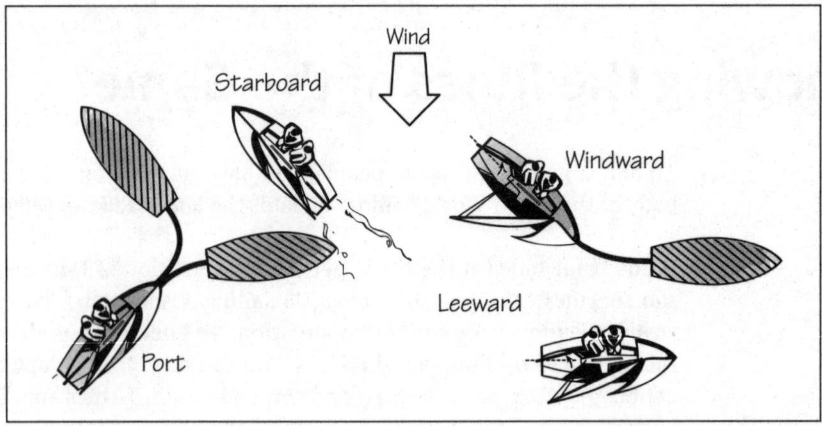

FIGURE 14-7: Racing rules: Port must avoid starboard; windward must avoid leeward.

© John Wiley & Sons, Inc.

How to Win — or at Least Get Started

To end this chapter, we offer our advice for mastering the basics of sailboat racing:

- **Become a student of the sport.** A great website for learning about racing is `www.speedandsmarts.com`. You can also read several outstanding books on sailboat racing, including *Expert Dinghy and Keelboat Racing* (Times Books), by maybe the best sailboat racer ever, Paul Elvström, winner of four Olympic gold medals; the *Sail to Win* series (from Fernhurst Books in the United Kingdom); and *Winning in One-Designs* (US Sailing Association), by Dave Perry, the author of the other must-have book, *Understanding the Racing Rules of Sailing*.
- **Enroll in a racing seminar.** Check with your local marine store, sail loft, or sailing club for local seminars. If your local college has a sailing program, it may offer racing classes too. Here are our favorite racing seminars in the United States:
  - *North U* (`https://northu.com`): North U offers a variety of seminars for racers on tactics and boat speed, and weather and cruising seminars too.
  - *J World* (`https://jworld-sailing.com`): J World runs on-the-water clinics on both U.S. coasts and offers offshore racing programs.
- **Find the right boat.** Most racing venues feature active fleets of one or two types of boats, such as a Snipe, Lido 14, Lightning, or Melges 15. Some popular fleets even have casual races on weekday evenings.
- **Know the rules.** Successful tactics depend on using the rules to your advantage. As you get close to a mark, for example, the boats converge, so being on starboard tack (which has the right-of-way) on the approach gives you a tactical advantage.
- **Practice, practice, practice.** To succeed on the race course, you must do many things well. You must sail fast, work well with your team, handle your boat and your sails smoothly, and acutely perceive the strategy and tactics of the race. The best racers spend much more time practicing than they do racing.
- **Sign on as a crew member or race-committee volunteer.** You can't improve your sailing skills unless you get out there. Certain regions and races have online crew-list "classifieds," or you can join local sailing groups. Or go to the marina, where the boats dock, and introduce yourself to the racers; sometimes, a boat will need a last-minute replacement or extra help on a windy day. If you want to go offshore, check out J World (mentioned earlier in this list) or the Clipper Round the World race (`www.clipperroundtheworld.com`). You can sign up for a complete circumnavigation or an individual leg of the Round the World race; no experience is necessary!

4

Sailing Away for a Year and a Day

IN THIS PART . . .

Deal with sailing mishaps and fix broken equipment.

Tackle boat maintenance.

Keep you kids safe on your sailboat.

Charter a boat and sail away.

IN THIS CHAPTER

» Running aground

» Mastering the jury-rig

» Handling sail problems

» Managing a fouled prop

» Breaking the mast and hull damage

» Abandoning ship

Chapter 15
Encountering Sailing Emergencies (And Handling Them)

Give me a spirit that on this life's rough sea

Loves t' have his sails filled with a lusty wind,

Even till his sail-yards tremble, his masts crack,

And his rapt ship run on her side so low

That she drinks water, and her keel plows air.

—GEORGE CHAPMAN

This chapter covers what to do when bad luck strikes and mishaps happen. Most sailors have their own great disaster stories about the time they were aground until the next high tide, or the time when the mast broke and bits of sharp aluminum rained down on the deck, missing them by inches. The best sailors have fewer exciting stories because they're prepared for most situations and can fix any minor problem before it turns major.

When something unexpected happens, you're under stress. You can't walk away and ignore the problem; you have to deal with it. Keeping your cool under pressure is invaluable when you're making important decisions that affect the safety of your boat and your crew.

Chapter 7 discusses basic safety preparedness on a sailboat, including practicing a man-overboard rescue and recovering from a capsize. This chapter addresses the not-so-common emergencies that you can't practice but that can happen in a sailboat. Don't worry — these mishaps are rare. But just in case your lucky day was yesterday, read this chapter so that you can be the one who stays calm, knows just what to do, and saves the day.

Running Aground

When any part of your boat touches the shore or the bottom, you've *run aground.* Usually, your underwater fin (keel or centerboard; see Chapter 1) is the first to hit, although we've seen boats run aground with their masts, capsizing in shallow water and sticking the tip of the mast in the mud. A grounding can be a gentle kiss (we hope) or an ordeal in which you're really stuck, with the tide dropping. Most experienced sailors run aground at some point — often in their home waters on a warm, sunny afternoon when they aren't paying attention.

Prevent those groundings

To prevent a grounding, you need to do more than just pay attention. The following tips can prevent the majority of groundings:

- **Brush up on your navigational skills.** Be familiar with the nautical chart of your sailing area, and if you're in unfamiliar waters or have shallow, tricky home waters, be able to *fix* (determine) your position on a chart and perform piloting skills (see Chapter 9).
- **Know how to raise your centerboard and rudder.** On a dinghy, you can often pull up the foils and slide over shallow waters. Just make sure that you're headed to deeper water!
- **Know how to "read" the bottom.** Chapter 9 covers how the color of the water and shape of the waves can help you spot shallow spots.
- **Know the depth of the water under your boat.** A good depth sounder is helpful for larger keelboats with electronics.
- **Know the exact depth *(draft)* of your boat.** How deep is your keel?

PLANNING FOR AN EMERGENCY

Having a clearly defined game plan for the crew to follow, with one person ultimately in charge, really helps in emergencies. A great example happened during the America's Cup races in windy Perth, Australia.

During one practice race, a jib blew out, and most of the crew (Peter included) rushed up to the pitching bow to help drag it down and set a new one. The waves were throwing the boat all around, and conditions were definitely "one hand for yourself and one for the boat." Despite the crew's talent and years of experience, they bungled the recovery so badly that the skipper, Dennis Conner finally turned downwind to give them a break, giving up the practice race.

On the way in, the crew discussed what happened. Everyone knew that they had to get the tattered sail down, but some of them stuffed pieces down one hatch and some down another, creating a hopeless mess that aggravated the issues. Finally, the crew agreed that in any future situations, Scott Vogel, the bowman, would decide on the plan of action.

Ultimately, that meeting won a race — maybe even the America's Cup — because another jib exploded during the Challenger Finals in a race against *New Zealand.* The crew not only got the mangled old sail down, but also got the new sail up so fast that they retained the lead!

- **Know the shape of your keel.** If you do run aground, knowing your keel shape is crucial for making the right assessment of how to get free, as we discuss in the section "When you go aground" later in this chapter.
- **Understand how the local tides and waves affect depth.** Chapter 8 shows you how to interpret the tidal information that's available online and in local tide books. In Chapter 7, we talk about how waves can build up and even break as they come into shallower water.

TIP

Don't push it, but if you absolutely must sail over a poorly charted area, sail slowly (at half speed or less). Doing so makes it easier for you to get free if you do get stuck.

When you go aground

So you're out on a nice, sunny day for an afternoon sail, and you run aground. What do you do? (No, don't cry into your coffee.) This section looks at ways to free your boat from a nice, soft bottom. Later in this chapter, in "Halting Hull Damage," we tell you what you should do in the rare event that you hit rocks and sustain serious damage.

To free yourself from a soft bottom, try these tips:

- **If you hit softly, slow down and immediately turn the boat to deeper water.** Ideally, you can sail free.
- **Send someone below to check for damage.** Look in the *bilge,* where the keel attaches inside the hull, for water leaking into the boat.
- **If your boat has a centerboard (lucky you), immediately pull it up partway.** A *centerboard* is the center, retractable fin on a dinghy.
- **Try to make the boat less deep.** Heeling works for all sailboats, except for those with a twin or winged keel, because it reduces the boat's draft. When you hit, immediately move all the crew weight to leeward, as Figure 15-1 shows. If you're on a reaching heading, overtrim the sails to generate heel from the wind.
- **Consider using the engine, but only in combination with some of these other remedies.** First, make sure that the rudder isn't stuck; you could break it by moving the boat. Depending on the situation, you may want to try forward or reverse gear. Watch the temperature gauge; silt can clog the water intake and cause overheating. And never put the engine in gear before ensuring that all lines are out of the water.
- **Take the sails down if they're driving you farther into shallow area.** First, let them luff.

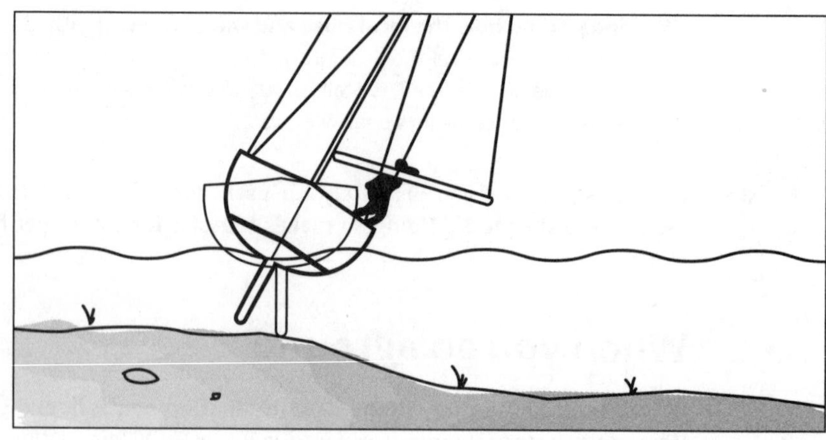

FIGURE 15-1: By creatively heeling the boat, you may be able to free the keel and motor (or sail) to deeper water.

Obviously, you should perform the preceding procedures as quickly as possible. If you're aboard a keelboat and still aren't afloat after trying these tricks, try one of these more involved actions:

- **Really heel the boat.** Drop and secure the mainsail. Then release the mainsheet and push the boom (supported at the outboard end by a halyard or other secure line) all the way out to the side the boat is heeling toward. Next, have some crew members climb up on it and slide as far outboard as they can. Lashing the boom to a shroud or tying it off to a forward cleat can free a crew member for other duties. Falling into the water is easy to do while performing this trick, so this act is only for the acrobatically inclined. Have the crew don life jackets first, and leave at least one person on board.
- **Get creative on ways to heel.** If you have a rowing dinghy, maybe you can suspend it (filled with water, if necessary) from the end of the boom to increase heel.

WARNING

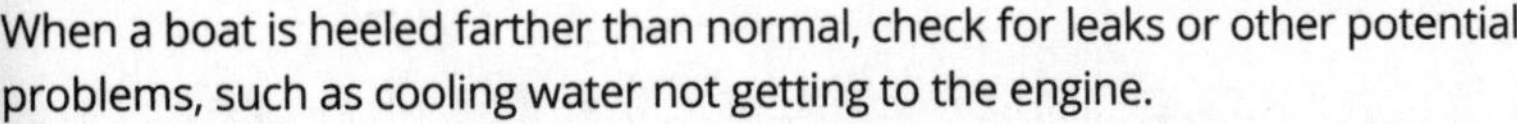
When a boat is heeled farther than normal, check for leaks or other potential problems, such as cooling water not getting to the engine.

- **Lighten the ship.** Offload extra crew and heavy gear into a dinghy to reduce draft. If you don't have a dinghy, try moving all the crew to the bow to see whether that helps.
- **Use the anchor to pull you off.** This system, called *kedging* or *setting a kedge,* requires sending a rowing dinghy (or other boat) out with an anchor to set. Put the anchor and sufficient anchor line (an all chain rode won't work very well here) in the boat, and head toward deep water, making sure that the end of the anchor line is tied to the dinghy or the sailboat. When the anchor is set (the farther away, the better the chance that it will hold), start pulling yourself free. Use a winch, if you have one. Meanwhile, keep heeling, powering with the engine or sails, and trying other measures.
- **Wait until high tide.** Unless you got stuck at the highest tide (assuming that you're on a tidal body of water), you'll eventually float free. Having an anchor set in deeper water hopefully keeps you from getting pushed farther aground as the tide comes in. If you're really high and dry, take heart: Most boats are built to withstand lying on their sides. Try to cushion the hull if possible.
- **As a last resort, accept a tow.** If your boat is hard aground, pulling it off can cause extensive keel and rudder damage, or the tow line can snap and hurt someone as it recoils. Hiring a professional towing service can be expensive (but not as expensive as salvaging a sunken ship). In case of a true emergency, contact the U.S. Coast Guard on VHF Channel 16. (For more on using the radio in emergencies and safe-towing tips, see Chapter 7.) The Coast Guard may refer you to a towing company.

BISCAYNE BAY BLUES

When Peter was part of a crew delivering a racing boat back to New England from Florida, the boat went hard aground at night while leaving Miami for the long sail north. Fortunately, the keel was stuck in nice, soft sand, and the boat was in the protected waters of Biscayne Bay. So after trying all the easy tricks, the crew gave up until morning and went to sleep with the boat on a 30-degree heel.

At dawn, the crew put up the spinnaker (to heel the boat more), put out an anchor, and ultimately flagged down a passing boat to add some towing power. When the tide rose, the crew finally clawed the boat off and got under way again.

Because going aground is kind of embarrassing, everyone agreed to keep the episode to themselves — until a friend mailed Peter a copy of the front page of the *Miami Herald*, with a beautiful spinnaker photogenically framing a boat that was clearly very hard aground!

Tip: Getting a tow or assistance from a commercial service can be costly. Fortunately, in many areas, there are towing services that you can subscribe to at a very reasonable cost. It's basically towing insurance. In the United States, BoatUS (`www.boatus.com/towing/gettowing/services.asp`) has a large network that can save you lots of money if you ever need their support.

Jury-Rigging Out of a Bind

A body of knowledge called *jury-rigging* (the fine art of replacing broken gear with a temporary fix) covers many possible emergencies. Covering all the possible jury-rig solutions is beyond the scope of any book, but this section lists the equipment and tools that are commonly used in many solutions, along with examples of how to use these items. Creativity is the key to effective jury-rigging. Keep in mind that you can't stuff as much equipment into a small dinghy as you can into a big keelboat. Here's a list of equipment and tools that are frequently employed when fixing things on your boat.

- **Knife:** A knife is a sailor's best friend. Use it to cut a heavily loaded sheet or halyard that's hopelessly tangled.
- **Duct tape:** Duct tape can fix just about anything, including a boo-boo on your finger when you run out of bandages.
- **Rope:** Sailors can do amazing things with rope. Besides an anchor line, all boats bigger than a small dinghy should have at least one spare rope that's

long and strong enough to serve as a sheet, halyard, or dock line. Additionally, a 15- to 30-foot (5- to 9-meter) length of ultrastrong, small-diameter rope (3⁄16 inch, or 4 millimeters) can be nearly as valuable as duct tape in an emergency. Braided rope with a low stretch core or single braid can be as strong as similar-diameter wire. For repairs in tight spots even smaller diameter single braid Spectra can be invaluable. (For more on rope, see Chapter 15). *Sail ties* or *webbing* (strong, ribbonlike straps available at sail lofts) can help with sail repairs and provide great lashing material.

- **Spare parts:** The list depends on your boat. But no matter how big the boat is, bring a few shackles (matching the size of common ones on the boat) and some appropriate-size clevis and cotter pins and/or a variety of machine screws with nuts. A couple of medium-size or large pulleys *(blocks)* are also great in your *ditty bag* (a bag for spare rigging).
- **Sticky-back:** This Dacron material is also called *insignia cloth*. This sail-repair material with adhesive backing comes in rolls, and you can use it to repair holes in boats and in sails. Even stronger and more waterproof is Dyneema repair tape, also known as Cuben Fiber.
- **Tools:** A dinghy may have only a screwdriver and small vise grips (although we recommend a multipurpose tool), whereas an ocean-circling cruiser may carry several toolboxes (mechanical, electrical, sail repair, and so on). Sailors often pull hammers, adjustable wrenches, wire cutters, and hacksaws out of the toolbox first in an emergency. A (precharged) battery-powered drill and angle grinder with spare batteries are aboard many boats headed offshore. Don't forget scissors, a few good sailmaker's hand-sewing needles, thread, and a *palm* (a leather device that fits over your palm, enabling you to push a needle through many layers of sailcloth). This list could go on and on, but you get the idea.

So what do you do with all these good things? Use your imagination, because that's what jury-rigging is all about.

Overcoming Sail Problems

Without functional sails, you can't do much sailing. Sails can blow out and rip — sometimes from misuse, sometimes from simple wear and tear. If your sail does blow out or tear, take it down right away, before any further damage can occur. Depending on the size of the rip, you may be able to fix it, sometimes as good as new. Your best friend in this procedure may be that roll of sticky-back cloth you brought aboard after reading "Jury-Rigging Out of a Bind" earlier in this chapter.

If you need to repair a hole in a sail or split seam, follow these easy steps:

1. **Make sure that the area you're working on is clean, dry, and salt-free.**

   You may have to rinse the sail in freshwater (or acetone) before it will dry completely.

2. **Lay the repair area on as flat a surface as possible.**

3. **Try to position the torn edges into their original positions.**

   Getting the edges into position may take several hands.

4. **Calculate the size of the sticky-back bandage (making sure to overlap the edges sufficiently), and cut it.**

5. **Apply the sticky-back.**

   Start at one end of the tear, and work slowly to the other end, trying to keep the sail as smooth and as close to its pretear position as possible.

6. **Press the applied tape firmly to the repaired area.**

   Using a solid object, rub hard on the repair, sandwiching it to the table or work surface. Really work the tape onto the repair, especially any stitched seams that are covered. For most small holes or seam tears, this repair will be enough. But if the problem is in a high-load area, such as a clew, you may have to get out your webbing, sail thread, and needles to rebuild the corner.

Furling blues

Although roller furlers are convenient for handling a big headsail or mainsail, they aren't foolproof. One common problem occurs while furling the sail after use. If a light amount of tension isn't retained on the jib sheet (or outhaul on the mainsail) while furling, the sail can end up with an uneven or unbalanced roll, which can cause a multitude of problems (sail damage, stuck in mast, and so on). Always make sure that your sails are furled smoothly. When in doubt, stop, unfurl, and start over.

Trouble getting your sail down

Occasionally, a sail gets stuck up when it's hoisted, often because the halyard has jumped the *sheave* (rolling part of a pulley) at the top of the mast and is pinched, unable to move. The first step in addressing a problem up the rig is hauling a person up the mast in a bosun's chair to inspect the situation and come up with a plan. (It's not always safe to go up the rig; see Chapter 16 for the proper use of a bosun's chair.) If the problem is a jumped sheave or similar issue, the person up the rig may have to attach a temporary halyard or jury-rigged rope to the sail's head and then disconnect the sail from the stuck halyard so that the sail can be lowered. You can try to fix the problem or put it on the list of jobs for your marine rigger.

Fouling the Prop

Sailors sometimes must use their boat's engine. A mishap known as fouling the prop proves that power and sailing don't mix all the time. Getting a rope tangled up in the propeller is a drag; when it happens on a boat with an inboard engine, the engine stalls, and the propeller gets stuck, unable to turn. Next thing you know, someone (probably you) has to jump in the water (probably cold) and untangle or cut the rope free. Usually, the culprit is a sheet (or dock line or tow line) dangling from your boat.

TIP

Preventing a fouled prop is simple: Keep your lines out of the water, and always look around both sides of the boat before putting your engine in gear.

Unfortunately, people aren't as vigilant as they should be, so here's how to deal with tangled ropes on an inboard engine propeller. (If you have an outboard, what are you waiting for? Pull it up and unwrap the rope!)

1. **Turn off the engine immediately (if it hasn't already stalled out).**
2. **Find the transgressing rope, and gently pull it with the gear shift in neutral.**

   Pull harder and pray, because if the rope doesn't release, you're swimming.
3. **Consider whether you really need the engine.**

   If you don't need the engine, or if the conditions are too rough and dangerous for anyone to go in the water, you just have to sail. Keep in mind that in big waves, the boat is going up and down fast, so swimming underneath it, near the propeller blade, is no fun. If you delay the swim until later, tighten the fouled rope, and tie it off on deck.
4. **As a last resort, try putting the engine in reverse (dead slow) for an instant and then pulling hard on the line.**

   We've never found this trick to work, but you never know.
5. **If the conditions are safe, or after you return to shelter, you can jump in.**

   Before swimming, stop the boat in a calm area (consider anchoring), and throw overboard a safety line that you can grab in the water. A mask, snorkel, and fins are nice.

CUTTING YOUR LOSSES

Have you ever noticed in the old pirate movies that every sailor carries a knife? Well, that knife isn't just for coaxing the good guy to walk the plank; it's a valuable tool for every sailor to have, especially in an emergency. A very sharp knife (with a blunt point to prevent any accidental perforation of boat or body parts) can cut through a highly loaded halyard or tangled sheet in a second. It can save you or the boat in an emergency, such as a sudden squall.

6. **Using the wrapped rope as a guide, swim down to the prop (the engine's off, right?), and try to untie the knot down there.**
7. **If untying the knot is impossible, use your knife to chop that stupid rope into tiny pieces.**

   Hey, be careful with that thing!

TIP

Having steering problems? Once every blue moon, the steering system feels stuck because, much like the problem we just described, a rope is wedged between the top of the rudder and the hull. Usually, you can get out of this situation with a good tug on the infringing line from the right direction. If not, turn the helm hard one way, and try again. (You may have to drop the sails in strong winds.) That trick usually works. If not, did you bring your swimsuit?

Surviving a Storm

Chapter 7 covers preparing yourself and your boat for strong winds. After following the safety steps in that chapter, here are some additional tips for a crew going into a really big blow:

- **Feed the crew.** Going into battle against the elements with the fuel tank full and fully hydrated is a good idea. Prepare the next meal, even if it's just sandwiches. It may be tough to find a volunteer for galley duty in the middle of a storm, and operating the stove or boiling water may be out of the question.
- **Fix your position.** Increase the level of your navigational energies, too. See Chapter 9 to find out how to fix your position.

» **Set a watch system.** If you're on a longer passage, you may already have established a rotation of the crew so that half the crew can get rest. A common rotation divides the crew into two *watches*, or groups (of equal ability), with each watch being on for two to four hours (you decide) and then off to get some rest down below.

Wearing a safety harness

A safety harness and its associated tether work like an extra hand to help keep you on board as you move around the deck on bigger keelboats. Wearing a safety harness leaves your hands free for boat-handling duties.

WARNING

Never use a safety harness and tether on a dinghy, which can capsize. They are only for bigger keelboats. Wear a life jacket.

Pick a safety harness that fits snugly and is the proper size. (Harnesses are often rated by body weight. The harness should have a tether (usually, a webbing strap) that clips onto a solid object, including jack lines. *Jack lines* are webbing or rope that runs along the deck on either side of the cabin for the length of the boat, specifically for use with safety harnesses (see Figure 15-2).

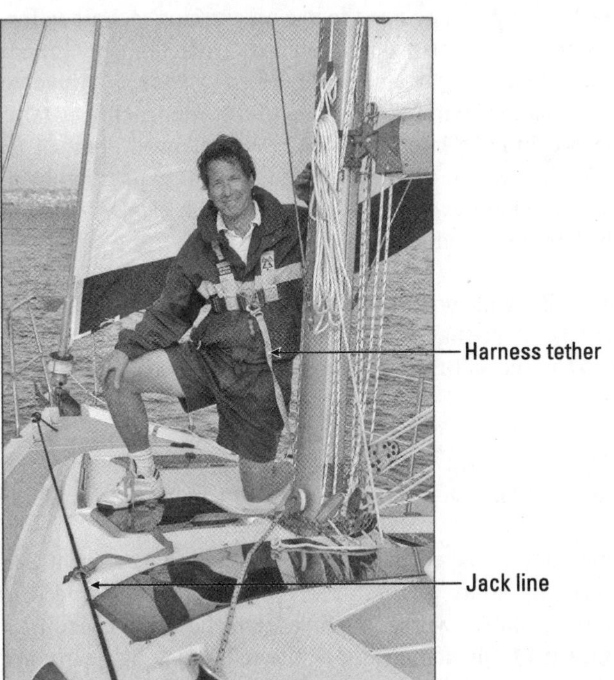

FIGURE 15-2: By clipping your harness tether onto a jack line, you can move around on the boat more safely and have your hands free.

Photo courtesy of Sally Samins

WARNING

Never attach a harness to a lifeline; lifelines put you closer to the edge of the boat and can break. Ideally, you clip into an inboard point where you'd still be on board if a wave washed you to the limit of your tether. Jack lines should be rigged so that you can clip on before you leave the cockpit and never have to unclip as you move around anywhere on deck.

Wear a harness and tether any time, especially when you're uncomfortable and during the following situations:

- Any time a man-overboard rescue would be difficult
- When you're on deck alone or short-handed
- When sailing at night, especially if you leave the cockpit
- When sailing in rough conditions - especially if you leave the cockpit to work up forward

REMEMBER

Safety harnesses can be great for kids. For more information, see Chapter 17.

Heaving-to and running before it

If you're ever in really heavy weather — when the wind is blowing the dogs off their leashes — you may need to use an extreme technique for survival. *Heaving-to* is a technique that also works (on boats with jibs) any time you want to "park" your boat, even in light air, as Figure 15-3 shows. It involves *backing* your jib (filling it backward with wind) while filling your main partially on a close-hauled or close-reaching course. The boat stays balanced, moving forward and to leeward very slowly. You can get into the heaved-to position by sailing along close-hauled and tacking over while keeping the jib cleated. Then adjust the mainsail until the boat feels comfortable.

WARNING

Look at the jib while you heave-to, and if it seems to be impaled on the windward *spreader* (the strut that holds the shrouds away from the mast), ease the sheet some to keep the sail from ripping; if you don't, you'll have to cancel your lunch break.

Heaving-to is a great way to take a break. When you employ this technique in extreme conditions, you should have your smallest jib and a reefed mainsail set.

Any time conditions are windy, moving around the boat can be difficult. The boat's heeling, spray and water are coming over the deck, and big waves are making the problem worse. Moving from the cabin cockpit can be difficult, and going forward to do something at the mast may be nearly impossible. A simple way to tame that wild beast if you're going upwind or tight-reaching is to bear away to a broad reach. The boat flattens out, the apparent wind calms, and the waves feel much smoother. Peter uses this technique in rough conditions all the time to keep things comfortable and safe for his crew when they want or need to move around on deck. Broad-reaching is your friend in rough conditions, which is why you don't want to be near a lee shore when the wind picks up.

FIGURE 15-3: Heaving-to: Cleat the jib on the windward side, and ease the mainsheet. This boat is on a close-hauled port tack heading. Now you can take a break.

Photo courtesy of Sally Samins

Running before it is a related extreme weather tactic used when it's just too windy to sail upwind or on a reach without getting into trouble. This technique entails sailing on a very broad reach, on a course with the waves, slowing the boat down with a minimal sail plan (small jib only). In really strong winds, it may help to drag ropes or any sort of object behind the boat to slow it down enough to be safe. It is not safe to take all your sails down in really big waves because of the danger of losing steerage and getting caught sideways to a breaking wave.

Avoiding thunder and lightning

In many parts of the world, the summer sailing season coincides with thunderstorm season. Sudden summer storms bring strong winds and lightning — a huge danger for sailors, because the mast on your sailboat puts you at risk of getting hit by lightning. Check the weather forecast before you go sailing (see Chapter 8). If you ever see a storm brewing or see lightning, head for shore as soon as possible. If getting to shore isn't feasible, you can anchor your boat. Go in the cabin, stay low, and stay away from any metal objects. Turn off the VHF radio and other electronics while the lightning is close.

Breaking the Mast

Breaking a mast is uncommon, but it's a real drag. Not only does it mean that you (or your insurance company) are out a good chunk of change, but also, it can be dangerous, especially in strong winds and big seas. Clearly, the best cure is an ounce of prevention. We cover the basics of care and maintenance in Chapter 16. But even with the best care, seemingly perfect fittings can fail, and the next thing you know — bang! — a gravity storm hits. Another cause of a dismasting is a violent capsize and subsequent *turtling* (a capsized position when the mast points straight down) in shallow water.

TIP

To avoid the risk of breaking the mast in a capsize, sail dinghies in deep water when it's breezy.

Every dismasting is a little different. Masts can break when standing rigging fails at a fitting (spreader or chain plate) or some other weak point. The broken mast may fall in the water, or it may dangle from the remaining stump. On a dinghy, you may be able to pick up and secure the broken pieces with one hand, whereas even lifting the standing rigging is a task on a big keelboat. Therefore, no one right way exists to deal with a broken mast. You must use common sense and creativity to solve the unique problem it creates. That said, here are some general rules to keep in mind:

- **Save the crew and the boat first.** If the process of retrieving and securing the broken pieces of the mast is endangering the safety of the crew or the boat, cut it away as fast as you can. Hacksaws, angle grinders, and bolt cutters can help.
- **Don't run the engine while rigging, sails and broken mast are in the water.** See "Fouling the Prop" earlier in this chapter if you don't believe us.
- **Be conscious of the loads.** Consider the direction of forces on things. As you clean up the broken gear, you're like a lumberjack cutting a tree; moving one piece may have a domino effect on other things.
- **Get the boat downwind of the mess.** If the mast falls into the water, try to maneuver the boat so that the mast is upwind. That way, the waves don't drive the hull onto the mast. Fortunately, Mother Nature should be on your side, because the mast and sails want to drag upwind like a sea anchor.
- **Recover all the wreckage, if you can.** If you're way out to sea, you may find that those pieces of mast, sails, and rigging come in handy for jury-rigging a new sail so you can get home.

THE RACE ISN'T OVER UNTIL . . .

In a famous incident in the Transpac Race (from Los Angeles to Honolulu), the 70-foot *Cheval* was 25 miles from the finish and in first place with a nice lead when the unthinkable occurred: The mast broke during a jibe.

As the disheartened crew rushed to clean up the mess before the boat blew onto the reef, the owner climbed on deck after doing some calculations at the chart table. "Hey, guys," he said, "we can still win this race. All we have to do is average 6 knots the rest of the way!" Rekindled with enthusiasm, the crew cut away the broken pieces and began jury-rigging halyards to the 15-foot mast stump sticking out of the deck. Soon, they had a small sail hoisted and were doing 5 knots — hardly the 20 knots or better that the boat was capable of doing, but movement at least.

After some more macramé and creative use of spinnaker poles and booms, the crew managed to set another, bigger sail sideways. The crew added more canvas as the boat began surfing the swells in the Molokai Channel. *Cheval* did win that race, and this story is a great example of how human creativity (and probably a fair amount of duct tape) can solve almost any problem.

TIP

If you must jettison the broken pieces for safety, being able to do so quickly is nice. Sharp hacksaw blades (several) and heavy-duty wire cutters are invaluable tools. Often, the easiest way to free the rigging is to remove the clevis pins at one end. See Chapter 16 for details on shackles with clevis pins.

Halting Hull Damage

Serious hull damage below the waterline can be a major problem. It can happen when you run aground, especially in rocks or coral, or if you run into a solid object floating just under the water's surface. Fortunately, this misfortune taken to its extreme is rare, but minor or medium-size leaks caused by a keel jarred loose in a grounding or a collision are more common. Here are some ways to stave the flow and save your boat:

- **Get out the pumps.** If leaking water is a problem, everybody should be bailing. Buckets work great.

- **Plug the hole with any available material.** On the inside, clothing or cushions might work, and so can a life raft or a rubber dinghy. You can use a paddle or convenient brace to secure the plug, as Figure 15-4 shows. A sail can be used as an external bandage lashed around the hole, and temporary external patches (collision mats) are available at marine stores.
- **Use heeling to your advantage.** This situation is one time when more heel can be good. If the hole is near the waterline along the side of the boat, you may be able to sail the boat on a particular point of sail (using the reverse of all the tips to limit heel, which we discuss in Chapters 11 and 12) so that the hole comes partially or completely out of the water. This direction may not get you to safety, but at least it gives you time to repair the damage.
- **Radio for help.** For information on using your VHF radio in emergencies, see Chapter 7. To get the attention (and assistance) of nearby boats, use the basic distress signal: Stand and wave your arms.
- **Get to safety/shallow water as soon as possible.** This tactic may mean sailing to a different port from the one from which you started. In an extreme case, when the boat is truly sinking, you may have to intentionally ground the boat (or beach your dinghy). If you must run aground, try to find a spot that's as sheltered (especially from waves) as possible and has a nice, soft sand or mud bottom.
- **Prepare to abandon ship if necessary.** We talk about more about this topic in the next section. If things are serious, make sure all the crew members are wearing life jackets, and prepare your *ditch bag* — a waterproof bag that you take with you when abandoning ship. Your ditch bag should include safety equipment such as a charged VHF radio, flares and lights, extra water, and equipment to supplement the gear in your life raft.

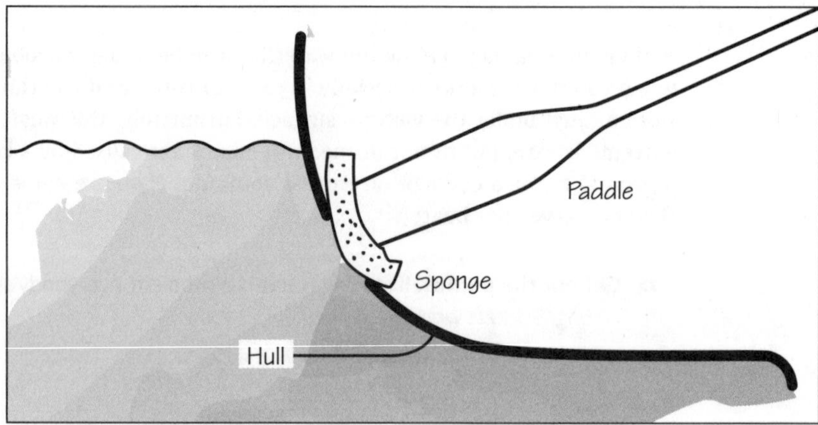

FIGURE 15-4: Plug a hole with whatever materials are handy and brace the plug.

Abandoning Ship

Between the two of us, we've been on boats that have run aground, blown out sails, been towed to safety, fouled a prop, been holed, dismasted, and sunk (in shallow water; Peter's cellphone was the only casualty). Peter even had to activate a personal locator beacon (PLB, which is covered in Chapter 7) and abandon ship into a rescue boat. But we're still enjoying our sailing. We hope that you'll be luckier than we've been, but remember the Boy Scouts' motto; it doesn't hurt to be prepared.

In Chapter 7, we discuss making emergency calls with the VHF radio and those invaluable emergency beacons (PLBs and EPIRBs). Make sure that you know how to operate your boat's communication and emergency equipment. In Chapter 7, we also recommend taking a formal Safety at Sea course, in which you'll learn more about a lot of the subjects discussed in this chapter.

You can't abandon ship into a life raft if you don't have one. A life raft is big and bulky, but carrying one when you're sailing a significant distance out of sight of land is wise. (Obviously, we're talking about keelboats; no one should sail a dinghy out of sight of land.) Make sure that the raft is rated for the number of people you have on board and was inspected recently. If not, or if you're unsure, check with your local marine store to find a company that specializes in inspecting and refreshing your life raft.

TIP

Heed this adage: "Don't abandon ship into a life raft until you have to step up to get into the raft."

This saying highlights an important fact: The situation has to be pretty darn desperate before you exchange your big sailboat for a glorified air mattress with K rations. Don't misunderstand; we believe in life rafts, and the modern ones are marvelous pieces of technology. Still, things have to be pretty bad before you'll be safer in a life raft than aboard your boat.

A modern life raft is packed into a hard plastic case and is very heavy. Therefore, you want to make sure that the raft is up on deck in a very accessible spot (and tied down securely) if abandoning ship is in the cards. In Safety at Sea courses (discussed in Chapter 7), you get to experience climbing into a life raft and pick up important information such as the following:

- You can find a cartoon-style description of how to deploy and inflate the life raft on the raft's case.
- Tie the life raft's bow line (which is outside the case) securely to the boat *before* throwing the raft into the water and inflating it.
- The K rations taste kind of like vanilla wafer cookies, and the water comes in cans.

ABANDONING SHIP MEANS ABANDONING YOUR CLAIM

Don't give away your boat! The law of the sea says that if someone finds an abandoned boat drifting along and tows it home (salvages it), the boat is theirs. So don't abandon ship. If you must leave your boat, leave a note saying that you intend to return. Even if you're aboard and in need of help, you don't want to risk any outrageous salvage claim, so clearly establish the terms of the helper's aid *before* you get too far along in the rescue process. Also, it looks better in the eyes of the law if you pass your rescuer a line (indicating a voluntary acceptance of aid) rather than have your rescuer pass a line to you.

For a great true story about this subject, check out Steven Callahan's best seller, *Adrift: Seventy-Six Days Lost at Sea* (Mariner Books).

Emergencies can happen to anyone. That's why it's important to monitor VHF Channel 16 at all times in case any nearby boats need help. We promise to keep the radio on whenever we're sailing and come to your aid if necessary, and we hope you'll do the same. We're all brothers and sisters out on the water.

IN THIS CHAPTER

» Maintaining your boat, all its parts, and the sails

» Checking the engine

» Storing your boat

Chapter 16

Caring for Your Craft

Mothlike in mists, scintillant in the minute brilliance of cloudless days, with broad bellying sails.

They glide to the wind tossing green water from their sharp prows while over them the crew crawls.

—WILLIAM CARLOS WILLIAMS

In the grand old days of Admiral Horatio Nelson's British Navy, the crew of a square rigger would *holystone* (scrub) the decks every day at dawn in all but the most extreme conditions. Unused sails had to be furled with a military precision rivaling the beds of today's U.S. Marines. This tradition of keeping your boat looking good, with everything in its proper place and stored absolutely correctly, is still in place today. Part of the tradition is simply good seamanship, and part is pride of ownership. Your boat and your sails are a reflection on you — and you don't walk around town with seagull poop on your head, do you?

Regular inspection of your boat for wear and tear helps prevent problems on the water. Many parts of the boat show signs of rust or stress cracks before breaking. The keys are knowing where to look for signs of a worn-out part — and remembering to look. In this chapter, we start by looking at the areas that require the most regular maintenance and replacement (the ropes, rigging, and sails) and then cover the mast, hull, and engine (if you have one).

A century ago, maintenance was a much bigger part of boat ownership, but today's boats are built of fiberglass and composites, not wood, and maintenance has become much easier. For those who prefer to leave the grunt work to others, you can choose among a plethora of boatyard and marine-maintenance professionals. Also, you can rent boats from charter companies and sailing clubs, thereby avoiding any maintenance work. (Check out Chapter 18 for more on chartering and Chapter 2 for more on finding sailing clubs.)

Doing basic maintenance on our own boat is fun, and we hope that this chapter makes you feel the same way. When it comes to the major repairs, however, we usually turn to the pros, not because we can't do the job (though sometimes we can't), but because that kind of project takes forever and never seems to come out as well when we do it ourselves.

Rapping about Running Rigging

Running rigging, as we cover in Chapter 1, is all the control *lines* (ropes) and gear (such as pulleys) you use to adjust the sails, including the sheets and halyards. Because running rigging gets a real workout every time you sail, you need to keep it in top condition; you can't trim a sail with a broken sheet.

In this section, we start by talking about something every boat has plenty of: rope. Then we focus on the blocks, winches, and cleats that help you work with those ropes and show you how to keep them functioning effectively.

A few lines about line

Line is rope with a purpose. Because most of the millions of ropes on a sailboat have some use, they're usually called *lines,* although in this book, we use the word *rope* often and interchangeably, with no ill effect (so far)!

When you're selecting or replacing a line, consider the trade-offs of the following characteristics in determining what's appropriate for the task at hand:

- **Strength:** All lines used as running rigging should be made of some sort of synthetic material. The strongest sailing ropes are stronger than the equivalent diameter of steel wire! High-tech fibers such as Dyneema, Vectran, Spectra, and PBO are very light and incredibly strong. The much cheaper (but less robust) polyester is quite popular.

  Different parts have different strength needs, depending on their application. A jib sheet must be stronger (and thicker) than a mainsail cunningham. An anchor or tow line should be strong but very stretchy, (so nylon is a common material). Your man-overboard retrieval line should float, as we discuss in

Chapter 7. A dock line should be strong and resistant to chafe. Some storage applications may call for incredibly stretchy rubber-filled rope called *bungee cord* or *shock cord.*

- **Diameter:** Any line increases in strength with its diameter. But those aforementioned high-tech fibers are so strong that some sailing ropes used with those materials are upsized for ease of handling. Comfort is most important in a line that you hold on to constantly; that's why you want a relatively thick mainsheet. If a line must pass through several pulleys and is usually kept cleated (like a block-and-tackle backstay adjuster), you can opt for much thinner line for less friction (and smaller, less expensive blocks).
- **Color:** If every rope on the boat is white, life gets pretty confusing (not to mention boring).
- **Cost:** Check out the rope department in your local marine store (most hardware stores don't stock good sailing rope), and you'll see why so many boats have white polyester line; all those fancy colors and high-tech materials are *expensive!*
- **Feel:** A rope that's softer and smoother is easier to hold but sometimes more expensive (and you can wear gloves anyway).

Comparing laid and braided rope

Rope that has three visible, primary strands twisted in a spiral is called *laid* rope. Laid rope, which is usually less expensive than its braided cousin, is common in dock lines and tow lines. For the running rigging in your boat, however, braided rope is the way to go. As the name implies, *braided rope* features fibers that are braided. Braided rope often has an inner core (where those low-stretch fibers can be used) that carries most of the load; this type is double-braid. Single-braid rope (like only the core of a double braid) is useful when you don't need the better handling properties of the braided cover. You can see laid and braided ropes in Figure 16-1.

Using splices

In Chapter 19, we show how to put a loop in a line by tying a bowline knot. Another, much more permanent way to make a rope loop is to make an eye splice. *Eye splices* are neater, stronger, and less bulky than knots, and are commonly found at the working end of a halyard (where the rope attaches to a shackle) and at the end of an anchor line. They're time-consuming for a beginner to create, but a professional rigger can whip one up in fewer than five minutes (but probably charges for an hour!). In some applications, you splice the loop around a *thimble* (metal or plastic teardrop-shape fitting) to distribute the load and prevent chafe. A webbed chafing sleeve is another option, especially for low-stretch ropes.

FIGURE 16-1: Laid line (left) and braided line (with core, on right) with their component parts exposed.

Photo courtesy of Sally Samins

Figure 16-2 shows an eye splice at the end of a double-braided halyard attached to a snap shackle (on the left) and an eye splice at the end of a laid-line nylon anchor rope with a thimble inserted to prevent chafe (on the right).

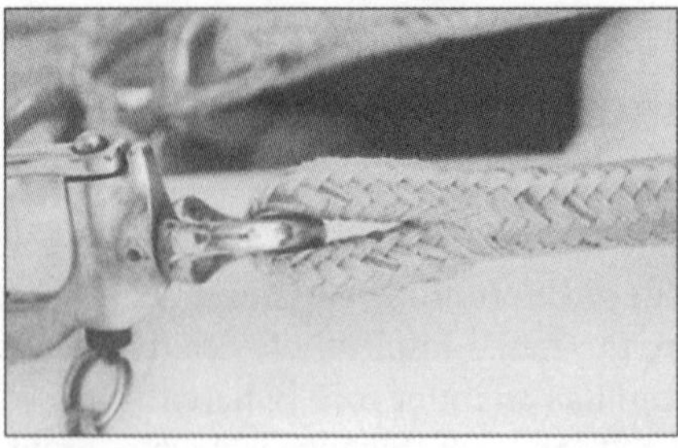

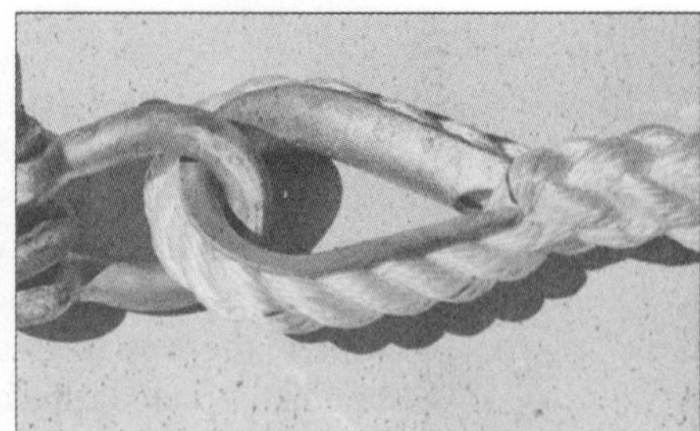

FIGURE 16-2: Eye splices. Left: braided line. Right: laid line.

Photo courtesy of Sally Samins

Browsing online, you can find more information about splicing and tying knots. More of this information exists than you can imagine!

Going to the bitter end

No matter what kind of rope you use, the end of it can be a problem area if it starts to fray because the usable part of the line gets shorter and shorter. The easiest solution for many ropes is to melt the end with a lighter, some matches, or a special *hot knife* (commonly found in the rope department of a marine store). With braided rope, sometimes, the inner core won't burn. So pull out and cut off an inch or two of the inner core; then milk the cover over and melt the end of the cover, as shown in Figure 16-3.

Whipping

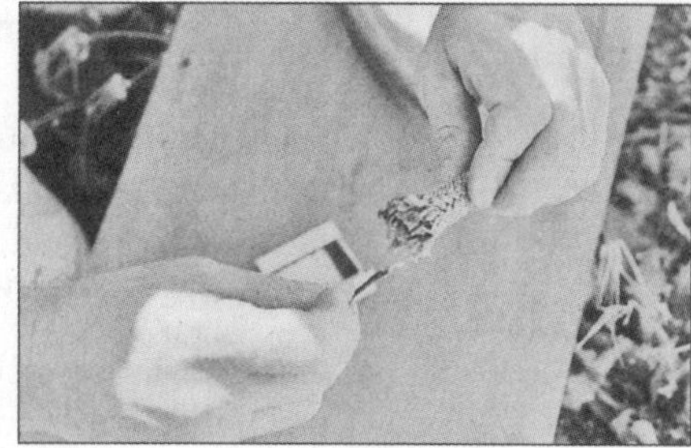

FIGURE 16-3: Finishing off the end. Left: Whipping on a three-strand laid line. Right: Melting the cover of a braided line).

Photo courtesy of Sally Samins

If burning doesn't work (some rope materials won't melt), you can always tie an overhand knot in the end (a temporary fix), wrap tape around it, or whip it. *Whipping,* the old-fashioned way to secure a splice or the end of a rope, requires the use of a special sailmaker's needle and strong synthetic thread. Wrap the thread tightly around the rope to hold it together and then stitch the thread securely through the rope so that it doesn't unravel during use, as Figure 16-3 shows. Melting the rope's end outside the whipping is still a good idea (if it'll melt!).

Caring for your lines

REMEMBER

When you're not using a line, securely coil and store it. (We discuss how to coil a line in Chapter 4.) If you sail in saltwater, flush the wet lines with freshwater after sailing. Hang wet line where it can dry, and store it (whenever practical) out of the incredibly damaging rays of the sun. Check lines periodically for wear, especially where they commonly load up on a pulley or other corner. Chafe on the cover is easy to spot and may indicate damage to the internal core. To extend the life of your lines, consider rotating your halyards and sheets end for end occasionally — sort of the yachting equivalent of rotating your tires.

Sailing gear

This section focuses on the fittings that help your lines do their work: the winches, blocks, shackles, and cleats. A key part of caring for this gear is visual maintenance — looking for hairline cracks in metal parts, signs of corrosion, or other indications that something isn't quite right.

Blocks

Your boat has many *blocks,* or pulleys; they're probably hanging from the boom, bolted to the deck, and built into your mast (see Chapter 4). Blocks come in all sizes and shapes, and they must be matched to the task at hand, or they might cause problems. Key considerations include

- **Strength:** The manufacturer provides information on the working load. Usually (but not always), the bigger the block, the stronger it is. A block that's too weak starts to deform. Often, a sticky *sheave* (the moving wheel that the rope turns over) is the first sign of problems.
- **Proper use:** Some blocks are designed specifically for wire; they often have metal sheaves. If you put wire on a block that's intended for rope, the sheave can crack or chafe and develop a groove. Also, don't use too thick a rope in a block. Err on the side of using a too-small rope diameter, and you'll have less friction.

Most sailing blocks are very low-maintenance. Rinse any block with freshwater after a day of sailing in saltwater, and all blocks appreciate being stored out of those ultraviolet rays. Some blocks require occasional lubrication, but check the manufacturer's directions first, because the lubricant may gum up the works. Often, the way that the block is attached to the boat — by its shackle or webbing strop — is the weakest link.

Shackles

Shackles (the metal fittings used to attach different parts of the boat, mast, and sails) are everywhere on your boat, just like blocks. Your boat may have twist shackles, snap shackles, brummel hooks, and/or captive pin shackles, to name a few. Keep the following considerations in mind when picking out, installing, and maintaining shackles:

- **Strength:** The shackle's manufacturer specifies the safe working load, but you can get a good idea of its strength by looking at the diameter of the metal.
- **Accessibility:** A *snap shackle* is the easiest type of shackle to open, but it can be large and expensive. The *D-shaped shackle* is by far the most common, but it's more difficult to open in a hurry.
- **Security:** Shackles, especially the ones attached to the corners of the sails, can really get flapped about when the sails are luffing. Wrapping plastic tape around a snap shackle keeps it from opening accidentally. D-shaped shackles are often secured by a screw pin; tighten the pin securely with a wrench.

  D-shaped shackles and other fittings can have a *clevis pin* with a *cotter pin* or *ring ding* securing it, as Figure 16-4 shows. Ring dings are easier to put on and take off, but you must tape them so that they don't catch something and open. Cotter pins shouldn't be too long and should be spread open, with the ends bent out just enough to facilitate removing the pins in an emergency; they should also be taped, because their points are very sharp.

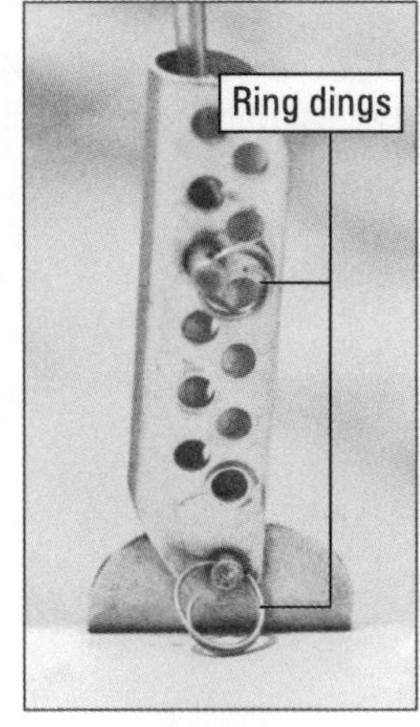

FIGURE 16-4: Clevis pins secured by ring dings (left) and by cotter pins (right).

Photo courtesy of Sally Samins

TIP

Gone are the days when metal shackles were the only solution for attaching parts to the boat or a line. Today's low-stretch fibers such as Spectra can be spliced into a loop that can do the same job as a shackle or pad-eye, which is much cleaner and easier to maintain and replace.

Winches

In Chapters 4 and 5, we discuss winches and techniques for using them. Because of their many moving parts, they need more attention than pulleys. The manufacturer's literature or the folks at the local marine store can help you pick out a winch (although most keelboats already have plenty) and maintenance supplies. In the following list, we provide the keys to maintaining your winches:

- **Clean your winch.** Take the winch totally apart at least once a year (sort of like disassembling something you built with an erector set; just remember where each piece goes!), and clean all the internal metal parts. A big bucket containing an inch or so of solvent-based cleaner such as mineral spirits or degreaser and a toothbrush make a great washtub and scrubber. Lay out a huge drop cloth, and have plenty of rags for this very messy job.
- **Keep your winch salt-free.** Flush it with freshwater after use, and make sure that all the drain holes around its base are open so that any rainwater can escape.
- **Lubricate your winch.** Check for any special instructions from the manufacturer. After taking the drum off and setting it aside, inspect and lubricate all the moving parts and bearing surfaces. Pay special attention to the *pawls,* which allow the winch to spin one way and not the other, as shown in Figure 16-5. The pawls should swing easily with the touch of a finger, with the spring providing sufficient power to return the pawl to the open position. If they don't move

freely after cleaning and lubrication, replace both spring and pawl. Inspect and lubricate your winches at least twice a year (more often if you use the boat frequently).

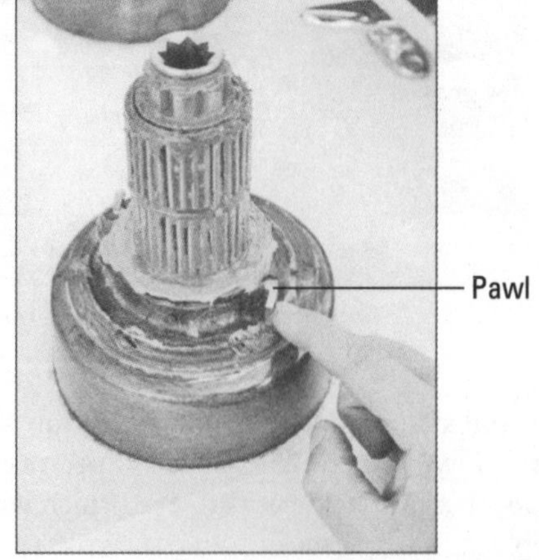

FIGURE 16-5: Remove the winch drum to inspect and lubricate the pawls, springs, roller bearings, and other parts.

Photo courtesy of Sally Samins

REMEMBER

Don't forget: Regular visual inspection is important. When sailing, pay attention to how well the winch works, and be especially concerned about any jerking under load or weird noises. Also, when you have the winch apart for lubrication, take a close look at all the internal parts for wear or signs of fatigue.

Inspecting the Mast

A mast is supported by wires (or fiber cables) called, as a group, the *standing rigging*, which we introduce in Chapter 1. And in Chapter 15, we discuss the potential hazardous consequences of one of a sailor's biggest nightmares: a dismasting.

First, make sure that your mast is straight (or *in column*) by sighting up the mast from the bottom. On a boat with shrouds, you can adjust the *turnbuckles* (devices used to adjust shroud tension) to get the mast straight. This "tuning" — getting the mast in column while at the dock — is easy. But you should also sight up the mast when you're sailing upwind in moderate winds, and make further adjustments as needed. If you're having trouble, ask a local rigger to help.

Depending on your use of the boat, you may have to inspect your mast and components twice a year, every month, or even more often — especially after sailing in heavy weather, when things get stressed to the maximum. On a dinghy or small boat, you can take the mast down to inspect it. For a larger boat, you have to send someone up the mast.

To hoist someone up the mast, you need a *bosun's chair* — a harness-type device that provides a seat and can be attached to the halyard, as Figure 16-6 shows. A winch is necessary if the person going up is heavy. Never trust your safety to a halyard shackle; always tie the halyard rope with a bowline to the bosun's chair. Avoid going up the rig when the boat is under way, especially in rough conditions: The ride can be wild because the motion of the ocean is accentuated at the top of the mast. Always ensure that any tools or hard objects (which can put a major dent in the deck if they fall) are secure when someone is going aloft. For that same reason, never stand below anyone who's working up in the rig.

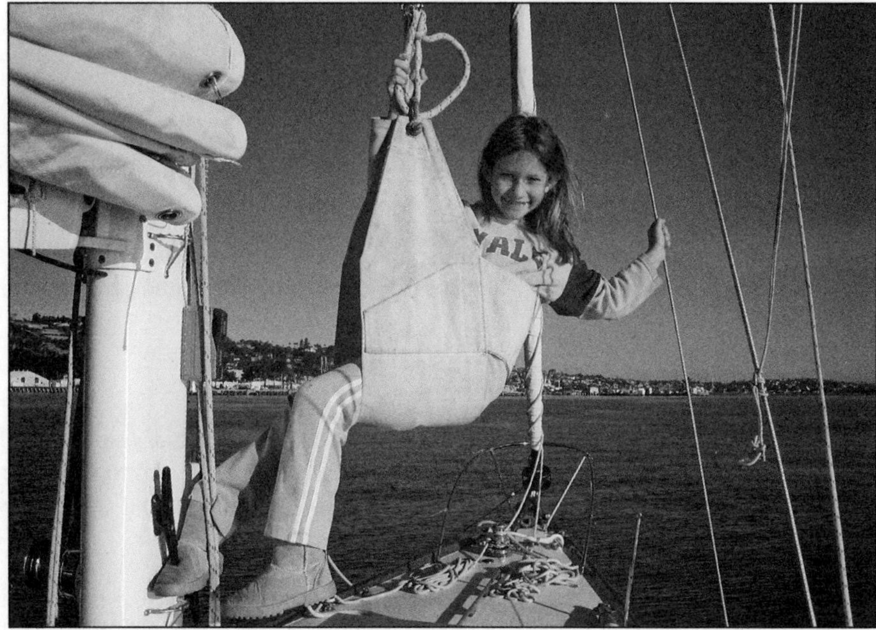

FIGURE 16-6: A bosun's chair provides comfort and safety for going up the mast.

Photo courtesy of authors

Whenever possible when going aloft, use a second halyard as a backup. You don't want to find out about a worn halyard when you're up the mast!

Examine the following areas for signs of stress or damage:

- **Mast section:** Dents and cracks are bad. So are missing rivets.
- **Sheaves:** Every halyard has a sheave that you need to examine.

» **Spreaders:** Try moving the spreaders by shaking them at the end. Movement is bad unless they're clearly designed to move laterally (fore and aft at the tip). Look for fatigue at the inside ends, and check the attachment to the shrouds.

» **Standing rigging:** The ends of the standing rigging, where they terminate on the mast and hull, are the first places to look. Check carefully, because a broken stay is a sure way to lose a mast. As with all metal fittings, look for cracks, signs of deformation, and corrosion.

» **Tangs:** *Tangs* are the attachment points for the standing rigging.

» **Turnbuckles:** Some turnbuckles — which are adjustment devices used primarily to tighten rods — are on deck; some may be aloft. You should lubricate turnbuckles when they're turned under load.

» **Water pockets:** Anywhere that water can sit is a prime location for corrosion. Look under taped fittings and anywhere else water might pool.

Maintaining Your Sails

Sails are your boat's engine, so keep them well oiled and in tune. With proper care, your sails will last longer and retain their designed shape when flying in the wind. In this section, we focus on how to fold, store, and care for your sails.

Folding sails

After using your sail, put it away in a manner that's easy on both the sail and you. Some racers on smaller boats roll their sails (from top to bottom) after a day on the water. Rolling may be easier on the sailcloth, but this task is cumbersome. An easier way is folding the sail.

REMEMBER

You can easily roll sails that are fully battened, like most catamaran mainsails, because the battens provide support, like a venetian blind. Rolling these sails is preferable to taking out all the battens and then folding the sail.

You can fold sails from bottom to top with creases horizontal to the foot, like an accordion. Mainsails on larger keelboats can be flaked in this manner right on top of the boom for easy storage, as Figure 16-7 shows.

FIGURE 16-7: A mainsail flaked on the boom and secured with ropes or sail ties.

Photo courtesy of Sally Samins

Follow these easy steps to fold your sails:

1. **Pick your spot, and stretch the sail out to its full size (if possible).**

TIP

   Find a spot that's at least as long and wide as a single fold on which to fold the sail. Grass lawns make great sail-folding surfaces; parking lots are bad because they're rough and dirty.

2. **Remove the battens from their pockets on the sail.**

   Except for the very short, permanently installed battens sewn to the leeches of some jibs, remove all the battens so that you can fold the sail into a smaller bundle.

3. **Stretch the foot out, and with one person at the tack and one at the clew, begin folding the sail like an accordion, starting at the bottom, as Figure 16-8 shows.**

   Pull against each other just enough to define the crease of the next fold.

4. **Work from bottom to the top.**

   Each fold should be approximately the same width: about 1 foot (30 centimeters) wide for a dinghy sail and 3 feet (1 meter) or more for a 50-foot (15-meter) keelboat sail.

5. **Roll up the folded sail, and bag it.**

   When you reach the head of the sail, begin rolling or folding the sail lengthwise into a shape that fits in the sail bag.

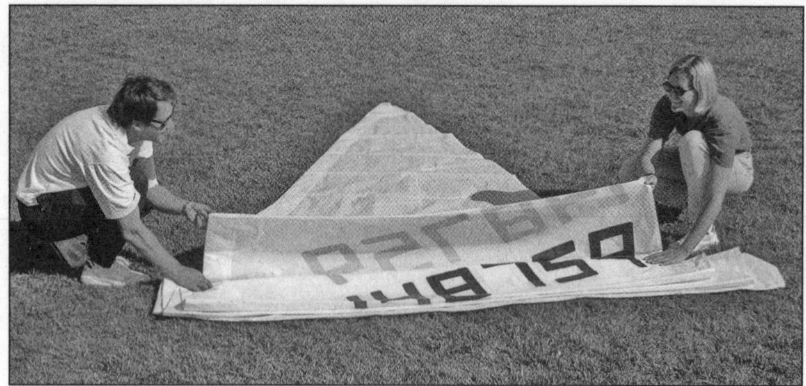

FIGURE 16-8: Keep tension on the sail to minimize wrinkles.

Photo courtesy of authors

Storing sails

Here are some tips to consider when you're putting sails away after a day on the water:

- **Keep all the pieces together.** If battens or other fittings come with the sail, store them with the sail in its bag.
- **Keep your sails out of the sun.** The sun's ultraviolet light degrades sailcloth and the stitching that holds the seams together. Therefore, cover the sails or store them away from the sun's rays while you aren't using them.
- **Minimize the creases.** If you don't have to roll them up into a tiny bundle, don't. Try not to crease any plastic windows.
- **Store your sails dry.** If you're going to sail again tomorrow, you don't have to dry your wet sails, but if you plan to store your sails for longer than a few days, make sure that they're dry. A lawn or the deck of your boat can be a good spot to spread the sails out to dry. If you're storing them for the winter, take the extra effort to rinse the salt off.

Caring for your sails

Most sails suffer their worst damage when they're hoisted under sail. You can take a few measures to protect your sails and to keep them looking good and holding together longer:

- **Don't let them flap too much.** Luffing degrades sails faster than the sun. In the America's Cup, crews actually keep track of the number of times a sail is tacked because it flaps when it tacks, shortening the sail's competitive life. Never leave your sails up and luffing at anchor or at the dock.

- **Don't sail without battens.** Without their support, the sail becomes overloaded in the region around the missing batten.
- **Don't use sails in too much wind.** Some sails, especially spinnakers, are made of lightweight cloth that can blow out in strong winds.
- **Inspect the seams, batten pockets, bolt rope or slugs, and corners for wear and tear.** Sails usually rip in these places. If they look questionable, take them to a sailmaker, drag out your needle and thread, or slap on some of that sticky-back tape we discuss in Chapter 15.
- **Protect sails from chafe.** Common chafe locations are where the sails hit the spreader and the lifelines. A layer of sticky-back tape applied over the at-risk location provides sufficient protection.

When your sails do get a rip or a hole, have a sailmaker fix them. But you can always refer to Chapter 15 if you're under way or in a do-it-yourself frame of mind.

Caring for the Hull

TIP

As you hose off your boat and fittings after sailing (an important part of boat maintenance if your boat sails in saltwater), take a good look at some of the high-load areas where serious structural problems may be apparent. Keep your eye open for cracks or signs of water leakage that indicate weak areas. Sometimes, supposedly stainless-steel fasteners attached to the hull begin to show signs of rust. If possible, apply a light amount of force and shake any attached fittings to see whether they're still secure.

The following list includes some parts of (or attached to) the hull and deck above the water line that come under high loads and that you should inspect after each sail:

- *Chain plates* (metal fittings to which the shrouds, forestay, and backstay are attached)
- Jib tracks
- Main traveler and mainsheet
- Cleats and jammers
- Mast step and *partners* (the point where the mast leaves the deck)
- Attachment points of other fittings

If your boat is stored in saltwater, its metal parts can turn it into a big battery, and chemical reaction can result in serious corrosion. To fend off the highly corrosive effect of saltwater on metal, you must give the saltwater something even more edible. If your boat has an inboard engine, you should have a zinc fitting attached to the propeller shaft. When dockside, you can also hang a plate of zinc (attached by a battery-type cable and clamp to the chain plates) overboard. Your local marine store has these sacrificial zinc anodes in stock.

Looking Under Your Boat

If your sailboat is a dinghy, you may be able to flip it upside down on shore to look at and work on the underside of the hull. You can most easily inspect keelboats on a trailer or other support on dry land, or you can always don a mask and snorkel. The same principles and guidelines apply under the waterline as above the waterline. Pay attention to the following high-load areas:

- **The attachment point of your foils (keel/centerboard and rudder):** Look for small horizontal cracks that can develop where the keel meets the hull or keel stub, or rust stains around the keel bolts. Ask a professional to look at any problem areas.
- **The steering system:** Check the rudder and its attachment points for signs of wear and tear. If the boat has wheel steering, check the *quadrant* (bracket around the rudder post that connects to the steering cables) and steering cables. The steering cables should be taut, not sloppy or overly tight.
- **The propeller shaft:** If you have an inboard engine, inspect the propeller shaft and its support structure.

Most composite dinghies and keelboats that are *drysailed* (stored out of the water) are happy with their original gel-coat bottom. If your boat lives in the water, it probably already has antifouling bottom paint on it. This stuff inhibits the growth of barnacles and slimy grass. If you're considering a new coat of antifouling bottom paint, check with a local boatyard to find out about any restrictions in your waters. Certain types of these toxic paints are restricted, especially in freshwater lakes.

TIP

When selecting a bottom paint, consider the manufacturer's information. Certain types of paints work better in different situations. For boat-maintenance-related research we often refer to *Practical Sailor* (`https://www.practical-sailor.com`), which has been the sailors' version of *Consumer Reports* for nearly five decades.

Most marinas have divers who scrub the bottom of your boat (and maintain the zinc on the propeller shaft) each month (or more) for a reasonable fee, compared with the hassle of donning that dive gear and doing the work yourself. Keeping your bottom clean is well worth the investment; a clean bottom is a fast bottom.

Keeping an Eye on the Engine

Hey, isn't this book about sailing? Yes, but most larger (longer than 25 feet, or 8 meters) keelboats have a noisemaker that can come in handy when you're docking in tight situations, in emergencies, and when (heaven forbid) the wind dies. This section focuses on using and caring for your engine.

Using the engine

Before you do anything with your engine, make sure to read your owner's manual, which is the best source of information on operation and maintenance. You also want to remember the following general operating rules for all types of engines:

- **Check the fluids.** Fuel, oil, and coolant (if any) are the big three.
- **Don't count on reverse.** We discuss operating a boat under power in docking situations in Chapter 6. Just remember that if you're moving forward at any significant speed, the reverse gear's effect is laughable, so don't count on a blast of reverse to stop the boat.
- **Look for water.** Most inboard engines are water-cooled and feature exhaust exit holes that are visible from on deck, often in the transom. When you start the engine, confirm that water is coming out (usually, a slow, pulsing flow) of the exhaust, which means that the cooling system is working properly. If not, stop the engine; something is plugged, or the water intake valve is closed.
- **Slow down to shift.** A boat isn't a rental car. Idle the throttle down to a bare minimum before shifting gears.
- **Ventilate first.** Explosive fumes from all sorts of sources can collect in the bilge of your boat. Make sure that the area around the engine (which can get hot and often has sparks involved) is ventilated before starting. If the boat has a *blower* (a fan in the engine compartment), run it for at least 5 minutes. Make sure that the cabin of the boat has been open for a while and check below for any funny smells before starting the engine.

» **Watch the temperature.** A high temperature may indicate a cooling-system problem (maybe a plastic bag sucked into the intake). Avoid operating your engine at maximum throttle; doing so may cause overheating. Watch the RPM meter if you have one, and keep the RPMs at or below the engine's safe operating limit. If your manual doesn't tell you this speed, check with a professional for advice.

Caring for the engine

As with a car, you probably want to leave the major (and maybe even the minor) stuff to a professional. Maintaining the engine in your boat is very important. The saltwater environment, often less-than-pristine fuel sources, and operation at various angles of heel can wreak havoc on the best power plant. Here are some important points to remember:

» **Change your oil.** Check and change it regularly; oil is the lifeblood of any engine.

» **Check your filters.** Along with having an adequate fuel filter, you should have a water separator in the fuel line; check and clean it regularly.

» **Rinse out that salt.** Saltwater corrodes metal. You can flush the cooling systems of most outboard engines with freshwater by using a special set of ears that attach to a hose. Ideally, you should flush an outboard after every saltwater use. Rinse off all the external parts of the engine with freshwater. Many inboard engines have sealed cooling systems like a car, so rinsing the salt after every use is not necessary.

» **Take along spares.** If you plan on making a longer trip, make sure that you have some common spare parts (such as drive belts, spare filters, and oil) and know how to install them. Ask your engine mechanic for a good list and instructions.

Leaving Your Boat

When the sailing is over and the time comes to go home, you want to make sure that your boat is happy and safe while you're away. This short section looks at the short-term and long-term concerns you need to remember.

Short-term

If you'll be back to the boat in the next few days or even within the month, you want to put your boat away securely, but not so securely that you'll need the whole weekend to prepare for your next sail. Here are some tips to help you make sure that your boat will be ready to go when you decide to take it out for another spin:

- **Minimize water collection.** Dinghies can be stored upside down if you take down the mast. If you leave the mast up, try to angle the dinghy so that rainwater drains out quickly. Many dinghies have drain plugs on the stern for this purpose. Most cockpits of keelboats drain automatically, but make sure that all hatches and openings to the interior are well sealed. A cover over the boom tied to the rails can also help keep the rain out.
- **Make no dents, please.** Be careful when storing your dinghy on land. If you store it with the mast up, make sure that the hull is supported in several locations, not a single point where the hull can depress and weaken. If you store your dinghy upside down, consider where the deck is strongest — often at the very bow, near the chain plates, and at the transom.
- **Protect your boat and its gear from the sun.** Store as much stuff (rope, blocks, sails, and so on) as practical out of those rays. A good trick is to hoist all your halyards to protect them. Tie a light retriever line to the halyard end, and secure it on deck or at the mast.
- **Protect your gear from the wind.** You know to tie down the hull, but consider other things that can loosen and blow on a windy day, such as any sail, including a roller-furled jib and halyards (which can cause a real racket).
- **Secure the hull.** If you store your boat on land, make sure that you tie it down securely. If your boat lives afloat, check the dock or mooring lines. In Chapters 6 and 10, we cover the best way to secure the boat.
- **Turn off anything electrical other than an automatic bilge pump.** You don't want to return to a dead battery. If your boat has an AC powered battery charger – then you should plug it in.

Long-term

Unfortunately, in many parts of the world, the sailing season isn't year-round. If you're going to leave your boat for longer than a week or two, consider making these further efforts to keep the boat happy:

- **Covering:** Whenever possible, cover your equipment to protect it from rain, snow, sun, and dirt.

» **Engine:** Ask your mechanic what, if anything, you should do to your engine, including winterizing to prevent ice from forming in the engine block. Disconnect the battery terminals unless the boat is stored in the water, where an automatic bilge pump is necessary.

» **Fluids:** Drain water tanks, and check with your mechanic about what to do with your fuel tank.

» **Haul out:** Most large keelboats are hauled out at a boatyard, cleaned (especially below the waterline), derigged, and covered with protective tarps for the winter. Make sure that the boat is supported and secured adequately.

» **Lubrication:** Consider lubricating all your moving fittings, including parts of the mast, to protect them from inactivity.

» **Mildew:** If you live in a wet area and plan to store your boat under plastic tarps, you're going to have a mildew factory under there. Take home for storage anything that's susceptible to damage. Some bigger keelboats even have a dehumidifier rigged up to drain into the sink.

» **Sails:** We talked about folding (or rolling) your sails in the "Caring for your sails" section earlier in this chapter. You may want your sailmaker to make an annual inspection of your sails at the loft.

WARNING

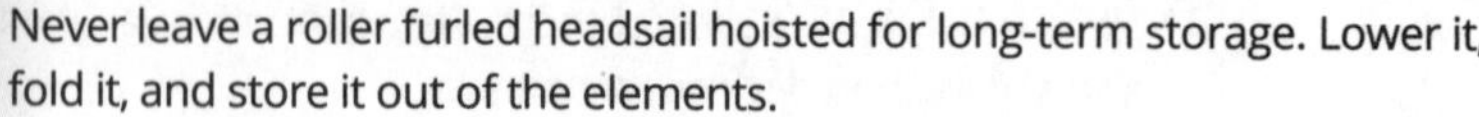

Never leave a roller furled headsail hoisted for long-term storage. Lower it, fold it, and store it out of the elements.

IN THIS CHAPTER

» Selecting the right boat and trip for your family

» Keeping kids safe and happy

» Earning the right to use the rowboat

» Having fun at anchor

Chapter 17 Cruising with Children

O, well for the fisherman's boy,

That he shouts with his sister at play!

O, well for the sailor lad,

That he sings in his boat on the bay!

—ALFRED LORD TENNYSON

If you have a family and love to sail, here's an important point: You get to sail more frequently if your family also enjoys the sport. Sailing can bring your family closer as you work together to keep the boat moving, and your kids may discover the joys of unplugging from technology.

In this chapter, we look at how to ensure that your sailing trip with your children goes as well as possible. We also share tips for planning a fun daytrip with some time at anchor. Kids come in all sizes and shapes, but we focus mainly on the younger, preteen years.

Preparing Your Family Crew

Probably every parent's biggest fear on a boat is a child drowning. One of the most important steps before taking your family sailing is *making sure that everyone can swim*. When children are confident of their swimming abilities and are comfortable in the water, they seem to pick up the basics of sailing much more easily because they're more relaxed and more likely to have fun.

After your kids have mastered swimming class and enjoy the water, check out sailing-school options in Chapter 2. Most children grasp sailing very quickly on small dinghies at a camp or sailing school.

Nonswimmers can enjoy sailing too, of course, but they should always wear a life jacket on all boats. And consider having them wear a safety harness with tether on a keelboat. For more information, check out the section "Wearing the right life jackets and safety harnesses" later in this chapter, as well as Chapter 3.

Picking the Right Boat and Trip

While your crew is getting shipshape, you can think about what kind of boat to ship them out on. The most important factor is the *experience level of the adult*.

We do *not* recommend that novice sailors ever take children sailing on boats that they're skippering. Novice sailors should try to go sailing with people who have *more* experience than they do. For intermediate sailors, the most important point is to pick a boat that they feel comfortable in — so that the children feel comfortable and enjoy the experience.

This section provides you with some quick pointers about selecting the right trip as well as the right boat for you, depending on your ability level, your crew's comfort level, and the length of your trip.

Choosing a keelboat

Beginning sailors, young and old, usually feel more comfortable on a *keelboat* than aboard a *dinghy*. (See the next section for more on dinghies.) A keelboat — check out Chapter 1 — has a heavy, ballasted keel fin under the boat that provides stability and prevents capsizing. Large cruising multihulls (which gain stability from having more than one hull) are also stable and comfortable. Here are some other reasons why these bigger boats are the best choice for families, even if your trip is just for the afternoon:

SAILING FOR TWO

So you think pregnancy rules out sailing? Not so. In fact, JJ not only sailed, but also raced in the United States, Japan, and Spain while pregnant. A quick tip for pregnant sailors: Your center of gravity is higher than usual, so be extra-careful when you step into a tippy dinghy.

Also, even if you haven't had any morning sickness or don't usually get seasick, the motion on a sailboat may make you feel queasy during pregnancy. For tips on combating seasickness, see Appendix B.

- Keelboats often have cabins down below that are handy for taking naps, storing snacks and cold drinks, and spreading out toys.
- Most keelboats have a deep cockpit, where kids are safest, as well as lifelines that provide extra security when walking on deck.

REMEMBER

If you're adamant about sailing with your kids, but you've completed only a basic sailing course and have little other experience, your best boat choice is a small keelboat (18 to 25 feet) — but *only* for day sailing in light and moderate winds in protected waters.

Table 17-1 offers some general guidelines for the *minimum* age of children on various types of boats, given the experience of the sailor.

TABLE 17-1 Suggested Minimum Age of Child on Different Boats

	Skill Level of Adult Skipper		
Type of Boat	Novice	Intermediate	Advanced
Dinghy shorter than 13 ft (4 m)	X	10 years old	5 years old
Dinghy longer than 13 ft (4 m)	X	6 years old	3 years old
Keelboat 18 to 25 ft (5 to 8 m)	10 years old*	6 years old	Newborn
Keelboat longer than 25 ft (8 m)	X	6 years old	Newborn

**For novice sailors, we recommend sailing with children on a small keelboat only if the children are good swimmers and are comfortable in new situations.*

Note: The table assumes light to moderate wind and sea conditions in protected waters. For the purposes of the table, a *novice* sailor has the equivalent of one basic sailing course and little practical experience. An *intermediate* sailor has completed basic sailing training and has six months to two years of practical experience. And *advanced* sailors have three or more years of experience in a variety of wind conditions. An X indicates that we don't recommend that novice sailors take children of any age on these boats.

Selecting a dinghy

Dinghies are usually smaller than keelboats (shorter than 20 feet, or 6 meters) and have a lightweight, retractable fin instead of a heavy lead keel; therefore, they're less stable and can flip over. In our experience, the scariest parts about dinghy sailing for small children are the sudden changes in *heel* (the tipping motion) and the fear of *capsizing* (tipping over). But if you're taking children out in a dinghy, here are tips to make the day a success, starting with things to do before you leave shore:

REMEMBER

- Make sure that you and your children are wearing life jackets.
- Make sure that your children dress warmly. Waterproof jackets or wet suits are nice so they stay warm even if they get wet.
- Have a towel and change of clothes on shore so they can get dry and comfortable as soon as you finish sailing.
- Before you leave the dock or beach, talk with your children about heeling. At the dock, show them how to move their weight to counteract heel.
- Run through what to do if the boat capsizes (see Chapter 7). While you're near the dock or a protected shore, consider doing a controlled capsize (in which you pull the boat over) so that the children can see how easy getting the boat upright is.
- Be prepared to move your weight around often to minimize heeling while sailing.
- If possible, let your children sit in the center of the boat in a secure spot where they can hold on.
- Be confident so that your children feel confident too.

Although dinghies offer the thrill of being close to the water, they have less room, and often, each crew member has a specific job. Those realities make caring for the comfort, entertainment, and safety of small children difficult, no matter how good a sailor you are.

Practicing Safety on the Water

This section covers important safety matters, including selecting the right life jackets and safety harnesses, keeping an eye on your children, and tips for childproofing a boat.

Wearing the right life jackets and safety harnesses

Do you let your small child go for a car ride without getting into a car seat? Probably not. The same consistency can help get your child to always wear a life jacket on the water. Insist that your child keep their life jacket on while walking on the dock or pier, too. (See Chapter 3 for information regarding life jackets.)

Children's life jackets have become so comfortable that we see lots of kids riding their bikes home after sailing class with their life jackets still on. When purchasing a small child's life jacket, look for the following specifics:

- **Bright color for visibility:** Reflective tape is great too. You want to be able to spot your child quickly if they fall in the water.
- **A strap between the legs and extra neck support:** The strap keeps the jacket from slipping off, and the neck support holds a younger child's head above the water.
- **Snug fit:** The life jacket shouldn't be so large that the child can't put both hands together in front (in which case they won't be able to hold on to the lifelines and handrails properly).

TIP

If you're still nervous about your child's being near the water, even in a life jacket, test the life jacket in the pool first.

Another option while you're under way is having your child wear a safety harness with a built-in autoinflatable life jacket. Clip the tether line to a strong attachment point in the center of the boat (*not* the lifelines). Make sure that the tether is short enough that the child can't reach the water. (See Chapter 15 for more on harnesses.)

So after you put your child's life jacket on, your job's over, right? As you know, a parent's job is never over, which is especially true while sailing.

Keeping tabs on the kids

WARNING

Watching your child play around a boat is like watching them play near a busy street: Real danger lurks close by, and you must know where your child is at every moment. *Never* leave younger children alone on deck for even a second, even if they're strong swimmers.

TIP

You can use the following safety rules and guidelines to get started:

- Even at the dock, allow children on deck only with an adult; require children to tell an adult when they're going down below.
- While sailing, don't allow children to go on deck without an adult's permission or without their life jacket and/or safety harness.
- Know all the ways that children can get on deck. They may surprise you by opening and climbing through the front hatch by themselves.
- Review with your kids the safety information in Chapter 7, especially the information about where the safe areas are on deck.
- Know when you're on watch. Always hand off the caretaker's responsibility verbally, and get verbal confirmation from the on-watch adult. Watch children just as carefully when you're at the dock as when you're sailing.
- Make sure that children sit safely below or quietly in the cockpit while you're leaving the dock and returning so you can dock the boat without risk of distraction or, worse, a collision.

Childproofing a cruising boat

Before your family steps onto a larger cruising sailboat, keep these safety precautions in mind:

- **Rule out running.** Rule it out everywhere, but especially on the marina docks or pier or while the boat is under way.
- **Establish appropriate safety rules, and be consistent in enforcing those rules.** Your rules might include "no go" areas such as forward of the mast while under way.
- **Consider weaving netting onto the lifelines.** Netting can provide a barrier between a younger child (and toys and pets) and the water. We recommend that you weave netting onto the lifelines of your boat if you have a toddler onboard. And even with netting, never leave a child unsupervised on deck.
- **Don't allow anyone to lean over or through the lifelines.** This rule applies whether you have netting or not.
- **Ensure that any lifeline gates have clasps that little fingers can't undo.** Close the gates securely as soon as you leave the dock.
- **Look at where a child would land if they fell down the hatch.** Do you need to pad any sharp corners in the cabin?

» **Put an awning over the cockpit while at anchor.** Sunburn can ruin a child's (as well as everyone else's) enjoyment of sailing. Awnings provide a shady, cool resting spot.

Enjoying a Longer Trip

Although keeping children happy on longer trips is quite possible, you're better off interspersing a short sail with a longer period at anchor or dockside — unless you don't mind being asked "When are we going to get there?" a million times. Planning ahead can keep those restless passengers entertained.

The most important items to bring are food and drinks. Nothing makes sailors grumpier than running out of food, even on an afternoon sail. And make sure that you have all the safety items listed in Chapter 3, including sunscreen, sunglasses, hats, and so on.

This section also has tips for sailing with a baby and keeping older kids entertained on a longer trip. Obviously, you have the best idea about what to bring for your kids, but we hope these suggestions will help.

Having Fun at Anchor

At some point, a child gains the maturity and the experience to be a valuable member of the crew, and many of the rules in the preceding section no longer apply. We don't think that this transformation occurs at a set age, but we encourage you to keep this fact in mind: Giving your child more freedom and authority on a boat (at the right time) is another great way to build their confidence and love of sailing.

Earning the right to go on their own

As a child, getting to go off in the rowboat by yourself or with your friends is a big step. As a parent, watching an older child head off in the rowboat for the first time is as nerve-wracking as letting them ride their bike to a friend's house a few blocks away for the first time (even though the peace and tranquility after they left made the experience worthwhile). The keys are teaching the kids about safety and setting guidelines.

WARNING

Your older children need to master the following skills before heading off on their own:

- **Ability to handle the equipment:** Children must know how to operate and get a boat onto and off a beach safely and how to tie secure knots if they're docking the boat.
- **Emergency preparation:** Practice a person-overboard drill, and teach the children what to do if the boat swamps and how to propel the boat if they lose one oar. Review the safety information we cover in Chapters 7 and 15.
- **Responsibility:** Responsible behavior includes being careful with the equipment and continuing to wear their life jackets even when they're out of your sight.
- **Knowledge of wind direction, tides, currents, and rocks in the area:** Rowing upwind or upcurrent can be exhausting or impossible. Before your child goes, review the information on navigation in Chapter 9, look at a chart of the area with them, and discuss boundary limits.

TIP

Having a kayak, paddleboard, or some other means of transportation while you're at anchor and your children are off in the rowboat is pretty nice for you and can be crucial for safety (in other words, a rescue) if they don't come back.

Essentially, you must make sure that your children feel comfortable and safe in the rowboat. Then you can trust them while they're off having fun — because as the Water Rat says in *The Wind in the Willows*, "There is nothing . . . half so much worth doing as simply messing about in boats."

Packing the right gear for a fun day on the water

Besides the items listed in Chapter 3, here are our suggestions for gear to make an afternoon at anchor enjoyable.

- Fishing poles and gear
- Snorkels, masks, and fins, as well as a "viewfinder" for watching the creatures on the bottom from a rowboat

TIP

While you're at anchor, a sudden puff of wind can sweep toys and towels overboard. Or a wave can rock the boat enough to knock over drinks. Even if it's calm, always secure everything, and bring a few clothespins so you can clip wet towels to the lifelines.

- An extra bucket for holding "beach finds"
- A sailing book or two

IN THIS CHAPTER

» Understanding chartering

» Recognizing chartering skills

» Looking at popular cruising destinations

Chapter 18 Chartering: Changes in Latitude

Whenever I find myself growing grim about the mouth; whenever it is a damp, drizzly November in my soul . . . then, I account it high time to get to sea as soon as I can. . . .

—HERMAN MELVILLE, MOBY DICK

Imagine spending a week's vacation with your closest friends and family in some of the most beautiful spots in the world. Thanks to sailboat charter companies, you can take short vacation cruises in sailing paradises around the world. In this chapter, we look at your options for chartering a boat and sailing away. We also help you prepare for the business side of the charter. Do you want to sail with a professional captain (and maybe a cook), or do you want to be in charge on a bareboat charter? We'll review the skills and any documentation you'll need. Last, we look at the top cruising spots around the world. So what are you waiting for? You don't even have to own a boat!

What to Expect When You Charter a Boat

Thanks to excellent charter companies around the world, chartering a boat doesn't require as much planning as you might expect. Hey, you can even go today; just log on or pick up the phone! The larger charter companies, such as Dream Yacht Charters (`www.dreamyachtcharter.com`) and The Moorings (`www.moorings.com`), can help arrange everything from air travel to hotel stays and side trips to provisioning. Very popular with newbies are the "cruise-and-learn" vacations to brush up on your sailing skills during the whole trip or just the first part. Some companies organize *flotillas*, in which a lead boat with a professional captain and other staff provide support and organize excursions and parties.

REMEMBER

The most common way to book your trip is directly with the charter company, but charter brokers can do the deal on your behalf. You can research the various charter companies by scanning the advertising sections in the back of some sailing magazines or going online.

A great magazine for charter aficionados is *Cruising World* (`www.cruisingworld.com`). The magazine has monthly features on different cruising locales, as well as an annual readers' survey of the best charter companies. Just to let you know how popular cruising vacations are, more than 90 percent of the respondents to *Cruising World*'s annual surveys feel that the cost was worth the experience and that their sailing vacation went smoothly. We think that the other 10 percent probably never came back from the islands!

This section specifically details what you need to do and what you can expect when chartering a sailboat. Follow our advice, and you should have a memorable experience.

Going bareboat cruising

The most common way to charter is through a *bareboat charter*, in which your group rents a *bare* boat from a charter company, fully rigged but without any skipper or paid crew members on board. But those latter options are available too; a *crewed charter* gives you more time to relax and learn from a pro!

Planning the trip

If you want to have a successful bareboat cruise, look into the following when you plan your vacation:

- **The type of boat:** Chartering enables you to try sailing different boats. The bigger charter companies offer a variety of monohulls and catamarans.

A catamaran has more space on deck (and that second hull for more space down below) than a monohull of the same length. If having a specific boat is important to you, make sure to get a commitment in writing from your charter company. Ask about the contingency plan if the boat you request isn't available or isn't ready when you arrive. If you're sailing with a large group, make sure that you get a plan of the boat's sleeping arrangements. (Pick the biggest cabin for yourself!)

- **The charter fee and contract:** When you book a charter, expect to pay a deposit (usually 25–50 percent of the total) upon booking and the remainder 30–60 days before the charter start date. Your charter contract should include a refund schedule, but expect to forfeit the entire charter fee if you cancel within 60 days. The average price of a weeklong bareboat charter (40-foot monohull) varies greatly ($2,500–$6,000, or more) with the season, type and age of boat, and location. All else being equal, bigger boats cost more, and catamarans are more than monohulls of the same length. Often, smaller charter companies offer more competitive rates (and sometimes older boats), so shopping around will pay if you're price-sensitive. You can also purchase travel insurance to cover you if you must cancel. You'll be asked to prove your sailing ability. Sometimes, a résumé is helpful, and so are any licenses or certifications you've earned at a sailing school (see "Checking out your craft" below about International Proficiency Certificates).

  Make sure that you read the fine print in the contract and are clear on basic things such as when you can get on the boat and when it must be returned. Try to negotiate a check-in schedule so you'll have time to do all the paperwork and housekeeping, including provisioning, and can leave the harbor and start your cruise that first day. Cruising time is a-wastin' at the dock!

- **Liability coverage:** Each charter company has its own policy on damage and loss. The typical policy is either a large, refundable deposit (about the price of a one-week charter) or a small, nonrefundable premium ($40–$60 per day for a 40-foot boat) that covers everything. We recommend going for the latter option.

- **Maintenance and repair services:** Keep in mind that a newer boat is probably less likely to have broken equipment, although the top charter companies have fantastic maintenance programs. Ask about the turnaround time between charters; the boat needs to be at the charter base for about a day for routine maintenance and cleaning.

- **On site support:** Make sure that you know how to contact the charter company by phone and VHF radio (see Chapter 7) and that you know its policy if you need assistance. Most charter companies have support networks throughout the cruising area.

- **Boat provisioning:** The charter company can organize partial or full provisioning, saving you a day of shopping in unfamiliar markets. When you get aboard, stow the food yourself so that you'll know where to find it. Unless cooking in a sailboat-size galley is your idea of a great vacation, we advise you to keep your menus simple and plan eating out a bit as part of your vacation budget.
- **Additional gear:** You need a *rowing dinghy* (usually, an inflatable equipped with a small outboard engine) to get to shore, and the charter company should include one.

  REMEMBER

  Throughout this book, we use the word *dinghy* to describe any sailboat with a centerboard. Here, we refer to a *rowing dinghy,* which is usually called a *dinghy* too; these boats usually aren't rigged with sails (although they can be). So for the rest of this chapter on chartering, when we say *dinghy,* we mean a rowing dinghy (which probably has an outboard). Okay?

  The charter company can organize snorkeling and other watersports gear such as stand-up paddleboards at a premium (except on high-end boats, where it may be included). We usually bring our own masks and snorkels, so we know they fit. Make sure to put any specific gear requests in writing, and get a confirmed response. Charter companies should also provide basic tools and navigation equipment, including nautical charts and a VHF radio. If you're in another country, a mobile hotspot might be a good add-on to consider. Check out the boat's equipment list to ensure that it has all the necessary goodies that you'll need (such as a way to charge a few cellphones at the same time and a Bluetooth stereo to play your song list).
- **Items to pack:** Pack lightly; the charter company can advise you on expected weather conditions. Space is at a premium, especially if you have a full boat. See Chapter 3 for tips on clothing needs afloat. And in the tropics, cover up lily-white skin no matter how warm the weather is. One charter company we know suggests that to ensure the perfect charter, bring half the clothes and twice the cash you think you'll need!

Checking out your craft

After you arrive at the front door of the charter company, ready to go cruising, you need to do the following:

- **Inspect your boat.** It's great if you can get on board the boat for an hour or so before the orientation meeting; that will give you time to look over the boat and make sure that all the required equipment is on board. You're bound to come up with some questions during this inspection. Make sure to point out anything you notice that's wrong. Ideally, the charter company should fix any broken equipment before you leave, but you have to balance repairs with your cruising schedule; it may be worth jury-rigging the outhaul to be able to leave the dock on time.

- **The all-important check-out/boat orientation.** The charter company's representative should give you a thorough orientation to the boat. This boat is new to you, and no matter how experienced you are, it's going to save you time and stress if you pay attention and ask questions. We recommend having a notebook, a pen, and one other experienced crew member with you for this session. We often film some of the demos (such as those on how to run the charging system and electric panel) on our phones for later reference. This orientation is your chance to make sure that you understand how all the systems work, including the engine, house electronics, fresh water and capacities, heads and holding tanks, sailing gear, safety equipment, anchor windlass, stove and fridge, sailing electronics and autopilot, navigation gear and radios, and (of course) the rowing (or outboard-powered) dinghy.
- **Get to know the cruising area.** Even if you've prepared well and studied the area, always take the time to sit down with a company representative to look over the nautical chart of the area and get recommendations on the best places to anchor or stop. You want to be briefed on the local attractions and any hazards. Even if you have a plan, ask for advice on planning your ideal itinerary, as well as backup plans in case of adverse weather.
- **Prove your ability to handle the boat.** These days, most charter companies have stringent requirements, and you should be clear about those requirements before you sign your charter contract. Certainly, certification to a recognized standard, such as the American Sailing Association's (ASA) or US Sailing's Bareboat Charter Standard, can be helpful, providing you the necessary skills in any event). In many European countries, a formal license or International Certificate of Competence (ICC) is required for the charterer or person in charge. We don't have boating licenses in the United States (yet), so qualified U.S. sailors should obtain an International Proficiency Certificate (IPC) from either the ASA (`https://asa.com` or US Sailing (`www.ussailing.org`) to charter in Europe. In other parts of the world, it's likely that paper proof of your skipper's (and crew members') proficiency will suffice. You could be asked to prove your skills on the boat, although that situation is kind of rare. If the charter company doesn't think that you possess the ability to handle the boat, it has the right to refuse your business or give you the opportunity to pay for a captain.

Cruising with a skipper

If you need pampering on your vacation, chartering a fully crewed yacht is for you. You can help with the sailing as much or as little as you like. Delicious meals appear at the proper times, and you can just relax and enjoy the sights. Your next bank statement will reflect this first-class treatment, of course. We've seen some truly *awesome* boats, 80 feet (24 meters) long and longer on fully crewed charters. The crew can even put away the sailboard for you after they hand you a cold drink!

One in-between option is to have a partially crewed trip in which you hire a skipper for the first half. Then, if you (and the charter company) feel that you're qualified, you can go the rest of the way bareboat. Some charter companies offer a free friendly-skipper service for a half day on your first day out to help you refresh your skills.

And as we mentioned earlier, in some popular destinations, such as the British Virgin Islands, it's easy to find a variety of "learn-to-sail" vacations in which you can earn certification while cruising. Introductory courses will likely start with day classes, followed by some cruising with an instructor.

Important Chartering Skills

What skills are needed to operate a charter boat safely for a week? The person in charge should have at least one full sailing season of experience skippering a similar-size boat in similar conditions. If you've mastered sailing on your lake aboard a two-person dinghy but have never been aboard a bigger keelboat, you need to take some lessons and build more experience. Not everyone on the crew needs to be an expert sailor, but at least two sailors need to be competent. You need to possess and be able to demonstrate the following ten pieces of knowledge and skills before chartering a boat:

- Experience as a skipper on a live-aboard cruise of at least 48 hours.
- Ability to anchor and pick up a mooring safely, using the equipment provided.
- Ability to obtain and interpret the weather forecast.
- Ability to perform coastal piloting by using a nautical chart and compass.
- Understanding of basic safety procedures for the type of boat you're aboard, including man-overboard rescue routines.
- Ability to handle the boat under power in confined areas.
- Understanding of onboard systems, including navigation equipment, engine, marine head, and galley facilities. Most cruising boats have a roller furler for the jib, a lazy jack system for storing the mainsail, and a windlass to help with the anchor; make sure that you understand these systems too.
- Understanding the how to's and the etiquette of anchoring in a crowded harbor.

- Ability to instruct and advise nonsailors and less-expert sailors on the operation of the boat and basic safety considerations.
- Ability to sail. (Just tell the charter company that you've read *Sailing For Dummies*!)

Using Your Dinghy

A key component of an idyllic cruise is having a dinghy tied behind the cruising boat. Because your dinghy is often your ticket to freedom on a cruise, you want to make sure that it doesn't float away. The following tips can make life afloat with a dinghy more enjoyable:

- **Bring a paddle.** An outboard engine may power your dinghy, but make sure that you have some alternate means of propulsion — just in case!
- **Stop that banging.** Assuming that your dinghy is a rubber inflatable, you can tie it so that the engine can't hit the hull of your sailboat. But kayaks and other water toys have a habit of banging against the hull as the wind shifts in the anchorage at 3 a.m., so you may want to pull them up on the boat at night.
- **Tie your dinghy securely.** Whether you're towing your dinghy behind the boat or leaving it at the dinghy dock for some exploring, make sure that you tie it up well. Use a bowline knot, or tie your dinghy around a horn cleat, as Chapter 19 shows.
- **Tow your dinghy safely.** We usually pull our dinghy up on deck for significant passages. But if you decide to pull your dinghy behind you from place to place, take everything out of the boat (oars, fuel tank, engine, swim fins, and so on) before you get under way. Check with the charter company for its recommendations on dinghy towing.
- **Watch out for surf.** Don't try landing your dinghy on a beach with breakers; even small waves can tip your boat. If you must beach your dinghy in waves, try to make your timing so that a wave washes you far up the beach. Then quickly climb out and grab the bow line so that it doesn't drift back. Always land bow first, and depart bow out. Avoid standing in the water between the dinghy and the beach, because a wave can throw the boat right at you.
- **Practice getting in and out of the dinghy.** When the water is rough, it may be safest to hold (with feet and/or bow and stern line) the dinghy alongside the swim step, perpendicular to the sailboat's centerline, and then sit down on the swim step and ease yourself into the dinghy from this seated position rather than step in like a rock star.

Eyeing Popular Cruising Grounds

So you think you're interested in taking a charter? This section provides a list of the ten nicest places we know to go cruising and some close runners-up. All places have great charter companies, but you can also sail your own boat there.

- **Australia's Whitsunday Passage:** Located in the Coral Sea between Queensland and the Great Barrier Reef, the Whitsunday Passage features great diving and a steady southeast trade wind, especially from August to October.
- **The Bahamas:** The Bahamas are popular and easily accessible from the United States. Some of the most beautiful islands are the Abacos (the Family Islands), Eleuthera, and the Exumas. Many safe anchorages in close proximity provide for variety and carefree planning when you're afloat.
- **Caribbean Islands:** Without doubt, the Caribbean is the top charter destination in the world. Especially popular are the U.S. and British Virgin Islands, which feature great year-round weather (although you may want to avoid hurricane season). These islands are especially good for novice charterers because of the predictable winds, deep waters, numerous protected sailing areas, easy navigation, and plenty of beautiful and safe anchorages.
- **Florida Keys:** With easy access from the mainland United States to the Sunshine State, the Florida Keys feature warm shoal waters.
- **Great Lakes:** Get out of the nearby big cities, and you'd swear that you're in the middle of nowhere when you're on the Great Lakes. Did you know that the water of northern Lake Huron is crystal-clear?
- **Mediterranean:** Spain, France, Italy, Croatia, Greece, and Turkey all have plenty of beautiful cruising grounds and lessons in ancient history.
- **Mexico:** The waters of the Gulf of California inside Baja, Mexico, can be magical.
- **New Zealand's Bay of Islands:** Summer — February and March (remember that New Zealand is in the Southern Hemisphere) — is the peak season for the Bay of Islands.
- **Pacific Northwest:** Uncrowded, scenic anchorages are the highlight in the Pacific Northwest. The protected waters of Puget Sound are great cruising grounds, but they have strong currents, big tidal ranges, and cold water.
- **South Pacific:** Tahiti, Tonga, and Fiji have big charter fleets. Watch out for cyclones in the South Pacific in the summer months.

Here are a few of the runners-up (fitting the world into a list of ten is hard):

- **Hawaii:** If you ever sail across the Pacific and make landfall on these islands — seeing the huge volcanic mountains and smelling the flowers — you'll never forget it.
- **California:** We love the Channel Islands of California, a pristine cruising ground just off Southern California.
- **Chesapeake Bay:** Peter loves the soft-shell crabs of Chesapeake Bay. Just make sure that you have a shallow-draft boat to get to all the neat little harbors on the Eastern Shore.
- **Maine:** Maine has beautiful cruising grounds, but they're not for beginners. Challenges for cruising include large tidal ranges, strong currents, possibility of fog, and the rocky coastline.
- **Scandinavia:** Can you say *fjords*? You may after sailing these waters — and you have some amazing archipelagos to explore.

[illegible]

[illegible]

[illegible]

[illegible]

[illegible]

[illegible]

5 The Part of Tens

IN THIS PART . . .

Master ten essential knots so you can keep that boat securely tied.

If you're shopping for a boat, ponder all the questions to ask the salesperson (and yourself) to get a boat that fits your needs.

IN THIS CHAPTER

» Securing the most common types of knots

» Mastering the more advanced knots

Chapter 19

Ten Nautical Knots and How to Tie Them

No one but an acrobat or a sailor could have got up to that bell-rope from the bracket, and no one but a sailor could have made the knots with which the cord was fastened to the chair.

—SIR ARTHUR CONAN DOYLE

Yes, you can tie the knot on a boat, but we're not talking about a wedding. This chapter reviews the basic knots on a sailboat and shows you how to tie them. On most boats, you can find a bowline, a figure-eight knot, a square knot, and maybe a couple of half hitches somewhere.

TIP

Knowing how to tie these knots (especially the bowline and the round turn with two half hitches) and using them properly can save you a great deal of time and make your life afloat safer. With a 5-foot length of rope, you can practice these knots at home and master them quickly. Master them, and you're well on your way to becoming an "able seaman."

Overhand Knot

An *overhand knot* is the basic knot you use to begin tying your shoes, and as you see in the following sections, it's the first step of many sailing knots. If you wear only slip-on shoes, Figure 19-1 shows you how to begin tying your shoes. (Also, you may want to buy *Getting Dressed For Dummies* as soon as it comes out.)

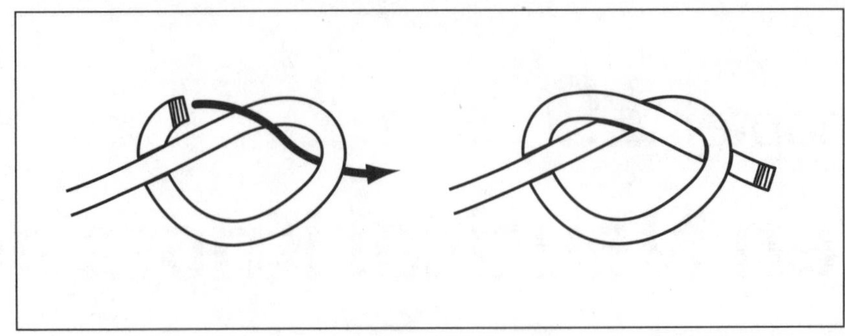

FIGURE 19-1: The basic overhand knot.

© John Wiley & Sons, Inc.

Figure-Eight Knot

The *figure-eight knot* is a lightweight, but it's fun to tie and can save you a great deal of aggravation. While you're sitting in the boat, let your eyes follow the sheets or halyards from start to finish. The "finish" is probably at some sort of cleat. On smaller boats, all these *running rigging* lines should have figure-eight knots (see Figure 19-2) at the very end to prevent the line from getting pulled out of its rigged path (that is, through pulleys and so on). Trust us — when a line "sucks" out of its normal path, it's a hassle, especially if the rope is a halyard!

WARNING

Note that with the additional loads on bigger boat lines, you don't want to tie knots in the ends of spinnaker sheets, because you may need to let the line run through the block in an emergency.

The reason to use a figure-eight knot instead of a simple overhand knot is that the figure-eight is easier to untie after it has been under load (a characteristic of most good sailing knots), whereas an overhand knot can get very tight. In addition, the figure-eight is a bulkier knot and thus is less likely to slip through a cleat or block.

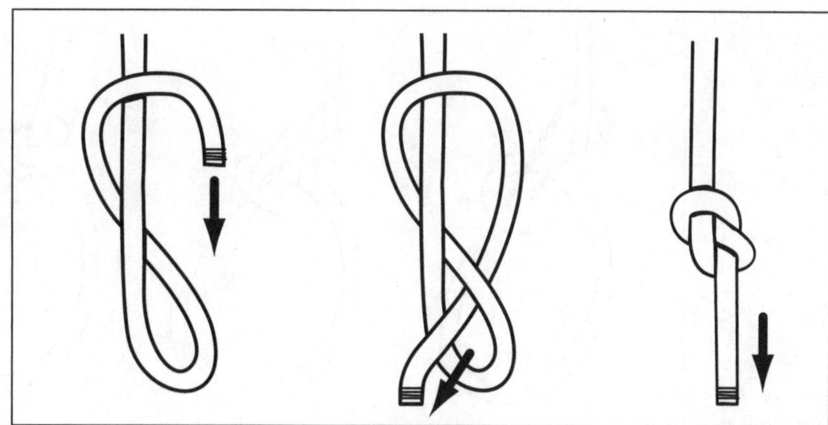

FIGURE 19-2: The figure-eight knot.

© John Wiley & Sons, Inc.

To tie a figure-eight knot, follow these steps:

1. **Make a loop in the end of the line.**
2. **Pass the end of the line under, back over, and up through the loop so that it looks like a figure eight.**

Bowline Knot

The *bowline* (pronounced *bow-lynn*, so it rhymes with *rollin'*) is a beautiful knot. You can call it the essential sailing knot: It's quick to tie and easy to untie, and it's a practical knot all around the boat. It forms a loop (of any size you want) at the end of a line, and sailors commonly use it to tie jib sheets onto the sail. On many dinghies, you use a bowline knot to attach the halyard to the sail.

The easiest way to remember how to tie a bowline is the kid's way: imagining a bunny rabbit coming out of his hole, as Figure 19-3 shows.

Follow these steps to tie a bowline:

1. **Make the rabbit hole, as Figure 19-3 shows.**
2. **Make the rabbit come up through the hole and around the back of the tree.**
3. **Make the rabbit go back down the hole.**
4. **Pull the three ends to tighten.**

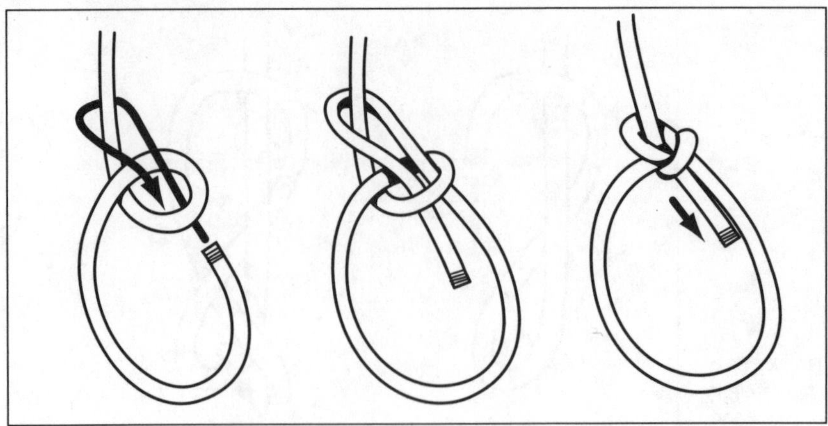

FIGURE 19-3: A bowline.

To untie a bowline, bend back the part formed when the rabbit goes around the back of the tree, and the knot loosens up nicely.

Square Knot

The *square knot* is just two overhand knots with the first tied right over left and the second tied left over right (or vice versa), as Figure 19-4 shows. Use a square knot to tie two lengths of the same type (or thickness) of line together.

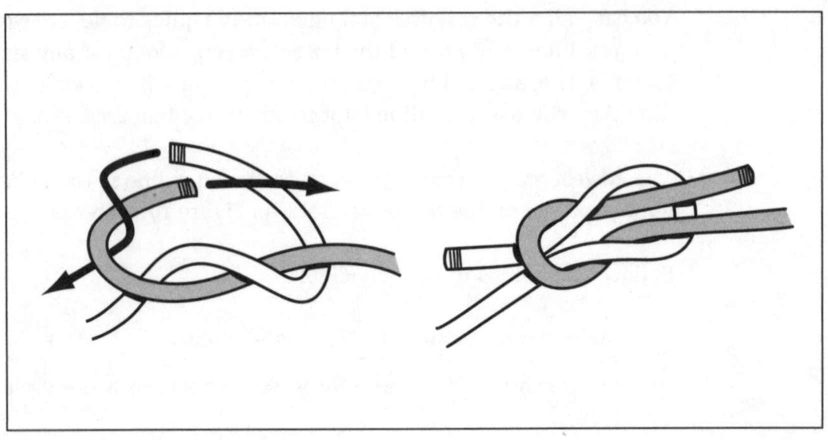

FIGURE 19-4: The square knot.

Tie a square knot like this:

1. **Tie an overhand knot (the first knot you tie when tying your shoes).**
2. **On the second overhand knot, tie it the opposite way.**

   If you put the left piece over the right on the first knot, put the right piece over the left for the second knot.

REMEMBER

You've tied the knot right if the ends of the lines are parallel to the *standing* (working) part of the lines, so that it looks like two symmetrical loops. (You make a *granny knot* when you tie both overhand knots the same way.)

Cleat Knot

Use the cleat knot in Figure 19-5 any time you find a horn or T-cleat, such as when you're tying off halyards and tying your boat to most docks. Make sure that you loop your line one full turn around the base of the horn cleat before tying this knot.

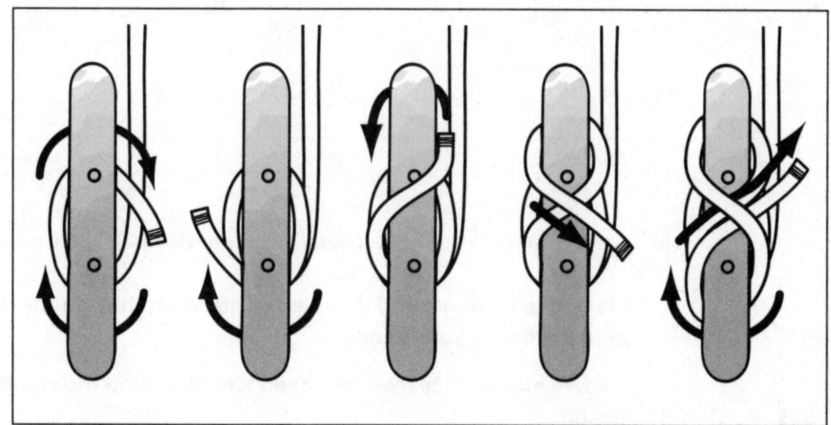

FIGURE 19-5: Securing a line around a horn cleat.

TIP

If your dock line is a very small diameter, it can slip off the horn cleat; in that case, you may want to tie a bowline through the center of the horn cleat instead.

Two Half Hitches

The *two half hitches* knot, also called the *double half hitch*, is really two overhand knots tied around the standing part of a line. This quickie knot has many temporary uses, including tying a tow line around your mast in a dinghy to get a quick tow. Tying two half hitches is a quick way to cleat off a line on a winch or other fixed object temporarily. If the rope is going to be under load, add the extra friction of a wrap or two around the object before tying the hitches (hence the term *round turn and two half hitches*). That way, you can untie the knot easily later, even if the rope has been stressed to its limit. Check out Figure 19-6 to see how to tie a round turn and two half hitches.

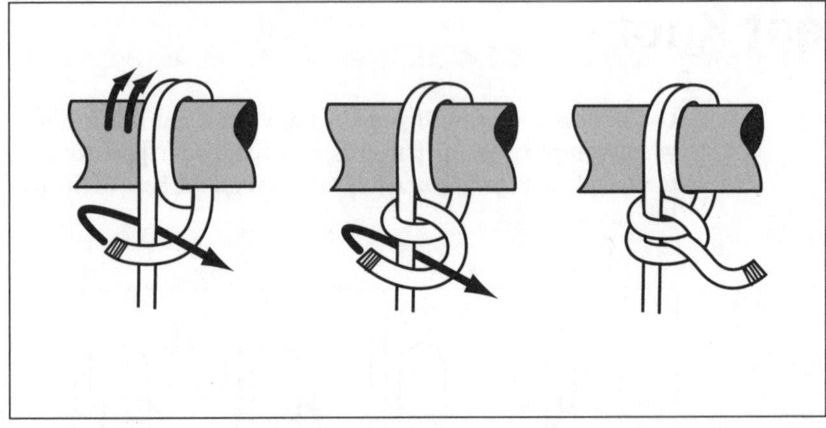

FIGURE 19-6: Round turn and two half hitches.

Here are the steps for tying a round turn and two half hitches:

1. **Make two turns around the mast or object so that you can comfortably hold the line in your hand.**
2. **Tie two half hitches (two overhand knots) around the standing part of the line.**

TIP

The round turn and two half hitches is, in our opinion, the most underrated of knots. It's the most practical knot there is; it's just so darn useful all over the boat. And the thing we like best is how easy this knot is to tie, even in pressure situations when you need to make that knot fast *now!*

Clove Hitch

You must tie the *clove hitch,* a close cousin to two half hitches, *around* something, such as a lifeline or piling. It's a quick knot for tying on fenders, tying a dock line to a piling, and anything you use temporarily. With the first loop, you can hold the line in place and then tie the second loop to be secure. Unlike a round turn with two half hitches, the clove hitch can get very difficult to undo under pressure. See the step-by-step details of tying a clove hitch in Figure 19-7.

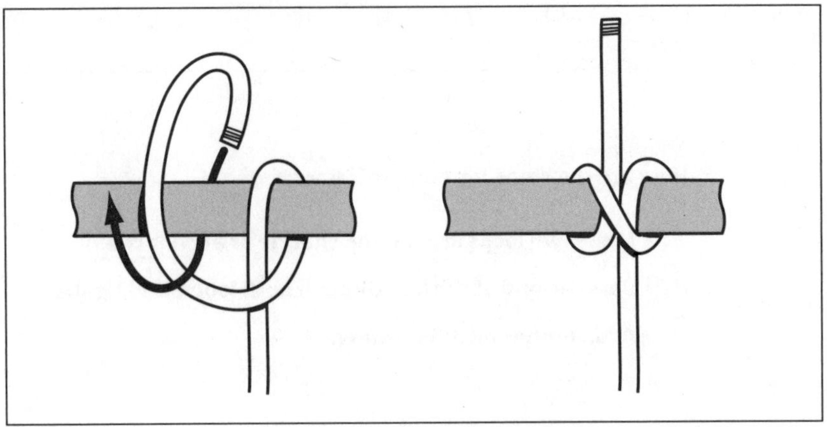

FIGURE 19-7: The clove hitch.

Follow these steps to tie a clove hitch:

1. **Make a loop around the pole or object.**
2. **Make a second loop by crossing over the first loop.**
3. **Put the tail under the second loop.**
4. **Pull both ends to tighten.**

Fisherman's Bend

The *fisherman's bend* isn't a common knot because other knots, such as the bowline and the round turn with two half hitches, can do the same job. This knot is less likely than a bowline to loosen but is more difficult to untie, making it a good one to use when you want to leave it in place for a long time. You often use the fisherman's bend to attach an anchor to its line, so it's sometimes called an *anchor bend.* Check out the how-to in Figure 19-8.

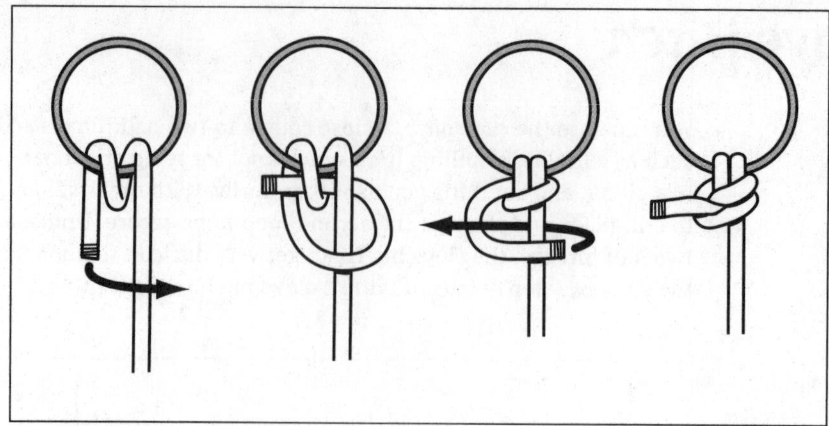

FIGURE 19-8: The fisherman's bend.

Here are the steps for tying this knot:

1. **Make two loops around the shackle or anchor chain.**
2. **Pass the end of the line through both loops, and tighten.**
3. **Add another hitch for safety.**

Rolling Hitch

The *rolling hitch* is an all-around great knot, one that can really impress your fans because you can use it to get out of trouble. You use it to tie one line to another. It grips so tightly that you can use it to take the load off the end of the other line in an emergency (such as a winch override; see Chapter 5). If you look closely at Figure 19-9, you see that a rolling hitch is a clove hitch with another twist or two.

Tie a rolling hitch like this:

1. **Make two loops around the rope or other item to be attached.**
2. **Put the tail over the two loops and then make a third loop.**
3. **Put the tail under the third loop, and tighten.**

TIP

Always wrap the first two loops of a rolling hitch on the side closer to your intended pulling direction. If you're tying a line to a halyard coming out of the mast, for example, wrap around the bottom first, because you intend to pull down. The third loop (the hitch that turns it into a real knot) wraps above the first two.

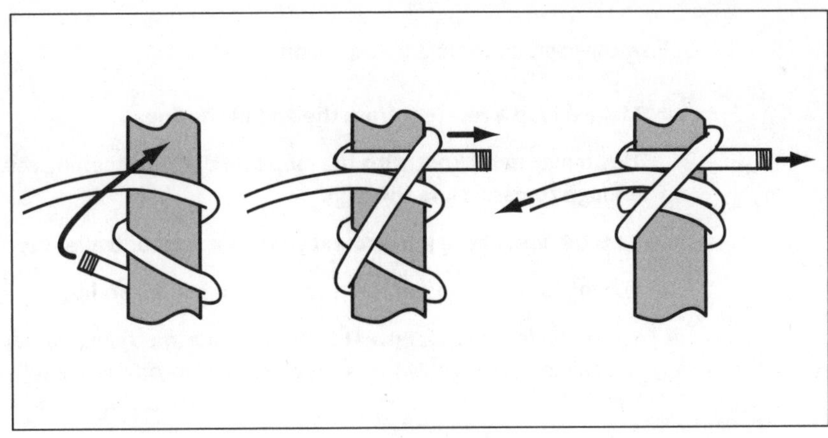

FIGURE 19-9: The rolling hitch.

Trucker's Hitch

We used to show the kids at sailing clinics a great old Warren Miller video in which a 15-foot dinghy flew off the roof of a car and slid down a ditch. Somehow, the music and Miller's dry humor made the scene hilarious, but having *your* boat fly off *your* car isn't funny. The *trucker's hitch* (a combination purchase system and knot wrapped up in one) makes the task much easier. For the how-to, see Figure 19-10.

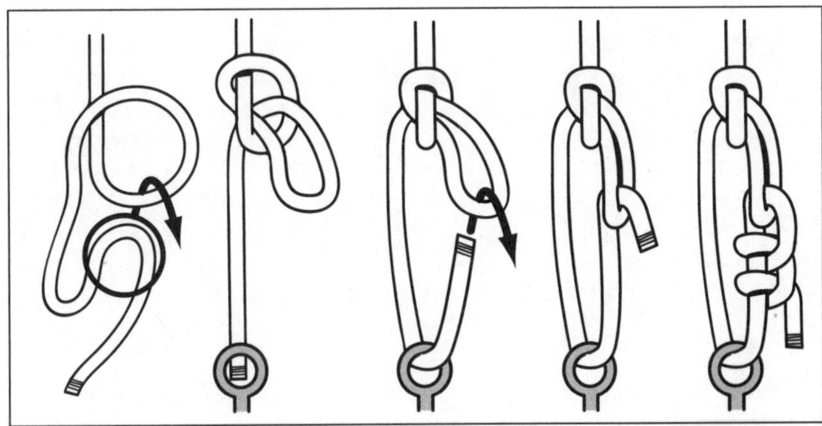

FIGURE 19-10: The trucker's hitch.

Follow these steps to tie a trucker's hitch:

1. **Make a loop a few feet from the end of the line.**
2. **Tie an overhand knot with the loop and tighten, keeping the loop big enough to pass a line through.**
3. **Pass the end of the line around your roof rack or trailer bar.**
4. **Put the line up through the trucker's hitch loop, and pull.**

   You've made a quick 2:1 (two-to-one) *purchase* (mechanical advantage), so you can pull that line tight twice as easily. You can tie off the line with two half hitches.

IN THIS CHAPTER

» Evaluating what a sailboat has to offer

» Looking at value

Chapter 20
Ten Questions to Ask Yourself When Buying a Sailboat

There was a great difference in boats, of course. For a long time I was on a boat that was so slow we used to forget what year it was we left port in. But of course this was at rare intervals.

—*MARK TWAIN,* LIFE ON THE MISSISSIPPI

We hope that by the time you read this chapter, you're hooked on sailing. In fact, we hope you're so hooked that you catch yourself daydreaming about having your own sailboat. You can window-shop for your dream boat in the pages of sailing magazines, at boat shows, online, and even by walking around the local marina.

Shopping for a sailboat can be intimidating, especially if you're new to sailing, and you may not want to rush the process. But if you decide to take that next big step and buy your own sailboat, this chapter can help you gather the information and better prepare yourself to make that big decision.

What Do You Plan to Use the Boat For?

Dinghy or keelboat? Catamaran or monohull? Big or small? It pays to narrow things down. Are you planning to day-sail locally or go on extended cruising trips? Do you want to start racing? Do you need to entertain (and impress) the boss? Are you into athletic exercise, or are you more of a couch-potato-type sailor? What other types of activities do you plan to engage in? If you're planning some overnight trips, you may want a *windlass*, a mechanical device to pull up the anchor (described in Chapter 10), for easy anchoring. An avid diver may want a large swim step. Do you envision fun outings with the whole family? If so, make sure that your family members have input in the selection process. Do you plan to make this new boat your "home away from home"? (Sadly, most sailboats spend most of their time tied up at the dock.) If so, you may require lots of headroom down below. Are you interested in racing? Check what fleets are popular in your area.

The answers to these types of questions can help you narrow your search.

Who Do You Want to Bring Along?

You can comfortably sail many dinghies and even some keelboats (if they're rigged with an autopilot and roller-furling sails) single-handed. Some high-performance dinghies and keelboats require a full contingent of expert crew and may not have room for extra bodies.

TIP

Lining up expert sailors for each and every sail can become a hassle, so be realistic about how big a boat you need. Make a list of your potential crew members, and make sure that you don't need every one of them before you can leave the dock. (This fact may surprise you, but some of your crew members may have other commitments from time to time.)

Where Do You Plan to Use the Boat?

Are you going to sail in protected waters, such as a small lake, or out on the open ocean? What are the heaviest winds and seas you expect during your sailing? Different boats work better for different locations. In Southern California, for example, a popular cruising destination is Catalina Island, a 20-mile (32-kilometer) sail from Los Angeles. Because sailing to Catalina requires an open-ocean crossing, you need a bigger, better-equipped boat to sail there than if you plan to stay inside the confines of the Long Beach breakwater.

Cruisers in Florida need lots of windows and hatches for ventilation, as well as a nice bimini cover to protect them from the sun. Cruisers in Maine or the Pacific Northwest may want a boat with a *pilot house* (high cabin with lots of windows surrounding the steering wheel) for protection from the rain and cold. If you live near a lake, you may want a boat that's easy to store on a trailer. Dinghies and small cats work, and you can find bigger boats with retractable keels for just that purpose.

A related question is "How deep is the water where you plan to use the boat?" Some manufacturers sell two models of popular cruising boats: a "shoal-draft" model, popular in shallow areas such as Florida and the Bahamas, and a standard full-draft model, which may be more appropriate on the West Coast.

Where Should You Buy a Boat?

If you're shopping for a used dinghy or a small catamaran or keelboat (shorter than 25 feet, or 8 meters), your best bet may be keeping an eye on classified ads and watching the bulletin boards at marinas and yacht clubs. Most often, this sort of transaction is handled privately. For a larger, more expensive used keelboat, you probably want to employ the services of a broker, as we describe in this section. If you're interested in a smaller (shorter than 25-foot, or 8-meter) racing-class boat, talk to local owners of the same class to find out your options.

REMEMBER

Boat shows are great places to shop for and even buy new boats — especially the bigger (longer than 25 feet, or 8 meters) more expensive models — because you have lots of boats to choose among, and dealers and manufacturers often offer deep discounts. But whether you want to buy new or used, do your homework before going to the boat show. Your first step may very well be to find a broker. A good (buyer's) boat broker should ask many of the same questions we do and will have lots of the answers you need to make the right purchase. They get their fee from the seller, and like real-estate brokers, they can help in all aspects of the purchase, including finding dock/storage space and financing.

Most new boats are sold by dealers, but some manufacturers sell their products directly to consumers. Some dealerships even offer personalized instruction in sailing or operating your new boat.

You can do a lot of your research at home by browsing sailing magazines and websites. Many of the big sailing publications run new-boat reviews and produce buyers' guides and listings. You can also search for boat brokers in your area and talk to a few; they may be able to help you navigate the seemingly endless options. As a sailor, you'll probably be looking at other boats all your life and dreaming about owning and sailing them, just as we do, so welcome to the club: It's time to become an expert browser.

Where Do You Plan to Keep the Boat?

Is a place available to launch your boat so that you can keep it on a trailer or put it on top of your car and store it at home? If you're planning to store your boat on a trailer in your yard, have you checked with your spouse, neighbors, and/or neighborhood covenants first? Do you have access to a *slip* (in-water dockside storage) at a marina or yacht club? The slip fees at your local marina may be as much as the loan payments on your new boat. Also, finding a slip can be hard, but boat brokers have good connections in this area too.

How Much Can You Afford to Spend?

Prices for a new 12-foot (4-meter) dinghy begin around $4,000, and prices for a new 25-foot (8-meter) keelboat begin in the neighborhood of $30,000. But you can spend many times as much, of course, which is one reason why a lot of buyers search for great deals on used boats. When you're calculating how much you can afford, don't forget to put together a realistic yearly operating budget, including storage fees, maintenance costs, and some replacement gear. For a dinghy, that jib sheet rope you need to replace may cost just a few dollars, but the same part on a keelboat or cruising cat can set you back $100, or more. In northern climes, you have to haul and store boats on land during the winter. Even in warmer areas, you should have a yearly haul-out for most boats for maintenance. Call the local boatyard to get a quote.

REMEMBER

As a rough guide, the bigger and more active a boat is, the more it costs to run and maintain.

FOR THE LOVE OF CLASSIC BOATS

Ever since Peter built a 13-foot (4-meter) Blue Jay wooden dinghy for his sister (during college, when he should have been studying), he's been enamored with wooden boats. We visit Mystic Seaport (the leading maritime museum in the United States) whenever we get to Connecticut; check out `www.mysticseaport.org` for more on the fascinating exhibits, which includes that famous Blue Jay!

Lately, Peter has been sailing and racing on *Spartan*, a Herreshoff-designed 72-foot sloop and a New York 50 class boat built in 1913. She's a joy to sail and incredibly beautiful to behold, with a cloud of sail area. With limited winch power and classic-boat-style rigging, it's much different to crew on than a modern boat. Unlike a modern 70-footer, which would go upwind with two sails (a headsail and a main), *Spartan* flies four sails, two headsails, the gaff-rigged mainsail, and a topsail.

Photo courtesy of Carlo Borlenghi

Are You Getting a Good Value?

As you gain experience, your taste in boats may change, so a rash purchase today may not suit you tomorrow. New boats are like new cars: They can lose a great deal of their value as soon as you drive them off the lot. Also, make sure that you have a complete inventory of what comes with the boat so that you'll know whether that cool depth sounder will still be there when you get the pink slip.

Is the Boat Seaworthy?

REMEMBER

An online search may turn up articles and/or forums on the merits of various types of boats. But the best way to find out whether a specific used boat is seaworthy is to pay for a marine survey, which includes (for a larger keelboat) a haul-out for inspection. A marine surveyor can give you a comprehensive report on the boat's seaworthiness and is also useful for insuring your new boat. Usually, a marine survey is more applicable to the sale of a used keelboat. With a dinghy, you may have to rely on your observation skills.

A *sea trial* (the nautical equivalent of a test drive) can also help you assess the boat's seaworthiness and decide whether you like the way it handles in various conditions. (Ideally, you'll get to test a boat on a windy day.) And ask the seller for the maintenance history of the boat.

What Equipment Do You Need?

The local conditions and your sailing plans affect what you need. Check out other boats at the local marina, or ask local sailors for gear recommendations. In San Diego, where the wind rarely exceeds 12 knots, you may never use a small, heavy-air jib, but if you're sailing in San Francisco Bay, such a jib is your go-to headsail. Wait to add equipment (except essential safety equipment and tools) until you day-sail the boat several times. But if you know you're planning to sail a larger sailboat short-handed, purchasing an autopilot and a roller furling headsail system (if it doesn't have one) right away is a smart investment.

What Kind of Keelboat Do You Want?

As you search for your perfect keelboat, you hear names such as *sportboat* and *blue-water cruiser.* These names are loose categories that can help you typecast a particular boat. Following are some of the common categories of keelboats:

- **Sportboat:** A *sportboat* is a fast keelboat (usually 20 to 33 feet, or 6 to 10 meters) with hardly any amenities, such as a *galley* (kitchen) or private *head* (cabin with toilet) down below. But in a sportboat, you get from point A to point B fast (and probably get a bit wet too).

- **Day sailer:** A *day sailer* is about the same size as a sportboat and also doesn't have many creature comforts below but is cheaper (and slower) than a sportboat.
- **Blue-water cruiser:** A *blue-water* (long-distance) cruiser is a sturdy, well-built keelboat (usually longer than 40 feet, or 12 meters) that's meant to make long passages, such as from New York to the Azores.
- **Cruisers:** Then you have all kinds of cruisers in between, from budget cruisers that won't break any speed records or have as many appointments but satisfy that urge to get out on the water to floating gadget palaces with watermakers, flat-screen televisions, and all the toys. A lot of our friends have been getting into cruising catamarans lately; these boats have tons of room for the same overall length.

Appendixes

IN THIS PART . . .

Peruse a handy glossary with all the important sailing terms that we use in this book.

Review some basic first aid in case someone on your boat gets sick.

Appendix A

Glossary

They say that when your ship comes in, the first man takes the sails,
The second takes the afterdeck, the third the planks and rails.

— ROBERT HUNTER

In this glossary, you can reference Figure A-1 to see where the parts of a keelboat are.

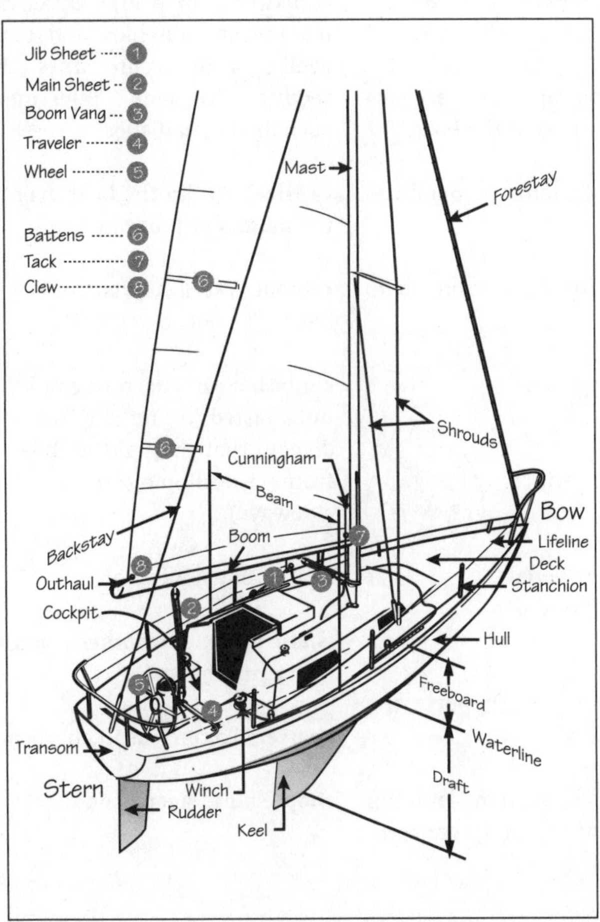

FIGURE A-1: The parts of a keelboat.

abeam: At right angles to the boat's center line.

aft: Toward the *stern;* opposite of forward.

apparent wind: The wind felt on board your boat; a combination of the wind from your forward motion and the *true wind* blowing onto the boat.

athwartships: Across the boat.

back: To *trim* a sail to *windward* so that it fills with wind backward.

backstay: The support wire between the top of the *mast* and the back of the boat.

battens: Slats inserted into pockets along a sail's *leech* to help maintain its shape.

beam: A measurement taken at the widest part of the boat; also, the widest part of the boat.

beam reach: *Reaching* on a heading perpendicular to the wind direction.

bear away: To turn away from the wind (or to turn to *leeward*).

bearing: The angle to an object, measured in degrees.

block: A pulley through which ropes run.

block

bolt rope: A rope (often covered with fabric) sewn to the *luff* or *foot* of a sail.

boom: The horizontal pole that supports the bottom edge of the *mainsail.*

boom vang: The control *line* system, running from the boom to the base of the *mast,* that controls *mainsail* twist.

bow: The front of the boat.

broach: A sudden, unplanned turning of a boat toward the wind that occurs in strong winds.

broad reach: *Reaching* at a wide or broad angle to the wind (greater than 90 degrees).

buoy: A floating (albeit anchored) object that can be a navigation aid or a *mooring.*

by the lee: Sailing *downwind* with the wind coming over the same side of the boat as the boom is *trimmed,* which can cause an accidental *jibe.*

cam cleat: A cleat with two moving "jaws" that allows for rapid adjustment of a line; optimized for use on dinghies and small keelboats to secure lines that require frequent adjustment, such as the mainsheet.

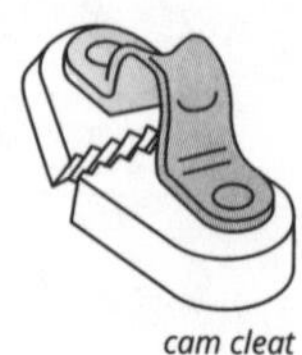

cam cleat

capsize: To flip the boat over so that the top of the *mast* is in the water.

catboat: A *keelboat* that doesn't have a *jib,* only a *mainsail.*

centerboard: The retractable, unballasted center fin on a *dinghy* that keeps the boat from sideslipping (moving sideways).

catboat

chafe: Abrasion; wear.

chain plate: Attachment point of the *standing rigging* on the *hull.*

charter: To rent (as in chartering a boat).

chop: Short, steep waves.

cleat: (1) A fitting used to tie off or secure a *line* under load so that the *line* doesn't slip. (2) To make fast or secure a rope.

clevis pin: A metal pin that secures a *shackle* or other fitting on a boat.

clew: The *aft*, bottom corner of a sail.

close-hauled: The closest course to the wind that you can sail effectively; also called sailing *upwind, on the wind*, or *beating*.

close reach: A reach at any heading between 90 degrees to the wind and *close-hauled*.

cockpit: The area where the crew sits to operate the boat.

cunningham: The control *line* system near the *tack* of a sail used to adjust *luff* tension.

current: Horizontal movement of water caused by tidal change, gravity, or wind.

cutter: A type of sloop with the mast set farther aft, about halfway back from the bow.

cutter

daggerboard: A *centerboard*-type fin that's raised and lowered vertically through a slot in the *hull*.

daymarks: Warning markers displayed on poles used in lieu of buoys, typically in shallower water.

dead reckoning: Plotting your position based on the course and distance from a previously known position.

death roll: A *capsize* to *windward;* generally occurs while sailing *downwind*.

deck: The top of the *hull*.

depth sounder: An instrument that measures depth of water below the boat.

deviation: The angular difference between the real magnetic heading and the one indicated by a compass; compass error.

dew point: The temperature at which the air becomes saturated with water vapor.

dinghy: (1) A sailboat with a *centerboard* (or *daggerboard* or *leeboard*); (2) a small rowboat.

dividers: An adjustable metal tool with two sharp points used in navigation.

downwind: (1) A run, but can mean any point of sail when the wind is *aft* of the *beam (broad reach)*. (2) The direction that the wind is blowing toward. (3) Any point that is farther from the source of the wind than another point.

draft: (1) The distance from the water's surface to the deepest point on the boat. (2) The amount and position of fullness in a sail.

ease: To let out (a rope or sail).

ebb: A tidal *current* flowing out to sea.

fender: Rubber cushion placed between a boat and a dock to protect the *hull*.

fetch: (1) The distance of open water that waves have to grow. (2) To sail a course that will clear a buoy without *tacking;* to lay.

flood: Tidal *current* coming inbound from the sea; a rising tide.

foils: The *keel* (or *centerboard*), *rudder*, and the sails; also, shaped underwater wings that allow a boat to lift above the surface of the water.

foiling (or *hydrofoiling*) Lifting a boat (or board) up above the water on shaped foils.

foot: (1) The bottom edge of a sail. (2) To sail slightly lower than *close-hauled* to go faster.

forestay: The support wire that runs from the *mast* down to the *bow.*

freeboard: The distance between the *deck* of the boat and the water; the height of the *topsides.*

furl: To roll or fold a sail and secure it.

gaff: The shorter boom at the top of the *gaff rig.*

gaff rig: A traditional type of *rig* with a four-sided *mainsail* attached to two *booms.*

galley: A boat's kitchen.

gaff rig

genoa: A large *jib* that overlaps the *mast.*

gooseneck: The fitting that attaches the boom to the *mast.*

GPS (Global Positioning System): A navigation system that uses satellites to plot location.

grommet: A small plastic or metal ring pressed or sewn into a sail, creating a hole.

guy: The *spinnaker sheet* (control rope) on the *windward* side that attaches through a fitting on the *spinnaker* pole to the *tack*; also called the *afterguy.*

halyard: The rope running up the *mast,* used to pull the sails up.

hanks: Snaps or clips at intervals along the *luff* of a *jib,* used to attach the sail to the *forestay.*

head: (1) The top corner of any sail. (2) The bathroom/toilet aboard a boat.

head up: To turn the boat toward the wind (to *windward*).

header: A wind shift that causes the boat to turn away from the old wind direction.

headsail: Any sail that sets up forward, in front of the *mainsail.*

headstay: See *forestay.*

heavy air: Strong winds.

heel: When the boat leans or tips to one side.

helm: (1) The wheel or *tiller* — the steering device. (2) A technical word for the balance of forces on the *rudder.* (3) The position of the *helmsperson* on the boat.

helmsperson: The driver or skipper of the boat.

hike: To lean over the side, usually to counteract the *heeling* forces.

hiking stick: See *tiller extension.*

hoist: To pull up the sails.

horn cleat: A common *cleat* shaped like a T; also called a *t-cleat* or *anvil cleat.*

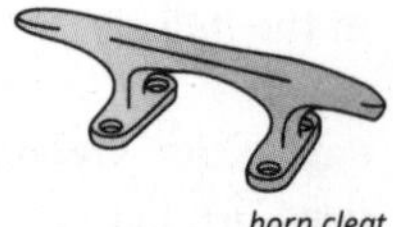
horn cleat

hull: The body of the boat.

in irons: When a boat has stopped moving and is stuck pointing directly into the wind.

jack lines: Ropes, webbing, or cables that run along the *deck* on either side of the cabin for the length of the boat, specifically for use with safety harnesses.

jammer: A mechanical fitting with a lever arm that cleats a rope.

jib: The most common *headsail.*

jibe: To change *tacks* by turning away from the wind.

jury-rigging: Temporarily fixing broken equipment.

kedge: To use an anchor to get a grounded boat back to deep water.

keel: A fixed, ballasted center fin that keeps the boat from sideslipping and provides stability to prevent capsizing, or tipping over.

keelboat: A sailboat with a *keel.*

ketch: An old-style *keelboat* with two *masts,* the front one being taller. The mizzen (smaller) *mast* must be in front of the *rudder* post (the attachment point for the *rudder*).

ketch

knot: (1) Nautical mile (6,076 feet) per hour. (2) A rope trick.

lateen: The top *boom* on a *lateen rig.*

lateen rig: An old-fashioned triangular *mainsail* arrangement with two *booms* that pivot the *mast.* The two booms meet at the front corner of the sail.

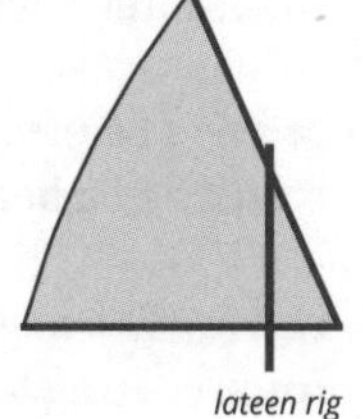

lateen rig

layline: The *line* beyond which you can *lay* (make) the destination on a *close-hauled* course with no more *tacks.*

lee shore: A shoreline to *leeward* of a boat onto which the wind is blowing.

leeboard: A retractable fin like a *centerboard* but attached to the side of the boat.

leech: The back edge of a sail.

leeward: *Downwind;* away from the wind.

lifeline: A wire supported by low poles called *stanchions* that encircle the *deck* to keep the crew from falling overboard.

lift: A wind shift that enables the boat to sail closer to the old wind direction.

line: A rope used on a sailboat with a specified purpose.

log: (1) A nautical record of a ship's voyage. (2) A device that measures distance traveled.

longitude: The vertical lines on a chart or globe designating the angular distance (0 to 180 degrees) east or west of the prime meridian.

LOP (line of position): A line through some point on which you presume your boat to be located as a result of an observation or measurement.

lubber line: Fixed vertical post(s) on the front edge of the compass.

luff: (1) The front edge of a sail from the *head* to the *tack.* (2) The flapping motion of sailcloth when a sail is undertrimmed (or not *trimmed* at all).

mainsail: The *aft*most sail on a boat with one *mast,* normally attached to the *mast* along its front edge.

mainsheet: The adjustment rope that pulls the boom (hence, the *mainsail*) in and out.

Marconi rig: The most common *rig,* in which the *mainsail* is a triangle shape with one boom. This *rig* became popular in the 1920s. It was called a

Marconi rig because with its supporting wires *(standing rigging)* and tall height (compared with the *gaff rig*), it resembled the radio towers built for Guglielmo Marconi's invention. This rig is so prevalent now that no one refers to it by a special name.

mast: The vertical pole that supports the sails.

mooring: A permanently anchored buoy to which a boat can be tied.

nautical mile: 6,076 feet; 1.15 times longer than a statute (regular) mile; equal to 1 minute (1/60th of a degree) of latitude.

no-sail zone: Zone where a sailboat can't sail; about 90 degrees wide, with the center point being directly toward the *true wind* direction.

off the wind: Sailing on a *broad reach* or run.

outboard: (1) Out to the side of the boat. (2) A removable engine.

outhaul: The control *line* system used to adjust the tension of the *foot* of the *mainsail.*

parallel rulers: A navigation tool with two straight-edged plastic slats or rulers connected by two hinges; used to measure and draw compass courses.

PFD (personal flotation device): A life jacket or other buoyancy device.

piloting: Navigation involving frequent determination of position.

pinch: Steering slightly closer to the wind than a *close-hauled* course.

plane: To skim along the water's surface.

pole lift: See *topping lift.*

port: (1) Left side while facing forward. (2) A small, round window on a boat, also called a *porthole.* (3) A commercial harbor.

port tack: Sailing with the wind coming over the left side of the boat.

puff: An increase in wind velocity.

purchase system: Block-and-tackle system that provides a mechanical advantage.

quadrant: Bracket around the *rudder* post that connects to the steering-wheel cables.

Quick-Stop method: A person-overboard rescue technique in which you instantly stop the boat as close to the victim as possible.

ratchet block: A block that turns freely when you pull the *line* but doesn't turn at all in the other direction.

reaching: Any heading between *close-hauled* and *running.*

reef points: Several horizontal reinforced holes in a row built into the sail to facilitate *reefing.*

reefing: Reducing the exposed area of a given sail.

regatta: A series of races with the cumulative race scores counting toward the final results.

relative bearing: A bearing measured in degrees relative to a boat's heading.

rig: (1) The *mast* and *standing rigging.* (2) A term for preparing the boat (or sail or fitting) for use.

righting moment: Leverage provided by crew weight or ballast that inhibits *heeling.*

roller furling system: System of sail storage and *reefing* where the sail wraps up on a narrow spool; most commonly used for *headsails.*

rope clutch: See *jammer.*

rudder: The underwater fin that steers a boat, controlled by a *tiller* or wheel on *deck.*

running: The course you're steering when the wind is behind you.

running lights: A boat's navigation lights.

running rigging: The ropes and pulleys used to raise, lower, and adjust the sails.

schooner: An old-style *keelboat* with two or more *masts.* The front *mast (foremast)* must be shorter than the main *mast.* If the sails are *rigged* in the old-fashioned, *square-rigger* manner (with rectangular sails set on booms crossing the *mast* like a T), you get into another family of *rig* names, which we kindly don't list here.

schooner

shackle: A metal fitting often used to attach a sail to a rope.

sheave: The moving "wheel" part of a *block* or pulley.

sheet: The primary *line* that adjusts the sail's *trim,* usually referred to with the sail it adjusts, as in "Pull in the *mainsheet.*"

shoal: A shallow area.

shock cord: Elastic rope; also called *bungee cord.*

shrouds: The support wires that run from the *mast* down to the edge of the *deck* on the left and right sides of the *mast.*

slip: A dockside parking space for a boat.

sloop: The most common type of *keelboat,* with only one *mast.*

sloop

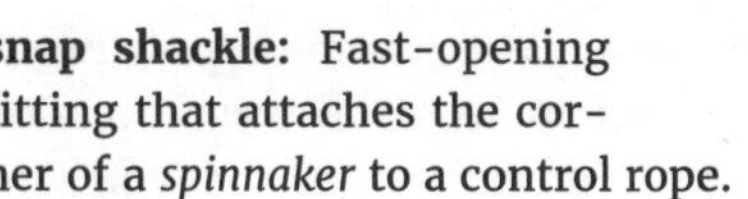

snap shackle: Fast-opening fitting that attaches the corner of a *spinnaker* to a control rope.

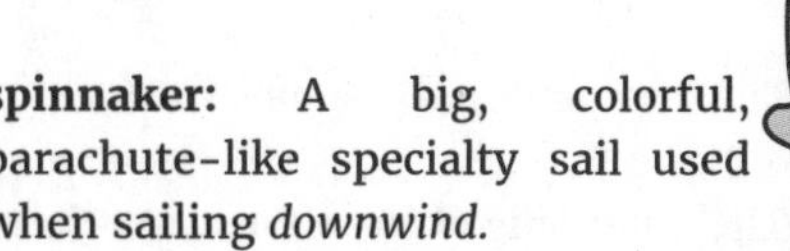

spinnaker: A big, colorful, parachute-like specialty sail used when sailing *downwind.*

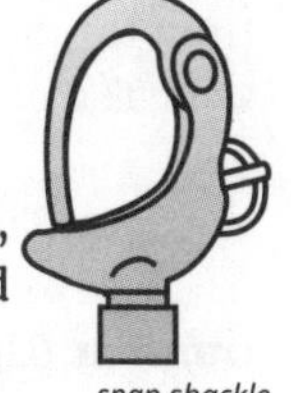

snap shackle

spring lines: Additional *lines* that are tied from the middle of the boat at opposing angles to the fore and *aft* dock *lines* to prevent the boat from surging forward or backward.

square rigger: See *schooner.*

standing rigging: All the wires that support the *mast,* including the *forestay, shrouds,* and *backstay.*

starboard: Right side facing forward.

starboard tack: Sailing with the wind coming over the boat's right side.

stern: The back end of the boat.

swamp: To fill with water.

tack: (1) The bottom-front corner of a sail. (2) The boat's heading in relation to the side of the boat that's closer to the wind (that is, on *starboard* or *port tack*). (3) To change tacks by turning toward the wind, entering the *no-sail zone* from one side and exiting on the other.

telltales: Strands of yarn or cassette tape that are attached to the sail or *standing rigging* to help the skipper judge the wind angle and whether the sails are *trimmed* properly.

tiller: The lever arm that controls the position of the *rudder.*

tiller extension: A device attached to the end of the *tiller* that enables a person to sit farther *outboard* while steering.

topping lift: *Halyardlike* control rope running from the *mast*, used to lift the *outboard* tip of the *spinnaker* pole.

topsides: The outer sides of the *hull.*

transom: The outer side of the *stern.*

trapeze: A system for adding *righting moment* by standing on the side of a boat wearing a harness with a hook, which is attached to a wire running down from the *mast.*

traveler: A sail-control system that can move the *mainsheet* attachment point on the boat from side to side.

trim: (1) To pull in a rope or a sail. (2) The set of the sails. (3) The bow-up or bow-down position of the boat when not moving.

trough: The low part of a wave.

true wind: The actual wind (as opposed to the *apparent wind*) that would be measured by a boat at anchor (that is, not moving).

turtle: A type of *capsize* in which the boat turns all the way over with the *mast* sticking straight down.

variation: The angular difference between true and magnetic north.

waypoint: The latitude/longitude coordinates of a point along your course.

whitecaps: Foamy crests on the tops of waves.

winch: A revolving geared drum turned by a handle that provides a mechanical advantage and increases the sailor's ability to pull on a rope under load.

windward: Toward the wind; the side the wind blows on.

wing the jib: When sailing on a run, to *trim* the *jib* on the opposite side as the *mainsail.*

wishbone boom: A two-piece *boom* shaped like a wishbone, commonly found on windsurfers and some small sailboats.

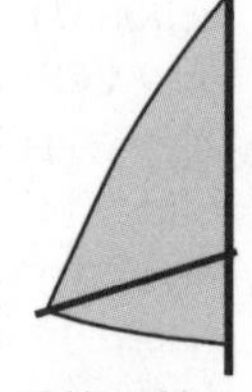

wishbone boom

yawl: An old-style *keelboat* with two *masts.* The mizzen (smaller) *mast* is behind the *rudder* post (the attachment point for the *rudder*). See *ketch.*

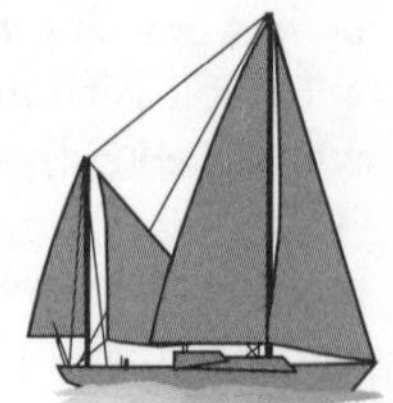

yawl

Appendix B

First Aid Afloat

Out of this nettle, danger, we pluck this flower, safety.

—WILLIAM SHAKESPEARE

This appendix is meant to give you an idea of what the most common afflictions aboard a boat are and the basic remedies for those ills. Obviously, anything can happen when you're out to sea, so you may need to help with a wide variety of medical situations. This appendix gives you some presailing advice and then covers the most common illnesses on board a boat, including hypothermia, seasickness, and sunburn.

If anyone on your boat requires prompt medical attention, call the Coast Guard (VHF Channel 16). Or you could call 911 on your mobile phone in an emergency. For more information on using your VHF radio, see Chapter 7.

Preparing for Sailing

We say this elsewhere in the book, but it bears repeating: It's best if everyone on the boat can swim. If they don't, they should wear a life jacket at all times.

We also strongly recommend that you know cardiopulmonary resuscitation (CPR), whether or not you plan to go sailing. Being on the water increases the amount of time that emergency personnel needs to get to you, and CPR is the best way to keep someone alive while rescue personnel are on their way. Teaching CPR is beyond the scope of this book, but your local Red Cross chapter can teach you the technique in only a few hours.

TIP

Be sure to ask your CPR instructor to show you how to use the technique with the drowning-victim recovery position.

In addition, smart sailors should strongly consider taking a first-aid course, and always sail with a first-aid manual and first-aid kit on a boat big enough to carry them.

Pick a first-aid manual

Even if you're not planning an extended cruise, investing in a good first-aid manual for your bigger keelboat makes sense. Ask your doctor and check online for a good first-aid manual.

Pack a first-aid kit

On any trip, even a short one, take along plenty of water, and if your boat has sufficient storage space, a good first-aid book, and a well-stocked first-aid kit. Ice can be used for a compress, and we also recommend those products that become cold compresses when you squeeze or shake them.

Stow a first-aid kit in a dry, watertight compartment with a list of contents visible for easy reference. Before you sail, familiarize yourself with your first-aid manual so that you know how to use the items in the kit to deal with burns, cuts, bleeding, and head injuries. If anyone requires medication for an ongoing condition, make sure that medicine is on board. If the medication needs to be kept cool, place it in a small cooler. You never know when the fickle wind may turn a three-hour sail into a late-night adventure, so be prepared!

Recovering from Hypothermia

We talk about the danger of losing body heat in Chapter 7. The loss of body heat is called *hypothermia* or *exposure*. Your body temperature cools 25 times faster in water than in the same temperature of air, so hypothermia is most common in people who have fallen overboard, but it can also affect people on deck when they're sailing in cold or wet weather. The symptoms of hypothermia start with loss of circulation to the extremities: fingers and toes. As your head gets cold, your mental and physical responses slow, and you may have difficulty speaking and get disoriented. Shivering is the body's attempt to warm up, and hypothermia is more dangerous when shivering stops.

WARNING

You must warm hypothermia victims *gradually*, and you need to warm their core area (around the heart) first. If the victim is unconscious and without a pulse, it's an emergency. Contact the Coast Guard, and use CPR until medical help arrives.

Here are the steps for treating hypothermia:

1. **Remove the victim's wet clothing.**
2. **Place the victim in a sleeping bag or wrap with warm blankets.**
3. **Have a crew member or two climb in the sleeping bag to warm the victim with their body heat.**

   REMEMBER

   You want to warm the core (chest area) first. This method of warming the victim may sound kinky, but it can be a life-saver. Don't apply direct heat.
4. **Give the victim warm (not hot) drinks and high-energy food.**

   Warm soup and warm sugary drinks are better than caffeine or alcohol, so the victim can generate their own internal heat.

Staving Off Seasickness

Having that seasick feeling can ruin an otherwise-great day afloat. To minimize your chances of feeling nauseated, we suggest that you take the following actions, some of them presail:

- **Avoid alcohol (and a hangover).** That woozy feeling isn't fun at sea.
- **Avoid rich, greasy foods.** Choose the bagel instead of the Eggs Benedict at breakfast.
- **Focus on the horizon.** Concentrating, such as steering the boat or helping with a job on deck, can help you feel better.
- **Keep some solid food in your stomach at all times.** Crackers or bread are good choices.
- **Sip small amounts of fizzy drinks.** It may be just an old wives' tale, but ginger ale and clear soft drinks work for us.
- **Stay on deck.** Stay in the fresh air, away from exhaust fumes (if your boat has an engine).

REMEMBER

If you throw up, try to do so in a bucket, downwind of everyone (including yourself). Leaning over the leeward rail isn't safe when you're feeling nauseated.

Several medicines can help combat seasickness, but in most cases, you must take them before the symptoms start. Don't take any of these medicines if you're younger than 12 or pregnant without consulting your doctor. Over-the-counter seasickness pills, such as Dramamine, must be taken an hour before sailing; keep in mind, however, that they can cause drowsiness and a dry mouth. Ask your doctor about a patch that administers Scopolamine, a prescription motion-sickness drug. Natural remedies include wearing wristbands and sucking on ginger lozenges. The latest remedy we've heard is to insert a foam ear plug in just one ear!

Keep an eye on anyone who's feeling seasick. Seasickness can make you weak, disoriented, and extremely sleepy — a danger when you're on deck. Help people who are seasick to a comfortable spot in the fresh air. If they're just feeling a little queasy, try letting them steer as a distraction. If you aren't feeling well, don't be ashamed; almost all sailors feel queasy at some point.

Steering Clear of Sunburn

The effects of being out in the sun all day, combined with the sun's rays reflected off the water and sails, make sailors prime candidates for sunburn. The following tips can help you avoid having a painful sunburn at the end of the day:

- **Put sunscreen on *before* you leave the dock.** Also, reapply it several times during the day — especially in wet conditions.
- **Always use sunscreen with a Sun Protection Factor (SPF) of at least 30.** We try to carry a sunscreen stick in our pockets at all times so that we can frequently reapply sunscreen to our noses, lips, and ears.
- **Always wear a hat and sunglasses.** Your skin and eyes will thank you in the long run.
- **If you're fair-skinned or are sailing in a tropical locale, wear a long-sleeved, lightweight cotton shirt (one with a collar will help protect your neck) and long pants.** Guarding your skin this way makes your trip much more enjoyable. You'll be amazed by how tan you'll get even when you're covered up all day.

WARNING

We have several friends (fellow lifetime sailors) who've battled skin cancer, and the fight isn't pleasant, so please be careful out in the sun. If you do have severe sunburn, aloe vera products help soothe the skin. Drink plenty of cool fluids and wear loose-fitting cotton clothes to help your skin heal.

Defeating Dehydration

Dehydration and heat exhaustion are two of the most dangerous illnesses for sailors because the body rejects the cure, which is to get cool and drink plenty of fluids. With severe dehydration, your body rejects any fluid intake by throwing up, making you further dehydrated. Severe dehydration can result in staying in a hospital hooked up to an intravenous drip to rehydrate. So try to drink as much fluid as you can while you're on the water.

In very hot conditions, you can get dehydrated even when you feel that you've been consuming fluids all day. One way to tell whether you're getting dehydrated is to consider how often you have to urinate. If you haven't had to use the *head* (marine toilet) all day, you need to drink a lot more water.

Index

Numbers

A

B

C

D

E

F

G

H

I

J

K

L

M

N

O

P

Q

R

S

T

U

V

W

Y

About the Authors

JJ Fetter grew up around boats in San Diego, California, learning to sail in a little 7-foot dinghy called a Sabot.

Peter Isler started out loving powerboats and fishing but took up sailing after his family moved to Connecticut when he was 13 years old.

JJ and Peter are well known throughout the sailing world as top competitors and teachers. They both have taught sailing to people of all ages and experiences. Peter played an important, early role in developing US Sailing's educational program. He also helped found the American Sailing Association, which accredits sailing schools and certifies sailors and instructors. In 2021, he founded the Isler Academy of Sailing Secrets, which features Marine Weather University, an online school.

Peter has sailed in five America's Cup campaigns, twice winning it serving as navigator aboard *Stars & Stripes* with Dennis Conner. An accomplished small-boat sailor, Peter was Intercollegiate Sailor of the Year while at Yale University. He was the top-ranked U.S. sailor on the professional match-racing circuit for five years, and as navigator, he has won many of the world's major ocean races, including the Bermuda Race, Transatlantic Race, and the Transpacific Race.

Serving as a TV commentator, Peter has been a member of two Emmy-award-winning broadcast teams covering six America's Cups. He is the author of several books on the sport and is presently Editor at Large of *Sailing World* magazine.

JJ is the only American female (so far) to have won two Olympic medals in sailing, and she has been inducted into the National Sailing Hall of Fame. With crew member Pamela Healy, JJ won the Bronze Medal in the Women's 470 class in the 1992 Olympics in Barcelona, Spain. In the 2000 Olympics in Sydney, Australia, she and crew member Pease Glaser won the Silver. JJ is a four-time Rolex Yachtswoman of the Year and has won three World Championships and numerous national and European titles in fleet racing and match racing. In 1995, she was the tactician and starting helmsman for the *America*^{3} Women's America's Cup team. She graduated from Yale University, where she was captain of the sailing team and a collegiate All-American.

JJ and Peter convinced their daughter, Marly Isler, a champion sailor, to contribute a chapter on windsurfing and kiting in this third edition of the book.

Dedication

To our daughters, Marly and Megan.

Authors' Acknowledgments

We first want to thank our respective partners, who were so patient through this revision. This book wouldn't be as good as it is without all the hard work and contributions from all the folks that helped us get this thing going with the first edition. This includes Peter Economy and our friends at IMG Literary who encouraged us get this project started when we wrote the proposal for the first edition a long time ago. For this edition, we are glad to have Brad Dellenbaugh back on board as technical reviewer. Brad is a super pro and has helped us for years both on and off the water!

We are very proud of the first and second editions of *Sailing For Dummies* and the success the book achieved, and we want to thank our acquisitions editor, Kelsey Baird, our development editor, Tim Gallan, and the rest of the Wiley's *For Dummies* team that worked so hard on helping us produce this new-and-improved third edition.

One of the things we're most pleased about in this third edition is the new artwork and photographs. And we definitely needed a little help from our friends to get the photos that we wanted. So in no particular order, our heartfelt thanks go to: Marie Rogers, Madison Mansour, Alexandra Foley, Betty Brandly, Monroe Melges, Pamela Healy, Sharon Green at Ultimate Sailing, Carlo Borlenghi of Borlenghi Designs, Martina Orsini, Chris Cameron of Photosport, Charlie Devanneaux with Lagoon Catamarans, West Marine, the Satellite Phone Store, and Trip Forman and the team at Real Watersports.

We greatly appreciate the efforts of many people whose help with the first and second edition still shines through in this edition. They include, Harry Munns, Jeff Johnson, Michael Boardman, and especially Sally Samins, who shot the book's original photos and helped us find the ones we couldn't shoot. Other people and organizations who helped with the first and second edition are Pat Healy, Doug Ament at H&S Yacht Sales, Geri Conser, Billy Black, Kristen Lawton, Doug Skidmore, and Matt Miller — the folks at Hobie Cat, Jason Campbell, Aine McLean Fretwell, Tom Leweck, Cam Lewis, Skip Novak, Mark Reiter, Marty Ehrlich, Rich Roberts, Dennis Conner, J World San Diego, Craig Leweck of *Scuttlebutt* (for loaning his camera to Peter when the perfect shot appeared one day while they were out sailing), Nick White, Emily Bohl, Andy Burdick, Harry Melges and the team at Melges Performance Boats, Tim Wilkes, Keith and Nigel Musto, the San Diego Yacht Club, US Sailing, and the American Sailing Association.

People who have played a key role in Peter's education as a sailor and a teacher include his mother, Marilyn Isler Brunger; Ted Jones, who bent some rules at Norwalk (Connecticut) Yacht Club so Peter could join the junior sailing program; Kendrick Wilson; Tyler Keys; Tom Whidden; Richard Hokin; Stan Honey; Steve Benjamin; Dave Perry; Lenny Shabes; Robert Hopkins; Gary Jobson; and John

Rousmaniere. And of course all his shipmates with whom he's traveled hundreds of thousands of miles over the water have been great teachers and kept him safe and fast.

JJ would like to thank her parents, Tom and Jane Fetter, for their steadfast encouragement, love, and support. And she would like to thank her first sailing instructors — Jack Wood, Mark and DeAnn Reynolds, and Dave Perry — for instilling an early and lasting love of the sport. Also, thanks to her many sailing teammates over the years — with a special thanks to Pease Glaser, Pamela Healy, and her Olympic and America's Cup team coaches — for giving her the opportunity to take her sailing to a higher level. And last but not least, thanks and love to her wonderful husband (and world-renowned naval architect) John Reichel.

Finally, we would like to thank you for your interest in "our" sport. May the wind always be at your back, and if it must come from ahead, may your sails be trimmed for speed!

JJ Fetter,
San Diego, California

Peter Isler,
San Diego, California

Publisher's Acknowledgments

Acquisitions Editor: Kelsey Baird
Development Editor: Tim Gallan
Copy Editor: Keir Simpson
Technical Reviewer: Brad Dellenbaugh
Illustrations: Brad Dellenbaugh, Mike Boardman

Production Editor: Mohammed Zafar Ali
Cover Image: © thakala/Adobe Stock Photos

Leverage the power

Dummies is the global leader in the reference category and one of the most trusted and highly regarded brands in the world. No longer just focused on books, customers now have access to the dummies content they need in the format they want. Together we'll craft a solution that engages your customers, stands out from the competition, and helps you meet your goals.

Advertising & Sponsorships

Connect with an engaged audience on a powerful multimedia site, and position your message alongside expert how-to content. Dummies.com is a one-stop shop for free, online information and know-how curated by a team of experts.

- Targeted ads
- Video
- Email Marketing
- Microsites
- Sweepstakes sponsorship

20 MILLION PAGE VIEWS EVERY SINGLE MONTH

15 MILLION UNIQUE VISITORS PER MONTH

43% OF ALL VISITORS ACCESS THE SITE VIA THEIR MOBILE DEVICES

700,000 NEWSLETT SUBSCRIPTI TO THE INBOXES OF *300,000* UNIQUE INDIVIDUALS EVERY WEEK

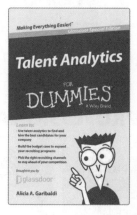

PERSONAL ENRICHMENT

9781119187790
USA $26.00
CAN $31.99
UK £19.99

9781119179030
USA $21.99
CAN $25.99
UK £16.99

9781119293354
USA $24.99
CAN $29.99
UK £17.99

9781119293347
USA $22.99
CAN $27.99
UK £16.99

9781119310068
USA $22.99
CAN $27.99
UK £16.99

9781119235606
USA $24.99
CAN $29.99
UK £17.99

9781119251163
USA $24.99
CAN $29.99
UK £17.99

9781119235491
USA $26.99
CAN $31.99
UK £19.99

9781119279952
USA $24.99
CAN $29.99
UK £17.99

9781119283133
USA $24.99
CAN $29.99
UK £17.99

9781119287117
USA $24.99
CAN $29.99
UK £16.99

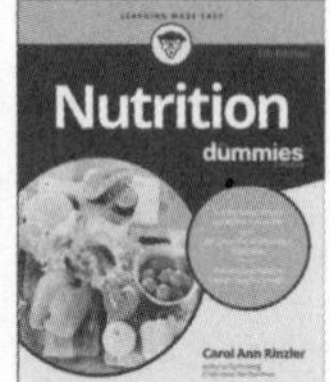

9781119130246
USA $22.99
CAN $27.99
UK £16.99

PROFESSIONAL DEVELOPMENT

9781119311041
USA $24.99
CAN $29.99
UK £17.99

9781119255796
USA $39.99
CAN $47.99
UK £27.99

9781119293439
USA $26.99
CAN $31.99
UK £19.99

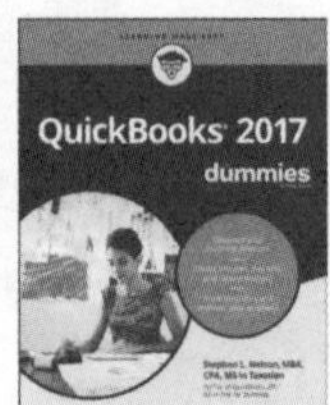

9781119281467
USA $26.99
CAN $31.99
UK £19.99

9781119280651
USA $29.99
CAN $35.99
UK £21.99

9781119251132
USA $24.99
CAN $29.99
UK £17.99

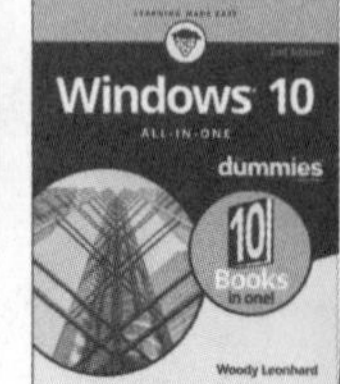

9781119310563
USA $34.00
CAN $41.99
UK £24.99

9781119181705
USA $29.99
CAN $35.99
UK £21.99

9781119263593
USA $26.99
CAN $31.99
UK £19.99

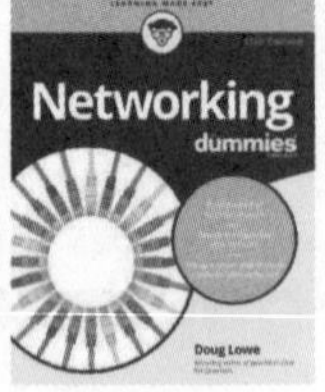

9781119257769
USA $29.99
CAN $35.99
UK £21.99

9781119293477
USA $26.99
CAN $31.99
UK £19.99

9781119265313
USA $24.99
CAN $29.99
UK £17.99

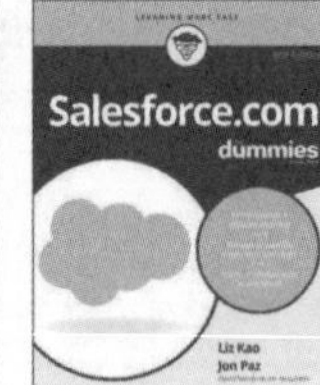

9781119239314
USA $29.99
CAN $35.99
UK £21.99

9781119293323
USA $29.99
CAN $35.99
UK £21.99

dummies.com

dummies®
A Wiley Brand

Learning Made Easy

ACADEMIC

9781119293576
USA $19.99
CAN $23.99
UK £15.99

9781119293637
USA $19.99
CAN $23.99
UK £15.99

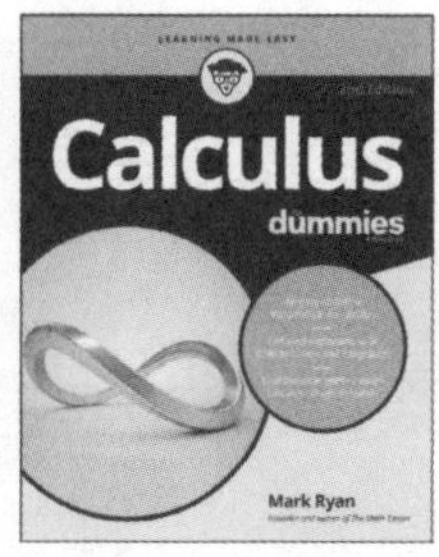

9781119293491
USA $19.99
CAN $23.99
UK £15.99

9781119293460
USA $19.99
CAN $23.99
UK £15.99

9781119293590
USA $19.99
CAN $23.99
UK £15.99

9781119215844
USA $26.99
CAN $31.99
UK £19.99

9781119293378
USA $22.99
CAN $27.99
UK £16.99

9781119293521
USA $19.99
CAN $23.99
UK £15.99

9781119239178
USA $18.99
CAN $22.99
UK £14.99

9781119263883
USA $26.99
CAN $31.99
UK £19.99

Available Everywhere Books Are Sold

dummies.com

dummies®
A Wiley Brand

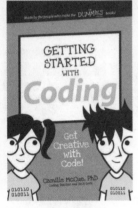

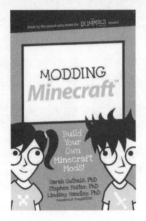

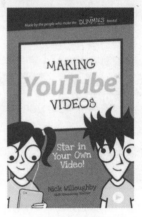

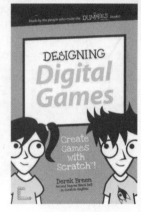

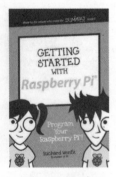

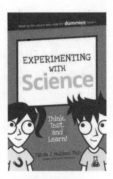

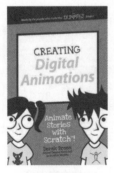

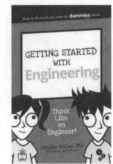

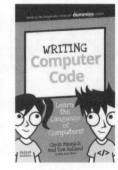